"*Transformational Teaching* is a valuable reference for those working in Christian schools. It is filled with practical and meaningful questions, ideas, and tools needed to guide Christian school leaders in their challenges for the future. This book provides school administrators a thorough awareness and understanding of their critical roles and responsibilities in leading their schools and staff. It's a great resource for establishing the school's philosophy on education and Christian school instruction. I highly recommend this book to everyone involved in Christian education."

—**Susan Banke**, director of graduate leadership, Gordon College

"*Transformational Teaching* is an education degree distilled into one book. Starting from the foundation of a biblical worldview essential for Christian educators, the authors cover key aspects, including learning and brain theory, instructional design, classroom discipline, diversity, and community. While our foundation stays the same, strategies must adapt and improve based on current research and a growing understanding of how God created people to learn, grow, and function in community. Get ready to be inspired and refreshed, as God will use this book to encourage, motivate, and teach you as a lifelong learner and educator."

—**Ellen Lowrie Black**, professor of education, Liberty University, and board member, Network of International Christian Schools

"*Transformational Teaching* is a must-read for all Christian educators and soon-to-be educators who desire to give their students an education with an eternal perspective. As an educational consultant serving Christian schools across Europe, I see a great need among Christian educators to have a well-developed Christian worldview effectively applied to all areas of teaching and learning. This book instructs and effectively engages the reader to grow and become successful in designing instructional approaches that are coherent and consistent with a Christian worldview, resulting in transformation in the learner."

—**László Demeter**, Europe regional director, Association of Christian Schools International

"This is a timely publication that is a must read for every person associated with teaching in Christian school at all levels. The research for this book is spot-on, and the authors certainly have the experience in Christian education to add their wisdom to the content. This is a practical resource that should be used daily in every instructional setting."

—**Tim Heaton**, professor emeritus of the School of Education, Cedarville University

"This book is the most thorough presentation of biblically based education that I've read in my 42 years of Christian school leadership. It covers a broad range of logically sequenced topics, from Christian education's unique philosophical foundations through current best practices for teaching and learning, to biblical integrated curriculum and lesson planning. This book is not only an 'essential read' for Christian classroom teachers and Christian home schoolers today, but it also contains the kind of resources that can be used again and again for the benefit of educators and their students for years to come."

—**Mark A. Kennedy**, retired director of ACSI Eastern
Canada and senior consultant, Paideia Inc.

"Although clearly intended as a textbook for college students beginning their vocation as schoolteachers, this book merits careful reading by parents of schoolchildren and other non-professional educators. Like those prospective teachers, they too need to know and differentiate among various educational philosophies and methods—especially if parents wish to sharpen their critique of the schools in which they enroll their children and the instruction those children are receiving."

—**D. Bruce Lockerbie**, chairman/chief executive officer, Paideia Inc.

"Master craftsmen recognize the importance of building on a solid foundation. The authors of *Transformational Teaching* demonstrate mastery of their craft by producing a resource that purposefully develops educators of all backgrounds and skill levels from a Christian worldview foundation. This scholarly work presents the most up-to-date research in the field of education in a way that is both approachable and engaging."

—**Max Stabenow**, assistant professor of Christian education, Gateway Seminary

"I don't recall, if ever, reading such a complete book for a Christian educator. The coauthors' unique blend of experience is noteworthy and evident throughout the book. They masterfully lay the biblical and philosophical foundation for transformational teaching. Their transition from the philosophical foundation to the practical application of instructional design is seamless. Teaching students to think critically about subject matter through the lens of a biblical worldview is our opportunity and responsibility."

—**Larry Taylor**, president, Association of Christian Schools International

"This book made me excited about the way Christ-centered education can lead to transforming the lives of students. Is there anything we need more in this present age? It takes you on a journey of how to develop a biblical foundation on teaching and learning, from thinking to acting. Thinking biblically about human learning will assist you in the task of selecting models and methods that contribute to effective learning. Throughout the book you find moments that engage you practically and spiritually to make the transition to your curriculum, classroom, and students. Studying this book will pay off, no matter where you are in your career as a Christian educator. It will help to pass on to students the habit of thinking Christianly, after first being immersed yourself."

—**Sjoerd van den Berg**, teacher educator at Driestar Christian
University for Teacher Education, the Netherlands

Transformational Teaching

Transformational Teaching

Instructional Design
for
Christian Educators

Kenneth S. Coley
+
Deborah L. MacCullough
+
Martha E. MacCullough

B&H
ACADEMIC
BRENTWOOD, TENNESSEE

Transformational Teaching: Instructional Design for Christian Educators
Copyright © 2023 by Kenneth S. Coley, Martha MacCullough, and Debbie MacCullough

Published by B&H Academic
Brentwood, Tennessee

All rights reserved.

ISBN: 978–1–0877–4891–7

Dewey Decimal Classification: 371.1
Subject Heading: TEACHING / TEACHERS--TRAINING
/ EDUCATION--AIMS AND OBJECTIVES

Cover design by Emily Keafer Lambright.
Cover images by ilyast/iStock and SirVectorr/iStock.

Printed in the United States of America

27 26 25 24 23 VP 1 2 3 4 5 6 7 8 9 10

To all Christian educators in any setting—
home, private, international, or public school; and church education—
who desire that their lives and work honor Christ
by being informed by a biblical worldview

CONTENTS

INTRODUCTION

Ken Coley

Laying a Sure Foundation

The plotline of the reality television series is a familiar one—a family needs a house that is different than where they are currently living, so the question becomes whether they will remodel their current home or search for a new one that meets their current needs. The participants always discuss a retrofit of the older structure with contemporary advances. Once the demolition begins, the made-for-television drama often includes discovering serious cracks in the basement foundation that results in costly delays and expensive repairs. But the result is a lovely, versatile flow throughout the house that is up-to-date and satisfies all the current construction requirements.

Now bring to your mind driving through a new neighborhood with houses in various stages of construction. Have you noticed the outline of a future house created by a large hole on the lot? Perhaps you noticed white pipes laid out in precise patterns and these pipes are resting on a bed of rock. Once these pipes have been carefully inspected, it will be time to pour a concrete slab that will bear the weight of the new house. The foundation will be laid that will support the structure while it is used for years by future generations.

Consider for a moment which of the two metaphors, the TV reality show featuring renovation or the new construction, represents the path you are embarking on—a journey that will produce a consistently strong and durable building. Starting fresh and basing practices upon a solid foundation is optimum for a young educator. However, whether you are a pre-service teacher just beginning to grapple with the process of building an effective philosophy and psychology of learning and determining related best practices, a homeschool parent designing a unique curriculum for each of your children, or a seasoned teacher wishing for needed renovation, this book is for you.

This second metaphor (new construction) expresses what the authors of this text desire for pre-service teachers who are in the process of developing their foundational commitments about the teaching profession and the teaching-learning process. Returning to the picture of the construction site, the authors want to connect a few symbols for the reader. We earnestly hope that you rest your hope and aspirations on Jesus, the Rock of all ages, building your educational principles and practices upon that sure Christ-centered foundation. Pipes, in this illustration, that might be stretched out on an unstable bed rather than on a bed of gravel and sand will crack and leak under pressure and seasonal temperature changes. This is why building codes require a gravel foundation. Education, too, requires a solid foundation.

Second, the flow of water to and from the home is crucial for the needs of the family. This, too, is a metaphor for developing sound educational practices. Throughout Scripture the picture of water, springs, and fountains represents the presence of life-giving refreshment. This flow will be strategic throughout your career. For this reason, this book is also suited for seasoned teachers who need a refreshing "flow" from the source of life to guide them forward in the profession.

Third, imagine pouring the concrete slab before the pipes are laid! It would take a jack hammer and hours of work to correct this error. It is, of course, easier to start to build the right way with a firm foundation than to have to undo practices that do not comport with a Christian view of humans and learning. However, reflective educators at all places of development shift their views from time to time with additional research and understandings. We resolutely want Christian educators to be acquainted with research and new understandings as they interweave their faith with their career.

Fourth, your mentor or instructor plays the vital role of inspector of your work as your philosophical foundation is laid. The authors assume that you have in place a supervisor, mentor, and/or colleagues with whom you can rehearse your developing thinking about what you are digesting as you read and interact with the authors on the various topics such as educational aims, instructional design for the curriculum, instructional techniques, assessment procedures, classroom management, and community building. Christian education has a rich tradition built on the foundation of God's Word. The authors are passionate about assisting you with the building of a firm foundation upon which you can connect every dimension of your career—from the broadest curriculum decisions to the everyday classroom management decisions.

In this book, each chapter is written by a team of experienced educators who present the latest research, including the most current debates from many different voices. Some of these viewpoints may surprise you because they presuppose a view of human nature that is not consistent with Scripture. We have carefully vetted the research findings and conclusions from biblical authors, from a second group who are silent about their faith, and even from those who disagree with a biblical approach to educational topics.

On the other hand, in many cases that which is considered effective practice is not in opposition to Scripture. Discernment is vital. For example, in the last decade, renewed calls for equality in education can certainly be embraced by faith communities. The creation of the term SEL (Social and Emotional Learning) may be the most frequently cited movement in educational circles. We can quickly agree that compassion and the support for each individual child is Christlike. Groundbreaking discoveries in mind, brain, and educational research celebrate the remarkable intricacies of God's design.

Educators need to wrestle with these issues, despite legitimate concerns about the theorist's philosophical orientation. Under the tutelage of your education professors or mentors, you can develop skills to unpack research findings and conclusions. These are skills you will need throughout your career as you continue to read and research in your field.

What You Can Expect Along the Way

The authors want to model for you what effective instructional approaches look like. In each chapter the writer addresses biblical truths that are tied to the topic of the chapter. We include twenty-first-century research that relates to each topic being addressed. The authors will encourage you to engage with the material and reflect on your own teaching experiences as you evaluate how the chapter concepts will play out in your personal context. We believe these three questions related to teaching and learning need to be asked and answered as you read this book:

- What does God's Word have to say about this issue or topic? (**Biblical integration**)
- What have others observed, researched, and reported about this topic or approach? (**Current research**)

- What has this looked like in my prior experience, and how might chapter discussions enhance and perhaps improve upon past experiences in education? (**Reflective practice**)

Be ready to interact with the concepts presented in each chapter. The authors will ask you to consider your prior experience in connection to the new material. We embrace Terry Doyle's statement about engagement: "The one doing the work is the one doing the learning."[1] So, we will ask you to put these new concepts in your own words and elaborate on the meaning for your context and situation. In addition, there will be space at the end of each chapter for you to describe how you plan to apply the concepts with the age group and discipline you are currently teaching or for which you believe God is preparing you. These instructional practices lead to deeper and more durable learning:

- Consider your prior experience and contrast or compare it with the new concepts. (**Schema—assimilation and accommodation**)
- How does this work out in educational practices? (**Active learning—"Engage" activities are designed to promote planning for real-life educational practices.**)
- Can you explain the new ideas in your own words? (**Elaboration**)
- What might the new ideas look like in your future classroom? (**Application**)

We will coach you along the way as you learn new concepts and terminology. Learning educational terminology is part of the experience of developing as a career educator. New terms will be used and explained as we go along. This chapter began with an emphasis on laying the proper foundation. This is the goal of the authors who want you to develop as a professional as you approach the planning of effective instructional events.

Returning to Our Opening Metaphor of Building Construction

It is our prayer that you will begin your career with a well-thought-out philosophy that has biblical wisdom as its underpinning. In addition, we hope the multiple voices of

---

[1] Terry Doyle, *Helping Students Learn in a Learner-Centered Environment: A Guide to Facilitating Learning in Higher Education* (Sterling, VA: Stylus, 2008).

educators that are included in these chapters will encourage you as you begin to build a planning model, active learning methods and techniques, and classroom management and student discipline procedures that represent the latest research in teaching and learning and fit with a biblical view of the human being and learning. In short, we want you to be prepared for God's call on your life to deliver *transformational teaching*!

We selected this ambitious title, *Transformational Teaching*, in the belief that God's Word will work powerfully in you, first, to remake you to be like Jesus. Then, second, your students will hear and experience God's truth, and the Holy Spirit will continue the process of renewal in each of them. The apostle Paul challenges believers in Romans 12:2, "Do not be conformed to this age, but be transformed by the renewing of your mind, so that you may discern what is the good, pleasing, and perfect will of God." The Greek word that is translated "transformed" is *metamorphoo* (which gives us our English word *metamorphosis*.) As you teach, you will be anticipating change. Author F. F. Bruce poses the challenge this way: "Instead of living by the standards of a world at discord with God, believers are exhorted to let the renewing of their minds by the power of the Spirit transform their lives into conformity with God's will."[2]

We trust that you will partner with God and invite your students to experience transformation.

---

[2] F. F. Bruce, *The Letter of Paul to the Romans: An Introduction and Commentary*, 2nd ed. (Grand Rapids: Eerdmans, 1985), 212.

SECTION 1
Foundational Perspectives

CHAPTER 1

Philosophical Perspectives on Education

Marti MacCullough

B e careful that no one takes you captive through philosophy and empty deceit based on human tradition, based on the elements of the world, rather than Christ" (Col 2:8).

What comes to your mind when you think of "philosophy"? I always ask this question on the first day of a philosophy of education course. While I get a myriad of responses—some of which are negative, perhaps because of an experience in a prior philosophy course—I do hear many positive comments. The response that thrills me most is that our philosophy of life should be informed by Christ and his Word rather than human tradition. If this is so, should we not also examine our philosophy of education to see if it is informed by a biblical worldview? Socrates famously said, "The unexamined life is not worth living." I will add that unexamined beliefs about education may not be worth carrying out in a classroom. Informing our beliefs about education from a biblical, Christ-centered worldview is the goal of this chapter.

History and Philosophy of Education

While the history of Christian education spans 2,000 years, almost from the beginning of Christianity, the concept of a philosophy of education is usually attributed to the Greeks and their views before the time of Christ. Western education in general has sided with either Aristotle or Plato in determining underlying beliefs about education. As depicted in Raphael's painting *The School of Athens*, Plato and his student Aristotle are standing in the middle of a vast number of prominent philosophers and scholars. Plato is depicted as pointing upward and Aristotle, by his side, is pointing outward. Western educational philosophies have traced their roots to either Plato's universal ideas, a world beyond that only the best and brightest can grasp, or to Aristotle's views that differed in some key areas from his mentor. Both believed that knowledge gained is a virtue. However, Plato focused on a growing body of knowledge for the elite class that would prepare them to be the philosopher kings to rule the citizenry.[1] His focus for education was society, the making of the "good citizen."[2] On the other hand, Aristotle held that schooling was for all, not just the elite.[3] The purpose for education was to move individuals toward happiness or *eudaimonia*, a Greek word meaning well-being or human flourishing, so that each one could contribute to the society as a virtuous person. Aristotle's focus on the use of reason and the senses to understand reality through observation of the natural world made his work attractive to the sciences. Plato's philosophy focused on ideas and ideals that make up reality. These two broad views have vied for acceptance in Western educational thought and, in recent decades, Eastern educational thought as well. Early philosophers of education are often described as espousing the Idealism of Plato or the Realism of Aristotle. The work of this pair continues to influence education today.

Christian Education

The history of Christian school education reveals that Christian educators have sometimes sided with one or the other of the Greek philosophers.[4] For example, Augustine was influenced by the work of Plato, and much later, Thomas Aquinas used the work of Aristotle in developing his philosophy. Both also focused to various extents on Christian theology and implications for education.[5]

---

[1] Gerald L. Gutek, *Historical and Philosophical Foundations of Education*, 2nd ed. (Upper Saddle, NJ: Prentice Hall, 1997), 23–24.

[2] Gutek, 12, 24.

[3] See "Aristotle's Ethics," *Stanford Encyclopedia of Philosophy* (orig. May 1, 2002; rev. June 2018), https://plato.stanford.edu/entries/aristotle-ethics/.

[4] Charles B. Eavey, *History of Christian Education* (Chicago: Moody Press, 1964), 102–10.

[5] Richard C. Sproul, *The Consequences of Ideas* (Wheaton, IL: Good News, 2000), 57–77.

Christian philosophers of education since the time of the Reformation have focused on the authority of the Scriptures over the ancient Greek philosophers. In so doing they have established well-grounded, biblically informed beliefs that focus on God and his created order.[6] This has allowed them to scrutinize views about education through the lens of Scripture to discern that with which they agree and that with which they disagree in underlying beliefs about education.[7] Examination and discernment are the work of developing a *Christian* philosophy of education. The authors of this book believe that Christian teachers in Christian schools, international schools, public schools, charter schools, and homeschools will benefit from developing a soundly biblical perspective on education that will impact their work with children and youth in any of these settings.

What Is a Philosophy of Education, and How Does It Relate to a Worldview?

A philosophy of education is a set of beliefs about the basic elements of education: the aim of education, the nature of the student and learning, the role of the teacher in the learning event, and the nature and purpose of the curriculum. While similar in content to opinions and views about these elements, a philosophy of education differs in that it has been examined, systematized, and intentionally accepted as a set of beliefs that one holds for the foundation of practice. The difference between a philosophy of education and simply opinions or views about education is much like the difference between a philosophy of life and a worldview. Worldviews are "messy" and usually have not been examined and organized as unified wholes. Contradictions may exist side by side in the mind without being realized. The same is true for educators holding to specific educational views. An educator may hold to conflicting beliefs about education that may not have been uncovered and examined, and this may lead to inconsistencies in practice. In developing a philosophy of education, current beliefs are examined and organized to clarify direction and goals. Teachers who espouse a developing biblical worldview have a set of beliefs to use in the process even though they may not (as most of us do not) have a full-blown theology or philosophy of life. This is one reason why the development of biblical worldview thinking is so vital for the Christian. Constant evaluation of ideas is essential for solidifying one's philosophy of life and one's philosophy of education if it is to be

---

[6] D. Bruce Lockerbie, *A Passion for Learning: A History of Christian Thought on Education*, 2nd ed. (Colorado Springs: Purposeful Design, 2007), 113–17.

[7] Eavey, *History of Christian Education*, 144–47.

informed by a biblical worldview. One's philosophy of education must be informed by one's worldview; however, one's worldview may not have been examined, evaluated, systematized, and intentionally accepted (as a philosophy of life). Worldviews often contain inconsistencies and even contradictions, while a full-blown philosophy is usually coherent and consistent.

Developing a philosophy of life takes a lifetime as we use God's Word as our standard to help make sense out of the world, make good choices in life, and make corrections where our thoughts are not in line with God's views. As we examine and clarify our worldview beliefs, we develop a sound and coherent biblical view of life, a philosophy of life. The same is true for educators in developing an educational philosophy. It takes time and the willingness to be open-minded as current beliefs about the elements of education are examined. It takes the willingness to change as education is viewed from a biblical perspective. This process is the subject of this chapter.

Common Beliefs of Educators

ENGAGE: Below are some common beliefs held by educators. They are not exhaustive but rather a sampling of beliefs within the three categories of teacher, student, and curriculum. Select the one (a, b, or c) with which you agree most and then think about *why* you selected that belief.

1. Do you believe that the teacher is more of (a) a dispenser of information to students, (b) a guide and facilitator who draws out of students their own knowledge through activities, or (c) a knowledgeable person who structures and facilitates student-learning of knowledge and skills?
2. Do you believe that the pupil is more of (a) a passive receiver of knowledge from external sources, (b) an autonomously active creator of knowledge and reality from within, or (c) an interactive participant in the learning event in which both inside and outside factors work together?
3. Do you believe that the curriculum should be (a) separate subjects—the basics and great books to be committed to memory, (b) whatever is of interest to the pupil that can be arranged around a theme, or (c) solid subject matter, integrated among and across subjects, integrated with real life and values?

Why We Do What We Do!

The answers alone to the above three questions about the teacher, the student, and the curriculum do not clearly convey one's philosophy without revealing the "why."

Why we do what we do as educators is an expression of our philosophy. If these beliefs have been examined for clarity, consistency, and internal coherency, and systematized or organized into a clear set of statements, they provide educators with a tool to guide and evaluate educational practices and results. A well-crafted philosophy of education also provides professional confidence.

You may be aware of the "Pot Roast Principle" portrayed in the story of the mom who was teaching her daughter to cook a pot roast. Together they prepared the vegetables, and when the pot roast was unwrapped, the mom cut off both ends before putting it into the pan. Her daughter asked her *why* she cut off the ends. To which the mom replied that her mother had always done it that way and she was a great cook. So, when the young girl had a chance to speak with her grandmother, she asked *why* she cut off both ends of a pot roast before putting it in the pan. The grandmother replied, "When your grandfather and I were married, we had just one pan to use and the roasts were always too big, so we cut off the ends." Hmmm . . . So, we ask why we do what we do as an expression of the reasons behind our practices. Perhaps our reasons need to be evaluated so that we do not "cut off both ends" without knowing why.

Reflective Christian Educators Know Why They Do What They Do!

Examining our beliefs is necessary if we are to become reflective teachers who evaluate our own progress based upon a clear set of beliefs. Reflective teaching is defined by the Yale Poorvu Center for Teaching and Learning as follows:

> Reflective Teaching (RT) is a self-assessment of teaching, wherein an instructor examines their pedagogy, articulates reasons and strengths for their strategies, and identifies areas for revision or improvement. RT involves an examination both of one's *underlying beliefs* about teaching and learning and their alignment with actual classroom practice, throughout a course and afterwards.[8]

The remaining chapters in this book unpack beliefs related to the elements of a philosophy of education informed by a biblical worldview and provide practical applications for education. In this chapter we provide a framework for developing a philosophy of education. Readers will be asked to "reflect" on their current beliefs and classroom practices as they "engage" with the material.

---

[8] "Reflective Teaching," Yale Poorvu Center for Teaching and Learning, accessed March 30, 2020, https://poorvucenter.yale.edu/ReflectiveTeaching (emphasis added).

Developing a Philosophy of Education

A philosophy begins with one's underlying worldview answers to the big questions of life and proceeds to relate these answers to education. Long ago, Herbert Spencer expressed the idea that developing a sound curriculum depends on the answer to the question, "What knowledge is most worth knowing?" He wrote: "Before there can be a *rational curriculum*, we must settle which things it most concerns us to know. . . . We must determine the *relative value of knowledges*."[9] As a naturalist, Spencer's answer to the question he posed was that science (natural and social) was the knowledge most worth knowing. He determined that the integrating core of a good curriculum, therefore, should be science because it "is that which most concerns us to know" and gives meaning to all of life. This was a direct reflection of his naturalistic worldview.

ENGAGE: How would you answer the question, "What knowledge is most worth knowing?"—that is, what knowledge gives meaning to all other knowledge and why? (Write your answer below.)

_____

_____

_____

Developing a philosophy of education should begin with our stated underlying worldview. It should differ significantly from Spencer's if we declare that we are Christians. His worldview starts with nature rather than God, the created order rather than the Creator. What is your answer to the above question?

A Christian worldview begins and ends with the living God our Creator. It is Christ-centered and informed by God's Word. The knowledge most worth knowing, the knowledge that gives meaning to all other knowledge and experiences, is the knowledge of God as revealed in his Son, in his Word, and in his creation.

The good news to so many who have never developed a philosophy of education is that we begin right where we are with our underlying biblical worldview. We do not have to be philosophers in the formal sense of the word. Dutch theologian Albert Wolters distinguishes between formal philosophy and what he calls the commonsense perspective on life provided by a worldview "which in one form or another is held by all normal adult human beings regardless of intelligence or education. In this sense,

---

[9] Herbert Spencer, *Education: Intellectual, Moral and Physical* (New York: D. Appleton, 1864), 29, emphasis added.

worldview does indeed precede science (philosophy), and is therefore quite different from philosophy in the strictly theoretical sense."[10]

Wolters goes on to say, "For Christian philosophers, the obvious implication is that they must *seek to orient their philosophizing to a Christian worldview*. Or to put the case a bit more strongly and accurately, the Christian must seek *to philosophize on the basis of the Christian worldview*—that is, the biblical worldview."[11]

So, we begin our philosophy of education with a biblical worldview clearly in mind. As we begin to look at the elements of education, relax and think of this as an exercise in seeing the implications for education of biblical answers to life's biggest questions (worldview questions). Most of the answers to these questions may already have been adopted by you as a Christ-follower, but perhaps never related to education.

An Organizational System for Examining Worldview Beliefs Related to Education

The goal of examining current educational beliefs in light of a Christian worldview is to promote education in which Christian educators have intentionally examined and accepted foundational biblical beliefs related to the basic elements of a philosophy of education. To organize our examination, we offer a framework of four key elements included in a philosophy of education.

1. Aim of education
2. Role of the teacher in promoting learning
3. Nature of the student as a learner
4. Nature and purpose of the curriculum and learning[12]

---

[10] Albert Wolters, "Dutch Neo-Calvinism: Worldview, Philosophy, and Rationality," in *Rationality in the Calvinian Tradition*, ed. Hendrik Hart, Johan Van Der Hoeven, and Nicholas Wolterstorff (Toronto: University Press of America, 1983), 114.

[11] Wolters, 115, emphasis added.

[12] See Martha MacCullough, *By Design: Developing a Philosophy of Education Informed by a Christian Worldview*, 2nd ed. (Colorado Springs: Purposeful Design, 2017). It is understood that in a brief section in a book on instructional design, a thorough presentation of a philosophy of education cannot be addressed. However, the author of this chapter has written an entire book for those who wish to follow up with a more in-depth study.

Starting Point for a Philosophy of Education

Formal philosophy of education documents open with a statement that identifies the "things that concern us most" or the "knowledge most worth knowing" that undergirds the perspective of the author or educator. This is a common practice when identifying a specific philosophy such as Spencer's statement (above). It is not a common practice among public or government-run schools today to state a specific starting point for their educational philosophy. Why might this be so? Could it be that the expression of a foundational philosophy is very difficult in pluralistic societies in which multiple life philosophies or worldviews are respected and protected? Could this be a valid reason for the establishment of private schools of all kinds, including Christian academies, International Christian schools, and homeschools and clusters of homeschools?

ENGAGE: Finish the statement: *My philosophy of education is informed by my worldview. I am a Christian and as such I believe* . . .

Try to finish the sentence above in a way that makes sense to you as a Christian, declaring several things you believe to be true about life in general. For example, do you believe in a living, loving God who created the universe, the earth, and all that inhabits it? Do you believe the human is created in the image of God and as such can think, feel, choose, create, and communicate? What do you believe about the external world, that is, the "natural world" we see and touch and hear, etc.? What do you believe about knowledge and how we come to know what we know? What do you believe about how humans know right and wrong? What do you believe about the purpose of life on this planet? What do you believe about life after death? State your opening beliefs as a form of preamble (introductory statement) to your philosophy. Keep it short. This first statement is a simple declaration of your underlying beliefs that are the basis for your developing philosophy of education. Now finish the statement: *My philosophy of education is informed by my worldview. I am a Christian and as such I believe* . . . You may wish to use the preamble as a bridge statement to declare, "all that follows in my philosophy of education is related to my foundational beliefs."

Framework Part 1: The Aim of Education

Many years ago, Robert Rusk wrote the following in his book *The Philosophical Bases of Education*: "The answer to every educational question is ultimately influenced by our philosophy of life. Although few formulate it, every system of education must have an aim and the *aim of education is relative to the aim of life*. Philosophy formulates what it conceives to be the end of life, education offers suggestions how this end is to be achieved."[13]

Rusk wanted educators to be aware that their own worldviews or views of their country will impact the aim of education. However, to decide on an aim of education, one must first decide on an aim of life. If you ask ten teachers working in a public or government school today to answer the question, "What is the aim of education?" you will hear several different responses. Why might this be?

Most readers of this book live in a pluralistic[14] or somewhat pluralistic society. This is true for much of the world today influenced by global communication. There are many different cultural answers to the broader question, "What is the aim of life?" This serves to confound the issue of determining an aim for meaningful school education. Rusk was aware of this problem in education when he wrote that "few formulate it" (meaning an educational aim). Why do you think that stating an aim for education should *not* be a problem for Christian teachers and administrators? The answer, I believe, is that the aim of life for Christians is singular.

The Need for an Aim of Education

In more recent years, Neil Postman addressed aims in his book *The End of Education*. This book is still read by many students in teacher education programs today. Speaking of American education, Postman declares, "Americans are now so different from each other, have so many diverse points of view, and such special group grievances that there can be no common vision or unifying principle."[15] This lack of a unifying principle was disturbing to Postman, who declared that schools need a common story or narrative to give meaning to all that is learned. What he is addressing is the need for a common worldview narrative. "Not any kind of story, but one that tells of origins and envisions a future, a story that constructs ideals, prescribes rules of conduct, provides a source of

---

[13] Robert Robertson Rusk, *The Philosophical Bases of Education*, 2nd ed. (University of London, 1956), 6, emphasis added.

[14] A pluralistic society is one in which there is "the existence of different types of people, who have different beliefs and opinions, within the same society." Cambridge Dictionary entry for *pluralism* as a noun, accessed January 5, 2022, https://dictionary.cambridge.org/us/dictionary/english/pluralism.

[15] Neil Postman, *The End of Education: Redefining the Value of the School* (New York: Random House, 1995), 196.

authority, and, above all, gives a sense of continuity and purpose . . . to enable one to organize one's life around it."[16]

For years, education in America and elsewhere in the world had overarching aims out of which to operate. Here is one example from one considered as a great American educator, Robert Maynard Hutchins. "Now wisdom and goodness are the aim of higher education. How can it be otherwise? Wisdom and goodness are the end of human life. How can we talk about preparing men for life unless we ask what the end of life may be?"[17] In the past, many writers used the term "end of life" to refer to the aim of life. Notice how Hutchins relates the aim of wisdom and goodness to the aim of life in general.

If Rusk, Hutchins, and Postman are correct in their assumptions that an aim for education is vital and that the aim of education is related to the aim of life, then a prior question must be asked before determining an educational aim. The question is, What is the *aim of life*? The answer should be clear for Christian teachers thinking biblically. Christian schools should be able to formulate a biblically oriented aim of education that coheres with a biblical view of the aim or purpose of life.

What Is the Aim of Life?

ENGAGE: What do you think is a biblically informed aim of life? Take a moment and think, and then write that aim. _____

_____

If you thought of the aim or "end" of life as described in the Westminster Confession of Faith, you would not be alone. When I speak on this topic and ask the aim of life question, many delegates will parrot, "The chief end of man is to glorify God and enjoy him forever." The Westminster Confession is a Reform document written in the 1600s. Much later in 1906, John Wesley revised the confession and kept the chief aim of man exactly as it originally read. But in an even better document, the Word of God, recorded many years before these confessions of faith, we find the words of Isaiah (43:7): "Everyone who bears my name and is created for my glory. I have formed them; indeed, I have made them." And in Rom 11:36, the apostle Paul declares, "For from

---

[16] Postman, 5–6.

[17] Robert Maynard Hutchens, *Education for Freedom* (Baton Rouge: Louisiana State University, 1943), 23–24.

him and through him and for him are all things. To him be the glory forever! Amen."
We were placed on this planet to bring glory to our Creator by reflecting his image.
God's glory is a display of his essence, his character, and his value.[18]

Human Flourishing as the Aim of Education

In *Not the Way It's Supposed to Be*, Cornelius Plantinga writes, "According to all traditional Christian wisdom, *human flourishing is the same thing as glorifying God* and enjoying him forever."[19]

Plantinga's view is a distinctively Christian view of human flourishing that connects it to the aim of life, to glorify God and enjoy him forever. This is not the case
for many espousing human flourishing as the goal of education today. The concept of
human flourishing has been adopted as the aim of education by many secular educators.
However, the description of the "what and how" of human flourishing varies greatly
according to the worldview espoused. Referring to the chief aim of life, John White,
a naturalist and educational philosopher, uses Aristotle's term *eudaimonia*, frequently
translated as "happiness," to refer to human flourishing. He expands the concept from
happiness to "well-being," "flourishing," and "fulfilment." He uses these terms inter-
changeably throughout his book, *Exploring Well-Being in Schools*. White declares that
there has been a "shift from a religious world-view to a largely secular one," and this
is the reason there are divergent accounts of 'well-being' or 'happiness' competing for
allegiance."[20] I would agree! Human flourishing has been described variously according
to the worldview held by the one using the term. Most of these views are man-centered
rather than God-centered and require evaluation by one thinking biblically about what
it means to flourish as a human being.

Human Flourishing Informed by a Biblical Worldview

Human flourishing is a powerful, biblical concept; it is what God intends for his creatures, created in his image. However, when sin entered the world through the choice of
humankind at the fall, the condition of human flourishing was stymied and the ability

---

[18] See Exodus 33 and 34.

[19] Cornelius Plantinga Jr., *Not the Way It's Supposed to Be: A Breviary of Sin* (Grand Rapids:
Eerdmans, 2002), 37–38, emphasis added.

[20] John White, *Exploring Well-Being in Schools: A Guide to Making Children's Lives More
Fulfilling* (New York: Routledge, 2011).

to reflect God's glory was marred. Thankfully, God's plan of redemption through Jesus Christ his Son makes it possible to flourish anew as an image-bearer of God. In John 10:10b Jesus said, "I have come so that they may have life and have it in abundance."

To express human flourishing, the writers of the Old Testament used the analogy of a green tree with roots that go down to the source of life—water and nutrients. To address a biblical view of human flourishing, you may wish to study the following passages and others you find that make use of the simile or metaphor of flourishing trees.

> The person who trusts in the LORD, whose confidence indeed is the LORD, is blessed. He will be *like a tree* planted by water: it sends its roots out toward a stream, it doesn't fear when heat comes, and its foliage remains green. It will not worry in a year of drought or cease producing fruit. (Jer 17:7–8, emphasis added)

> But I am like a *flourishing olive tree* in the house of God; I trust in God's faithful love forever and ever. (Ps 52:8, emphasis added)

> How happy is the one who does not walk in the advice of the wicked or stand in the pathway with sinners or sit in the company of mockers! Instead, his delight is in the LORD's instruction, and he meditates on it day and night. He is *like a tree* planted beside flowing streams that bears its fruit in its season, and its leaf does not wither. Whatever he does prospers. (Ps 1:1–3, emphasis added)

What Does It Mean to Flourish as a Human?

The *Oxford Dictionary* defines *flourishing* as "to grow or develop in a healthy or vigorous way, especially as the result of a particularly congenial environment."[21] The term *flourishing* is a companion concept to the Hebrew term *shalom*, often translated into English as "peace." *Shalom* carries the idea of wholeness, completeness, maturity, and overall well-being in every aspect of human development: spiritually, morally, socially, emotionally, physically, and mentally. *Eirene*, the Greek word translated as "peace" in the New Testament, comes from the root word that means "to bind together that which has been separated or divided."[22] Cornelius Plantinga writes in his insightful book, *Not*

---

[21] "Flourishing," Oxford English and Spanish Dictionary, UK edition, accessed January 5, 2022, https://www.lexico.com/definition/flourish.

[22] Precept Austin, *Peace-Shalom* (Hebrew word study), accessed March 14, 2022, https://www.preceptaustin.org/shalom_-_definition; and *Peace-Eirene* (Greek word study), https://www.preceptaustin.org/peace_eirene.

the Way It's Supposed to Be, that shalom is the way things ought to be.[23] One might say: Shalom, then, is human flourishing with an undivided heart that loves God and others.

In Psalm 1, the human who is blessed and flourishing will "yield its fruit in season." Christian education is not only about human flourishing now during the years in school but also for life in the future. In the past some educators have declared that school is preparation for life while others have declared that school is life now. If we are to view flourishing as a biblical concept, it is for daily living in school now and for life beyond school in the future.

An all-encompassing educational aim might be expressed like this: The aim of education is to promote student flourishing: students will experience life to the full, becoming all that God intends for them to be, as they study and learn about God and his created order, all to his glory!

Or perhaps like this: The aim of education is to promote human flourishing, the full development of each human being as he/she was intended to be as an image-bearer of the God of the Bible.

Or perhaps a little more in-depth expression might be: The aim of education is to promote human flourishing, the living out of what God intended his created image-bearers to be, by pursuing truth about God, his universe, and humankind (ourselves and others); by knowing, understanding, and effectively using knowledge and skills for wise and moral living, thereby growing personally and serving and benefiting society—all to the glory of God, the ultimate aim and first principal of life![24]

The charge to educators is to enhance student **development** in all areas: cognitively, socially, emotionally, physically, and spiritually, and to promote optimal **learning** and human flourishing.

Reflect and write: Think about how you would describe the aim of education and write a first draft here. _____

_____

_____

_____

_____

---

[23] Plantinga, *Not the Way It's Supposed to Be*, 10.

[24] Adapted from Martha MacCullough, *By Design: Developing a Philosophy of Education Informed by a Christian Worldview*, 33.

Framework Part 2: The Role of the Teacher

There is no need to examine the nature of the teacher as a person because teachers are humans too! What is true of their students as human beings is equally true of them. Human nature is addressed in the next section of this chapter. Teachers, too, are created in the image of God and have a glorious purpose in life on this planet. They are thinkers, communicators, and decision-makers. They are creative and inventive. However, they have different *roles* to play in the educational experience than do students, and it is important to know these roles as one enters the teaching profession.

ENGAGE: Early in this chapter, under the heading "Common Beliefs of Educators," you were asked to select answers provided (a, b, or c) with which you agree most. Which of the answers did you select about the teacher's role and why? Here are the options briefly stated: Do you believe that the teacher is more of (a) a dispenser of information, (b) a guide to the learning process, or (c) a knowledgeable person who structures and facilitates learning? If you were asked to explain why you selected (a, b, or c) what would you say?

We are going to examine several biblical passages that help us view the role of the teacher in the teaching/learning process. But first, read some typical beliefs about the teacher's role stated in the chart below that are the general beliefs of two different broad views of educators. In speaking about general philosophies of instruction, teachers often declare that they are traditionalists or progressivists. John Dewey declared that "mankind likes to think in terms of extreme opposites." In educational philosophy he referred to these views as traditional (older views) and progressive (newer views). He describes these two views in his book, *Experience and Education.*[25] We will develop a contrast as we use these two broad views. The chart below shows how some traditionalists and some progressivists might answer our question about the role of the teacher. With which set of beliefs do you agree most and why? Select the beliefs that fit your own thinking at this time and write them.

---

[25] John Dewey, *Experience and Education* (London: Macmillan, 1938), 17–23.

Traditionalists Believe the roles of the teacher are...	Progressivists Believe the roles of the teacher are...
• Authority/boss • Central figure in instruction • Dispenser of knowledge • Example/role model	• Friend/guide • Not the central figure in instruction • Facilitator of learning • Fellow learner

What is the primary purpose or role of the teacher? _____

_____

_____

When I have asked my university students early in their teacher education program to finish the sentence "When I walk into the classroom my *primary* role is _____," I hear a plethora of answers: to be a role model, a guide, a friend, a co-learner, and one who loves kids. I rarely hear that *my primary* role is "to teach!" By the time they are seniors, these students usually respond to the same question saying that their primary role is to promote learning through effective teaching. What would you have said about the primary role of a teacher?

ENGAGE: Pause and do this activity: Using the passages of Scripture provided below, make a list of the roles of the educator you glean from the verses and then compare them to the traditional and progressive views in the chart above. You may wish to read the entire passage in addition to the verses provided. This will provide a broader picture of what the author is conveying in the cited verses.

Deut 6:5–9: "Love the LORD your God with all your heart, with all your soul, and with all your strength. These words that I am giving you today are to be in your heart. Repeat them to your children. Talk about them when you sit in your house and when you walk along the road, when you lie down and when you get up. Bind them as a sign on your hand and let them be a symbol on your forehead. Write them on the doorposts of your house and on your city gates."

1 Cor 11:1: "Be imitators of me, as I am of Christ" (ESV).
(Some translations use the term *example*: "Follow my example, as I follow the example of Christ" [NIV].)

2 Cor 10:8: "For if I boast some more about our authority, which the Lord gave for building you up and not for tearing you down, I am not ashamed" (HCSB).

1 Thess 2:7b–8: "We were gentle among you, as a nurse nurtures her own children. We cared so much for you that we were pleased to share with you not only the gospel of God but also our own lives, because you had become dear to us."

1 Thess 2:11–12: "As you know, like a father with his own children, we encouraged, comforted, and implored each one of you to walk worthy of God, who calls you into his own kingdom and glory."

Mark 10:42–45: "Jesus called them over and said to them, 'You know that those who are regarded as rulers of the Gentiles lord it over them, and those in high positions act as tyrants over them. But it is not so among you. On the contrary, whoever wants to become great among you will be your servant, and whoever wants to be first among you will be a slave to all. For even the Son of Man did not come to be served, but to serve, and to give his life as a ransom for many.'"

1 Pet 5:2–3: "Shepherd God's flock among you, not overseeing out of compulsion but willingly, as God would have you; not out of greed for money but eagerly; not lording it over those entrusted to you but being examples to the flock."

Luke 6:40: "A disciple is not above his teacher, but everyone who is fully trained will be like his teacher."
(The NIV translates the word for *disciple* as "student.")

Your list should include several key roles of the teacher. The Deuteronomy passage was listed first to point out that the primary role of the teacher is to teach in various ways so that students learn. The educators referenced in this passage are parents, however the principle may be applied to teachers who serve in schools as well. Here is a possible list from which to determine implications for the classroom. You may have found others. Teacher-roles are:

- to teach
- to serve
- to be in charge
- to be a role model

Each category, and others you may have gleaned, should be addressed briefly in your philosophy of education.

Category One: To Teach

What does it mean to teach? (1) Does it mean to dispense information using a model of telling, testing, and reinforcing correct answers to questions? (2) Does it mean to be a fellow-learner and simply address whatever the students desire to learn, using a drawing-out model in which the teacher simply draws out of students what they are thinking or what they are doing? (3) Or does it mean that a knowledgeable teacher who loves learning organizes and facilitates the learning of solid subject matter and skills, integrated among and across subjects, and integrated with real life and values? These are three different views that are foundational to the instructional process. If you selected number 3, you are close to the view of the authors of this book, and if so, there are some key prerequisites to promote effectiveness, all of which are addressed more in depth later in this book. Teachers must:

1. Know the subjects they teach and how each subject should be learned (see the nature or structure of the subject matter and skills in section 4). This requires the teacher to be one who loves to learn and is willing to study.
2. Know the students and how they learn and be able to build a caring learning community (see the nature of human learning in chapters 2–4 and section 3).
3. Be able to bring 1 and 2 above together to create and deliver lessons that promote learning (see the development and delivery of the curriculum in chapters 5–6).

In the next three chapters we explore how the nature of the student and learning impacts the role of the teacher in teaching. You may wish to refer to this section again after reading the next few chapters. Toward the end of this book, you will find an entire section that examines each basic subject area, addressing the underlying structure of that subject and how it should be learned so that teaching a particular subject can be adapted to fit with the structure of that subject.

Category Two: To Serve

What does it mean to serve? Are we to be doormats for students to walk all over, or is service much more complex than that? As Jesus taught his disciples who were going to lead the greatest movement in history—Christianity—he washed their feet, yet he was their master and Lord! He called them to do likewise to others in John 13:14–15. "So if I, your Lord and Teacher, have washed your feet, you also ought to wash one another's feet. For I have given you an example, that you also should do just as I have done for you." In Mark 10:45 we read, "For even the Son of Man did not come to be served, but to serve, and to give his life as a ransom for many." Teachers are not placed in their role to have their own needs met or even to be loved by their students. They are there to love, serve, and care for students as they live together in a caring learning community. Building a caring learning community is addressed in section 3.

Category Three: To Be in Charge

What does it mean to be in charge? What does it mean to have authority in the classroom? Does this mean that the teacher is the boss? Is "authority" something to be ashamed of in the twenty-first century? We might get some help from the apostle Paul who wrote, "For if I boast some more about our authority, which the Lord gave for building you up and not for tearing you down, I am not ashamed" (2 Cor 10:8 HCSB).

All human authority is delegated, whether it is the authority of the school board over the head of school, the authority of the head of school or principals over teachers, or teachers over students. Ultimately all authority is sourced in God and delegated to others. It is not a good idea to view ourselves as the boss! However, we are responsible both legally and morally for our students. Government sets up certain legal responsibilities for teachers and we must serve under these. For a Christian, however, there is a moral or ethical authority as well.

Children are a sacred trust and therefore we must care for each one of them. This includes their safety, their emotions, and their learning. Moral and legal authority were the norm in early American education and in much of the world, but the situation has changed drastically during the last five or six decades and the focus is now on legal authority alone. However, both moral and legal authority impact how we discipline. Sociologist Richard Arum, addressing the problems of discipline in America's government schools, claims that the loss of moral authority in the schools began in the 1960s and '70s with the focus on autonomous individual rights. He believes that to understand the erosion of moral authority in school discipline "requires one to consider how the expansion of individual rights has come into conflict with the schools' prerogative to control student behavior."[26] He concludes that US court litigation (he calls it adversarial legalism) and a sense of student entitlement have led to the problems

---

[26] Richard Arum, *Judging School Discipline: The Crisis of Moral Authority* (Boston: Harvard University, 2003), 5–6.

in classroom discipline we have been experiencing in recent years. Legal authority has remained, but moral authority has been lost.[27] This is sad and should not be true in Christian schools. More on this topic will be addressed in the chapters on classroom management and student discipline in section 3.

Category Four: To Be a Role Model

What does it mean to be a role model? If you ask several teachers what or who teachers are to model, you will get various answers. When I was a child in elementary school, the answer might have been the teacher was to be a model of the most upstanding citizen. During my years of serving as a dean of a school of education, the concept of what teachers were to model was a person of high morals and a lifelong learner. Recently, teachers have been encouraged to develop self-acceptance and the acceptance of others through mindfulness and then model mindful skills.[28] The answers vary from year to year depending on the prevailing worldview of the general culture of education.

Young people will usually name their role models as athletes, music stars of the day, or popular people on TV or social media. The character traits these models portray are moving targets. What is morally good seems to change from year to year. What people in the last century considered an upstanding or moral person is radically different from a description of a moral person today. The characteristics of good role models might be considered as moving targets because the concept of "good" or what is best to model changes periodically. There is one person to model, however, who never changes. That person is Jesus Christ. He is the same today as yesterday and will be the same tomorrow. First John 1:6 declares: "If we say, 'We have fellowship with him,' and yet we walk in darkness, we are lying and are not practicing the truth." The NIV translation of the next chapter succinctly translates 2:6, "Whoever claims to live in him must live as Jesus did." The apostle Paul wrote, "Be imitators of me, as I am of Christ" (ESV).[29]

What does it look like to model Christ? The apostle Paul, writing to the Colossian church, encouraged Christians to be clothed in Christ and provided a list of characteristics to "put on": kindness, humility, gentleness, patience, bearing with one another,

---

[27] Arum, 6.

[28] Patricia A. Jennings, *Mindfulness for Teachers* (New York: W. W. Norton, 2015), xxv, 183–84.

[29] This is referenced in the list used for this activity—see 1 Cor 11:1 (ESV), "Be imitators of me, as I am of Christ." Some translations use the term *example*: "Follow my example, as I follow the example of Christ" (NIV).

and forgiving as the Lord has forgiven us (Col 3:12–13). These characteristics are very similar to those that God revealed to Moses when he asked him to lead his people and Moses asked God to show him his glory. "The Lᴏʀᴅ passed in front of him and proclaimed: The Lᴏʀᴅ—the Lᴏʀᴅ is a compassionate and gracious God, slow to anger and abounding in faithful love and truth, maintaining faithful love to a thousand generations, forgiving iniquity, rebellion, and sin" (Exod 34:6–7a).

Reflect again on the aim of life for the Christian: "to glorify God and enjoy him forever." We glorify him by reflecting his character; we enjoy him as we flourish as image-bearers. If these characteristics of love, grace, compassion, and care were consistently lived out in any school by teachers and staff, we might turn the small part of our world upside down as did the early church leaders. What or who to model is not a mystery for the Christian! It is Christ.

Framework Part 3: Nature of the Student as Learner

This section of a philosophy of education is vital to "teaching that matters." Therefore, several of the following chapters build upon the broad foundation provided in this section. To engage the mind related to the nature of the student and learning, please complete the activity below:

ENGAGE: "If you were asked to address the question "What is a human being and how do humans learn?" what would you say? Think for a minute and then write your thoughts.

_____

_____

Some possible answers may be found in the chart that follows. These are just examples from present-day philosophies of education that have been characterized under the headings: "Traditional View" and "Progressive View,"[30] which are two very different views of human learning. Although these broad statements in the chart do not express the complete beliefs of educators who might label themselves traditional or progressive, the examples may trigger your thinking in describing human learning. You may wish to check the statements with which you agree on either side.

---

[30] Martha MacCullough, _By Design_, 49.

Human Nature and Learning:[31]	
Traditional View: humans are...	**Progressive View: humans are...**
• Rational creatures: Natural capacity to think, to know, to seek truth, and to acquire knowledge. (The most important aspect of learners is their intellect or the mind.) • Sensory learners. (Realism) • Psychologically passive rather than active in the learning event. They take into the central nervous system information from outside. They are considered a blank tablet to be written on by the environment. (Behaviorism) • Morally flawed or morally neutral and in need of moral instruction and guidance. • Subject to natural law and therefore not free in their choices. Morally neutral (Behaviorism) and can be shaped for good by reinforcement. Early traditionalists held that the human is morally flawed and in need of intervention. • Part of a great universal machine that can be programmed. (Behaviorism; Determinism) • Microscopic selves who are in the process of becoming more like the Absolute Self. (Idealism)	• Curious, possessing a natural desire to learn and discover things about the world around them. The student is autonomously active, rather than passive, in the learning event. Learning emerges primarily from within the learner. • Experiencing individuals, capable of using their intelligence to resolve problematic situations and contribute to society. (Pragmatism) • Choosing, free, and responsible agents. (Existentialism) • Capable of increasing self-awareness and finding and being or creating themselves. • Morally good or neutral. If good, restraint is not good. Children should be able to unfold their natural goodness. If neutral, children need moral education, usually through modeling. (Dewey)

Anticipating a Third View

There is a third view to consider that will be addressed in the next chapter. Various worldviews answer these key questions concerning human learning very differently. How do Christians answer these questions? This will be the focus of the next several chapters. Here is a template to help organize your thoughts as you read the next two chapters:

---

[31] I created this chart and have used it for many years. Adapted from MacCullough, *By Design*, 49.

Template for the Nature of the Student and Learning[32]

I. *Commonalities* (things that are true of all humans because we are born into the human family, rather than into the family of plants, animals, angels, or God)
  A. Special category of living things (If so, why special?)
  B. Moral nature (good, bad, or neutral at birth?)
  C. Actional nature (psychologically passive, autonomously active, or cognitively interactive—these are mutually opposed inborn conditions and only one can be true)
  D. General developmental nature

II. *Differences* (human differences by birth or developed over time, both individual and cultural)
  A. Individual developmental variance from the norm (statistical curve)
  B. Individual preferences and capacities in learning—brain or experience-related (for example, learning styles, multiple intelligences, and cognitive processing capacities)
  C. Cultural and social forces that affect individuals and groups of individuals
  D. Various other abilities and disabilities

The above template is provided for you to examine what it is you believe about these educational issues. With further examination you may change your mind or word what you believe differently. This is part of the process of developing a philosophy of education.

ENGAGE: Write one thing you believe about each of the items A through D from the two categories above, commonalities and differences. Come back to these beliefs at the end of this book to compare them with any new insights.

_____

_____

_____

_____

---

[32] My own template. Adapted from *By Design*, 85.

A Biblical View of the Human Learner

When I ask a group of teachers which of the two, human similarities or differences, was the focus of their teacher education program, the response is almost unanimous—individual differences. However, an effective teacher must address those things that all humans have in common as well. They are foundational for effective planning and delivering of the curriculum in accordance with human nature *and learning*, and they promote learning that is more natural and less of a struggle for students. Understanding human individual differences as well as commonalities will help the educator in the development of relationships, in adaptations or differentiation, in assessment, and in carrying out classroom management and student discipline. These areas are addressed later in this book.

Without a doubt, the most important truth about the human being is the fact that humans are created in the image of God. We are special! We are not plants, animals, angels, and certainly not gods or God. We are in another category altogether according to God's Word. We are human! Only of humans did God declare, "In the image of God he created them" (Gen 1:27). Certainly this is special! Yes, students must know that scientists who observe external and cellular characteristics have classified humans in the animal kingdom as mammals. But God has added something that science apparently cannot observe, the image of God in humanity. Our students must understand this specialness!

Blaise Pascal, a seventeenth-century mathematician, warned in his *Pensées*: "It is dangerous to show a man too clearly how much he resembles the beast, without at the same time showing him his greatness. It is also dangerous to allow him too clear a vision of his greatness without his baseness. It is even more dangerous to leave him in ignorance of both."[33]

Our **greatness** as humans is the reality that we are image-bearers of the Living God. What does that mean? Among those characteristics that image God seem to be these: I can think, feel, choose, create, communicate, relate to others in love and companionship, and I have a work to do in caring for, sustaining, and enjoying the earth.

---

[33] As cited in Malcolm Jeeves, ed., *Rethinking Human Nature: A Multidisciplinary Approach* (Grand Rapids: Eerdmans, 2011), 192.

Genesis 1:26–27; 9:6; Psalm 8:4

Genesis 1 records the clear statement of God himself about his creation of humans in his image and likeness. "Then God said, Let us make man in our image, according to our likeness. They will rule the fish of the sea, the birds of the sky, the livestock, the whole earth, and the creatures that crawl on the earth. So God created man in his own image; he created him in the image of God; he created them male and female."

The declaration of the image of God in man is made again in Genesis 9 after the fall of humankind and after the horrendous wickedness that led to the flood in the days of Noah. Humans were still described as image-bearers, and although given the right to kill animals for food in Genesis 9, they were forbidden to kill each other. The reason given: "for God made humans in his image" (v. 6).

In Psalm 8:4–6, the writer asks, "What is a human being that you remember him, a son of man that you look after him?" He then answers his own question: "You made him little less than God and crowned him with glory and honor. You made him ruler over the works of your hands; you put everything under his feet." Human "greatness," it seems to me, is related to being created in the image of God with the purpose of reflecting that image on this planet and living as God intended, ruling for good "over the works of God's hand."

Human "baseness," to use Pascal's term, is no doubt related to the fall when Adam and Eve sinned, and this resulted in a flawed, sinful nature that prevents the human from reflecting God's image, his glory, as God intended. We could not fix ourselves. We could not fulfill the purpose for which we are made; could not flourish as God intended. We all "fall short of the glory of God" (Rom 3:23). What a sad commentary on the human predicament. The fall made necessary an outside intervention in the person of Jesus Christ, God's Son, who provides salvation and restored relationship with God through his death and resurrection. This is God's grace at work for all those who, by faith in his finished work, believe.

God's Spirit is at work recreating his image and the glory from which we have fallen so that we can once again reflect the God of the universe as he intended. "We all, with unveiled faces, are looking as in a mirror at the glory of the Lord and are being transformed into the same image from glory to glory; this is from the Lord who is the Spirit" (2 Cor 3:18). This is the process of human flourishing and fits with the overall aim of education.

The other issues in the template are addressed in the next chapters beginning with the nature or "born-with" capacity to make sense of the world. In closing this chapter on philosophy of education we turn to the nature and purpose of the curriculum.

Framework Part 4: Nature and Purpose of the Curriculum and Learning

Describing the nature of the curriculum is not straightforward to many teachers. When asked to define or describe the curriculum, many still refer to the curriculum materials and guides that describe a course of study. Some just say the curriculum is "my textbook." However, the curriculum includes all of the *planned* experiences designed to bring about learning in any school setting (including homeschool). It includes the plans and resources, the planned delivery, and the planned learning environment. This broad definition is important in creating a cohesive experience for students.

As you work through the process of examining, clarifying, and systematizing your beliefs, it will become apparent that all parts of your educational philosophy are interrelated. The strong connection between the curriculum, the nature of the pupil and learning, and the role of the teacher will be evident as you think and write about the nature of the curriculum. Your developing philosophy of education should be an internally consistent set of beliefs that coheres in such a way that it makes sense as a unified whole. To highlight this process, answer the following questions. You may not be sure of your answers at this point. That is just fine. These questions will be addressed in the next several chapters and throughout this book for your evaluation.

ENGAGE: **Think about your answers to the questions below:**
1. What will I do differently in my curricular plans and delivery if I believe the student is an active participant in learning with an interactive actional nature, rather than either a passive receiver of information or an autonomously active creator of personal knowledge or reality? (The concept of the "actional" nature as active, passive, or interactive will be addressed in the next chapters.)
2. What will I do differently in my plans and delivery if I understand my students' developmental limits and potentials as a group and as individuals? What will I need to consider, and how will these considerations affect the curriculum?
3. How will I respond to students if I believe humans are created in the image of God? What value will I place on each life? How will my behaviors reflect my beliefs as I work with the poorest child, the most gifted, the learning disabled, the ELL (English Language Learner), the worst behaved, or the brightest and the best academically? These questions relate to the curricular planned learning community.

Beliefs about the Curriculum

ENGAGE: Examine two sets of beliefs in the chart below and determine with which one you agree most and why. How would describe your own beliefs at this point?

_____

_____

_____

Category	Traditional Curriculum	Progressive Curriculum
Lesson/unit plans	Outlined content or skills to be developed: facts, skills, quizzes Curriculum is **subject**-centered or teacher-centered	List of processes, activities, or experiences for students Curriculum is **student**-centered
Delivery of the lesson	Dispense information: tell, put in outside information, and test	Student activities: draw out inside creation of knowledge
Environment	Rigid, stern, business-like	Permissive, relaxed, free

The curriculum should promote student learning, and therefore the teacher must examine how humans learn as a primary consideration. You may wish to return to this section after reading the next three chapters on students as learners. When our primary concern is for student learning, it might be best to use the labels below for the curriculum instead of using subject-centered (content focus) or the opposing view, student-centered, as descriptors for the curriculum. As you see, each element of the curriculum begins with the word "learning."

ENGAGE: Why might these labels be better than student centered or subject centered?

Learning Plans: Overall approach to teaching based on a theory of learning

Plans for promoting student learning that focus on content that is student-processed and understood for retrieval and use in problem-solving, decision-making, and growing as a learner.

Learning Activities: Delivery methods

Impressive and expressive methods to carry out a cognitive interactive learning plan.

Learning Community: Planned classroom environment

Planned environment that enhances student learning and human flourishing in a caring community (see section 3).

Perhaps the label Learning or Learner-Centered might be better than the other two common labels of Student-Centered or Subject-Centered!

The Nature of the Human and Learning AND the Content of Learning

When we think about the curriculum in any school, we must address not only the general nature of the student as a human being, but also the nature of humans as learners. We must also address what kind of learning we espouse. Do we focus on content from outside the knowing mind as an object of learning, or do we focus on the inside capacity and processes for learning of the student? Is this an either/or issue or something else?

There is a mind (inside factor) and an object (outside factor); there is a human learner with inside capacities, prior experiences, and prior knowledge, and there is outside information to be learned. Both are equally important, as you will see in the next chapters. James Porter Moreland writes, "In thought, the mind's structure conforms to the order of the object of thought."[34]

> The Old Testament proclaims that the same rational God who reveals Himself to the prophets also created the world as an orderly, understandable cosmos. And the Old Testament assures us that this God made our minds to be apt for gaining knowledge and understanding so as to avoid foolish and ignorant beliefs. For those willing to pay the price of exercising their minds and studying diligently, there is knowledge and wisdom found in Scripture (Ps 119); in the natural world and its operations (Isa 28:23–29); and in the accumulated insights embedded in the art, literature, and science of the different cultures of the world (Isa 19:11–13; Jer 49:7; Dan 2:12–13, 5:7).[35]

When Christian educators consider the curriculum, they must also answer the question, "What is the nature and source of knowledge?" They must understand that something is *there to be learned*, an objective and knowable world in all its complexities, and the God who created it. There is, as well, *someone* doing the learning. Christian

---

[34] James Porter Moreland, *Love Your God with All Your Mind* (Colorado Springs: NavPress, 1997), 67.

[35] Moreland, 66–67.

educators must also realize that coming to know is messy and involves a measure of subjectivity because of human limits in vocabulary, prior knowledge, processing capacities, and other complex cognitive and emotional/social factors. Teachers must be aware that standards of knowledge do matter, and cognitively interactive humans can misconstrue and misunderstand for a variety of reasons. Ongoing assessment is vital for effective learning and should be a form of feedback that provides information about how students are doing. Are they getting it? Do they need more instruction or time to digest new information? Are they meeting the criteria or standard? Assessment is also feedback to the student that indicates whether they are getting it—that is, whether they understand the information or can use the skill effectively. This is vital to adjusting one's teaching and to promoting effective effort on the part of the student.

The implications for considering one's view of the content we teach is related to one's developing philosophy of education and the beliefs related to several issues: (1) standards of knowledge versus personally constructed knowledge; (2) assessment for understanding versus self-assessment alone with little assessment of content, or the opposite, the assessment of parroted-back content/information alone without checking for understanding; and (3) truth as correspondence to reality versus truth as a creation by the mind. You might be able to name other implications.

Why might a person think that a view of knowledge *and* knowing that includes both inside and outside factors fits best with a biblical view of knowledge and knowing? Or does it? The Christian, informed by a biblical worldview, must reject the postmodern epistemology with its omission of the objective existence of outside factors that impact learning. (For more on the discussion of the nature of knowledge and knowing and the relationship to a current philosophical theory, Radical Constructivism, refer to my book *By Design*, chapter 11.)

Purpose of the Curriculum

Examining the purpose of the curriculum brings us back, full circle to the aim of education. The curriculum—that is, all the planned experiences of the school—is designed to move toward the overarching aim for schooling that may be described in terms of human flourishing. How will you incorporate your stated aim of education into the purpose or "aim" of the curriculum in a Christian school? How will the target of human flourishing be fleshed out in your classroom through the curriculum?

Developing biblically minded students through the process of worldview integrative teaching is a curricular issue. It is not accomplished through devotions or chapel periodically or prayer at the beginning of class alone. Rather, it is achieved when the curriculum is strategically designed to develop biblical worldview thinking that transforms the disintegrated and culturally affected mind into a mind that grows in love for God and others as well as in appreciation for all of God's created order. It is the human mind that must be integrated until we develop God's perspective on all of life, learning, and living that coheres with his answers to life's biggest questions. It takes time, a lifetime!

A popular model that is used for "biblical integration" is the framework of the Big Story of Scripture: Creation, Fall, Redemption, and Restoration. I prefer to begin with God first to make it a five-element story because I use a questions approach, the first question of which is, "Is there a higher being or does God exist?"

Example:

God: God exists from everlasting to everlasting—eternally. "In the beginning God . . ." This answers the question, Is there a being higher than we? Is there a God? This is foundational to a biblical worldview. His existence is not only verified by his works as seen in the Bible but also his works in his created order.

Creation: God determined to **create** the universe; this story is recorded in Genesis 1 and 2. This answers the big question: How did the world and humans come into existence? The "what" he created, the "who" did it, and the "why" are universally accepted by Christians. The exact "how" and "when" are not only a mystery but open to interpretation. The creation part of the story also addresses the questions, What or who is a human being, specifically, the difference between humankind from other creatures because we are created in the image of God, and what gives us worth and purpose?

Fall: God reveals the answer to the questions, What happened? What went wrong? In Genesis 3, humanity, endowed by the Creator with a mind to think, emotions to desire, and a will to choose, made a terrible choice to disobey the one command God gave to them, and sin entered the world. We see the wrong immediately in broken relationships not only with God but between man and woman and between their sons, Cain and Abel. This part of the story is called "the fall." Yet at that very time, God promised a solution to the problem (Gen 3:15). Humans, created in the image of God, were thereafter born with a marred and flawed image of God, but that image was not eradicated. Much of the book of Genesis up to chapter 9 reveals the result of sin and the culmination in the flood in the days of Noah. But that was not the end of sin as is seen and addressed in the rest of the Bible.

Beginning in Genesis 12, God begins to unfold his plan through Abraham and a nation through which he would send his Son, Jesus, into the world. The story of the Israelites, their struggles and God's work, their rebellion because of sin, their exile from and restoration back to the promised land, and finally their inability to follow the law of God in their own strength displayed in the Pharisees, among others, continues in the New Testament.

Redemption: Fast-forward from the fall and God's promise of redemption to the time of Christ. God sent his Son to redeem humanity who had already proven, even with God's care and his law, to be unable to keep God's commands. The problem of sin and humankind's separation from God could not be solved by humanity alone. God's intervention is absolutely necessary. The Israelites were stiff-necked and disobedient. The Pharisees tried to meet God's requirements but were filled with pride, and their good deeds were not enough. The story of redemption and reconciliation takes up most of the rest of the story of God's work recorded in the Bible.

Restoration: Restoration of our relationship with God is immediate at salvation (redemption); however, ultimate restoration is foretold in the last two chapters of the book of Revelation, which reveal God will make all things new—a new heaven and a new earth. Compare these two chapters in Revelation with Genesis 1 and 2. This is an aid in remembering that restoration is all about God restoring humanity and all of creation that was affected by the fall. We will not be disembodied creatures or angels in the "afterlife." We will forever be humans and live and eat and be in the presence of God who will dwell forever with all of those who have believed.

A wonderful story! But how do we teach the subjects of math and science, social studies, and the language arts, PE and health, and the arts using the story? This has been the dilemma for many years in understanding what has been called biblical integration that I now prefer to call biblical thinking and acting (see Rom 12:1–2).

Teaching to Develop Biblical Worldview Thinking

I have used a *questions* approach for teaching biblical worldview thinking for many years and have found this to be helpful as teachers develop lessons in which the students learn to critically think about the material they are learning by practicing biblical thinking. That is, by using God's answers to basic worldview questions to appreciate and connect to the subject matter in the curriculum including resources and research materials. Teachers can develop lessons in which the students learn how to also detect and distinguish worldview answers to basic questions that are not biblical. This is the process of critical thinking.

Answering questions is a form of "apologetics." The word is derived from the Greek word *apologia*, "to give an answer or defense." Christians are encouraged to develop this process, "but in your hearts regard Christ the Lord as holy, ready at any time to give a defense to anyone who asks you for a reason for the hope that is in you" (1 Pet 3:15).

The first set of questions I used were found in a resource book, *The Human Adventure: Four World Views*, published by Allyn Bacon in 1971, for middle school social studies. Later, I found and used the questions from James Sire's book *The Universe Next Door*. The questions approach seems to fit with the process of critical thinking that is required in Rom 12:2, "Do not be conformed to this age, but be transformed by the renewing of your mind, so that you may discern what is the good, pleasing, and perfect will of God." This worldview approach can be used together with the framework addressed briefly above: God, creation, fall, redemption, and restoration.

Teachers and students work together in the task of biblical thinking. This is accomplished, in part, through the strategic design of the curriculum as the teacher plans and the teacher and students learn. In the last chapter in this book, the concept of developing biblical worldview thinking will be further addressed. For in-depth information, see the book *Undivided: Developing a Worldview Approach to Biblical Integration*[36] by the author of this chapter. The best book I have read and used on the topic of apologetics, especially for science and history teachers, is *I Don't Have Enough Faith to Be an Atheist*.[37]

In my university philosophy of education classes we explore together three types of integrative thinking: (1) **subject-to-subject**, often called multidisciplinary or interdisciplinary learning, thematic units and the like; (2) **subject-to-life** that includes authentic learning and assessment and helps students to understand the connections between learning and life; (3) **subject-to-worldview** integrative thinking in the strategic design of the curriculum in which the teacher plans for the students to examine worldview answers to life's biggest questions found in the subjects of the school curriculum. Students are prompted to see if these answers fit with a biblical worldview or do not fit and must be distinguished from a biblical view. The goal is that students view

---

[36] Martha MacCullough, *Undivided: Developing a Worldview Approach to Biblical Integration* (Colorado Springs: Purposeful Design, 2016).

[37] Norman L. Geisler and Frank Turek, *I Don't Have Enough Faith to Be an Atheist* (Wheaton, IL: Crossway, 2004).

all of life and learning from God's perspective as a unified whole. God's perspective found in his Word is the "knowledge most worth knowing," that forms the integrating core for developing biblical thinking and gives meaning to all else we learn.

Worldview integration is the process of bringing together into a whole the things that we are learning that fit with a biblical worldview; it is the task of bringing together both special and general revelation into a unified and wonderful whole. Things that do not fit with a biblical view are learned and stored as information in the mind and enable us to understand and appreciate and respect others who hold to these beliefs. However, their beliefs are not a part of our growing and developing biblical worldview; they are a contrast to biblical views. This process of critical thinking based upon the standard of God's Word leads to discernment and human flourishing as characterized by Scripture.

Are we willing to take the time to study and prepare so that both we and our students grow in our understanding of God's Word and his world?

> For those willing to pay the price of exercising their minds and studying diligently, there is knowledge and wisdom found in Scripture (Ps 119); in the natural world and its operations (Isa 28:23–29); and in the accumulated insights embedded in the arts, literature, and science of the different cultures of the world (Isa 19:11–13; Jer 49:7; Dan 2:12–13; 5:7).[38]

Conclusion

This book is about developing biblically minded teachers, integrative thinkers who can promote student learning. How should we view our scholarly activity related to becoming a teacher? A teacher who views all of life and learning from God's perspective will see every student as created in the image of God; one who can think and feel and choose and create; one who was created to reflect the God of the universe; one who is a special creation of incredible worth. Compare that to the perspective that humans are merely machines or highly complex animals but with no qualitative difference from the animal kingdom. A teacher's overall approach to the teaching profession will be informed by his or her understanding of human nature and learning.

Christian teachers will not only study hard and know their subject and students well but will also promote learning in a way that helps students process and internalize new information into their scheme of meaning. Compare that to a teacher who

---

[38] Moreland, *Love Your God with All Your Mind*, 66–67.

holds that humans are passive in the learning event. These teachers use a telling-testing approach, reinforced only with stickers and/or grades, and so often the information is never internalized, integrated, and remembered.

Christian educators who practice biblical integrative thinking view their role as a teacher as one who models a nonmoving target, the Lord Jesus Christ, whose compassion, love, and forgiveness we are instructed to imitate. Even in classroom management and discipline, Christian teachers see that what they do is for the "profit of the child" and not to prove their own power. I will never see myself as the "boss" but as one with delegated authority, a servant leader. The goal is that my students, whether in first grade or college, will see learning and life as an integral whole framed by biblical answers to life's biggest questions. This kind of intentional education will impact the church, society, and the world to really know our great God and our place in his story as we live on the planet. This is what we will unpack throughout the rest of this book.

ENGAGE AND REFLECT:

Read the conversation below. Identify the speaker that seems to believe things about education that fit with how you think. Select Amos, Bogard, or Carpet, or enter the conversation based upon what you have understood from this chapter about the nature of the student and learning. Discuss these alternatives with a fellow teacher.

Mr. Amos: I think that the most important things in school emerge from within the students themselves. School should be student-centered and provide for the natural unfolding of human creativity. Schools should not stifle the student by imposing a structured curriculum.

Mrs. Bogard: Yes, student motivation from within is vital in the learning process and some teachers do stifle kids; however, a teacher must provide a scaffolding or framework to help the student make sense out of information. Students need a knowledge base in order to creatively process and use information for real-life.

Mr. Amos: Okay, but I believe a person needs to be, first of all, fulfilled as a human and allowed freedom from an imposed structure. Skills and knowledge will be picked up naturally as students feel a need for them and when they feel positively about themselves.

Miss Carpet: Dreamer! Can you imagine a whole school of little self-actualized humans who feel good about themselves even though they can't say their timetables, don't know state capitals, and can't even count change at the store?! Give me your kids! I'll get them to learn the basics they need to know, and they will pass their standardized tests. Our school will show high test scores. How? Simple: Set up specific objectives. Expose the kids to the information or skill they need, drill them, test them, reward them (grade them). No big deal. That's school learning.

Mrs. Bogard: But will they be able to retrieve and use the knowledge or know when and how to use the skills in a variety of real-life situations rather than just to pass a test? What do you think Mr. A.?

Mr. Amos: I think we need more coffee!

What is missing in the conversation above according to your own thinking? What would you add to the conversation? With what do you agree and not agree and why?

Much of what is written in the remaining part of this book will unpack elements of a philosophy of education informed by a Christian worldview. Your answers to the above questions may be enriched by what follows.

Reflection and Possible Educational Task: It is worthwhile to take a few minutes to reflect on the four basic elements of a philosophy of education—the aim of education, the nature of the student and learning, the role of the teacher, and the nature and purpose of the curriculum—and write several beliefs under each category. This could be the beginning of writing your own philosophy of education.

This chapter has outlined a basic structure for developing one's philosophy of education. The remaining chapters in this book explore in depth some of the topics outlined here. It may be worthwhile to review this chapter after reading the entire book and then write your philosophy of education.

Extended Research and Reflection: If you or your school use InTASC Standards, how does developing a sound philosophy of education help to meet the issues addressed in Standard 9?

Professional Learning and Ethical Practice. The teacher engages in ongoing professional learning and uses evidence to continually evaluate his or her practice, particularly the effects of his or her choices and actions on others (learners, families, other professionals, and the community), and adapts practice to meet the needs of each learner.[39]

---

[39] "Interstate Assessment and Support Consortium," Council of Chief State School Officers 2013 (Washington, DC).

Two Educational Philosophers Who Have Impacted Education

John Dewey (1859–1932), Pragmatist and Progressive Educator

John Dewey was born in Burlington, Vermont, in 1859 and became a philosopher. He promoted pragmatism, an American philosophy that claims that truth is tentative and not universal and absolute. The test for truth is to find out if something works in practical use.[40] It was this philosophy that became the underlying foundation of his views on education. Dewey was against the practice of reacting negatively to traditional ideas without basing new educational ideas (labeled "progressive") on an underlying philosophy.[41] Therefore, his ideas about education are an extension of pragmatism, a philosophy that promotes relativism.

Dewey did not believe that philosophy should begin with metaphysics, such as the existence of something or someone higher than humankind. Rather, pragmatists hold "that truth is tentative, a warranted assertion, rather than universal and absolute. Further, truth is derived from human experience which involves the testing or verification of an idea by acting on it and determining if the consequences of such action resolve the particular problem."[42]

Teachers in the twentieth and twenty-first centuries have selectively borrowed key Deweyean phrases such as "learning by doing," the "activity method," and "problem-solving," without adopting his entire underlying philosophy. Sometimes they have gone well beyond Dewey's intentions.[43] Others, including many Christian educators, opposed Dewey's philosophy because of their own differing philosophical convictions. Many think that his views encourage relativism, the death of truth that is universal and unchanging, and denial of a personal God as the ultimate authority for life.[44]

---

[40] Gutek, *Historical and Philosophical Foundations of Education*, 321.

[41] John Dewey, *How We Think* (Buffalo: Prometheus Books, 1991), viii.

[42] Gutek, *Historical and Philosophical Foundations of Education*, 321.

[43] George R. Knight, *Philosophy & Education: An Introduction in Christian Perspective*, 4th ed. (Berrien Springs, MI: Andrews University, 2006), 105.

[44] Gutek, *Historical and Philosophical Foundations of Education*, 327.

To Dewey, life is an experiment, truth is what works. One must wait to see if what one does and believes works—if it works, it is true. Humankind's final authority is experience rather than God; "experience itself is the sole ultimate authority."[45] His faith was in humankind to work out this philosophy of experience.[46]

Dewey's focus for schooling was not so much on the individual but rather on the individual in a group, the society, or the community. While his educational philosophy has been labeled "child-centered" by some educational psychologists, Dewey always referred to the educational focus as the student actively experiencing the environment; inside factors interacting with the outside factors found in the culture and society. He saw school as a microcosm of society at large.[47]

The experience of the student was his focus in methodology, and this led to his pedagogical contribution of "active learning."[48] Teachers should be trained, he thought, to use the scientific method of problem-solving and to use student activities that fit with the design of the curriculum or related pursuits of the student, rather than activity for activity's sake alone. He scolded teachers for the latter. He addressed advocates in the "newer schools" for abandoning organized subject matter and for proceeding as if "any form of direction and guidance by adults were an invasion of individual freedom."[49]

Frank Gaebelein (1899–1983)

Frank Gaebelein was born in 1899 to parents who had emigrated from Germany to Mount Vernon, New York during the last quarter of the 1800s. He grew up in a Christian home in which the Bible was honored and obeyed, art and music were promoted, and all of God's creation was appreciated. Frank became a talented musician and lover of literature. During his undergraduate

---

[45] John Dewey, "What I Believe," in *The Later Works of John Dewey*, vol. 5, *1925–1953: 1929–1930, Essays, The Sources of a Science of Education, Individualism, Old and New, and Construction and Criticism*, ed. Jo Ann Boydston, *The Collected Works of John Dewey* (Carbondale, IL: Southern Illinois University Press, 1984), 267.

[46] Dewey, 22.

[47] Ronald F. Reed and Tony W. Johnson, *Philosophical Documents in Education*, 2nd ed. (New York: Longman, 2000), 110–11; Nel Noddings, *Philosophy of Education* (Boulder, CO: Westview Press, 1995), 31.

[48] Lois E. Lebar, *Education That Is Christian* (Old Tappan, NJ: Revell, 1958), 36.

[49] See Dewey, *The Collected Works of John Dewey*, 69–72.

studies at New York University and graduate work at Harvard, he honed his writing and speaking skills.[50]

Gaebelein served in World War I, and shortly thereafter was recruited to start a new school by a group of men who were interested in developing a Christian college preparatory school for boys on Long Island, New York. The Stony Brook School began in September of 1922 as a Christian private school. Gaebelein served there for forty-one years, during which time he wrote on the topic of Christian education among other biblical topics. His two books on philosophy of education, *Christian Education in a Democracy* (1951) and *The Pattern of God's Truth: Problems of Integration in Christian Education* (1954), impacted Christian education during the second half of the twentieth century and still are read and appreciated in the twenty-first century.[51]

The public school system in the first half of the twentieth century largely adopted the philosophy of John Dewey. Many private church-related schools at various levels were being influenced by the anti-supernaturalistic philosophies of Dewey as well as liberal theology.[52]

John Dewey and Frank Gaebelein were contemporaries; the latter was four decades younger but living at the height of Dewey's popularity. While Dewey, a naturalist who followed pragmatic philosophy, wrote the book *Democracy and Education* (1916), Gaebelein, a Christian, wrote the book *Christian Education in a Democracy* (1951) in which he outlined his philosophy of education that centered on God and his Word. He focused on the integration of all of human knowledge in the arts, sciences, and humanities with God's perspective on life and learning. To Gaebelein, "all truth is God's truth" wherever it is found.[53]

Gaebelein insisted that a full education should be holistic and include the arts as well as the sciences and humanities. Above all, he held that all of life and learning should be related to the God of the Universe, and he declared that wherever there is truth, if indeed it is true, it is God's.[54]

---

[50] Cheryl L. Fawcett and Jamie Thompson, Database: Christian Educators of the Twentieth Century, Talbot School of Theology, accessed March 5, 2021, https://www.biola.edu/talbot/ce20/database/frank-ely-gaebelein.

[51] Lockerbie, *A Passion for Learning*, 326.

[52] Lockerbie, 325.

[53] See Frank E. Gaebelein, *The Pattern of God's Truth* (Chicago: Moody, 1968), 21–26.

[54] Gaebelein, 23.

CHAPTER 2

Psychological Perspectives on Education

Human Development and Learning

Marti MacCullough

In Lewis Carroll's book *Alice's Adventures in Wonderland*, Alice asks the Cheshire Cat for directions, and the cat asks Alice where she wants to go. Alice replies that she does not much care where she is going as long as it's *somewhere*. So, the cat responds that if you don't care about a destination, "then it doesn't matter which way you go."[1]

An operating assumption of the authors of this book is that educators do care about where they are going and where they want to take their students. This is the reason the chapter on philosophy of education preceded this one. In that chapter we addressed the worldview answer to where we want to go by addressing the aim of education from a biblical perspective. That aim informs why we do what we do as educators. How we can be effective at this task is the subject of the next two chapters. Chapter 2 introduces the key issues related to human development and learning, and chapter 3 addresses human learning theory.

---

[1] Lewis Carroll, *Alice's Adventures in Wonderland* (London: MacMillan, 1865), chap. 6.

Worldview Questions about Human Development and Learning

Under philosophical foundations we briefly addressed the major worldview question, "What is a human being?" Sub-questions include, "How did we get here on planet Earth?" (our existence) and "What is our purpose in life?" (why are we here?). These two questions are essential to the development of an authentic philosophy of Christian education. Additional sub-questions that fall under the big question, "What is a human being?" undergird psychological foundations addressed in this chapter. They are:

- How do humans develop over time?
- How do humans learn?
- Why are human beings of great worth and value, so much so that their education is important?

While a philosophy of education is basically a set of beliefs, assumptions, or truth claims about the major areas of schooling, the psychology of human development and learning that informs the design and delivery of the curriculum is based on the nature of the human being and learning derived from both underlying beliefs *and* psychological research. We address both in the next two chapters.

Keeping the Aim of Education in View as We Study Research

It is imperative that we keep in focus the aim of education informed by a Christian worldview as we examine available educational research. A possible aim of education that emerges from the discussion in the previous chapter will help the Christian educator to determine, in part, what we accept or reject from the research and why. Here is a broad summary of the aim addressed in the last chapter: The aim of education is to promote the full development of each human being as he/she was intended to be as an image-bearer of God, one who reflects his character. This aim is the path to human flourishing from a biblical perspective.

Christian educators are charged with the task of enhancing student ***development*** in all areas: cognitively, socially, emotionally, physically, and spiritually, and charged with promoting optimal ***learning*** for the purpose of growth in relationship to God, others, self, and God's created order. Notice that in this charge to teachers both student development and student learning are included. In addressing the psychological foundations for education, both human development *and* human learning are explored as separate but related key sets of information for the teacher to know and understand. Changes that are relatively permanent in students occur through the processes of maturation, learning, or a combination of the two. This chapter addresses primarily developmental changes, while the chapter that follows addresses human learning theories.

Biblical Answers to Worldview Questions Matter!

As Christians, we begin with God's view of human existence and purpose. However, many researchers begin with humankind or nature and leave God out of their views altogether. While we read and study current research and conclusions and benefit greatly from these studies, we must be aware that the choice of research subjects, questions to investigate, conclusions, and suggested applications are filtered through the worldview of the researcher. No research stands with absolute objectivity. It is imperative that the Christian view research with an open mind but also through a lens of God's view of human nature.

Francis Schaeffer addresses the objectivity of scientific research in his book *He Is There, and He Is Not Silent*. He credits Michael Polanyi, a Hungarian-British scientist of physical chemistry, as one of the first to write that science is never absolutely objective. Schaeffer wrote: "The observer sets up the experiment and the observer observes it—then the observer makes the conclusion. Polanyi says the observer is never neutral; he has a grid; he has presuppositions through which he feeds the thing which he finds."[2] This is a good reminder as we briefly explore research related to human development and learning. We often hear the expression "Trust the science!" as though science is always objective and void of contradictions. However, there are multiple scientific investigations with varying outcomes on many different questions about which humans are curious. These outcomes may be in conflict and demand further study. This is the nature of dealing with the science of human learning.

When we consider school education, we must be aware of not only the nature of the learners (including development and learning), but also the nature of what is there to be learned. For example, are humans seekers of truth or creators of truth? Can truth be known? Beliefs about both the knower (learners) and the known (that which is learned) must be considered when examining the work of researchers who bring to their work worldview answers to the questions about the nature of the learner *and* the nature of knowledge and knowing.

---

[2] Francis Schaeffer, *He Is There, and He Is Not Silent* (Wheaton, IL: Tyndale, 1972), 49.

Beliefs about the human from a biblical viewpoint are not subject to change when they are clearly revealed over and over again in Scripture. God has spoken! One such belief is vital to the Christian teacher. It has to do with why humans are of such great value that we study and teach them in the first place.

What Gives the Human Being the Quality of Great Worth?

Before addressing human development and learning, we take a brief look at an important question to answer before adopting an instructional theory. The question is, "What gives human beings the quality of having *great worth* as individuals and as a group?" A second question is, "How should our answer impact our understanding of development and learning and why?"

Worldviews vary in answering the question about value and worth of human beings, and these answers predict, to some degree, how researchers handle questions related to the aim of teaching. Are we simply a speck of dust on a larger speck of dust called planet Earth? Or are we simply a combination of molecules that exist for a while and then return to dust, ending life, period? Or are we angels in the making? Or what?

What Gives a Person Worth?

A brief summary of the answer from God's perspective using four key issues may help.
Humans may be considered as . . .

special created beings with a
special purpose, but hindered by a
special predicament, but salvaged by a
special plan, God's plan to restore relationship with him through his Son, Jesus.

Humans are very special beings created in the image of God (Gen 1:26–27). King David asked a question about human nature and offers his answer in Psalm 8:4–8: God made humans, crowned them with glory, and gave them a work to do. There are several things that give humans incredible worth; however, the most important is that God created us in his image. We have a **special existence or "being"**; we alone are the recipients of God's declaration, "made in my image."

A second and very important reason for assigning worth to humans is that God gave us a purpose for living. We have a work to do, and to do it we must understand the things that God created. We study nature and humans for a purpose. We have a **special**

purpose, to live for God's glory as we live and work here on earth. However, because of the fall of humankind, sin entered the world and death came by sin. This led to a **special predicament**.

Because of sin, we are separated from a holy God and, were it not for God's **special plan** to save us and to restore our relationship with him, we would be without hope and life would be meaningless. Through God's gracious provision and our faith in his Son, Jesus, our relationship with God is restored, and the potential to bring glory to him by reflecting his image is possible. Ephesians 2:10 declares, "For we are his workmanship, created in Christ Jesus for good works, which God prepared ahead of time for us to do."

All humans, those who have not yet understood God's gracious plan and those who have, are of great worth. God sent his Son to give us new life and a restored relationship with our Creator. As we grow spiritually, little by little, we are more and more capable of being the person God wants us to be. This is the process of human flourishing.

ENGAGE: Using the four key biblical truths—special created being, special purpose, special predicament, and special plan—discuss with a friend or fellow teacher why we treat *all* humans, including *all* of our students, with dignity and great worth, no matter their age, gender, current relationship with God, developmental level, learning capacities and differences, background, or their current worldview. How will this biblical perspective inform what I do as a classroom teacher or administrator? Determine at least two implications for the classroom.

If we truly believe that every individual student is of great worth, we will treat each one with dignity and respect. This includes how we speak about them to parents and to other teachers and how we treat them as individuals.

Made in God's Image: What Does This Mean, and What Does This Say to Educators?

Task: What are some of the key characteristics of God that human beings also possess? Obviously, we are not omnipresent (all present), omniscient (all knowing), or omnipotent (all powerful). These are characteristics only of God. Below are some characteristics that theological scholars have suggested. You may wish to pause and ask how understanding these characteristics, true of all your students, might impact teaching, student learning, and relationship building in your classroom.

1. Responsible and accountable choosers—moral responsibility (the **will**)
2. Vice-regents—stewardship to care for God's creation (earthly task)

3. Rational—thought is internal processing of the external world (the **mind**)
4. Communicators—external verbalization of thoughts (language facility)
5. Relational—social creatures created for relationships
6. Emotional—feelings (**emotions**)
7. Creative—create and invent
8. Possess self-awareness or self-consciousness (know we exist as an individual and can think about our own thoughts and the thoughts expressed by others)

Note the three characteristics in bold: will, mind, and emotions. For many years, theologians have identified these three key human characteristics that mirror some of God's characteristics as a personal God. These characteristics are used to explain human *personhood*. Keep these in mind as you evaluate theories of development and learning.

The characteristics above in combination seem to be present in humans because we are born human. However, God's design is for humans to develop these characteristics *over time*. Our capacity to think, to choose, to feel, to create, to communicate, to relate to others, while present at birth, seem to develop as we grow. Even Jesus developed over time: "And Jesus increased in wisdom and stature, and in favor with God and people" (Luke 2:52). The apostle Paul used the concept of human development when he said in 1 Cor 13:11, "When I was a child, I spoke like a child, I thought like a child, I reasoned like a child. When I became a man, I put aside childish things." Human development over time is God's idea!

What Is the Difference between Human Development and Human Learning?

ENGAGE: Read the definitions below and then summarize the difference between developmental maturation and learning.

Maturation is a developmental process within which a person from time to time manifests traits whose "blueprints" have been carried in the person's cells from the time of conception.

Learning, in contrast with maturation, is an enduring change in a living individual that is not heralded by genetic inheritance. It may be considered a change in insights, behavior, perception, motivation, or a combination of these. It always involves a systematic change in behavior or behavioral disposition that occurs as a consequence of experience in some specified situation.[3]

---

[3] Morris Bigge and Samuel Shermis, *Learning Theories for Teachers* (Boston: Allyn & Bacon, 2004), 1.

In summary, **human developmental maturation** answers the question: "How do people change while growing from infancy to old age because of inborn patterns that are present at birth?" On the other hand, **learning** is a relatively permanent change in thinking and acting that is not a specific product of genetics or inborn patterns of unfoldment but occurs through experience, planned or unplanned. School education qualifies as planned learning for groups of various sizes. Therefore, educators must have a theory of learning to guide in the process of schooling while also accounting for developmental characteristics for the grade level they teach.[4] Individual differences within a group and the effect of these differences on learning are also important to consider. There are individual differences in maturational rates and, also in learning capabilities. The chapter on the diverse learner will address these differences.

Human Development as a Field of Study

Nature or Nurture Controversy

Among educational psychologists who study human development, there exists a basic disagreement over how humans develop. This disagreement has been labeled the Nature/Nurture Controversy. Can human development be "forced" by the *environment* (by nurture) or must it *simply unfold* (by nature) over time because of inborn patterns? The controversy raged between these two views during the twentieth century and continues, to some extent, in the twenty-first century.[5]

The **nature** (or heredity) point of view would lead one to think that we should let kindergarteners play and they will naturally develop human characteristics, such as social, emotional, and positive willful behaviors. They will also develop language as well as their creative and cognitive capacities. What humans are to be is primarily a matter of genetics. The environment is simply a location for *unfoldment* of what nature has provided.[6]

The **nurture** point of view, however, might lead one to think that all kindergarteners can be pushed to learn equally well by the teacher or parent, and therefore, kindergarteners should have a strong academic program with multiple stimuli and reinforcements. The focus is on the environment rather than the inborn capacities of each student. The environment (teacher) can "make" student outcomes rather equal.

---

[4] Bigge and Shermis, 3.

[5] Anita Woolfolk, *Educational Psychology*, 11th ed. (Columbus, OH: Merrill, 2010), 27.

[6] Bigge and Shermis, *Learning Theories for Teachers*, 31.

Equality in living and learning is a goal of this view, and therefore it has been attractive to some democratic societies that seek equality of opportunity and to some extent, equality of outcomes.[7]

There is a third, more up-to-date and commonsense point of view that helps to settle the nature-nurture question. This view sees the human as one who is born with certain potential patterns of development (nature) that must mature over time *as they interact* with the environment (nurture).[8]

The third view might be labeled **interactionary**, or simply interactive, in that it takes into consideration inborn patterns of development as these interact with an environment that is, hopefully, encouraging and supportive. In considering human development, the primary emphasis is on developmental patterns that emerge *over time*. Many who study human development are "stage theorists" who observe the developmental characteristics of groups of children over time and then suggest certain *average*, general characteristics of which teachers should be aware. This leads to the practice of "developmentally appropriate" strategies in the classroom.

While humans develop in several categories, cognitive development has been a major focus for school education as it relates to mental, moral, emotional, social, and language development. We will focus on this aspect of human development and related research.

Cognitive Development

JEAN PIAGET

Jean Piaget, a twentieth-century Swiss cognitive developmentalist, studied children (his own and others) and observed and recorded several stages of development to help parents and teachers provide a good environment for cognitive growth. While his observed developmental stages have been challenged by more recent research, his theory of how humans develop has been a powerful influence on the study of human development in the twentieth and twenty-first centuries. Piaget declared that cognitive development occurs through the processes of (1) **Maturation** (of inside factors and inborn capacities), plus (2) **Acting on objects** (outside), plus (3) **Social Interaction** (outside and inside factors including language), all leading to the process of (4) **Equilibration.**

---

[7] Woolfolk, *Educational Psychology*, 27.
[8] Woolfolk, 28.

Equilibration is an internal two-pronged mental process of **assimilation** (the adding to existing schemes or categories in the mind) and **accommodation** (the modification of schemes or developing categories).[9]

I like to use the process of a young child mentally processing the concept of dog as an illustration for equilibration. As my firstborn daughter matured during the first two years of her life, she saw our dog, she acted on our dog by touching it in a variety of ways, and her parents gave her a label for that "object." "We call this a dog, and his name is Snoopy." He is an animal (a larger category she was also developing). So Sheryl developed the scheme or category, "dog." One day we visited a friend who had a cat. Sheryl pointed to the cat and said, "Look, Mommy, a fuzzy doggie!" She was trying to *assimilate* or fit into an already existing category (dog), the object she was now seeing. Did I say to her, "Isn't that cute? Let's call this animal a fuzzy doggie!" Of course not! I said, "No, honey, we call that a cat. It is another kind of animal." She pointed again and said, "cat." And so, she now accommodated that new information and inside her mind developed a new category for cat still under the larger category of animal. We purchased animal books for her to see, and she continued to grow in her understanding of the animal world, a large category with many sub-categories such as cat and dog. Piaget created a model for development based upon these inside and outside elements.

Piaget's work had great promise were it not for his epistemology (theory of knowledge). Piaget's theory is called a theory of genetic epistemology. It is clear that while he was against a teacher pushing a child forward—and he held to outside and inside factors operating together—his clear emphasis was inside (genetics). He would say that *development leads learning*, and therefore, inside factors are *more* important than outside. While his work with cognitive development was an improvement and contrast to theories that were behavioristic in orientation (nurture—outside factors alone are key to development), he had his detractors. One who benefited from, but also challenged his work, was Lev Vygotsky.[10]

Lev Vygotsky

The work of Lev Vygotsky, a Russian psychologist and contemporary of Piaget, is an important contribution to educational psychology. His work was not recognized for

---

[9] Woolfolk, 16, 33–34.

[10] Bigge and Shermis, *Learning Theories for Teachers*, 18.

many years in his own country and was not translated into English until the 1980s. Vygotsky died in 1934 at the young age of thirty-seven.[11]

Vygotsky was not appreciated for years in the former Soviet Union. His views at one time were labeled "anti-Marxist,"[12] perhaps because he wrote against socialism as a young Russian-Jew who was keenly aware of his Judaic background. This all changed after the Russian Revolution in 1917 with the abolishing of the Pale of Settlement, which kept Russian Jews in a geographical location and limited the vocations they could enter. With the freedom to work as a psychologist, Vygotsky began to study how humans develop, and he submitted to the Marxist ideas of his day in order to share his theory. However, Marx did not deal with the mind in his writings, and this alone may have caused many in his home country to undervalue his work.[13] In the 1960s his writings were uncovered and taken seriously in the Soviet Union and his work spread worldwide.[14]

The translation of Vygotsky's work helped to promote the interactive view of cognitive development and helped to quell the age-old controversy between nature and nurture. Perhaps because Vygotsky lived and worked in a nation that encouraged research that supported Marxism with its clear social perspective, his theory is more social-oriented than the individual-oriented focus of Piaget. The living context and time-period of researchers often impacts their work and should be taken into consideration with an open mind as their work is critiqued by Christian educators.[15] There will always be things with which one can agree and other ideas with which one disagrees on biblical grounds.

Outside factors are real and important. In his book, *Thought and Language,* Vygotsky took an entire chapter to challenge Piaget's view of human knowing called "genetic epistemology." Piaget dismissed an objective reality that exists outside the knowing mind that can be delivered by social elements (such as teachers) and understood as true reality. Piaget's view that humans create their own reality has propelled modern-day

---

[11] Lev Vygotsky, *Thought and Language,* trans. Alex Kozulin (Cambridge, MA: MIT, 1986), xliv.

[12] Vygotsky, xliii.

[13] Vygotsky, xliii.

[14] Vygotsky, xxii, xxiii.

[15] For an in-depth presentation of Vygotsky and Marxism, see Uwe P. Gielen and Samuel S. Jeshmaridian, "Lev S. Vygotsky: The Man and the Era," *International Journal of Group Tensions* 28, nos. 3/4 (1999), especially pages 276–79 and 283–96, http://lchc.ucsd.edu/mca/Mail /xmcamail.2007_04.dir/att-0170/TSHC_-_LEV_S._VYGOTSKY_THE_MAN_AND _THE_ERA.pdf.

Radical Constructivism, which opposes the truth that a real, existing world can be known. Vygotsky disagreed with Piaget on this point. He wrote: "If we were to summarize the central flaws in Piaget's theory, we would have to point out that it is reality and the relations between the child and reality that are missed in his theory."[16]

While Piaget's work on how humans develop has had a profound impact on today's cognitive theories, his view of knowledge must be carefully evaluated from a Christian perspective. Piaget has been crowned today as the Father of Constructivism. His view of knowledge and reality is embraced by adherents of Radical Constructivism,[17] a philosophical theory (epistemology) of learning that focuses on inside factors while acknowledging some measure of outside factors in learning.[18]

Vygotsky's chief contribution to education: Zone of Proximal Development. Vygotsky[19] held that as children develop, they operate within a range of potential learning he called a "zone of proximal development" that spans from what they can do alone to what they can do with help. When there is a teacher or other advanced student (a mismatch of abilities) who can nudge the student toward growth, the student can move forward in learning and development. Inside developmental factors interact with outside factors. The human innate capacities and the environment are vital. Outside social factors include the teacher and other students and the immediate cultural experiences. To Vygotsky, *learning leads development.*[20] Therefore, teachers, who nudge or pull students toward what they can do with help are important in promoting learning.[21] I believe this was an important improvement on the work of Piaget.

Differences between Piaget and Vygotsky. Both Piaget and Vygotsky held to the belief that humans have an innate capacity to make sense out of incoming information, a powerful view and precursor to cognitive interactive learning theories presented in the next chapter. However, Piaget thought it best to teach to the unfolding level of children and not rush them forward while Vygotsky held that children should be nudged or pulled forward through the interaction of a teacher or advanced students. The social

---

[16] Vygotsky, *Thought and Language*, 51–52.

[17] For more on the topic of Radical Constructivism for a primary source, see Ernst von Glasersfeld, *Radical Constructivism: A Way of Knowing and Learning* (Washington, DC: Falmer Press, 1995).

[18] For more on Radical Constructivism, see my book *By Design*, 65, 70, 127–35 (see ch. 1, n. 12).

[19] Vygotsky, *Thought and Language*, 87–96.

[20] Saul McLeod, "Vygotsky's Sociocultural Theory of Cognitive Development," Simply Psychology, updated 2020, https://www.simplypsychology.org/vygotsky.html.

[21] Bigge and Shermis, *Learning Theories for Teachers*, 129–30.

context is important. Cooperative learning, mixed-level grouping, and scaffolding are applications of Vygotsky's theory.

Piaget[22] considered acting on objects a key to cognitive development, while Vygotsky held that language was the key.[23] Piaget held that "learning is subservient (a servant) to development" while Vygotsky held that "learning leads development."[24] Both of these early views that acknowledge inborn factors and development are in sharp contrast to Behaviorism that focuses on outside factors alone. Behaviorism dominated education in America during the first half of the twentieth century and has remained influential even today around the world. Most behaviorists do not focus on inside factors nor on human development. Vygotsky considered himself a developmentalist; however, his work has been classified more recently as a theory of learning. Living as a contemporary of Piaget, he was influenced somewhat by his work but created a very different theory.

Other Human Developmentalists Who Built upon the Work of Piaget and Vygotsky

Lawrence Kohlberg created stages for moral development that represented growth toward higher levels of moral reasoning. Cognitive development was essential to his theory. His theory was an interactive theory—that is, outside and inside factors work together in moral development.[25]

Human developmentalist Urie Bronfenbrenner was responsible for the initiation of the Head Start program in America.[26] His ecological system of development demonstrated the importance of the environment interacting with the child's nature. Prior to the 1960s, the nature or unfoldment view reigned in early childhood studies. Bronfenbrenner's work was a much-needed improvement on the unfoldment,

---

[22] Bigge and Shermis, 9.

[23] Vygotsky, *Thought and Language*, 53.

[24] For an overview of Piaget and Vygotsky, see McLeod, "Vygotsky's Sociocultural Theory."

[25] Cheryl E. Sanders, "Lawrence Kohlberg's Stages of Moral Development," Britannica, accessed January 10, 2022, https://www.britannica.com/science/Lawrence-Kohlbergs-stages-of -moral-development.

[26] Sharon Tregaskis, "50 Years Later, Recalling a Founder of Head Start," *Cornell Chronicle*, May 15, 2015, https://news.cornell.edu/stories/2015/05/50-years-later-recalling-founder-head -start.

nature-alone view. His view promoted the idea that teachers and early experiences were important in early childhood education.[27]

While most twentieth-century developmentalists studied, primarily, the childhood period, including the psychoanalytic theory of Sigmund Freud, Erik Erikson was an exception. He researched human identity, presenting eight stages of psychosocial development throughout the life span. While his theory was built upon the psychoanalytic theory of Freud, it included a strong environmental element. His life-span theory is also interactive, the third position that has challenged the nature-nurture controversy of the twentieth century. From this brief historical overview of research, it can be shown that the nature-nurture controversy was challenged during the twentieth century and the interactive theory has become the prevailing theory of the twenty-first century.

How Do Human Development Experts Conduct Their Research?

Human development research is done through observation. Physical development is easy to observe and measure. Humans start out at 5–8 pounds (2.27–3.63 kilograms) on average and continue to grow physically all through the teen years and beyond. While not as easy to observe and measure as physical characteristics, evidence for social, emotional, and cognitive growth (including language) is observed as well. A true picture in these areas is more complex than the physical. Nevertheless, human development researchers use observation, direct and indirect, to determine patterns of growth and development and write about these maturational characteristics *using averages*.

Teachers must be aware of statistical (average) norms in order to understand the level of development of their general population of students. However, the very nature of a statistical (normal) curve requires that some of the population will be above and some below the average characteristic at the same age level.

Caution: Educators who have memorized a list of typical human characteristics for the age level they teach must realize that these are simply averages, and some of their students in the same classroom will be above or below the average. This awareness must influence the teacher's lesson preparation, in general, as age-appropriate content and methods are planned for a specific level, but also adaptations or differentiation for those that fall above or below the average. Teachers must be committed to teach all students well.

---

[27] Olivia Guy-Evans, "Bronfenbrenner's Ecological Systems Theory," Simply Psychology, November 9, 2020, www.simplypsychology.org/Bronfenbrenner.html.

ENGAGE: Research a list of developmental characteristics for the grade and age level you teach. You may wish to put these under categories: physical, social, emotional, cognitive. Write at least one implication for each category that will affect your teaching. How will these characteristics impact your classroom community?

A little quiz from what has been addressed so far will help you identify flaws in the two views that were strictly heredity or environmental. List any flaws you find.

From your understanding of the differences between those who advocate nature (heredity only) over nurture (environment only), try the following activity!

> Label numbers 1–9. Use H for heredity (the nature position) and E for environment (the nurture position).

1. This theory of human development doomed humans; it locked them in without much hope.
2. This approach perpetuated racism, sexism, and fixed intelligence.
3. This approach to human development would say that "teachers are made, not born."
4. This approach was attractive to a democratic society that believed that factors in the environment could lead to utopian change.
5. This approach might be called the genetic theory.
6. This theory would hold that teachers are born, not made.
7. This view would hold that the teacher or parent is the most important factor in human development.
8. This view would hold that the presence of the teacher in the classroom is just for safety; the school provides a location for "unfoldment" of what is already there in the individual.
9. This view might allow students to claim about their behavior, "It's not my fault. I am a victim."

   Answers: 1. H; 2. H; 3. E; 4. E; 5. H; 6. H; 7. E; 8. H; 9. H and E

   Number 9 should be marked as both H and E: "It's my genetic makeup that *made me* do it." Or, "It's my environment (family, culture etc.) that *made me* do it." Both views lead to victimhood.

As you may have discovered from the answers above, the last issue in #9 identifies a glaring flaw in both of the two positions: "it's all heredity" or "it's all the environment." The flaw is that students can legitimately claim that any negatively developing characteristic is either the fault of their genetic makeup or of the environment in which they have been reared. This attitude kills effort and hope to improve. The third position, the interactive position, gives the student hope for change, with help, and promotes effort on the part of the student to grow. It also encourages the teacher to teach all children well.

Summary of "interactive" view. A more commonsense and reasonable view that developed out of research during the last half of the twentieth century with the work of developmentalists Piaget and Vygotsky recognizes that heredity and genetics do play a part in who we are and how we develop. So, too, does the environment. This view is not a synthesis of the other two, but rather a view that from birth humans are interactive by nature. God created us to interact with his created order. When we include both genetics/heredity and environment, we refer to this view as **interactive** whether we are discussing *human development*, with a huge amount of heredity, inborn patterns of development, and time, or when we are discussing *learning*, with a huge amount of the environment and experience involved. Time plays a vital role in development; experiences play a vital role in learning. Both developmental patterns and learning are important in understanding students. Human development and learning work together. Teachers and parents or caretakers are a part of the environment. What we do with what we observe, in terms of human developmental patterns, matters. So, here I offer a principle to help us serve our students. Strive to maximize potentials and minimize limits!

ENGAGE AND REFLECT: Relate the following principle to the academic expectations of a classroom teacher: "Maximize potentials and minimize limits." With this in mind, evaluate the statement below and discuss your thinking with others with whom you are working through this book.

What is known about a person through present observation may not include actual genetic potential because the environment may not have been optimal or ideal.

Teachers must determine their role in promoting optimal student development for all of their students, some of whom have not experienced the best environment in which to grow and develop prior to entering their classroom. We start where they are in their development and nudge as needed to help them develop from where they are on their own to where they can be with help. For example, a child may come to your classroom well behind most other students in social development. It will take patience, encouraging communication, and nudging to help the child close the gap between appropriate and inappropriate behavior for the age level. This is true for all areas of development.

ENGAGE: You are in an interview for a new position in a school, and the head of school asks the following questions related to human development implications for the grade level of the open position. Answer as you would in the interview. Keep in mind the interactive view of humans. How will your teacher behaviors help or hinder the development of your students?

1. Do you teach to the middle of your grade level? Yes or no, and why?
2. Do you treat children equally or fairly? Why?
3. Do all children process your lessons and learn in exactly the same way? Why? Or why not? What will your answer mean for your teaching prep and delivery?
4. Are all the children in one classroom at the same developmental level? Why did you answer as you did?
5. Do you plan to the middle and hope others at both ends of the growth continuum will pick up some of the new material as best they can? Or do you plan for differentiated instruction? Why?
6. How will you view a class of students? As a group or as individuals?

In answering the above, you will reveal some of your broad understandings of human development required to be an effective teacher. Here are a few comments about the above questions and answers. If you are blessed to have the privilege of teaching a class or several classes of students, you are charged to teach *all* students in the class regardless of their developmental and learning characteristics. Therefore, you do not **teach** to the middle only. You must, however, **plan** a lesson and you do **plan** to the middle, that is, prepare your lesson based on the development level of the average students in a particular class and subject area and then add adaptations and differentiation for diverse learners. You will see in chapter 5 that a cognitive interactive model for teaching provides natural opportunities for differentiated learning because it is open to the greatest number of methods.

Differentiation may mean that you are treating your students fairly, rather than equally. How might this be so? Understanding that all students do not develop and learn in the exact same way and determining to meet the needs of all while exposing all to different ways of learning is important. You cannot differentiate everything you teach; however, being aware of differences in learning preferences, learning styles, and limits and potentials of individuals may allow the teacher to insert specific methods into a lesson that might appeal to, and allow for growth in, an individual or several individuals that otherwise might not experience optimal learning.

Personally, I never enjoyed working in groups in high school but preferred individual study and research. I had one teacher in my post high school experience that had nothing but group work for every session. While I learned to enjoy and learn through group work, I would have preferred a variety of methods! How about you? Even preferences must be considered in classroom instruction rather than simply teaching "just the way the teacher likes to learn." We will fail to optimize the learning experience of some students when we deliver lessons using the exact same method each day even if it is a personal favorite. For example, I now use group work as one method for learning.

The answer to whether you consider your class as a group or individuals is best answered as a "group of individuals." This will impact how the teacher will treat each one and organize and plan for learning for all.

The questions above were designed to stimulate thinking related to teacher attitudes and behaviors that impact development and learning from an interactive point of view in which both the students and what they bring to the classroom experience, and teachers in what they do, matter! More will be addressed related to this issue in the chapter on the diverse learner in section 3.

ENGAGE: Think about or read about how Jesus differentiated the learning experiences of his disciples. He modeled much of what educators today think are important characteristics of learning-centered teaching. From the beginning of his ministry, Jesus manifested relational qualities as he called twelve apostles "to be with him" (Mark 3:14). He spent three years teaching them and observing individual differences. His teaching was relational, so much so that he recognized individual differences—the boldness and impulsivity of Peter, for example, that Jesus recognized and used in teaching Peter and was later used mightily by God after the resurrection of Christ. Jesus saw the intellect and learning of Saul (Paul) who was an early opponent of Christianity to say the least. However, after his conversion he was used by God to take the gospel to Gentiles and teach Jews in synagogues and philosophers in Athens. While Jesus worked with a group of twelve and large groups of other followers, he saw individual needs and potentials. See if you can find examples for these two qualities of needs and potentials as you think through the research below.

Extended Reflection: Which of the following in each pair would you rather have in class and why? First, read and determine the general characteristics of each one in each pair below and find needs and potentials. We illustrated this briefly with Peter and Paul in the paragraph above when we looked at the boldness of Peter and the intellect of Paul. Describe what those personal characteristics might look like in a classroom today. Select the one of each pair that you might wish to have in class and share why. The "why" may reveal your own bias toward certain student characteristics. However, you will have some of each type of the "student" you see in pairs below! Be ready to fight against your own biases and to teach all students well.

Moses	Daniel	Deborah	Peter
Aaron	David	Barak	Paul

Introducing the Next Chapter

Next, we address human learning theory, paying specific attention to the two theories that are considered scientific: *behaviorism* and *cognitive interactive theory*. Keep in mind the content of this chapter as we address the corollary to human development, human learning.

Extended Research and Reflection: If you or your school use the InTASC standards for effective teaching, ask yourself, How has this chapter addressed and helped to meet the first standard?

Standard #1: Learner Development. The teacher understands how learners grow and develop, recognizing that patterns of learning and development vary individually within and across the cognitive, linguistic, social, emotional, and physical areas, and designs and implements developmentally appropriate and challenging learning experiences.

CHAPTER 3

Psychological Foundations for Education

Human Learning Theories

Marti MacCullough

Human development and human learning are two different processes. However, they work together in the learning event. Teachers must be committed to understanding both development and learning if they desire to be effective in maximizing the school experience for all students. The previous chapter introduced the two processes and then focused on human development. This chapter addresses theories of learning.

ENGAGE: Read the following situation and respond to the questions that follow. This illustration was shared by educational psychologist William James in his *Talks to Teachers on Psychology*.[1] It involves a visit to a class that had been studying geography and the earth's interior. The visitor was encouraged to examine the class to see how they were learning.

The visitor asked: "Suppose you should dig a hole in the ground, hundreds of feet deep. How should you find it at the bottom—warmer or colder than on top?"

No hands went up.

---

[1] William James, *Talks to Teachers on Psychology* (New York: Henry Holt, 1899), 150.

The classroom teacher said to the visitor: "I'm sure they know, but you don't ask the question rightly. Let me try." Looking at the book, she asked the class the following: "In what condition is the interior of the globe?"

Together the class responded in recitation fashion: "The interior of the globe is in a condition of igneous fusion."

Thinking about the above scenario, do you agree or disagree with the statement, "These students are learning"? Share why you agree or disagree.

- If you answered, "Yes, I agree that these students are learning," please suggest, as best you can, what *kind* of learning this situation illustrates.
- If you disagree with the statement, why do you think the students were not learning? Write or share your thoughts with at least one other person.
- Now answer these questions according to the account: How do we know that the students did not understand what they were memorizing? How do we know they could not use the information to solve a simple problem? Briefly share your thoughts.

What would learning theorists say about this event? Learning theorists would agree that these students are learning *something*, but they would strongly disagree about the benefits of this *kind* of learning for much of education. The learning portrayed in the situation above is called "rote learning." Rote learning may be defined as memorization by repetition, without necessarily understanding the reasoning or relationships inherent in what has been learned. In this kind of learning, it may be difficult to retrieve and use the information in a variety of settings or when a question is asked in a slightly different way as in the example provided by Dr. James.

Rote memorization is an essential skill and important, especially when the learning needs to be automatically recalled and paired with a stimulus. Here are a few examples: a person needs to rehearse and learn the alphabet or the counting numbers in order, or a kindergartner needs to memorize a home phone number and respond when asked, "What is your home phone number?" Or, perhaps, "What is the number you dial for an emergency?" However, when to use these numbers must also be learned! Rote memory is useful and necessary but never sufficient in human learning.

Theories of Learning

Learning theorists ask the question, "How do humans learn what they need to learn?" A variety of answers are offered to this age-old question. Teachers, however, have not always examined the question or the possible answers and are therefore, at times, swept away by every new "innovation," or worse, become closed-minded to new research and new ideas. Bigge and Shermis state: "Each learning theory implies a set of related classroom procedures. The ways in which an educator develops instructional techniques depend on how that educator defines the learning process."[2]

Do learning theorists agree that memory is vital to learning? Both *scientific* theories of human learning addressed in this chapter hold that memory is important to learning. However, they disagree strongly about the process of human learning that leads to remembering. *The two broad scientific theories are Behaviorism and Cognitive Interactive Theory.* There is a popular philosophical theory that we will address as well because of its importance in the twentieth and twenty-first centuries. While not considered a scientific theory, it is a contrast to both Behaviorism and Cognitive Interactive Theory. It is often labeled Humanistic Theory.

What Is a Theory of Learning?

According to Morris L. Bigge and Samuel S. Shermis in their classic book, *Learning Theories for Teachers*, "A learning theory is a systematic integrated outlook in regard to the nature of the learning process."[3] These two authors declared that each theory implies a set of related classroom procedures and instructional techniques. It seems reasonable to think that gaining some understanding of the broad theories from which to select should be a task in which all educators happily engage if they desire to maximize learning.

What Is Human Learning according to Learning Theorists?

Learning is a relatively permanent or enduring *change* in thinking and acting. Behaviorists do not include "thinking" in their definition, declaring that "learning is a change in behavior (acting)," period. All cognitivists include both, thinking and acting. Current-day cognitive theorists hold that change occurs when the student takes in new information, processes it (understands), and creates a disposition to remember and apply or use it in some way. Behaviorists, on the other hand, hold that learning is

---

[2] Morris Bigge and Samuel Shermis, *Learning Theories for Teachers*, 6th ed. (Boston: Allyn & Bacon, 2004), xv.

[3] Bigge and Shermis, 3.

a response to a stimulus that has been conditioned by reinforcement, much like the example of the classroom above in the illustration provided by William James.[4]

How we determine the best model or overall approach to teaching is based on our understanding of how humans learn; this is a major worldview issue addressed in this book. In this chapter, we provide a broad overview of theories of learning and an exploration of which one fits best in an integrated way with a biblical worldview. The goal is to bring our biblical view of the human and learning to the findings and conclusions of researchers and use the knowledge available for effective teaching.

How Do We View Learning Theory from a Biblical Perspective?

When we ask questions about learning, we are asking how it is that humans come to know (learn) what is available to be known or learned. A biblical answer to these questions, in short, is that humans are created in God's image with the capacity to know. We have been given something to know, God himself, and his created order. God reveals himself to us through his Word, his Son Jesus, and his creation. God and his created universe—this is reality!

Humans can come to know at least a measure of reality (what is actually the case) even if limited by our humanity and our inability to know exhaustively. Inherent in this view are two factors: (1) the inborn God-given human capacity to learn; something is there inside at birth that enables learning, and (2) something is objectively there, outside the knowing mind, to be learned. A real and knowable world exists. In learning theory and its applications, it is vital to understand that there is a knower and that which is known. Views related to both influence our selection of a theory out of which to operate. Both behaviorism and cognitive interactive theories hold that a real, knowable world exists. Both are interested in learning; however, how humans come to know and learn varies greatly, as we will see.

God's Word implies that we can learn. Scripture was written for our *learning*. The statement in John 20:31 is very specific to the book of John. "But these are written so that you may believe that Jesus is the Messiah, the Son of God, and that by believing you may have life in his name." Romans 15:4a declares, "For whatever was written in the past was written for our instruction" ("for our learning" in some translations). The Word of God is God's revelation to humans in language form. God-given language

---

[4] James, *Talks to Teachers on Psychology*, 150.

facility and the relationship of language to learning is assumed in his Word. God communicates; humans, created in his image, are communicators by nature.

God gave us a work to do to care for his creatures and the land, and he gave us the capacity to understand nature (the world around us), and other humans. We have the capacity to discover scientific principles and mathematical patterns and relationships, and to reason and infer related principles. God has revealed some things we could not know any other way, through his Son, the living Word, and through his recorded Word, the Bible. It is interesting to note that God chose to create humans with language capacity and then communicated information about himself and his work in language, first oral and then written.

Learning is a wonderful human process designed by God. We have lots to learn! To maximize each student's learning, we need to understand, as best we can, how humans learn in general (commonalities) and in particular (diverse learning capacities and styles).

ENGAGE: Two teachers discuss the question, "What should be our focus in teaching?" If you were listening to this conversation and they asked for your opinion, what would you say?

Their conversation might go something like this:

Teacher One: "Well, I teach children. My focus is always on the child and how they are developing. I try to draw out what is already there within the child."

Teacher Two: "Well, I teach my subject. The focus in school is on math and science, etc. We are not here for play or for therapy! I try to provide something to be learned."

Teacher One: "Well, I am teaching my students to learn and to think, so they can be lifelong learners."

Teacher Two: "Yes, but think about what? Learn what? When you think and learn it is more than a process; it must include content. Students must think about something and learn something. Content is vital! Don't you think so?"

Teacher One: "The student is the most important, their feelings and their thinking, and not just the content. They need to respond to their own promptings to learn. Don't you think so?"

In the conversation above, it may be clear to you that one teacher is focusing on child development as unfoldment, a developmental approach to learning that holds that humans simply unfold like a flower the characteristics that are there by nature.

The other teacher is focusing on content coming from outside the learner. Just as in our review of human development and maturation referred to in the last chapter with adherents on each side of the Nature/Nurture or Heredity/Environment controversy, the same is true for learning theory. There are those who think that learning is motivated by human inside factors *alone*, while others believe that outside factors trump anything inside. These two sides, one philosophical and one scientific, have been vying for the minds and hearts of teachers for well over 100 years. Who is right, or is there a better third option that is both scientific and more recent in Western education? I think there is.

Bigge and Shermis review multiple learning theories held before and after the twentieth century in their book *Learning Theories for Teachers*.[5] They list proponents of each as well as typical beliefs about the nature of humans and learning. About these views, they write, "Prominence does not guarantee validity. Less well-known persons may be more nearly right. Furthermore, in the field of psychology it is common for top-ranking authorities, who have spent lifetimes in research, to disagree. Such disagreement is, in part, *the result of differing basic assumptions*."[6]

If indeed psychologists who study human learning bring their basic assumptions about human beings to their research (and they do), we should be careful to do likewise when evaluating their theories.

Three Different Views Described

The basic way to describe the major difference in theories is to declare what the researchers believe about one of three views of human nature and learning based upon the "actional" nature. The actional nature describes one's belief about the nature and source of human motivation. "Such motivation arises from some kind of relationship between people and their respective environment."[7] There are three views of the actional nature: (1) **psychologically passive**, (2) **autonomously active**, and (3) **cognitively interactive.** These three views are mutually opposed and only one can be true because they express belief about what humans are like in this regard at birth. The terms are related to psychological events rather than to physical activity or passivity or a balance of both.[8]

---

[5] Bigge and Shermis, *Learning Theories for Teachers*, 8–9.
[6] Bigge and Shermis, 6, emphasis added.
[7] Bigge and Shermis, 13.
[8] Bigge and Shermis, 15.

Psychologically Passive View

One view is that the human is **passive** (psychologically) in the learning event and reacts to outside factors such as the teacher, the textbook, a video, other students, etc. in a stimulus-response fashion. This is much like the students who could give a memorized response to the stimulus question provided by the teacher in the exact words they had memorized. The response was followed by the teacher's reinforcement, "Wonderful; that is correct!" Learning, to this way of thinking, is a product of the environment acting upon the student and the student reacting. This view leads to absolute determinism, meaning that all human characteristics or all that a person becomes is the result of the environment or outside forces alone.[9] It can lead to victimhood as well. "It's not my fault! It was my environment."

The psychologically passive view is associated with the work of behaviorists such as Burrhus Frederic Skinner (1904–1990) who described himself as a radical behaviorist. His research on rats, cats, and pigeons was generalized to human beings because he saw little difference between animals and humans in how they learn.[10] Skinner's research was of good quality following scientific methods of his day. As a scientific theorist, he used observable behaviors as data, such as the answer given by a student to a stimulus question about the interior of the earth. The answer, "The interior of the globe is in a condition of igneous fusion," was considered *the* learning. The fact that the students could not retrieve the memorized information given a slightly different question is not considered a major problem by the teacher at the time of learning.

My Early Experience with the Science of Behaviorism

When I was a child, I put a nickel into a slot attached to a small cage at the local park. When I pushed the slot, immediately a light went on, and a chicken came out and walked across a toy piano keyboard just like she was playing the piano. Then the chicken would turn to a slide where she awaited a piece or two of corn as reinforcement for the behavior of "playing the piano." These clever events were the result of Skinner's operant conditioning techniques. The chicken, in the presence of the light (discriminate stimulus) was associating the playing of the piano (response) with the reinforcement (the piece of corn).

---

[9] Bigge and Shermis, 102–3.
[10] Bigge and Shermis, 97–102.

While chickens and humans do learn through conditioning, Skinner's theory applied to human learning is only as good as his underlying assumptions (beliefs) about humans. If there is more to a human being than simply an animal to be trained or machine to produce mechanical responses, and if human behaviors are not determined by outside forces alone, then his view is incomplete and limited for much of learning.

Motivation and Behaviorism

Skinner did not believe in inner motivation and did not believe that humans act on purpose. Because he believed that humans are morally neutral (neither good nor bad at birth), he believed they could be conditioned to behave in good ways and therefore the potential for a utopian society would follow. This view is expressed in his book *Waldon Two*. When I read the novel, I was challenged to think about questions such as: (1) "Who determines goodness?" In the utopian society portrayed in the book, there was no place for religion. Goodness was determined "scientifically" by the community as whatever led to happiness. (2) "Who is the conditioner and does the conditioner play God in determining what is right?"[11]

The psychologically passive view of the human was also held prior to the twentieth century by Johann Herbart, a German psychologist, who believed that ideas (rather than humans) were active and were constantly associating with new ideas.[12] Knowing ideas automatically brought about change in a person. He was ahead of his time in suggesting that students learn by starting with the known and moving to the unknown.[13] Input of material in interesting ways was a key to his teacher education instruction.[14] While some of his ideas have stood the test of time, his belief that the learner is a passive recipient of ideas much like a container into which a teacher pours information (ideas),[15] is flawed, and his theory leads to a basic teaching model that is much like that of behaviorism.

---

[11] These questions are addressed by Skinner as his characters explain the function of the community; certain human beings are assigned to condition others in the community to do as the conditioner "thinks" best. See B. F. Skinner, *Walden Two* (Toronto: MacMillan, 1948), chapters 29–32.

[12] Bigge and Shermis, *Learning Theories for Teachers*, 35.

[13] Lois E. LeBar, *Education That Is Christian* (Old Tappan, NJ: Revell, 1958), 30–31.

[14] Bigge and Shermis, *Learning Theories for Teachers*, 40.

[15] Bigge and Shermis, 35.

Herbart's work was brought to and adopted in America before John Watson, credited as the Father of Behaviorism, used the term "Behaviorist." In the article, "Psychology as a Behaviorist Views It," Watson launched behaviorism as a new American theory of learning. In his article, published in the *Psychological Review*, he wrote: "Psychology as the behaviorist views it is a purely objective experimental branch of science. Its theoretical goal is the prediction and control of behavior. The behaviorist in his effort to get a unitary scheme of animal response, recognizes no dividing line between man and brute."[16]

Watson's underlying assumptions that humans are qualitatively the same as brute animals and there is no dividing line between human and animal have permeated much of behavioristic research.

Early Twentieth Century: Association Is the Key to Learning in Behavioristic Theories

Watson used the concept of classical conditioning (pairing of ideas) following the pattern of Russian physiologist Ivan Pavlov's conditioning of his famous dog.[17] He conditioned the dog to associate the regular clicking of a metronome[18] with a response "that was already there"—salivation in the presence of meat. The dog did not salivate when hearing the clicking metronome before he was conditioned. In the conditioning process, when Pavlov presented meat to the dog, the dog responded by naturally salivating. Concurrently, Pavlov clicked on the metronome. Soon, the dog salivated when he heard the clicking sound without the presence of meat. (Maybe you have a dog that comes running to the kitchen when he hears you opening a bag or can of dog food, or any bag or can of food. Our dog, Cindy, did that.) Pavlov's dog "learned" to *associate* the clicking of the metronome with the meat and responded with salivation.

Pavlov's work impacted both Watson and B. F. Skinner. However, Skinner understood that much of school-learning involves responses that are not "already there." You

---

[16] John Watson, "Psychology as a Behaviorist Views It," *Psychology Review* 20 (1913), https://psychclassics.yorku.ca/Watson/views.htm.

[17] Associationism "is any of several theories that explain complex psychological phenomena as being built up from the association of simple sensations, stimuli and responses, or other behavioral or mental elements considered as primary," Dictionary.com. s.v. "associationism," accessed January 10, 2022, https://www.dictionary.com/browse/associationism.

[18] A metronome is a device with a regular clicking sound as it moves back and forth and is used to help a musician keep regular time to music.

must teach the response in order to condition it. For example, the response to "What is the capital of the State of Pennsylvania?" is not a natural inborn response. Skinner took one principle, the Law of Effect, from the work of Edward Thorndike, a brilliant American scientific psychologist, and developed a process called operant conditioning. The law or principle he used states that responses immediately followed by satisfaction will more likely reoccur. The law of effect also suggests that behaviors followed by dissatisfaction or discomfort are less likely to occur again.[19]

In operant conditioning, a response (behavior) of the student elicits a reinforcement from the teacher, much like the teacher who first exposed her students to what the interior of earth was like—hotter than on top—by "telling them." Then she provided a stimulus for them to memorize so that she could reinforce the response. The stimulus was "In what condition is the interior of the globe?" They repeated it, and she reinforced their response. The learned response was "The interior of the globe is in a condition of igneous fusion." The reinforcement, which is the key to the student responding the same way again and again, is what the teacher says after the response, "Wonderful! That is correct!" What gets associated? In the presence of a certain stimulus ("In what condition is the interior of the globe?"), the learned action/response is associated with the reinforcement that follows.

In most cases of teaching content, the response is *not already there* and must be provided, usually by a textbook, video, internet, or by the teacher. In classroom management, the teacher might try to "catch them being good" and then reinforce that behavior in hopes that they will be good tomorrow as well. However, most school content and skills are not something you can "catch the student saying or doing," so, the teacher tells, the student repeats, and the teacher reinforces. This is the essence of the methodology of behavioristic theories.

Both the behavioristic and the Herbartian views lead to a model of teaching: teacher tells, students take notes, and the teacher tests and reinforces students with a comment, grade, or sticker. Herbart's view had potential if he had considered the student as a psychologically *active participant* in the learning of incoming ideas; however, he did not.[20] Behaviorists challenged Herbart's view of active ideas and remained committed to looking at behaviors only as research data.

---

[19] Bruce W. Tuckman and David M. Monetti, *Educational Psychology* (Belmont, CA: Wadsworth Cengage Learning, 2011), 234, 236.

[20] Bigge and Shermis, *Learning Theories for Teachers*, 35.

The Active/Passive Pendulum Swing in Education

Skinner challenged the autonomously active view of the human that was expressed in philosophy in the eighteenth and nineteenth centuries and eventually impacted education in the twentieth century as a challenge to behaviorism. Opposite poles were created and the active/passive controversy (inside vs. outside factors) that has haunted teachers for years was born. About this controversy, Skinner wrote: "It is in the nature of an experimental analysis of human behavior that it should strip away the functions previously assigned to autonomous man and transfer them one by one to the controlling environment."[21] However, the "active self" theorists fought back.

Autonomously Active View

A second view of human nature and learning popular in the twentieth century and today declares that the human is **autonomously active** in the learning event. Everything needed for learning is already there inside the learner and must be drawn out or allowed to emerge naturally. Furthermore, early proponents of this view declared that humans are morally good. Therefore, what emerges from within a person should be "good" or positive. Restraints should be avoided. You may see how this led to extreme permissiveness in classroom management and student discipline.

There was a slight modification in this romantic view of the human simply because of human observation; humans are sometimes bad. What were teachers to do with bad behavior? An eighteenth-century Swiss philosopher, Jean-Jacques Rousseau, suggested that any bad individual behavior was the result of the environment or society. His famous line in *The Social Contract*, published in 1762, was "Man was born free, and he is everywhere in chains."[22] He held that humans born "morally good" are corrupted by society. To Rousseau, what humans need is to be free from the restraints of bad social environments.[23] Reason would ask, if humans are born morally good, then how has society, made up of morally good people, become corrupt? Of course, his underlying assumption does not meet the criteria of the Word of God that tells us that all humans born after the fall of Adam and Eve are morally flawed and need intervention from

---

[21] Burrhus Frederic Skinner, *Beyond Freedom and Dignity* (New York: Alfred A. Knopf, 1971), 198.

[22] Jean-Jacques Rousseau, *The Social Contract* (n.p., 1762), bk. 1, chap. 1.

[23] Bigge and Shermis, *Learning Theories for Teachers*, 31.

outside rather than to simply let a "good nature emerge." Rousseau's ideas, however, have influenced education primarily through his book, *Emile, or On Education*.[24]

Schools in the early to mid-twentieth century were thought to be bad environments by some who were influenced by romanticism and the view of the autonomous human. This was, in part, progressives argued, the result of practices and principles of behaviorism that squelched human freedom and creativity and led to a determinism that diminished humanity.[25] This reaction to behaviorism gave birth to the Free School Movement of the 1960s and '70s. Radical autonomy was the answer to the development of the human and to learning. "Get kids out of current-day schools" was a mantra of that era.[26]

The autonomously active view of the human is a purely developmental and natural unfoldment view of learning that results in the teacher using multiple activities to draw out what is already there present or constructed by the student. Theoretically, no student's knowledge-based comment is incorrect. Students are responsible for changing a view based upon their own processing. Motivation comes from inside. Students are expected to learn through the promptings of their own interest.

The autonomously active view is not considered scientific, nor does it use observable data in research. It is, rather, a philosophical view of learning that expresses the ideas of romantic naturalism suggested by Rousseau and Frobel long before the twentieth century. "Devotees of this position tend to place great emphasis on the study of child growth and development and to minimize the study of learning."[27] However, the view that all that the child becomes lies within the child has taken hold in many schools in America and around the world. The theory was promoted in the twentieth century by proponents of existential humanism championed by A. H. Maslow, Paul Goodman, and John Holt and may be presented under several titles: humanistic theory, unfoldment theory, educational humanism, and more recently, existential humanism.[28] We will use the label "humanistic theory" when we refer to this *philosophical* (nonscientific) theory.

---

[24] George Knight, *Philosophy & Education: An Introduction in Christian Perspective*, 4th ed. (Berrien Springs, MI: Andrews University, 2006), 20, 104. See Jean-Jacques Rousseau, *Emile, or On Education*, trans. Allan Bloom (New York: Basic Books, 1979).

[25] Knight, 103–6.

[26] Knight, 138.

[27] Bigge and Shermis, *Learning Theories for Teachers*, 32.

[28] See Bigge and Shermis, 31.

Critique of the Theory Based on the Autonomously Active Actional Nature

Because this theory focuses on the student and inside processing alone rather than content and outside factors such as the teacher, textbook, and resources, many Christian schools have not adopted it beyond, perhaps, the early childhood years. As well, many secondary schools that are charged with preparation for government or standardized tests have not adopted it. They may have adopted some of the tenets of human autonomy but retain the belief that content from outside the human must be learned. These decisions are more pragmatic than a decision based upon the examination of underlying presuppositions of adherents. The latter, I believe—to examine underlying assumptions—is far better in decision-making for Christian settings.

With just two views of the actional nature from which to choose during the first half of the twentieth century, active or passive, it was natural to reject one over the other for various reasons. For many Christians, who understand that God and his revelation in language form (the Bible) and his created order exist outside the knowing mind, the autonomously active view did not make sense and did not meet the criteria of a created, knowable, and objective world. For some educators, Christian or not, who accepted the importance of new information, that is, "content" to be learned, this view of the active actional nature was simply "romantic" and not practical for school education.

Neither of the two views, psychologically passive or active, fits with a biblical view of the human and learning. Thankfully, a third view entered the conversation in the last third of the twentieth century. It is a second scientific view. Elements of this theory were acknowledged long before it became a fully accepted theory of learning. So we ask, does it fit better with a biblical worldview?

Cognitively Active View

During mid-twentieth century, the passive and active views were challenged by a third view of the actional nature (born with) of the human being. This third view of the actional nature, referred to as psychologically or cognitively interactive, affirms that humans are born with a capacity (inside factor) to reach out to a real existing environment (outside factor) and make sense out of information that is there and available to be processed and learned. It is scientific in nature because behaviors are used to infer learning.[29] This third view holds that the human is neither psychologically passive nor

---

[29] Bigge and Shermis, 86.

autonomously active in the learning event, but rather, **cognitively interactive**. This simply means that inside factors and outside factors are essentially of equal importance and work together in learning.

Each of the three views attempts to describe how we learn because we are born human beings. Each theoretical view takes a position related to the actional nature of human beings at birth. The actional nature describes the psychological nature and source of human motivation that comes from "some kind of relationship between people and their respective environments." Each position related to human learning is mutually opposed and therefore only one of the positions can be true.[30] Some teachers who have been educated to think in terms of physical activity and physical passivity only have misunderstood the concept of cognitive interaction. The third view, interactive, is not a synthesis of the other two, as some may think, but a wholly different view that leads to different applications in the classroom.

The Third Theory Dominates Educational Theory Today

Cognitive interactive theory is not only the most prominent today and a more reasonable view than the other two, but it also *fits best with a biblical view of human learning* in its primary assumption of the basic "actional" nature of the student. This third view, however, has been seriously misunderstood by educators who view active, passive, and interactive as physical concepts (activity or passivity) rather than psychological characteristics describing how the mind works in the learning event.[31]

This confusion may be the result of the concept of "active learning," attributed to pragmatic philosopher John Dewey, often equated with physical activity and a minimized view of the teacher in learning. A close reading of John Dewey's work on education, however, reveals that he did not advocate the autonomously active human in which the teacher simply draws out from the student their own construction of knowledge, nor did he view activity as a replacement for teacher instruction of content. He wrote about the two views of the early twentieth century:

> The older type of instruction tended to treat the teacher as a dictatorial ruler. The newer type sometimes treats the teacher as a negligible factor, almost as an evil, though a necessary one. In reality, the teacher is the intellectual leader

---

[30] Bigge and Shermis, 15.
[31] Bigge and Shermis, 15.

of a social group. He is a leader, not in virtue of official position, but because of wider and deeper knowledge and matured experience. The supposition that the teacher must abdicate its leadership is merely silly.[32]

"Active Learning" and What It Means for Interactive Theorists

When referring to a theory of human learning that includes "active learning," it is far better to indicate that the student is an *active participant* in the learning. The activity of the mind is the focus in cognitive interactive theory. Of course, both physical and social activities engage the mind; they are important! You will see this as you continue to read this book. However, to be psychologically interactive means far more than social interaction, cooperative learning, or doing something alone or as a group.

A Challenge to the Cognitive Interactive Views: Radical Constructivism

Cognitive interactive theories such as cognitive information processing and social cognitive theories have been challenged by a prominent worldview that insists that all we can know of reality is what we construct with our own minds. To some extent this is an outgrowth of the autonomously active self as well as the seminal work of Jean Piaget. Truth, these postmodern thinkers declare, is my own constructed view of the world. This view has been labeled by one of its leading adherents, Ernst von Glasersfeld, as Radical Constructivism in his book with the same title.[33] This view is considered a philosophical view, an epistemology (branch of philosophy that studies knowledge) rather than a scientific view of learning.[34]

While adherents of radical constructivism hold to elements of the cognitive interactive theory described in this chapter, their view of knowledge must be evaluated. Constructivism has become a theory encouraged by a postmodern view that declares that humans create their own reality and their own truth, and that all of reality or truth

---

[32] John Dewey, "What I Believe," in *The Later Works, 1925–1953*, vol. 5, *1929–1930*, ed. Jo Ann Boydston, The Collected Works of John Dewey (1984; Carbondale: Southern Illinois University Press, 2008).

[33] Ernst von Glasersfeld, *Radical Constructivism: A Way of Knowing and Learning* (Washington, DC: The Falmer Press, 1995).

[34] See the book *By Design*, by the author of this chapter, for a more extended view of Constructivism and its problems and potentials. Martha MacCullough, *By Design: Developing a Philosophy of Education Informed by a Christian Worldview* (Colorado Springs: Purposeful Design, 2017), 65–68, 128–35.

can be known. As a theory of learning, it leans toward the views of the "active self" more than toward the interactive learner.[35] This is true primarily because of the view of knowledge held by its proponents and the heavy focus on inside factors.[36]

Does Our View of the Learner Matter in Approach to Education?

ENGAGE: It might be worthwhile to take the two early views, active and passive, briefly described above, and determine what the focus of teaching would be in each one. Would the focus be on the teacher or the student or something else? You may wish to refer to the previous conversation between the two teachers, several pages back, to review the focus of each one. In the conversation between the two teachers, one would focus on presenting outside information to students (stimuli), soliciting a response, and reinforcing it. The other would focus on the students and the promptings of their own interests as they unfold what they are developing from inside capacities. What approach to teaching would each of these views engender?

Focus of Cognitive Interactive Theory and Its Implications for Learning

ENGAGE: Thinking about the third view, cognitive interactive theories, what do you think would be the focus of teachers in their preparation and delivery of lessons if they really operated under cognitive interactive learning theory? We will use a cartoon to determine an answer. Read and respond to the message of the cartoon described below. (While this is one of my favorite cartoons to use in theories of learning presentations, I could not obtain permission to reprint it in this book.)

The cartoon is a Classic *Peanuts* cartoon in which Lucy represents the teacher who is reading the story of *Goldilocks and the Three Bears* to Linus, the student. The story has the little girl, Goldilocks, knocking at the door of the home of the three bears. The bears have gone for a walk while their morning porridge cools. Hearing no response, Goldilocks enters the house. When she sees the table set for three and the three bowls

---

[35] For a philosophical explanation of the epistemological problem related to radical constructivism, see Mortimer J. Adler, *Ten Philosophical Mistakes* (New York: MacMillan, 1985), 18–29, 89.

[36] Ernst von Glasersfeld, *An Introduction to Radical Constructivism*, originally published in *Die Erfundene Wirklichkeit*, ed. P. Watzlawick (Munich: Piper, 1981), 16–38. English translation in *The Invented Reality* (New York: Norton, 1984), 17–40. https://app.nova.edu/toolbox/instructionalproducts/ITDE_8005/weeklys/1984-vonGlaserfeld_RadicalConstructivism.pdf.

of porridge, she tastes each one. The great big bowl is "too hot," the middle-sized bowl is "too cold," but the wee little bowl is "just right and she ate it all up."

In the cartoon, Linus, the student, cannot allow this seeming error to occur. He says to the teacher/reader, Lucy, "I have a question."

Of course, Lucy says, "ABOUT WHAT!"

Linus replies, "It's about cooling. It would seem to me that if the middle-sized is cold, then the little bowl would be cold too, and—"

Lucy interrupts him with a good smack—*pow!* Linus is shocked and left lying on the floor.

The cartoonist uses the story to depict how Lucy treats Linus when he thinks and responds to what she is reading. She smacks him! *Pow!* Linus, left lying there with an injured look on his face, thinks, *I never even brought up the far more obvious point of unlawful entry.*

I have used this cartoon in my educational psychology classes for years to help students discover a principle of interactive learning clearly portrayed by the "learning theorist" Charles Schulz.

Read the description of the cartoon again and determine the following:

1. What is Linus doing? Remember he is the student.
2. What is the teacher's role in the learning? Lucy is the teacher.
3. What is the result of the teacher's response to the processing and questioning of the student?

Work in pairs if you are reading this book as a group. Cite evidence that Linus was doing the following:

1. Attending to and understanding the words and meanings of the author as read by the "teacher"
2. Locating related information (What was the information he located and from where did he locate it?)
3. Comparing to/contrasting some criteria (prior knowledge or beliefs)
4. Arriving at a conclusion, making a judgment, and communicating that conclusion
5. Seeking more information
6. Experiencing cognitive dissonance (something did not make sense!)

Note: 1–5 above are the elements of the critical thinking process and mirror key processes undertaken in learning according to cognitive interactive theorists.

Try to answer these questions: Why do you think the student (Linus) did *not* seek more information by asking another question or making a statement of judgment? How do you know that he *did not* stop thinking (from the cartoon description above)? How do you know he did stop communicating his thoughts to his teacher (Lucy)? (Exception: When he gets home that night, he might tell his mom that the teacher does not know anything about cooling and thinks that breaking into a house when someone is not home is just fine.)

What conclusions can you draw from this activity? Write or share these.

One sure thing can be inferred from Linus's experience that captures the concept of interactive:

Something is going on inside in response to something outside!

Now determine: What would be the focus of a classroom operating under the assumption that outside and inside factors are both important in human learning?

We will come back to this cartoon a little later to see how we might diagram what is happening.

Cognitive Interactive Theory

The theories of learning that are considered scientific because they use observable data are just two broad types: behavioristic and cognitive interactive theories. In behavioristic theories, the behavior as an answer to a stimulus question equals the learning. The learning *is* the response of the student. However, for the cognitive interactive theories, behaviors (responses such as answers) are evidence for some learning, but not the total picture.[37]

The two scientific theories are often referred to as (1) reactive theories (behavioristic) and (2) constructive theories (cognitive interactive). The latter is not to be confused with constructivism. Constructive theories hold that the learner does not simply react to input but rather uses inside capacities to make sense out of incoming information. The capacity to process information and create and use mental or cognitive categories helps to build (construct) meaning and understanding. This does not mean that humans construct reality, but rather that they construct their understandings of reality. They could be wrong. This is the assumption that is essential for the assessment element of teaching. Humans can make sense of, organize, and retrieve and use new

---

[37] Bigge and Shermis, *Learning Theories for Teachers*, 11.

information. In cognitive interactive theory, this capacity is thought to be inborn as one selects from the environment (outside) and processes what he or she is taking in using this inside capacity.[38]

Prior knowledge and categories are vital in future learning; therefore, teachers are encouraged to engage students' prior knowledge in introducing new information. Linus possessed prior knowledge to create a question about the science of cooling and an issue about the law or ethics of entering a home when no one is there. Something was going on inside when he retrieved prior knowledge and then asked a question (behaved). Behaviorists that focus on outside factors alone do not attempt to address what is going on in the mind. Skinner famously said about learning that it is simply a change in behavior because you can't see the mind, and "he doubted that there was anything inside that needed to be changed!"[39]

Key Psychologists Who Introduced Cognitive Interactive Learning

The first book I read on cognitive theory was written by Ulric Neisser, the Father of Cognitive Psychology. His work *Cognitive Psychology* was considered a scientific refutation of Skinner's behavioristic theory. Neisser presented cognitive psychology as the empirical investigation of mental processes and activities used in perceiving, remembering, and thinking, and the act of using those processes. It was Neisser who coined the term "cognitive psychology."[40]

JEROME BRUNER (1915–2016)

The book *Process of Education* influenced my own thinking toward a cognitive approach to learning. It was written by educational psychologist Jerome Bruner, who, in his early research and writings, developed a cognitive interactive information processing theory. The major metaphor used in early cognitive theories is the computer: input, input processed, and output. However, Bruner's theory was not as mechanical as the early versions of information processing theory.[41] His theory included a reciprocal and fluid relationship between outside and inside factors.

---

[38] Bigge and Shermis, 55.

[39] Daniel Goleman, "Embattled Giant of Psychology Speaks His Mind," *New York Times*, August 25, 1987.

[40] See Ulric Neisser, *Cognitive Psychology* (New York: Appleton-Century-Crofts, 1967).

[41] Jerome S. Bruner, *The Culture of Education* (Cambridge, MA: Harvard University, 1996), 1–6.

Bruner asked key questions about learning summarized here: (worldview questions added in italics)

1. What is the nature of persons as learners? *What is a human being as a learner?*
2. What is the nature and structure of knowledge and how is it developed for optimal, insightful comprehension? *What is the nature of knowledge and knowing?*
3. What is the nature of the knowledge-getting process, and how might that be structured for optimal insightful comprehension? *How do humans come to know what they know? How do we teach?*[42]

For Bruner, "an individual is best viewed as neither a mystical active self nor a passive recipient of information."[43] He was one of the first to express the cognitive interactive theory that held that the human is a processor of incoming information (stimuli) and not just a reactor. He held that current processing is built upon previous learning much like the processing of Linus in the cartoon reviewed above. Linus used what he understood about an aspect of science and law to "behave," that is, to ask a question. Bruner viewed the result of effective learning as the ability to transform and use information, activating higher mental functions that allow the learner to go beyond the information given.[44]

Recall the class visited by the friend of William James in which the students could not solve a very easy problem. The visitor to the class asked them, if one dug deep into the earth would they find it hot or cold. They could not go beyond the memorized statement to provide an answer. However, they could answer the question (stimulus) when it was given exactly as memorized. Bruner offers a theory that predicts that students will be able to go beyond memorized answers stored in their memory toward using the knowledge in new and different ways. This is essential for the transfer of learning, a goal of school learning that enables the student to use knowledge and skills gained in multiple areas of the curriculum in school, and in life outside the classroom.[45]

Bruner viewed learning as the act of connecting things that are related and combining them into structures that give significance. His early theory of learning is called Categorization Theory. Thinking is the process of conceptualization and

---

[42] See Jerome Bruner, *The Process of Education* (Cambridge: Harvard University, 1960). These questions also appear in the discussion of Bruner in Bigge and Shermis, *Learning Theories for Teachers*, 144–45.

[43] Bigge and Shermis, 135.

[44] Bruner, *Process of Education*, 17–20.

[45] Bruner, 6.

categorization.[46] He was influenced by the work of Piaget, who also used categories or schema to label what the learner is developing inside the mind. He differed from Piaget in that he believed that children could begin to learn a subject at a young age, if taught the "right way."[47] Bruner famously said, "We begin with the hypothesis that any subject can be taught effectively in some intellectually honest form to any child at any stage of development."[48] In this statement, Bruner advanced cognitive theories well beyond cognitive developmentalists such as Piaget and Vygotsky. In his more recent writing, Bruner refers to Vygotsky as contributing to his developing thinking that focuses on social/cultural learning as integral to individual learning.[49]

Bruner believed that a stored knowledge base, organized into categories, is the key to learning. Teaching the structure of a subject aids in the process of developing big ideas (categories) into which related facts can be stored. Learning, he believed, is "constructive" rather than "reactive." While Bruner takes a constructive approach, he does not rule out a reality that exists outside the knowing mind as radical constructivism does. Bruner wrote: "But the 'rightness' of particular interpretations, while dependent on perspective, also reflects rulers of evidence, consistency, and coherence. Not everything goes."[50] The human reaches out to what is there to be learned, takes it in, and tries to make sense of it by fitting it into present categories or constructing new categories in the mind. The environment provides what is there to select, take in, and process. Therefore, the teacher, the textbook, other learning resources, and other students are very important in learning. Inside and outside factors work together.[51] Bruner's later works, especially his book *Folk Psychology*, added a strong element of social and cultural factors and personal narratives that give meaning to life.[52]

Information Processing Theories

Below is my replica of a model used by information processing theorists.[53] The diagram focuses on the inside factors that are a part of learning after the learner takes in

---

[46] Bigge and Shermis, *Learning Theories for Teachers*, 142.

[47] Bigge and Shermis, 133.

[48] Bruner, *Process of Education*, 33.

[49] Bruner, *Culture of Education*, xiii, 11.

[50] Bruner, 9–14.

[51] Bruner, xi.

[52] Bruner, 1–43.

[53] Anita Woolfolk, *Educational Psychology*, 11th ed. (Columbus, OH: Merrill, 2010), 237.

new information (outside stimuli) through the "sensory register." There is a working or short term (ST) memory, the place where processing occurs, and the long-term memory (LTM) where the processed information may be stored. This model was developed by Atkinson and Shiffrin and was based on an analogy of the computer: input, processing, and output. It is a linear (straight line) model and rather mechanical. The model was improved upon through the work of other information processing theorists such as Bruner and Albert Bandura. Below are several diagrams that depict variations in cognitive theories. The first one depicts the original basis for Information Processing Theory and includes three inside processing mechanisms: sensory register, short-term or working memory, and long-term memory.

Information Processing Theory
(Original—rather mechanical)

Three systems
Atkinson and Shiffrin[54]

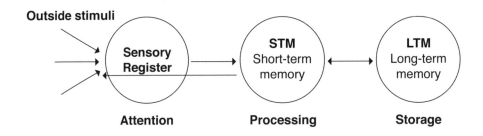

First theory to use the computer analogy

Diagram 1

[54] See "Atkinson & Shiffrin Information Processing Model," Teacher-Librarian Association, accessed January 12, 2022, https://teacherlibrariansassociation.wordpress.com/2014/02/19 /atkinson-shiffrins-information-processing-model/.

Albert Bandura Helped to Improve the Original Model for Information Processing Theory

Canadian psychologist Albert Bandura (1925–2021) began his work as a behaviorist but soon recognized the value in cognitive interactive theories. As he continued to develop his theory, he retained some of the terms and principles of behaviorism but added a strong social and personal component. His theory is labeled Social Cognitive Theory.[55] In this view humans are neither driven by inner forces (as in the autonomously *active* view), nor automatically shaped by the environment and external stimuli (as in the psychologically *passive* theories).[56] Social cognitive theorists, in contrast to other views, give about equal weight to "both aspects of the person-environment relationship."[57]

Bandura held that humans act on purpose.[58] This was in stark contrast to B. F. Skinner's behavioristic assumption that states humans do not act on purpose. However, another behavioristic psychologist, Edward C. Tolman (1886–1959), had already challenged the idea that humans do not act on purpose. Tolman developed a theory of *purposive behaviorism* that attributes behaviors to cognition rather than reinforcement.[59] His work was a forerunner to Bandura's.

Bandura held that "the model of the person is that of an active processor of information organizing and constructing experience into meaningful internal representations and behaving not as an automaton but as a thoughtful, purposeful being."[60] He explained human learning in terms of what he called a *triadic reciprocal model*. Triadic refers to three factors: (1) the person (prior knowledge and experiences, emotions, etc.), (2) the behavior, and (3) the environment. To Bandura, behavior, cognitive and other personal factors, and environmental events interact with each other in the learning event. Inside and outside factors work together. Bandura's theory focuses on human nature (related to how we learn) as interactive rather than passive or autonomously active. I have diagrammed his model below.[61]

---

[55] Bigge and Shermis, *Learning Theories for Teachers*, 154–55.

[56] Bigge and Shermis, 158.

[57] Bigge and Shermis, 158.

[58] Bigge and Shermis, 154–58.

[59] Stephen B. Klein, *Learning Principles and Applications*, 5th ed. (Los Angeles: Sage, 2009), 30, 272–73.

[60] Bigge and Shermis, *Learning Theories for Teachers*, 155.

[61] Adapted from Tuckman and Monetti, *Educational Psychology*, 391.

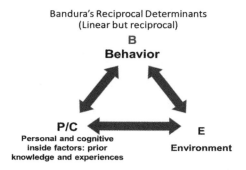

Diagram 2

More recent cognitive theories may be diagrammed using a more robust version of information processing theory that adds *perception* to the original "attention" as elements of the sensory register. Perception begins immediately when the person attends and in nanoseconds (fast) finds connections (vocabulary, concepts, etc.) in the long-term memory to help the learner begin to make sense of incoming information. I have diagrammed it this way.

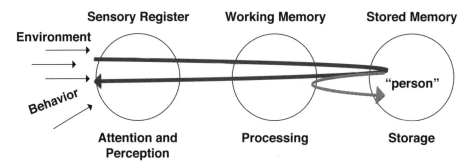

Diagram 3

Notice in diagram 3 that the original three inside systems, sensory register, short-term or working memory, and long-term (stored) memory are present. However, there is a major difference. Notice that perception has been added along with attention.[62] The long line goes immediately to the stored memory (what the person has stored) to find any prior knowledge, categories, or vocabulary to help make sense of incoming information or stimuli. Think of Linus hearing about the hot and cold bowls of porridge. Notice as well that this same line may lead to a behavior such as asking a question or making a statement or doing something. (Linus asked a question.) Some or all of the processed information may simply be stored or lost. In this diagram the shorter line indicates that information is stored for later use. (Linus told his mom about it at home that night.)

In the cognitive information processing view illustrated above, the environment provides input (think: teacher, video, other students, books, computers, etc.). When the student attends to and selects from what is provided, perception (a way of understanding something) begins. The learner tries to find in his stored memory anything that relates to or connects with what has been taken in—such as concepts, vocabulary, images, prior experiences—that will help him to begin to make sense of the new information. This is one reason we use prior knowledge and experiences of the learner as an aid to learning new material. At this point, in nanoseconds (fast), the student processes the information and either "behaves" (asks a question, makes a statement, does something observable) or stores the new information with a disposition to think about it or use it at a later time. If this does not happen, it may be lost.

Bruner's theory of categorization makes the point that if the student has classified and organized prior knowledge into categories, he is better equipped to learn something new related to the subject and to store it in the right place for later recall. This idea relates to Bruner's concept of "structure of the subject" that is addressed later in the book. Understanding structure, including major categories and concepts, enhances learning.[63]

ENGAGE: Let us see how the cognitive interactive model works by referring again to the cartoon described above with Linus and Lucy. Study the diagram of the cognitive information processing theory below and explain the behavior of Linus (he asked a question). The question he raised with the teacher is considered a "behavior" in learning theory. See if you can make sense of this diagram. Think about the cartoon.

---

[62] Bigge and Shermis, *Learning Theories for Teachers*, 63.
[63] See chapter 2 of Bruner, *The Process of Education*.

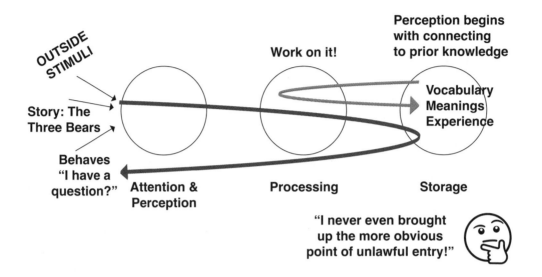

Explanation:

1. Teacher reads the story of the three bears; this is the outside stimulus.
2. Student pays attention and takes in the story through his sensory register: sees and hears.
3. He begins to try to make sense of the story (perception) by locating prior knowledge and understandings, in this case about science and the law or ethics.
4. When his prior knowledge about science and cooling do not match what he is hearing, he "behaves" (does something). He asks a question. His behavior indicates some of what might be going on inside that the teacher needs to address.
5. Lucy's response is very negative. Instead of a *pow!* she might have said, "This is just a make-believe story, Linus." And then she could have explained the genre of literature, or she could have asked Linus for clarity, "What are you thinking; please explain your question," allowing Linus to give his conclusion about the science mistake in the book and perhaps the moral issue of entering a house when not invited. Instead, she just responded with a *pow!*
6. So Linus stored in his long-term memory (category: law) his other issue about this story advocating breaking and entering with no one home. Notice the lighter arrow that shows sending this information back to storage until he got

home later that day and spoke with his mom. (This is not in the cartoon but added by me.)

7. At home Linus tells his mom that the teacher knows very little about cooling (he had stored her response to his question) and furthermore she must believe it is okay to enter a home without being invited. He had stored information that he was able to retrieve and use as he conversed with his mom in trying to make sense of the day's learning event.

    (The teacher may have shared at home that night that she has a student who simply cannot think about make-believe stories and asks crazy questions—this is what she processed and stored. We might say that "the student and teacher were not on the same page.")

If you can explain this cartoon in the terms of a cognitively interactive human, you are well on your way to understanding this theory of learning and will be able to understand the model for teaching that is derived from it.

Which View Fits with a Biblical View of the Learner?

Which of the three views of the nature of humans and learning fits best with a biblical worldview? We have reviewed briefly some of the work of key theorists that has led to a cognitive interactive approach to learning. We have also kept in mind the importance of a biblical view of the human and learning. Behaviorism is extremely deterministic and holds that the human does not act on purpose. It is a theory that dehumanizes human beings and views humans as more like machines than creatures with personhood (will, emotions, thinking, acting on purpose). Much of behavioristic research was conducted on animals. Findings were generalized to humans because researchers saw little essential difference between humans and the animal kingdom. On the other hand, cognitivists have used humans, primarily, in their research. The philosophical theory—humanistic theory—promotes the belief that the human is basically good and autonomously active and therefore there is little need for correction of constructed knowledge or need for character development. Outside information is not really the focus. Unfoldment of what is already there is the focus.

Cognitive theories, just like all theories, are man-made. Researchers bring their own worldviews to their work. As we evaluate these theories, including cognitive interactive theories, we bring our Christian worldview to the research and conclusions to determine what to accept and use and what to reject. Christian apologist Francis Schaeffer put it this way: "The same reasonable God made both things, the known and the knower, the subject and the object, and he put them together."[64] God can be trusted to help us understand how he intended for humans to learn.

A Christian view suggests that truth (true information) exists *outside* the knowing mind and can be known, even with the human limit of not being able to know exhaustively. The mind (*inside*) has been created by God with the capacity to learn, to come to know. Humans can and do learn what is there to be learned. If this is true, then reason would inform us that the best fit from a Christian viewpoint would be the third choice, the position that acknowledges both inside *and* outside factors equally. One who is seriously viewing learning theories through a biblical lens cannot agree with the autonomously active or psychologically passive views as they appear in their stated forms.

Furthermore, humans may construe incoming information correctly or incorrectly. We do not create our own truth or reality, but rather we construct a representation of reality and knowledge that must be subject to ongoing assessment. While we may misconstrue new information because of our own limits and prior knowledge or lack thereof, assessment and further learning enhances cognition and the reorganization and changes in thinking that are vital in learning. The cognitive interactive view, with a focus on inside and outside factors, preserves the concept that reality/truth exists outside the knowing mind and humans have the capacity to process it and respond. This view is the most compatible of the three possibilities with a biblical view of the human and learning. It is, by no means, exhaustive and should not be viewed as a "Christian" view but rather as a view that is compatible with a Christian view in its basic form. As we read cognitive theorists and bring our biblical worldview to inform our reading, we will certainly not agree with all each one has to offer. Thinking biblically about human learning will assist the educator in the task of selecting models and methods that contribute to effective learning.

The Christian mind operates under the belief, then, (1) that there is something outside of ourselves that we must take into account, and (2) there is something inside, built in the human by our Creator, that allows us to learn. If this is a true statement, there should be some evidence in the teaching ministry of Jesus.

In the book *Educating for Human Flourishing: A Christian Perspective*, Spears and Loomis make a very interesting statement:

---

[64] Francis Schaeffer, *He Is There, and He Is Not Silent* (Wheaton, IL: Tyndale, 1972), 69.

The most intelligent man who ever walked the earth—the sage of Nazareth, studied and followed by millions and millions of people, arguably having more influence than any other intellectual in history—informs no part of educational theory or practice. The greatest teacher who ever taught has little or no voice at the table of teacher preparation or educational policy. Plato, Aristotle, Karl Marx (e.g., through the critical pedagogues) and Charles Darwin (through the psychological behaviorists) have more residual influence over American education agenda than does Jesus.[65]

Christians should certainly bring to the "table" the "voice" of the greatest teacher who ever lived. Exploring how Jesus taught his disciples may help us to select a theory of learning that leads to an effective model for teaching. How does the teaching ministry of Jesus fit with the principle that inside and outside factors work together in learning?

ENGAGE: Review the following worldview statement and then complete the activity below to determine how this claim is evident in Scripture.

> *Humans, created in the image of God, are born with the innate capacity to learn, to know, to understand, and to act. God has provided something to know, himself and his creation, that is, reality and it can be known! Inside and outside factors are equally important in human learning!*

As you complete this "Engage" activity, ask why you think Jesus taught his disciples and other individuals as he did, and then answer the questions at the end of this section. Read the full passage and take some notes before you discuss each teaching event with a group or pair. These are just a sampling of incidents in the teaching ministry of Jesus. In each passage below the teacher is Jesus.

1. *Mark 8:27–30 (Matthew 16 and Luke 9)*
    Teacher: "Who do people say I am?"
    The Learners: "Some say you are John the Baptist, Elijah, or one of the prophets."
    Teacher: "Who do you say that I am?"
    Peter the Student: "You are the Christ." (Right answer, but did he understand?)
    Teacher: Designs an activity—field trip to a mountain (he took three students).

---

[65] Paul D. Spears and Steven R. Loomis, *Educating for Human Flourishing: A Christian Perspective* (Downers Grove, IL: IVP Academic, 2009), 158.

What happened on the mountain that aided the understanding of the students? In what ways does this example fit the concept of interactive learning? How does it fit with the answer to the question: How does God intend for his creatures to learn?

2. *Mark 4:35–41*

Teacher is asleep in the boat. Storm arises.

Students need help and ask a question.

The teacher stills the storm and arouses a key question in the minds of the students: "What manner of man is this that the winds and seas obey him?"

The teacher then begins to answer that question throughout the "unit of study"—that is, the rest of the time he had with his students (disciples) on earth.

What did the actions of the teacher do to create questions from the learners? (While we cannot create this kind of activity—calm a storm—we can create activities that engage the mind toward the lesson at hand.)

3. *Luke 10:25–37*

Student asks the master teacher: "What must I do to inherit eternal life?"

Teacher: "What is written in the law?" How do you read it?

Student answers correctly, quoting the greatest law. ("Love the Lord your God with all your heart, soul, and mind, and strength and love your neighbor as yourself.")

Student asks (wishing to justify his own thinking): "Who is my neighbor?"

Teacher tells a story: Then, at the end of the story, Jesus did not tell him the answer but rather, asked a question to be answered by the student that required him to draw a conclusion.

Teacher encourages the man to respond to the story and live accordingly.

The student was challenged to live according to the conclusion he had drawn from the story.

4. *Matt 22:23–32*

Students tell the teacher a made-up story about a woman who had seven husbands (one at a time, all brothers). In the story, each husband died without leaving children, and they said that Moses "told us that if a man dies without having children, his brother must marry the widow and have children for him." They posed a question for the teacher about the afterlife: "Whose wife will she be, of the seven, since all of them were married to her?"

Teacher's response: "You are in error because you do not know the Scriptures or the power of God." He then proceeded to do some direct instruction. These "students" needed some information.

Perhaps you can think of other teaching incidents in the life of Jesus. Discuss these with others if possible and then discuss the four incidences in the teaching of Jesus outlined above.

REFLECT: Using these passages, how would you defend the concept of interactive learning, that is, that something inside the learner and something outside the learner work together in the learning event? Ask yourselves, What is the content or information to which Jesus was referring or teaching? What was the processing and response on the part of the student to the content? and What was the result? This is the heart of interactive learning in which information, processing, and response result in thinking, actions, and attitudes. The result of learning should lead to human flourishing, that is, to living to the fullest and becoming more and more the person God intended.

Write a brief defense of the roles or place in the learning event for the classroom teacher and the student. Who is more important and why?

What Can We Infer from the Teaching of Jesus?

Jesus was concerned with the inside processing of the student as well as with the information to which he was referring as he taught. He often used the prior knowledge and experiences of the student to engage minds to actively process what he was saying. He asked students to draw conclusions as well. Is it too much to infer that Jesus knew best how to teach because he knew how we were created to learn?

Both teacher and student are important in learning!

School curricula written with the cognitive interactive view in mind are designed to be learning-centered rather than simply "child-centered" or "subject-centered." This statement assumes that the student is learning something a certain way and that the teacher is teaching in such a way as to promote the learning of that something! Content, teacher, and human processing are all important contributors to be considered in determining a teaching model. Learning theory should lead to a teaching *model* consistent with one's chosen theory.

The Theory Behind a Teaching Model

REFLECT: If both inside and outside factors are important in learning and working together, and if content and student processing are both important, what should a teaching model include? Think like this:

1. If something inside matters in the learning of new information, I must plan to engage that inside "something" to activate prior knowledge and motivate toward learning the lesson at hand.
2. If something outside matters, I must study and organize content and skill development strategies to deliver these, taking into account the students' prior experiences and current skill and knowledge base and developmental level.
3. If learning occurs as information is taken in and processed by the individual, I must create student processing activities, both group and individual, that are designed to help the student fit into their current understandings, make sense of new information, construct adequate understandings, and practice skills.
4. If learning occurs inside as a development of understandings and meanings, and I am a teacher who must assess learning to see how well the student has made sense of new material, I must create ongoing assessment activities that provide feedback to the teacher that answers the question, "Are they getting it?" and feedback to the students answering their question, "Am I getting it?"

A Personal Journey

As a young teacher of teachers, I was acquainted with inquiry learning. My very first article was written on inquiry learning. I used the approach but added the adjective *directed*—as in "directed inquiry"—to try to depict the concept of outer (directed) and inner (mental processes—the curious inquiring mind). This was an outgrowth of my education under Drs. Lois LeBar and Lawrence Richards at Wheaton College and was first represented by an outline for Bible teaching: Hook, Book, Look, and Took. I revised the model for directed inquiry for all school subjects and used the labels Motivation, Input, Closure, and Evaluation. I have since developed other, more up-to-date and more accurate labels, and my students have improved the model as well. Chapters 5 and 6 identify a teaching model that fits with the cognitive interactive learning theory and answers the "how to" in expressing the theory behind the reflections above. They are written by one of my former students (my daughter, Debbie).

In the twenty-first century, the concept of the interactive actional nature, with its applications for learning and teaching, has opened the door for a robust framework for teaching that seems to take into account a reasonable view of human learning as well as one that fits with a biblical view. We owe a debt of gratitude to both mid-twentieth century educators such as Lois LeBar and to educators as early as John Amos Comenius (seventeenth century) who understood that outer factors (books, pictures, the teacher, other media, other students) and inner factors (the inborn capacity to reach out to the world and try to make sense of it using cognitive processes) were essential to learning. Comenius was way ahead of his time, coming as he was from a broad Christian world-view. He is often referred to as the Father of Modern Education.[66] See sidebars on John Amos Comenius and Lois LeBar for more information. We owe much to cognitive theorists for this more recent paradigm that helps to verify the attempts of some educator/practitioners in the past to answer the question, "How do humans learn?"

Conclusion

In this chapter we have addressed the psychological foundations of effective teaching and contrasted and compared three distinct approaches using the psychological labels of (1) psychologically passive, (2) autonomously active, and (3) cognitively interactive. Three broad views have been addressed from a biblical viewpoint. You will find a summary of proponents of these theories at the end of this chapter.

We have encouraged the reader to adopt the third position that promotes the understanding that humans are interactive learners who must actively participate in the learning process of new information coming from outside (books, internet, teacher provided, and so on). A teaching/learning model will be developed in chapters 5 and 6. Before that task is undertaken, new research in brain-based learning will be addressed in the next chapter. While this present chapter has explored the psychological aspects of learning, Dr. Ken Coley will address the physical or biological aspects that are a part of a developing theory of learning based upon recent research in brain physiology with potential applications in education.

Extended Research and Reflection: If you or your school are using the InTASC Standards (Interstate Teacher Assessment and Support Consortium), review Standard #1 and discuss or write how the content of this chapter has addressed the standard, at least in part.

---

[66] See KYTKA, "The Father of Modern Education," Everything CZECH, August 6, 2016, https://www.tresbohemes.com/2016/08/father-of-modern-education/.

Standard #1: Learner Development. The teacher understands how learners grow and develop, recognizing that patterns of learning and development vary individually within and across the cognitive, linguistic, social, emotional, and physical areas, and designs and implements developmentally appropriate and challenging learning experiences.[67]

John Amos Comenius (1592–1670), The Father of Modern Education

Comenius was born in Moravia (current-day Czech Republic) in 1592. He was exiled because of his Protestant beliefs during the persecutions of the Thirty Years' War (1618–1648). He fled to Poland and several other European countries, where he began to focus on education rather than his prior pastoral ministry. He thought that all people should be educated so they could read the Bible for themselves. He declared that the education of his day was not conducive to the joy of learning. He was keenly aware that the condition of education in the seventeenth century needed much improvement, calling schools "slaughterhouses of the mind."[68]

In one of his most famous works, *The Great Didactic*, he wrote that the main object of his work was "to seek and to find methods of instruction, by which teachers may teach less, but learners may learn more."[69] Comenius disliked the method of student recitation of memorized information while standing at the teacher's desk. He advocated for memorizing only that which the student understood. He was ahead of his time in promoting active participation of the student in learning rather than a dictatorial telling by the teacher. He was also ahead of his time in promoting compulsory education for all, for girls as well as for boys, for rich and for poor, and he held that it should take place where children lived, in the small hamlet or the big city.[70]

LeBar suggests that Comenius was one of the first to focus on both inner and outer factors in the learning event. "He found that inner factors (in his

---

[67] "Interstate Assessment and Support Consortium," Council of Chief State School Officers 2013 (Washington, DC), 8.

[68] LeBar, *Education That Is Christian*, 39.

[69] LeBar, 41.

[70] See Lockerbie, *A Passion for Learning*, 177–84 (see chap. 1, n. 6).

day) were being almost entirely neglected."[71] LeBar also suggested that he was keenly aware of God's creatorship of the human and the natural world. His views on education reflected his understanding that there is a God-created learner and something objectively there to be learned, and both must be addressed by teachers because they work together in learning. He was the first to use illustrations and pictures in school textbooks and to suggest using the prior knowledge of the student to create interest. His famous first illustrated textbook was *Orbis Pictus*.[72]

Dr. Lois LeBar

Lois Emogene LeBar was born in Olean, New York, on October 28, 1907. Lois observed her mother, a schoolteacher, whose love for teaching and learning influenced her the rest of her life. Right after high school, Lois entered a normal school for training to be a teacher. However, a major change occurred in 1932 when her sister, Mary, attended a teachers' Bible study and shared with Lois the message of the gospel. Both sisters put their faith and trust in Jesus as Savior and decided to attend Moody Bible Institute, where they studied the Bible and Christian education. Church education became her passion as she continued her education and teaching positions at Moody and later, in 1945, at Wheaton College where she and her sister, Mary, remained until retirement in 1975.[73]

While progressive educators who championed the active involvement of the student in learning had a profound influence on LeBar's developing educational philosophy, she also developed a keen interest in seventeenth-century educator John Amos Comenius, whose views on education were informed by his Christian worldview.

What LeBar appreciated about Comenius was his ability to balance what she called "inner factors" (the needs, desires, and motivations of students) and "outer factors" (the content of Scripture, the person of the teacher, and the classroom environment) without losing the importance of either. It remained

---

[71] LeBar, *Education That Is Christian*, 42.

[72] See KYTKA, "The Father of Modern Education."

[73] David P. Setran, "Database: Christian Educators of the 20th Century," Talbot School of Theology, accessed March 4, 2021, https://www.biola.edu/talbot/ce20/database.

a continual project for LeBar to cultivate an educational theory that embraced both realities.[74]

LeBar instituted the lesson plan concept of boy/girl; book; boy/girl (originally boy/book/boy) as an approach to planning a lesson. Later, Lawrence Richards, who also taught at Wheaton College during the last decade of LeBar's tenure, developed the model into Hook, Book, Look, and Took. It was this model that Dr. Marti MacCullough, one of the authors of this book, developed and used in this book under more up-to-date labels. MacCullough studied under Drs. Lois and Mary LeBar in their last several years at Wheaton. We owe a debt of gratitude to Lois LeBar for developing an early version of interactive teaching in which inner and outer factors work together in learning.

Proponents and Views of Theories of Human Learning

	Autonomously Active	Psychologically Passive	Cognitively Interactive
Relation to Environment	Underlying human characteristics are inborn. Environment is merely a location for unfoldment of what is within. Motivation is solely from within.	Human characteristics are primarily products of the environment. Behaviors are the result of outside forces. Humans are non-purposive. "Motivation" must come from outside in the form of reinforcement.	Human characteristics result from the person making sense of the physical and social environment. Person-environment is a reciprocal relationship. Motivation may be a reciprocal process. Inside is often triggered by outside factors.
Proponents	Rousseau, Pestalozzi, Froebel, Maslow	Skinner, Thorndike, Watson	Dewey, Tolman, Vygotsky, Bruner, Bandura, Bigge and Shermis, developmentalists such as Piaget

---

[74] See LeBar, *Education That Is Christian*, 40–41.

	Autonomously Active	Psychologically Passive	Cognitively Interactive
Teaching Model	Draw out: Activity, activity, activity with the focus on the enjoyment of thinking and doing	Put in: Tell, explain, test, reinforce (grade) with the focus often on the reinforcer, the grade	Engage the mind: Provide (make available) new information through exploration and explanation Student processing activities and construction of meaning and understanding Ongoing assessment (MacCullough)

Adapted from Martha E. MacCullough, *By Design: Developing a Philosophy of Education Informed by a Christian Worldview*, 2nd ed. (Colorado Springs: Purposeful Design, 2017).

CHAPTER 4

The Perspective of Mind, Brain, and Education Research

Ken Coley

Introduction

Teaching and learning in the twenty-first century have been transformed at a rapid pace in large part due to what is referred to as mind, brain, and education research (MBE). Incredible advances in the field of neuroscience have led to a much deeper understanding of how the brain functions when exposed to new stimuli. One author/educator famously describes the process of teaching and learning as "the art of changing the brain."[1]

This chapter addresses the biological aspects of learning related to the brain and focuses on the mental activity of the student. The learning process involves both outside stimuli and inside activity as was addressed in the previous chapter. Learning is an interactive process, and the human being is interactive by nature; that is, God created humans to be able to process new information from the environment. Human activity in learning is the focus of brain research and this chapter. In the chapter that follows, a planning model will be addressed that takes the MBE research into account.

---

[1] James E. Zull, *The Art of Changing the Brain: Enriching the Practice of Teaching by Exploring the Biology of Learning* (Sterling, VA: Stylus, 2002).

Many creative and complex studies have been conducted over the last two decades making use of extraordinary advances in brain research made possible by MRI scans (magnetic resonance imaging), EEG mapping (electroencephalogram), and PET scanning (positron emission topography). These medical advances have provided ample evidence to erase the misconception that was widely held by previous generations that each person is born with a given number of brain cells and this number decreases as the individual ages.[2] Many forward-thinking teachers of generations ago, including the authors of this text, did not embrace these limitations placed on their students' academic abilities but lacked the technical and scientific means to speak out against this myth. Now we can!

The process of impacting the size and shape of the brain may best be described by the term *brain plasticity* or *neuroplasticity*. One educator describes the process this way:

> All learning is characterized by plasticity, or the connection of brain cells that were not previously linked. Plasticity challenges old views that the brain is a fixed structure; instead we now know that it is malleable and that different parts can be used for different things. . . . Every time the brain learns something new, it experiences physical change and demonstrates its plasticity.[3]

Mind, Brain, and Education Science

The most basic explanation for the experience of teaching and learning is the single word *change. Where no change has taken place, no teaching and learning have taken place.* The change may be an increase in factual knowledge, an increase in comprehension, or a change in attitude or perception. But over time our goal as educators is a change in the heart that will lead to a change in behavior.

How does this change come about most effectively? When the learner is engaged. Rich Felder refers to engagement as *active learning*. Felder defines it this way: "Active learning consists of short course-related individual or small-group activities that all students in a class are called upon to do, alternating with instructor-led intervals in

---

[2] Judy Willis, *Research-Based Strategies to Ignite Student Learning: Insights from a Neurologist and Classroom Teacher* (Alexandria, VA: ASCD, 2006).

[3] Tracey Tokuhama-Espinosa, *Mind, Brain, and Education Science: A Comprehensive Guide to the New Brain-Based Teaching* (New York: W. W. Norton, 2011), 120.

which student responses are processed and new information is presented."[4] Doyle puts it succinctly: "The one doing the work is the one doing the learning."[5]

ENGAGE: Before you go any further in this chapter, rate your level of understanding of each term below. If the term is completely unfamiliar to you, rank it one (1). If you have some previous knowledge of it, rank your knowledge as two (2). If you have previously encountered the idea and believe that you are currently using it in your teaching, score it as three (3):

schema	chunking	formative assessment
durable learning	differentiation	reflective practice
scaffolding	cooperative learning	metacognition

Now pause for a few moments and reconsider each term you rated as 1 or 2. Jot down a *prediction* about what each word has to do with education and your teaching; you may be surprised by this activity as you move through this chapter.

The above list is composed of terminology frequently discussed in the literature related to the teaching-learning process. These terms and others will be discussed in this chapter and will be presented in the order an experienced teacher would consider them as he/she plans a curriculum unit and daily lesson plans. To put this another way, we will present concepts from MBE research based on the beginning, development, and wrap-up of your daily teaching plan.

Connecting MBE Research to Instructional Approaches in the Gospels

At this point we want to draw your attention to the connection between these twenty-first-century advances and research findings to instructional episodes found in the Gospels. A systematic comparison of these concepts to the active learning techniques used by Jesus during his ministry is startling—nearly all the techniques discussed in the pages of this text and in the books cited for support can be found in the Gospels. But we want to quickly clarify that these connections do not validate the teaching ministry of our Lord. He needs no validation. However, these correlations highlight the power

---

[4] Richard M. Felder and Rebecca Brent, "Active Learning: An Introduction," *ASQ Higher Education Brief* 2, no. 4 (2009): 2.

[5] Terry Doyle, *Helping Students Learn in a Learner-Centered Environment: A Guide to Facilitating Learning in Higher Education* (Sterling, VA: Stylus, 2008).

of the Master Teacher and give us insights into how we can teach as he did. Coley states it this way:

> Long before modern teaching-learning theory, Jesus understood and demonstrated unique educational prowess, utilizing techniques that now fill academic textbooks. Millennia before the concepts of multiple intelligences and learning styles were formally conceptualized, Jesus mastered the ability to challenge people to embrace new thoughts, beliefs, understandings, convictions, attitudes, values, choices, behaviors, and lifestyles. The teaching-learning approach practiced by Jesus remains peerless.[6]

Here are just a few examples of Jesus engaging his disciples in the teaching-learning process:

- Jesus engaged their imagination: "Consider the birds of the sky: They don't sow or reap or gather into barns" (Matt 6:26).
- Jesus engaged them in discussion: "Who do people say that the Son of Man is?" (Matt 16:13).
- Jesus engaged them in problem-solving: "Why are you troubled? . . . Touch me and see . . ." (Luke 24:38–39).
- Jesus engaged them with tests: "Whoever does not bear his own cross and come after me . . ." (Luke 14:27).
- Jesus engaged them in active learning: "You give them something to eat" (Mark 6:37).

Echoing throughout contemporary MBE research is the need for engaging our learners. Well-known educator Robyn Jackson titled her book on effective teaching *Never Work Harder Than Your Students,* and in it she asks this penetrating question of herself: "Was it more important that my students be quiet and cooperative, or was it more important that they actively engage with the material and learn to be critical thinkers and effective communicators?"[7] In a different context, Gary Newton, Professor of Discipleship and author of *Heart-Deep Teaching: Engaging Students for Transformed Lives*, endorses this concept of engagement: "Learning happens most effectively

---

[6] Kenneth S. Coley, *Teaching for Change: Eight Keys for Transformational Bible Study with Teens* (Nashville: Randall House, 2017), 119.

[7] Robyn R. Jackson, *Never Work Harder Than Your Students and Other Principles of Great Teaching* (Alexandria, VA: ASCD, 2009), 93.

through active engagement of every aspect of the person. The more engaged and active a person is in the learning process, the greater potential for learning to take place."[8]

REFLECT: Consider your most recent opportunities to teach a group. Why do you teach the way that you do? Reflect on this while you continue working through this chapter, and we'll return to this question in a few pages.

Begin by Making Connections

Teachers who lead effective instructional episodes begin their planning and their presentation of new content with a simple question: *Where are the students going to put this?* Every learner brings prior learning and experiences to which new concepts can be connected. This mental framework is known as the learner's *schema*. Jesus modeled this for us in every interaction, whether the group was a massive crowd or a private one-on-one discussion. In a memorable discussion with Nicodemus, Jesus took a profound theological doctrine concerning salvation and put it in terms of an experience common to all humans: "You must be born again." In his conversation with the Samaritan woman, Jesus preceded a profound truth about himself being living water with a simple request, "May I have a drink?"

ENGAGE: Before using a search engine to look up the complete list, try jotting down as many of the "I am" sayings of Jesus presented in the Gospel of John as you can recall. (Hint: there are eight.) Most people can spontaneously recall 2–3 and many can even list 6–7. Why is this? Jesus packaged some of the most significant statements of theological truth about himself in everyday, concrete pictures that connect with our prior learning and experience. Make your list and then check your answers.

In *How Learning Works*, Ambrose and others support the significance of connecting new information to prior learning and experience:

> Students connect what they learn to what they already know, interpreting incoming information, and even sensory perception, through the lens of their existing knowledge, beliefs, and assumptions. In fact, there is widespread agreement among researchers that students must connect new knowledge to previous knowledge in order to learn. However, the extent to which students are

---

[8] Gary Newton, *Heart-Deep Teaching: Engaging Students for Transformed Lives* (Nashville: B&H, 2012), 107.

able to draw on prior knowledge depends on the nature of their prior knowledge, as well as the instructor's ability to harness it.[9]

Educator and author Eric Jensen expresses the value of connecting with a learner's schema as he describes the brain's four primary input pathways in his latest book, *Brain-Based Learning: Teaching the Way Students Really Learn.* The first pathway or input is what he terms *pre-existing input* or previously constructed learning. He summarizes this concept by stating, "Pre-existing input simply means you are using what you already know to generate insights, solutions, or action steps."[10] Felder and Brent assist teachers in understanding the brain wiring associated with this discussion. They explain:

> A schema is stored in clusters of neurons distributed through different regions of the brain. When it is initially stored, the connections between the neurons in each cluster and the linkages among the clusters are relatively weak, so the brain may have difficulty when it tries to retrieve the contents of clusters and reassemble them into the original schema. However, if the schema is reinforced through rehearsal . . . the connections within and among clusters are strengthened.[11]

These concepts of connections and rehearsal will be discussed in more detail later in this chapter. I have vivid recall of the Boy Scout Law committed to memory over a half century ago. The list of twelve characteristics of a Scout comes back at a moment's notice when he hears two or three of the standards mentioned. Perhaps you memorized lines from a favorite song or poem. Hearing some of the words or phrases, even in a different context, can take you back to cherished lines like, "It looked extremely rocky for the Mudville nine that day" from Ernest Thayer's *Casey at the Bat.*

[9] Susan A. Ambrose et al., *How Learning Works: 7 Research-Based Principles for Smart Teaching* (San Francisco: Jossey-Bass, 2010), 15.

[10] Eric Jensen and Liesl McConchie, *Brain-Based Learning: Teaching the Way Students Really Learn* (Thousand Oaks, CA: Corwin, 2020), 18.

[11] Richard M. Felder and Rebecca Brent, *Teaching & Learning STEM: A Practical Guide* (San Francisco: Jossey-Bass, 2016), 71.

Next, Make Comparisons

Closely related to the discussion on schema is the technique called *drawing an analogy*. A team of researchers/educators from Stanford University assembled a carefully vetted collection of MBE concepts and created "The ABCs of Learning," limiting their choices to just twenty-six. The first chapter is "A is for Analogy." Creating an analogy involves challenging learners to discover similarity between varied objects or concepts. Schwartz, Tsang, and Blair argue that "analogies can be a powerful way to learn new concepts and principles. Providing tasks where students find the analogy between two examples improves understanding of the underlying principle. It also increases the chances that students will spontaneously use that principle in a novel situation."[12]

If you have spent any time at all around veteran coaches, you can call to mind their efforts to teach new skills by comparing two seemingly unrelated things. When a basketball player's shot lacks proper trajectory, the coach may say, "Down the chimney." A young baseball player may swing with his back foot and heel flat on the ground and his coach will say, "Squish the bug." A soccer player may need to disguise the flight of the ball toward the goal and will slice across the ball and execute a "banana kick." But the researchers referenced above encourage teachers to challenge learners to find the analogous structure themselves. This leads to exploring the comparison and uncovering the deep structures.[13]

Think of the parables spoken by Jesus as presented in the Gospels. The word *parable* in Greek meant to place beside or toss alongside. Jesus would take an accepted truth and place it beside a profound theological truth and weave them together in a story with a familiar setting. One man built his house upon the sand; another built his house upon a rock (Matt 7:24–27). On other occasions Jesus challenged his listeners to an even higher order of thinking by placing two parables side by side: "No one tears a patch from a new garment and puts it on an old garment. . . . And no one puts new wine into old wineskins" (Luke 5:36–38). On one occasion recorded in Luke 15, Jesus wove three parables about lost items together—a lost sheep, a lost coin, and a lost son.

ENGAGE: Look up the three parables about lost items just referred to in Luke 15. Develop a visual representation of the similarities and differences in the three stories.

---

[12] Daniel L. Schwartz, Jessica M. Tsang, and Kristen P. Blair, *The ABCs of How We Learn: 26 Scientifically Proven Approaches, How They Work, and When to Use Them* (New York: W. W. Norton, 2016), 1–2.

[13] Schwartz, Tsang, and Blair, 6.

Create a Venn diagram by sketching three overlapping circles. Find at least one thing all three parables have in common.

As you design effective instruction for your class, do not limit the power of your instructional techniques to simply the content at hand. McTighe in *Teaching for Deeper Learning* presents the impact that this approach can have for your students. "When learners engage in purposeful comparison, they are constructing meaning and growing their understanding during the learning process. Comparing is a foundational thinking skill and a necessary underpinning to more complex processes such as argumentation, decision making, and problem solving."[14]

Explain How You Mastered These Concepts

Now that you have introduced your learners to new course content by connecting with their prior learning and experiences and challenged them to discover new meaning in an analogy, your next MBE instructional technique could be explaining to your class how you mastered the concepts in today's lesson. As a part of your lesson preparation, reflect on the mental processes that you engage when encountering new information. This is called *metacognition* or thinking about your thinking.

I have asked hundreds of audiences to pause and consider what they do when they need to remember a ten-digit phone number. In response I have dozens of examples of metacognition as adults share procedures like repeating the numbers over and over out loud, chunking the ten numbers into smaller units, creating a melody that contains the numbers, and typing the numbers on an imaginary touch screen on my leg. One response particularly stuck with me: I imagine the football team picture in the yearbook, and the numbers are on the jerseys of the players seated in the front row. My favorite, however, came from my wife, who is strong in geometry. She memorizes the angles on her touch screen as she visualizes each number and pretends to type in the numbers in order.

Wilson and Conyers describe it this way: "Thinking about one's thinking with the goal of enhancing learning. In its simplest terms, metacognition involves being mindful of one's thinking processes. . . . The goal of teaching students to be metacognitive

---

[14] Jay McTighe and Harvey F. Silver, *Teaching for Deeper Learning: Tools to Engage Students in Meaning Making* (Alexandria, VA: ASCD, 2020), 44.

is to guide them to consciously recognize when and how to employ the thinking and problem-solving strategies that work best for them."[15]

Here's another example of metacognition. What do you do when you discover you are "lost" while reading a chapter in a text, particularly containing material you find difficult and will be quizzed on the next day? The most popular response—I go back to a place in the text that was clear and reread from there. Some might say, "I start over from the beginning." Or perhaps, "I take a break and come back when I'm ready to focus." My son majored in philosophy and has an entirely different approach—he forges ahead until he has the scope of the entire argument and then returns to the place that gave him trouble.

Researchers advocate for teaching your learners to be conscious of their thinking and to take charge by applying cognitive strategies in new ways. Such steps include self-monitoring and self-teaching. Consider this research finding for your setting:

> A crucial finding in the research about metacognition and executive function is that skills and strategies that permit students to take charge of their learning can be taught. Through explicit instruction, modeling, and encouragement, students can learn to identify and overcome deficiencies in comprehension, reasoning, problem solving and communication.[16]

ENGAGE: You are preparing to teach a particular subject area or have been doing so for a while. Select a skill or concept that is rudimentary to that discipline and describe your thinking processes related to learning and performing that activity. For example, when I need to remember the location in the New Testament of Galatians, Ephesians, Philippians, and Colossians, I say to myself, "**G**eneral **E**lectric **P**ower **C**ompany." Or maybe you recall how you committed to memory your multiplication tables or the light cycle for photosynthesis. Recruit a partner and practice the articulation of your thinking with him/her.

Jesus teaches us in Luke 6:40 that when the disciple is fully trained, he will be like his teacher. Have you thought about coaching your students to become self-directed, independent learners? Ambrose and others break the process down: "To become self-directed learners, students must learn to assess the demands of the task, evaluate their

---

[15] Donna Wilson and Marcus Conyers, *Five Big Ideas for Effective Teaching: Connecting Mind, Brain, and Education Research to Classroom Practice* (New York: Teachers College, 2013), 110.

[16] Wilson and Conyers, 117.

own knowledge and skills, plan their approach, monitor their progress, and adjust their strategies as needed."[17]

Rollins outlines three strategies that help students monitor their own comprehension, summarize key ideas, and stay engaged in and focused on the content:

VIP (Very Important Point)—as your students work through a chapter of new material, they can use a highlighter to indicate a VIP phrase or sentence. After completing that section, they can go back and explain why the highlighted portions were selected.

Sticky Notes—as individuals study the chapter, they jot down reactions, questions, or summary statements on sticky notes. The limited space requires more effort to comprehend and articulate the ideas in just a few words.

Coding—this strategy works well when the selection has two or three main ideas for which a student can create his or her own code for repeating concepts.[18]

But don't stop with sharing your metacognitive stories and challenging your students to think about their own. Provide ample class time for students to voice their insights about their thinking processes. Research has found when this final step occurs, learning can become almost immeasurable.[19]

Neurologist and middle school teacher Judy Willis sums up the MBE research this way:

Metacognition—knowledge about one's own thoughts and the facts that influence one's thinking and learning—can optimize learning. Despite all the information neuroimaging and brain mapping have yielded about the acquisition of information, some of the best strategies are those that students recognize themselves. Research has demonstrated that optimal learners practice distinct behaviors. After a lesson when students are prompted to recognize a breakthrough success in the learning processing that they experienced that day, they should reflect on what they did right. . . . Students benefit from multiple opportunities to practice the metacognitive process of making the unconscious conscious.[20]

---

[17] Ambrose et al., *How Learning Works*, 191.

[18] Suzy Pepper Rollins, *Teaching in the Fast Lane: How to Create Active Learning Experiences* (Alexandria, VA: ASCD, 2014), 101–2.

[19] Wilson and Conyers, *Five Big Ideas for Effective Teaching*.

[20] Willis, *Research-Based Strategies to Ignite Student Learning*, 32–33.

Develop a Mindset of Individualization and Diverse Instructional Techniques

I have asked countless audiences this question: If you are a parent and have two or more children at home, do they learn the same way? The response is universally laughter. It is as if this is a silly question. "Of course not!" follows the chuckling. Let's look at this for a moment—children with the same hereditary background (unless they are adopted) and with the same family environment learn best in different ways. (My son loved reading and preparing for tests alone; my daughter craved social interaction and profited from group study sessions.) But what do we generally do? We herd children and teens of the same age together, line them up in a classroom, and expect them all to learn and grow uniformly.

Differentiation is the approach to teaching that acknowledges that "one size doesn't fit all."[21] Just as the root word in this term suggests, students come to our classrooms with varying levels of knowledge, readiness, and skills. Educator and author Carol Ann Tomlinson has spent decades unpacking the concepts related to differentiation. Tomlinson states that "differentiation stems from the research-based perspective that students will engage more fully with learning and learn more robustly when teachers proactively plan with their differences—as well as similarities—in mind."[22] She presents a five-part argument foundational to effective teaching:

1. The environment students are asked to learn in must invite learning, including being safe, challenging, and supportive.
2. A teacher must be able to identify what constitutes essential knowledge, understanding, and skills in a unit and the daily lessons. Where necessary, the teacher will create a scaffolding of knowledge and skills as needed.
3. Teachers must regularly assess student performance.
4. Teachers will use assessment data to adjust instruction so that students will continue to progress toward overall curriculum goals.
5. Teachers must guide students to understand and support a classroom that has the flexibility needed to address a range of student differences.[23]

---

[21] Gayle H. Gregory and Carolyn Chapman, *Differentiated Instructional Strategies: One Size Doesn't Fit All* (Thousand Oaks, CA: Corwin, 2013).

[22] David A. Sousa and Carol Ann Tomlinson, *Differentiation and the Brain: How Neuroscience Supports the Learner-Friendly Classroom* (Bloomington, IN: Solution Tree, 2018), 8.

[23] Sousa and Tomlinson, 9.

ENGAGE: Recall a question that was previously asked in this chapter—why do you teach the way that you do? Many teachers respond, "I teach the way that I do because that's how my favorite teacher taught me." Another favorite, "I teach the way that I do because that's how I learn best." And a different perspective, "I recall how many poor teachers presented to my class and decided to approach things very differently." But at this point in our discussion I want to pose a bold challenge for you to consider—**I teach the way that I do because that is what my students need in order to be at their best.**

Tomlinson recently stated, "Research psychology has long indicated that treating students of a given age as though they were essentially alike is likely to fail many, if not most students. In diverse classrooms, especially, we must individualize how we teach learners."[24] Given this principle, effective teachers know how to differentiate (1) the *content* (what students are expected to learn), (2) the *process* (the instructional activities in which they participate), (3) the *product* (what a student demonstrates or produces as a result of the learning experience), and (4) the *affect* and *learning environment*.[25]

Let's go back to scaffolding mentioned in a previous discussion. You are perhaps most familiar with this concept from watching a construction crew lay block or brick on the outside of a building. As the bricks are laid, the scaffolding is erected to assist the brick layers. Once the wall is complete, the scaffolding is dismantled. If you used training wheels to learn to ride a bike, a tee ball stand to learn to hit, or short skis before trying long ones, then you have experienced learning through scaffolding. "A common barrier to beginners is the sheer complexity of orchestrating multiple novel subskills simultaneously. Reducing the cognitive burden for one task can help."[26]

ENGAGE: Educator Suzy Pepper Rollins challenges teachers to assist students with their remedial deficits by scaffolding the steps to the target outcomes of your unit.[27] Accept her challenge and prepare a response to one target outcome in the discipline you are preparing to teach: Students can master the new standard if they just knew _____.

Think about an imaginary forest in which you travel a short distance to determine an ideal site to leave provisions that you will want to retrieve in the future. Each time

---

[24] Carol Ann Tomlinson and David A. Sousa, "The Sciences of Teaching," *Educational Leadership* 77, no. 8 (2020):18.

[25] Sousa and Tomlinson, *Differentiation and the Brain*, 13. Note: Special attention will be given to number 4 in a later chapter, titled "Social and Emotional Learning."

[26] Schwartz, Tsang, and Blair, *The ABCs of How We Learn*, 198.

[27] Rollins, *Teaching in the Fast Lane*, 14.

you venture back, the path becomes worn and develops into a trail. As you have occasion to return over and over, you begin to connect this storage area to other locations and need to return many times. Your trail develops to a well-traveled road and eventually a highway on which major ideas flow.

Quoting Willis once again, we have a succinct description of the storage and retrieval process created by learners when they have the opportunity to embrace new ideas through a diverse array of instructional techniques:

> Multiple stimulations mean better memory. The more regions of the brain that store data about a subject, the more interconnection there is. This redundancy means students will have more opportunities to pull up all those related bits of data from multiple storage areas in response to a single cue. This cross-referencing of data strengthens the data into something we've learned rather than just memorized.[28]

REFLECT: Gregory and Chapman discuss the mindset of teachers who are differentiating in their classrooms. Rate yourself on a scale of 1–5 with 5 being "strongly agree" and 1 being "strongly disagree" as you consider each statement:

- All students have special strengths.
- All students have areas that need to be strengthened.
- Each student's brain is as unique as a fingerprint.
- It is never too late to learn.
- When beginning a new topic, students bring prior knowledge to the learning.
- Emotions, feelings, and attitudes affect learning.
- Students learn in different ways at different times.[29]

Differentiation not only means adjustments for those students who lack prerequisite knowledge or skills and require scaffolding. It also means multifaceted instructional episodes where all learners engage with new concepts in multiple ways. "Cells that fire together, wire together"[30] is a well-known MBE phrase that describes durable learning. "When neurons fire in sync with one another, they are more likely to form new

---

[28] Willis, *Research-Based Strategies to Ignite Student Learning*, 4.
[29] Gregory and Chapman, *Differentiated Instructional Strategies*, 2–3.
[30] Willis, *Research-Based Strategies to Ignite Student Learning*, 7.

connections. As the connections grow stronger by repeated stimulation, a given neuron becomes more likely to trigger another connected neuron."[31] Here is a suggested list:

- *Thinking*: Ask your class to reflect on a recent situation or consider alternatives.
- *Reading*: Ask students to look for/listen for a particular concept or fact found in the verses as the passage is read (out loud or silently). Never ask students to read a passage without describing a specific idea for which they should look.
- *Writing*: Ask students to put ideas in their own words. Writing greatly increases engagement with the text and the likelihood of memory retention. The product need not be tightly organized or grammatically precise. Distribute note cards and consider collecting their responses.
- *Discussing: Think-pair-share* gives everyone the chance to talk without feeling intimidated by a teacher or a large group. First, challenge everyone to craft a response to a question or problem. Next, each student shares that idea with an elbow partner. Finally, the pairs get a chance to present their best idea to the full class.
- *Cooperative learning:* Design a task that is clear and doable in a brief time period. Assign participants to groups in which each person has an assigned task. The assigned task includes a work product and the group is held accountable for completing it.
- *Full group interaction and movement*
  Gallery walk: Groups present a final product that is hung like art in a gallery. A member of each group stays with the "artwork" and serves as a docent to explain the process and their group's thinking.
  Graffiti wall: Students write random responses on the board or easel paper. Just like the popular urban art form, the responses need not be in complete thoughts nor added in a linear or formal format.

ENGAGE: Review Deuteronomy 6:4–9 and identify the intersections between the preceding discussion on differentiation and the teaching strategies recommended by Moses to parents.

We want to conclude this discussion on differentiation by connecting Tomlinson's basic beliefs about leading a classroom with the preceding chapter on philosophy of Christian education.

---

[31] Willis, 7.

First, Tomlinson states, **"Every student is worthy of dignity and respect."**[32] We celebrate each learner that crosses the threshold of our classroom as God's workmanship. Ephesians 2:10 uses an interesting Greek word, *poiema*, that can be translated masterpiece or craftsmanship. Our English word *poetry* has its etymology in this word. The verse tells teachers that God has special plans for each person. It is our calling to direct each learner to Christ so each one can begin the transformation process to be like him and walk in the plans he has for us.

Second, Tomlinson states, **"Diversity is both inevitable and positive."**[33] Both in Ephesians and 1 Corinthians, Paul exhorts believers to identify and rejoice for our differences. In our classrooms we encounter a variety of developmental differences as well as diversity in gifting. How can you make the most of each student's strengths as you plan instructional episodes?

Third, Tomlinson challenges teachers, **"The classroom should mirror the kind of society in which we want our students to live and lead."**[34] As we embrace this mindset, how much more should we be committed to modeling the body of Christ? Paul challenges us in 1 Cor 12:12, "For just as the body is one and has many parts, and all the parts of that body though many, are one body—so also is Christ."

Fourth, Tomlinson concludes, **"Most students can learn most things that are essential to a given area of study."**[35] God has called us to inspire students to persevere and develop a growth mindset.[36] Angela Duckworth presents in *Grit* that the most important characteristic a learner can develop is passionate persistence.[37] Scaffold the most important knowledge and skill, and teach to the strengths of your students.

Have Them Put It in Their Own Words

As learners encounter new information, they should do more than copy notes on an outline. Much more. When the learner is challenged to put the new concepts in his or

---

[32] Carol Ann Tomlinson, *Leading and Managing a Differentiated Classroom* (Alexandria, VA: ASCD, 2010), 27.

[33] Tomlinson, 28.

[34] Tomlinson, 29.

[35] Tomlinson, 31.

[36] Carol Dweck, *Mindset: The New Psychology of Success: How We Can Learn to Fulfill Our Potential* (New York: Ballantine Books, 2006).

[37] Sarah McKibben, "Grit and the Greater Good: A Conversation with Angela Duckworth," *Educational Leadership* 76, no. 2 (October 2018): 6.

her own words and connect it to prior knowledge, it is called elaboration.[38] Research states that when a student is able to repeat new information in his or her own words, then greater learning and memory retention take place. "Elaboration is the process of giving new material meaning by expressing it in your own words and connecting it with what you already know. If you practice elaboration, there's no known limit to what you can learn."[39]

A related skill is summarizing, "the process of distilling information down to its most salient points to aid in understanding, memorizing, and learning the relevant material."[40] Comprehension of the new concepts is a must, but then higher order thinking is required to sort, organize, prioritize, and express in wording that is personally meaningful. If your students need assistance with summarizing, here is a list of steps:

1. Take out material that is not important to understanding.
2. Take out words that repeat information.
3. Replace a list of things with one word that describes them (example: "Peter, James, and John" with "disciples").
4. Find a topic sentence or create one if it is missing.[41]

Wormeli and Stafford present an approach that encourages summarization throughout a 45-minute or 90-minute class. Students can be asked to summarize their prior knowledge on the new topic for the class, which may influence your starting point or the pace of your lesson (see chapter 7 on formative assessment). Inserting the opportunity for summarization in the midpoint in the lesson gives students a chance to monitor their own progress. Practicing summarization at the close of the lesson allows students a final opportunity to articulate new information in their own words and in so doing move it into long-term memory.[42] He also emphasizes the value of chunking lectures in 15–20 minutes, followed by a brief period during which students summarize their notes before the teacher moves on to the next section.[43]

---

[38] Schwartz, Tsang, and Blair, *The ABCs of How We Learn*, 52.

[39] Peter C. Brown, Henry L. Roediger, and Mark A. McDaniel, *Make It Stick: The Science of Successful Learning* (Cambridge: Belknap Press, 2014), 5.

[40] Ceri B. Dean et al., *Classroom Instruction That Works: Research-Based Strategies for Increasing Student Achievement* (Alexandria, VA: ASCD, 2012), 78.

[41] Dean et al., 80.

[42] Rick Wormeli and Dedra Stafford, *Summarization in Any Subject: 60 Innovative, Tech-Infused Strategies for Deeper Student Learning* (Alexandria, VA: ASCD, 2019), 5.

[43] Wormeli and Stafford, 5.

Dean, Hubbell, Pitler, and Stone present the process for executing *reciprocal teaching*, an instructional activity that includes summarizing. After experiencing new material (read, heard, or seen), student one summarizes the main idea(s). Others may participate. Student two, the questioner, poses questions that push the group to deeper levels of thinking. Student three, the clarifier, points out vocabulary or key ideas that may be confusing. Student four, the predictor, leads a brief discussion on the participants' predictions of what comes next.[44]

Lang describes an interrelated skill called *self-explaining*, in which "learners benefit from explaining out loud (to themselves or others) what they are doing during the completion of a learning task."[45] As learners talk through the steps of learning new procedures, processes, or skills, they put the discrete stages in their own words and can even fill in gaps that were omitted in the instructor's instructions.

Divide New Material into Smaller Pieces

Do you recall trying to take notes in a class and working feverishly to keep up while the instructor avalanched the group with massive amounts of new information? Of course, we've all been there. Molecular biologist John Medina points out that most adults lose focus and stop listening after ten minutes.[46] Felder and Brent argue that teachers need to break up large quantities of material into digestible pieces so that students can absorb unfamiliar concepts. In addition, learners need opportunities to retrieve and reflect and practice applying.[47] More on practice in the next section. "When people's cognitive load at a given time exceeds the processing capacity of their working memory, their brain is in a state of *cognitive overload*, and they will be unable to process new incoming information without losing information already present in working memory."[48] This instructional technique is known as *chunking* or dividing the material into units that the brain can retain. The practice established by Moses in

---

[44] Dean et al., 89.

[45] James M. Lang, *Small Teaching: Everyday Lessons from the Science of Learning* (San Francisco: Jossey-Bass, 2016), 138.

[46] Carmine Gallo, "Your Audience Tunes Out after 10 Minutes: Here's How to Keep Their Attention," *Forbes*, February 28, 2019, https://www.forbes.com/sites/carmine gallo/2019/02/28/your-audience-tunes-out-after-10-minutes-heres-how-to-keep-their -attention/?sh=3745f3f47364.

[47] Felder and Brent, *Teaching & Learning STEM*, 72.

[48] Felder and Brent, 92. See also Jensen and McConchie, *Brain-Based Learning*, 171.

Deuteronomy 6 of storing bits of the Torah in phylacteries beautifully illustrates this educational concept.

Barkley presents another related insight to research on working memory—the average adult can handle five to nine items of information at once. For example, consider how numbers for a credit card, Social Security, or cell phone are chunked in groups of four. He suggests that teachers limit topics or items to seven, chunk smaller and similar components together, and break up lectures into sections with engagements intermingled.[49]

Wormeli and Stafford provide a strong summary for the technique of chunking:

> Long text passages can be daunting to someone learning to summarize. The brain will more effectively process information that is "chunked" into shorter segments for a summary in route to understanding the full passage. Breaking text into segments does not dilute its message; rather, it presents the message in a way that enhances student learning. When students encounter information in these smaller segments, more of it goes into their long-term memories.[50]

ENGAGE: Based on my years of experience of presenting to hundreds of groups and classes, I imagine that many of the terms and concepts in this chapter are new to most readers. Therefore, I purposely created divisions in this new material and interspersed activities. Skim back through this chapter and identify how the material has been carved into chunks.

Include Time for Practice

Two of my favorite book titles are *"Sit and Get" Won't Grow Dendrites* (2012) and *Worksheets Don't Grow Dendrites* (2015) both by Marcia Tate. For students to experience the chemical reactions in the brain that result in the growth and connection of dendrites to existing networks, the learner must be engaged and needs to have active participation in practicing the new concepts. Such approaches lead to durable learning. But how can you assist your learners in moving their recall of new facts in their working memory to long-term retention?

---

[49] Elizabeth F. Barkley, *Student Engagement Techniques: A Handbook for College Faculty* (San Francisco: Jossey-Bass, 2010), 102.

[50] Wormeli and Stafford, *Summarization in Any Subject*, 25.

Authors Brown, Roediger, and McDaniel discuss three types of practice that result in durable learning in their book, *Make It Stick*. Before we break it down, here is their conclusion: "Practice that's spaced out, interleaved with other learning, and varied produces better mastery, longer retention, and more versatility. But these benefits come at a price . . . it requires more effort."[51]

First, they argue that the rehearsal must be *spaced* out, as opposed to being packed together in massed practice. Most of us recall using note cards to review information over and over. Memorizing names with dates; trying to remember vocabulary words by repetition. That's massed practice. But spreading out the practice sessions over several days allows for some forgetting—then we must work harder to find and retrieve that new information. When discussing spaced learning, Carey wrote in *How We Learn* that "nothing in learning science comes close in terms of immediate, significant, and reliable improvements to learning."[52]

Next, practice should not only be spaced, it ought to have other learning activities mixed in or *interleaved*. Lang illustrates *interleaving* an instructional unit with four major concepts. He recommends teaching one concept and moving on to the second concept before having mastered the first. After introducing the second, go back to the first before moving on to the third—and so on. The goal is to have them master the four ideas by the end of the semester by spacing out the instructional episodes over time and mixing up the specific skills the learners are focusing on.[53]

Third, practice should be varied. The coaching here is, don't approach your practice in the same way each time you do it. Don't shoot your jump shot from the same spot each time. Sometimes off the dribble; sometimes catch and shoot; sometimes after a head fake.

> The evidence favoring variable training has been supported by recent neuro-imaging studies that suggest that different kinds of practice engage different parts of the brain. The learning of motor skills from varied practice, which is more cognitively challenging than massed practice, appears to be consolidated in an area of the brain associated with the more difficult process of learning higher-order motor skills.[54]

---

[51] Brown, Roediger, and McDaniel, *Make It Stick*, 47.

[52] Benedict Carey, *How We Learn: The Surprising Truth about When, Where, and Why It Happens* (New York: Random House, 215), 76.

[53] Lang, *Small Teaching*, 68.

[54] Brown, Roediger, and McDaniel, *Make It Stick*, 51.

Agarwal discusses a fourth type—*retrieval practice* is the intuitive idea of encouraging students to "pull out" information they have learned from memory.[55] Much like the discussion related to spaced practice, the brain activity related to retrieval produces a strengthening of memory. For example, an instructor who includes references from a previous unit of study in a discussion or includes questions on an exam that are cumulative. The authors of *Make It Stick* define it as "self-quizzing."[56] They argue that asking yourself questions as you study should become your main study technique as opposed to rereading printed material. While students may find this more tedious and even frustrating at times, the struggle strengthens the mental pathways and makes future recall durable.

A fifth approach to practice is *predicting*. When learners have the opportunity to predict meaning or outcomes, their minds are challenged to look for connections that will assist them to make an accurate prediction.[57] Carey describes the power of predicting this way:

> Predictive activities reshape our mental networks by embedding unfamiliar concepts into questions we at least partly comprehend. . . . Even if the question is not entirely clear and its solution unknown, a guess will in itself begin to link the questions to possible answers. And those networks light up like Christmas lights when we hear the concepts again.[58]

Asking students to predict gives them a clear target for where the instructional episode is going, and the learners are focused on what the teacher thinks is important. In addition, predicting introduces us to things we don't know and may struggle to connect to prior learning and the lesson at hand.[59] And we can celebrate even those predictions that are incorrect. "Unsuccessful attempts to solve a problem encourage deep processing of the answer when it is later supplied, creating fertile ground for its encoding, in a way that simply reading the answer cannot."[60]

---

[55] Pooja K. Agarwal, "Retrieval Practice: A Power Tool for Lasting Learning," *Educational Leadership* 77, no. 8 (2020): 76.

[56] Brown, Roediger, and McDaniel, *Make It Stick*, 201.

[57] Lang, *Small Teaching*, 49.

[58] Benedict Carey, "Why Flunking Exams Is Actually a Good Thing," *New York Times*, September 7, 2014, https://www.nytimes.com/2014/09/07/magazine/why-flunking-exams-is -actually-a-good-thing.html.

[59] Lang, *Small Teaching*, 50–51.

[60] Brown, Roediger, and McDaniel, *Make It Stick*, 88.

ENGAGE: Do you recall early on in this chapter that you were asked to rate your level of understanding of nine terms related to this chapter on a scale of 1–3? Following this activity, you were asked to predict the definition of any term that you rated 2 or 3. Go back to your notes and evaluate the accuracy of your predictions. Do the claims in the preceding paragraph appear to be valid?

We close this discussion on the value of making predictions with a powerful quote from neuroscientist Judy Willis:

> Through observations, experiences, and feedback, the brain increasingly learns about the world and can make progressively more accurate predictions about what will come next and how to respond to new information, problems, or choices. This ability for prediction, guided by pattern recognition, is a foundation for successful literacy, numeracy, test taking, appropriate social-emotional behavior, and understanding.
>
> Successful prediction is one of the brain's best problem-solving strategies.[61]

Provide Time for Collaboration

What was your reaction when you read the subheading to this section? Would you agree that your prior experience with classmates in various settings strongly influences your response? Often the ambivalence toward group work focuses on the assignment being too vague, undoable in a reasonable timeframe, or too easy or too difficult for the skills and knowledge of the group. Sometimes disapproval revolves around the group process; some students watch while those considered stronger performers do all the tasks. Or maybe the knot in your stomach is a result of the product that the group produced was not accurately connected to the focus of the assignment, or worst of all, the teacher never asked to see your work product. From a teacher's perspective, the concerns include wasting of valuable class time and the class/groups becoming chaotic.[62]

But the overwhelming weight of MBE research supports the extraordinary benefits that can result from cooperative learning done well. For example, when stress levels created by individual competition are lowered, the release of stress hormones that inhibit learning is reduced. The basic components that lead to productive learning

---

[61] Jay McTighe and Judy Willis, *Upgrade Your Teaching: Understanding by Design Meets Neuroscience* (Alexandria, VA: ASCD, 2019), 9.

[62] David Francis, Ken Braddy, and Ken Coley, *Shepherd: Creating Caring Community* (Nashville: LifeWay, 2017), 48.

experiences (both personal knowledge and group/teamwork skills) were first articulated by David Johnson and Roger Johnson (1975), and their five elements are included in italics below. Others have embraced these initial characteristics of effective cooperative learning and added their own descriptions.[63] A sixth element is included here.

1. *Positive interdependence*: The group's success depends on everyone's cooperation. Each participant is assigned a role.

2. *Individual accountability*: All students in a team are held accountable for contributing to the work and for mastering the material covered in the assignments. (Some instructors include a peer evaluation of each team member.)

3. *Face-to-face promotive interaction*: Although some of the assigned work may be parceled out and done individually, some is done interactively. In the interactions, team members provide one another with feedback, debate solution strategies and conclusions, and most importantly, teach and encourage one another.

4. *Interpersonal and small group skills*: The students are helped to develop the skills required for high-performance teamwork, such as communication, leadership, decision-making, time management, and conflict resolution.

5. *Regular self-assessment of team functioning*: The students set team goals, periodically assess their progress toward meeting the goals, identify what they are doing well and where they may be falling short, and decide on changes they will make to function more effectively in the future.

6. *Provide a meaningful task*: The goal or work product needs to connect with the learners, so they view their efforts to be relevant and the work product authentic.[64]

As teachers embrace the concepts listed above, they need to reflect on the readiness of their class, collectively and individually. Many students will need coaching and practice, particularly if the overall school environment is one that is competitive and individual achievement is celebrated. It would be overly ambitious for most classes to begin with a lengthy project that requires several hours of work and has a significant grade attached to it. Teachers are encouraged to scaffold the necessary teamwork skills by using a variety of active learning techniques.

---

[63] See Nancy Frey, Douglas Fisher, and Sandi Everlove, *Productive Group Work: How to Engage Students, Build Teamwork, and Promote Understanding* (Alexandria, VA: ASCD, 2009), 15–20; Felder and Brent, *Teaching & Learning STEM*, 247; and David A. Sousa, *How the Brain Learns* (Thousand Oaks, CA: Sage, 2017), 315.

[64] This element was added by Frey, Fisher, and Everlove, *Productive Group Work*.

- Begin by using *Think-Pair-Share*: each student *thinks* about a problem or question and formulates a response. Then each one *pairs* with a nearby partner and expresses that idea. This involves articulating your thoughts and listening to the idea of another classmate. The pair then formulates a response to *share* with the entire group.

- A more challenging Active Learning Technique (ALT) with a larger group is called *Think-Pair-Square-Share*. This ALT begins the same as the previous approach but adds a step—two pairs unite and the square exchanges ideas before sharing with the full class. Students who are ordinarily reluctant to address the entire class can develop confidence as they speak to a group of three others. Also, students who tend to dominate can learn to listen and incorporate the ideas of others.

- A third step could be a "jigsaw assignment" with a defined work product required at the conclusion of a tight timeframe. Each group of 3–4 students is responsible for producing a piece of information that is important to the whole of that day's lesson. These pieces are generally isolated and unique—investigating that chunk does not require "seeing the whole picture."

REFLECT: Reread a familiar Gospel story found in Matt 14:13. The disciples approached Jesus and asked him to dismiss the crowd for dinner at the end of a long day. He said, "You give them something to eat." How does this learning experience compare the previous discussions on cooperative learning?

Conclusion

While we are learning much from brain research, the field itself is relatively new and there is much more to learn. It is suggested that teachers who are involved in professional development stay abreast of new research in this area and use what seems to fit with their developing philosophy of education. This indeed will make us better teachers. Remember, the God who created us to learn created the brain and gave humans the capacity to invent new extended senses, such as MRIs, to use for his glory in medical advances and in situations such as teaching his creatures.

Effective Instructional Design Based on the Foundations of Teaching and Learning

CHAPTER 5

Developing a Model for Teaching Based on Cognitive Interactive Learning

Debbie MacCullough

What Is a Model?

When you think of the word *model*, what comes to your mind? For some, it might be a model airplane that was put together and displayed as a child; for others it might be a man or a woman posing in a clothing fashion magazine, on TV, or on the internet, displaying a product. An architect's plan is used to create a model for one wanting to build a house or develop land. Sometimes we refer to teachers as role models. Whatever the case, a model is a replica or picture of what is the ideal or the real thing. In this chapter an overall *model* for teaching that flows out of cognitive interactive learning theory is developed. The model is what we think is the "ideal" plan or approach to teaching based on how humans learn.

A model or theory for learning, such as was described in chapter 3, logically leads to a model for teaching that is used to develop unit and lesson plans. When a teacher believes a child learns in a particular way, then the lesson should be designed to maximize the learning. Lesson plans were promoted using the work of German educator Johann Herbart.[1] Since that time, teachers have been encouraged to use lesson plans.

There are various elements for lesson delivery that are logically inferred by examining different theories. Some of these elements are (1) **engagement**, motivation, or activation of the students' minds; (2) providing new **information** for the students to learn; (3) **student activities** to aid in learning; and (4) **assessment** or evaluation of learning. In addition, objectives, standards, materials needed, and a variety of other elements comprise planning.

ENGAGE: Think about the delivery of a lesson using the four elements listed above. Your task is to determine which of the elements in the chart below would be included in a lesson plan prepared by an advocate of one of the three theories summarized in chapter 3. These theories (listed across the top of the chart) are related to the actional nature of the human and learning. Adherents hold one of three views about the human and learning: the student is psychologically *passive*, autonomously *active*, or cognitively *interactive*. We have labeled these theories as Behavioristic (passive), Humanistic (active), and Cognitive Interactive.

Circle the elements in the chart below that would be in a lesson plan for each theory.

Elements of a typical lesson plan:

Behavioristic *Passive*	Humanistic *Active*	Cognitive *Interactive*
Motivation Engage the mind	Motivation Engage the mind	Motivation Engage the mind
Information provided	Information provided	Information provided
Student Processing Activity	Student Processing Activity	Student Processing Activity
Assessment	Assessment	Assessment

Behavioristic theories would definitely include "information provided" and "assessment"; these should be circled. Since behaviorists such as B. F. Skinner do not believe humans act on purpose, the concept of motivation or engagement at the start of a lesson is not necessary; however, they do provide reinforcement after the assessment.

---

[1] Johann Friedrich Herbart, *The Science of Education: Its General Principles Deduced from Its Aim; And, The Aesthetic Revelation of the World* (UK: S. Sonnenschein, 1892).

Humanistic: minimally, "student processing activities" should be circled. The student is already actively motivated by nature unless restrained by the teacher or circumstances. Motivation comes from inside alone; however, the materials and the activity may arouse motivation. Assessment is individual and not a part of the delivery plan other than perhaps self-assessment (such as: "Write in your journal how you felt about today's lesson"). While there is information, it is usually what the students bring up in class and want to pursue.

Cognitive interactive: all four elements should be circled. This activity may help you understand a model that is derived from cognitive interactive theory that holds that something inside the learner and something outside work together as a unit in learning. More on these elements as we develop the model for teaching later. But first let us address the term "interactive," as it applies to a model of teaching derived from a theory or model of learning.

ENGAGE: What comes to your mind when you think of the term "interactive learning" in relation to practice in a classroom setting? Which of the statements below seem to imply interactive learning as you view it? (Yes will mean "yes, I believe this is interactive learning"; no will mean "it is not interactive learning.")

1. The students are frequently in cooperative learning groups using project and discussion methods.
2. There is a class discussion where all are involved together.
3. At least some time for questions is planned into the lesson (at the beginning or at the end).
4. The teacher plans creative activities for the curriculum.
5. Technology in the classroom
6. A lecture to 300 in a huge lecture hall at a university or a webinar to hundreds

All the above statements except for #6 represent methods of instruction that include *human social interaction*. However, when thinking about human learning as an interactive process, #6 may also qualify. Why? Because interactive learning refers to what the mind is doing with outside information. If we confuse models and methods, we will miss the key factor in today's most prominent theory of human learning, and we might think incorrectly like this:

"Well, sometimes students are passive when I am talking, and at times they are active when they are doing something or talking. Don't you think they can be both passive and active? And isn't that what interactive means?"

The answer to that question is no. The opposite of passive is not interactive! The opposite of passive is autonomously active. Interactive learning involves observing and listening to the teacher as well as writing and speaking and more. Many articles that address interactive learning focus primarily on *methods* of social interaction rather than on an overall approach that views inner and outer factors as a unit in learning. For an example, one author states: "While in school, the teacher may use interactive learning instead of traditional methods, such as lecturing, to engage and involve the students in the educational process. Interactive learning involves group projects, small group settings and the use of manipulatives and technology in the learning process."[2]

Notice that the author, while trying to help fellow teachers, has confused models of learning based upon the passive, active, or interactive "actional" nature, with methods for teaching such as group projects, small groups, and manipulatives, all of which are appropriate for interactive learning but do not define it. They are methods to work out the plan. An architect draws the model or plan to build a deck and lists tools and materials that are needed to carry out the plan. Teaching methods are the teacher's tools and strategies to work out the model or plan for learning. The model is the plan or approach outlined and the methods are the tools to deliver the plan.

Broad categories of methods include:

Impressive and Expressive Methods

Impressive	Expressive
Listening	Speaking
Reading	Writing
Viewing	Doing

Those who believe that the human is psychologically **passive** in learning use impressive methods for the most part, while expressive methods are used almost exclusively by those who hold to human nature being autonomously **active** in the learning event. On the other hand, the **cognitive interactive** view uses all of the *language arts* in almost every lesson. Humans are communicators by nature, and language and learning are interrelated.

---

[2] See "Classroom, Definition of Interactive Learning," eHow, accessed June 2017, http://www.ehow.com/about_6703584_information-interactive-learning.html.

ENGAGE: See if you can identify which of the following sets of methods and concepts might be used by teachers who hold to either the passive or the interactive view of human nature and learning and label the set as Passive or Interactive. Then try to determine the similarities between the two sets, if any.

Set One: Label _____

Impressive methods only

Notes taken in exact form; answers required exactly as in the notes of the teacher

Focus on grades

Content very important

Memory is vital

Set Two: Label _____

Impressive and expressive methods

Notes and answers worded in the words of the learner

Focus on understanding, retrieval, and use

Content very important

Memory is vital

Set One represents a **passive view** of the human and learning. Set Two represents an **interactive view** of the human and learning. The autonomously active view is not represented above. While there are significant differences in the two sets, notice the similarities found at the bottom of the lists above: *Content and memory are very important.* Keep this in mind.

Set Three, below, represents the **autonomously active view** of the human and learning. Read the focus and methods typically used by those who hold this view and determine the major difference between this view and the other two.

Set Three: (Autonomously active)

Expressive methods only

Focus on feelings about learning

Journal how one feels and what one is passionate about

Focus is on enjoyment in the learning environment

Content is unimportant

Memory is not an issue

In the set above, the major difference between this view and the other views is the fact that content and memory are unimportant or not a major issue. One holding to the cognitive interactive view might agree with all the other items listed—expressive methods, concern for feelings about learning, journaling those feelings and responses, and enjoyment in learning. In fact, the cognitive interactive theory of learning leads to the most versatility in methods and to the most comprehensive view of the student while also considering content and skills as vital to learning. Learning has not occurred unless one remembers; therefore, memory is also important.

Developing a Model of *Teaching* by the Model of *Learning*

In developing lesson plans we use our understanding of human learning theory (cognitive interactive learning model) to develop a teaching model. The teaching model then leads to how we develop both unit and lesson plans. Let us consider how the three views of the actional nature (passive, autonomously active, and interactive) lead to different models for learning and teaching. Consider behaviorism (a passive view of the nature of the student and learning) as an example. When interviewed by Daniel Goleman for the *New York Times* in 1987, B. F. Skinner's response to an inquiry related to cognitive interactive and information processing theories was to declare: "The cognitive revolution is a search inside the mind for something that is not there. You can't see yourself process information. Information processing is an inference from behavior and a bad one at that."[3] So, his view was that only outside factors are important in learning and, therefore, this was true in teaching as well. Books and media and most importantly, the teacher, are central in the behavioristic classroom. The teacher is the professional reinforcer that affects learning. The teaching model is: Tell and Test (and reinforce):

- Teacher tells.
- Teacher expects students to take notes exactly as given.
- Teacher tests, expecting exact answers as given in the notes.
- Teacher reinforces (after the lesson); motivation, if any, is after the lesson in the form of reinforcements (stickers, grades, cheers, etc.).

No wonder this view is called Teacher or Content-Centered.

On the other hand, German philosopher Friedrich Froebel (Father of the Kindergarten) held that all the child is ever to be and become lies in the child and is attained through the process of unfoldment of what is there at birth—"preformation."

---

[3] Daniel Goleman, "Embattled Giant of Psychology Speaks His Mind," *New York Times*, August 25, 1987.

Development is from within, outward. He believed, "The purpose of teaching and instruction is to bring ever more out of man rather than to put more and more into man."[4] He also compared human development to flowers that unfold over time from processes within.[5]

Thus, a teaching approach for Unfoldment (autonomously active) Theory might look like this:

- <u>Student</u> interests and needs guide activities as the child unfolds.
- <u>Students</u> learn through their own prompting and need little prompting from outside.
- <u>Student</u> activities involve students in their own learning and development.
- <u>Student</u> enjoyment and fun are the focus! Feelings and emotions are central.
- <u>Students</u> are naturally motivated. There is no need to motivate.
- Classroom environment is simply a location for <u>student</u> activity.

No wonder this approach is called Child or Student-Centered.

Neither of these two views clearly accounts for learning as a process that involves both inside and outside factors.

Deciding Which Model Is Best

Assuming that an educator is interested in examining various views before committing to a teaching approach, *how does one decide?*

How might one determine which of the three views of human nature, for example, fits best with the view of humans espoused by the educator? Does the teacher believe that the human is simply a set of matter/material highly organized and determined by cause and effect in the environment that provides and uses a stimulus (response and reinforcement event)? Or does the teacher hold that the human is an autonomous chooser who makes or creates his own world, knowledge, and reality? These are two very common answers to the worldview questions, "What is a human being?" and "How do we learn?"

After reading the first four chapters of this book, the reader should be aware there is a third view. This view is held by many current-day researchers who bring their own

---

[4] Friedrich Froebel, *The Education of Man*, trans. W. N. Hailmann (New York: D. Appleton, 1887), 311.

[5] Froebel, 152.

worldview to their research and conclusions that may not reflect a biblical worldview. This third view may fit best with a biblical worldview and understanding of human nature and learning. This third view is the cognitive interactive theory of learning described in chapter 3. Here are some of the categories of educational issues that must be addressed consistently with one's selected theory.

1. **Teaching Model** (overall approach to teaching plan)
2. **Teaching Methods** (what kind and why?)
3. **Motivation** (engagement toward learning, or no need to engage; or reinforce at the end)
4. **Focus of the Curriculum** (content, or process only, or content processed and understood)
5. **Objectives** (behaviorally stated, affective only, or big idea stated in observable format)
6. **Discipline** (outside factors/behavior change only, inside factors/feelings or motivational change only, or inside change that affects outside behavior—a right behavior for a right reason)
7. **Worldview Integration** (a telling view, a view that each one decides, or a view that there is an outside standard—the biblical information—to be internalized and lived by each student)

A learning model based upon the interactive nature of the human is not just passive telling and testing—nor is it unguided activity, simply drawing out. Rather it is an orchestration of four basic elements (not just ordered steps). You will see in the lesson later on constellations that student processing activities can be included in the engagement part of the lesson, during the input of new information or skill development, or in the assessment. This is why these elements are not called steps. Early cognitivists often developed lesson plans that were organized into steps. This is a rather sterile approach to a teaching/learning model. In our suggested model, we encourage the view that these are elements that can be navigated throughout the lesson and may sometimes be in the order as above but not always.

Cognitive Interactive Teaching Model

1. Engaging the mind (inside factor) of the student using an activity planned by the teacher (outside factor).

2. Providing new information by *giving it* (outside the student) or creating a student activity that requires the *student to get* the new information from some outside source. For example, a read to find out activity.

3. Creating student processing activities to help the student make sense out of new material or a new skill, to form closure (fit it in), make connections, generalize, draw conclusions, or practice and use a skill.

4. Assessing learning by using student expressions of inside-constructed understandings in their own words as feedback to see if students are getting it. The model includes formative assessment for each lesson as well as summative assessments for units and lessons.

Notice that with these elements, the focus is not solely on the teacher, nor is it solely on the student, rather the focus is on *learning* and requires both the teacher and the student to be actively involved as participants in the learning event. To better understand how this model (and its elements) flow within a lesson plan, we will examine a sample lesson on constellations later in this chapter.

A teaching model will convert into a unit and a lesson template, making sure that all the elements of the model are included. Here is the suggested template:

- Motivation (engage or activate the mind toward the lesson at hand)
- Information or skill development
- Student processing activities to help students fit into schema or categories of the mind and make sense of new information
- Assessment

For each element, the teacher plans the methods to carry out the model. Let's look at each element.

First, to begin a lesson or to reintroduce a lesson suspended from the day before, an engagement activity should be planned.

ENGAGE: Why do we begin a cognitive interactive lesson with an **engagement** activity to get the **mind activated** toward the lesson of the day and the student **motivated** to want to learn? Formulating your answer to the "why" engagement of each student's mind is important.

Read the story below and answer the question, Who or what is Rocky? Write your answer.

Rocky got up slowly from the mat, planning his escape. He hesitated a moment and thought. Things were not going well. What bothered him most was being held, especially since the charge against him had been weak. He considered his present situation. The lock that held him was strong, but he thought he could break it. He knew, however, that his timing would have to be perfect. Rocky was aware that it was because of his early roughness that he had been penalized so severely—much too severely from his point of view. The situation was becoming frustrating; the pressure had been grinding on him for too long. He was being ridden unmercifully. Rocky was getting angry now. He felt he was ready to make his move. He knew that his success or failure would depend on what he did in the next few seconds.[6]

How did you answer the question above? Write it down so that you commit to the answer.

This story was used in research at the University of Illinois in 1976 to find out whether the reader's background might lead to a different understanding of Rocky's identity. Thirty female music students and thirty weight-training male students were given the story and asked the same question. There was a statistically significant difference in the overall understanding of Rocky's identity. Most of the female music students claimed he was a prisoner; most of the male athletes claimed Rocky was a wrestler. The researchers concluded that schemata are needed to begin to make sense out of (perceive) material read or heard.[7]

To show you how this works, this story has been used in professional development workshops around the world. Near Lexington, Kentucky, the number one answer to Rocky's identity was a horse. Can you guess why? In Philadelphia, the most often cited answer was a boxer. Can you guess why? Kentucky is known for its horses and horse racing. A very popular film made in Philadelphia was about a boxer named Rocky. However, Rocky in the story above is a wrestler; but if you know little or nothing about wrestling, you try to fit the elements of the story to your prior knowledge or experience and try to make sense of it.

---

[6] Richard C. Anderson et al., "Frameworks for Comprehending Discourse," *American Educational Research Journal* 14, no. 4 (1977): 367–82.

[7] Richard C. Anderson et al., *Frameworks for Comprehending Discourse* (Urbana, IL: University of Illinois, 1976), 10.

Many teachers who lecture as their primary or exclusive method begin their lecture assuming that all students will be mentally aware of the main point of the material being dispensed as they proceed through their notes. Some students may not understand because they were thinking that the lecture was about a prisoner or about a horse or a boxer and the teacher was talking about a wrestler. This is frustrating and simply discourages students.

With the above research in mind, we can answer the question about the need for an activity to begin a lesson that engages the mind toward the lesson at hand. Sometimes it is called a motivation activity because motivation relates to what is going on inside the student's mind; sometimes it is called engagement as we have used the term in this book; and sometimes it is called activation with the goals of activating prior knowledge and schema that will enhance the learning of new material.

A Science Lesson on Constellations Using Interactive Learning

Let's look at an example of a lesson based on cognitive interactive learning that includes these elements in an effective lesson.

Element 1: Activation, Motivation, Engaging the Mind toward the Lesson at Hand

ENGAGE: Which of the two approaches fits best with human learning and why?

Teacher One shows the pictures below and says, "We call these constellations and will be studying constellations this week. Open your science books to page 85 and copy the definition of constellation."

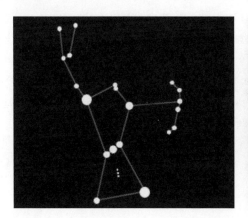 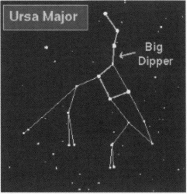

Teacher Two uses another way to start this lesson—this connect-the-dots activity.

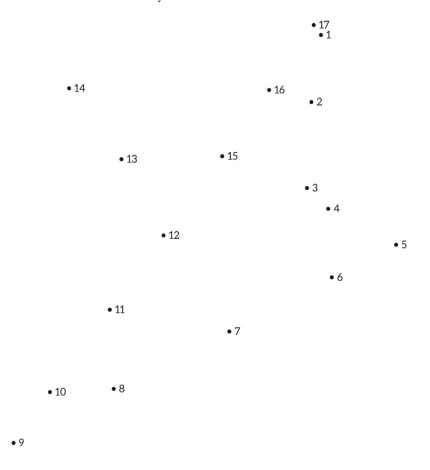

Provide a copy of the above dot-to-dot. Have the students connect the dots beginning with number 1 and going in order to 17, then connect number 17 to number 1 to form a picture of an object. Have the students turn the picture any way they wish and name their picture (airplane, peeled banana, star fish with missing leg, etc.) Let them share what they name their object. Then have them write a three-sentence story about the object and have some of them tell the name of their object and read their story. This later part in writing the story will be used in a lesson several days later when students study myths about some of the constellations written by the Greeks.

Element 2: Concept Development and New Information Developed by Teacher and Students

The teacher begins this way: "Hundreds of years ago in Mesopotamia (near Iraq today), ancient people looked up in the night sky and began to connect the dots. When they did, they saw images and named patterns of stars; later, they made up stories about them (so did the Greeks). We call the stories myths. Does anyone know what the patterns of stars are called?" The teacher should allow time for responses, and if no one answers correctly, say, "Constellations" and write this word on the whiteboard, on PowerPoint, or on the chalkboard.

Element 3: Student Processing Activity

Let's see if we can write a definition of constellations before we look at our science book. Have the students write a definition using just the dot-to-dot activity and the teacher's few comments. Give prompts to individuals as necessary. Most of the definitions will sound very much like the text, but do not turn to the text before they write and share their definitions. Many of your students will write and share that a constellation is a group of stars that form a picture when your mind connects the dots—stars. Below are possible definitions that will be found in a textbook:

1. Constellations are easily recognized groups of stars that appear to be located close together in the sky and that form a picture if lines connecting them are imagined.
2. Any of the groups of stars in the sky that seem from earth to form a pattern and have been given names.
3. "An easily recognized group of stars that appear to be located close together in the sky and that form a picture if lines connecting them are imagined."[8]

After sharing their definitions, direct them to the page in their science books on which they will find the text definition. Have them compare their definition to the one in the book and make any necessary adjustments needed without copying directly.

Let us review the methods used to work out the plan that have been used so far:

---

[8] *The New Dictionary of Cultural Literacy*, 3rd ed., s.v. "constellation," Dictionary.com, accessed June 20, 2022. https://www.dictionary.com/browse/constellation.

- Connect-the-dots
- Name the picture—share names; write a brief story about it and share
- Teacher shares about ancient viewing of stars in the night sky and those that "connected the dots to form pictures"
- Students write a definition for constellations and then compare theirs to the science text

ELEMENT 2: DEVELOPING THE CONCEPT OF CONSTELLATIONS

After determining the definition, teach the specific content for the day. Use your text or other supplemental resources such as YouTube videos related to the topic of the day. What is your learning objective for this first lesson in the mini-unit? While lesson objectives are not a part of the delivery of the lesson, they are essential. We will address the writing of objectives later. For this introductory lesson, the objective might be as simple as: The student will be able to define constellations and name and identify several that might be visible on a clear night in his or her geographical location.

Continue input of new information: "What are stars? (from previous lessons). How far away are they? Where do we find them first mentioned in history?" The text will usually have level-appropriate paragraphs about these questions. Here is one example:

> Constellations were part of the historical record in Mesopotamian culture around 4000 B.C. In the 8th century B.C. Homer mentioned a few now familiar constellations in his epic poem, the Odyssey. Four hundred years later Eudoxus of Cnidus wrote about 43 constellations (or 45 or 48 depending on one's interpretation) which survive today. Eudoxus' original work was lost but his ideas were kept alive by Aratus in a poem called Phaenomena (around 270 B.C.).[9]

"Where else might constellations be mentioned that might surprise you?" Just see if anyone knows, and if so affirm or say, "We will find out later."

---

[9] "To 88 Modern Constellations," The Seven Worlds, May 25, 2015, https://theseven worlds.wordpress.com/2015/05/25/to-88-modern-constellations/.

To aid with input of new information, search YouTube for overall explanations of constellations and show these brief presentations. For example: The one suggested here uses the idea of dot-to-dot and is called "Connect the Dots in the Sky!"[10]

"What constellations are visible where we live (Northern or Southern Hemisphere, all year long or seasonal)?" Students discover which ones, research on the internet or the teacher tells them, and they draw several that are visible to them using pictures in the text or provided by the teacher. Using a pencil to punch out the stars and a flashlight to shine from the back of their paper in a darkened room, they can see what the constellation might look like. Or, for this first lesson, the teacher will show which constellations are visible in the hemisphere in which they are living and have the students create cards with pictures they create on black paper and using gold stars. Just the key ones for this first lesson, and encourage the students to check the sky that night.

Later in the unit you can use a black umbrella or old overhead projector (if one is available) to create the night sky. You can turn the umbrella to show the movement in the night sky and find the location of the constellations at a particular time of the year. Students can draw a particular constellation and then punch out the stars like a dot-to-dot, then project these on an overhead projector or other light source. The light will show through the punched-out holes. You can create a game in identifying these. This activity gives the student the opportunity to begin to be curious about the night sky and the possibility of observing a constellation. If you have no light source available, just make flash cards for several of the constellations that are visible in your geographical area.

Natural inclusion of biblical worldview thinking during concept development. Within this second element, there are several ways in which the teacher can naturally include biblical worldview thinking. This thinking can be encouraged through different types of activities. Two such activities are those which connect to the biblical worldview and those that distinguish the biblical worldview from a competing worldview. The teacher will have the students connect the existence of constellations to the Creator by having them read Job 9:9. Constellations are mentioned in the Bible several times by name, and this may surprise your students. Have them write the names of those mentioned and identify who named them from the passage. Job names Bear, Orion, Pleiades. "He makes the stars: the Bear, Orion, the Pleiades, and the constellations of the southern sky. He does great and unsearchable things, wonders without number"

---

[10] "Constellations: Connect the Dots in the Sky!" SciShow Kids, April 30, 2015, YouTube video, 3:44, https://www.youtube.com/watch?v=1sZ15SUeS9w.

(vv. 9–10). (Who is "He"?) Amos 5:8 declares, "The one who made the Pleiades and Orion, who turns darkness into dawn and darkens day into night, who summons the water of the sea and pours it out over the surface of the earth—the LORD is his name." This is not tacked on at the end of the unit but part of new information—element 2 of the model and is a student processing activity as well.

Teacher: "The Bible is a very old book, and the book of Job is considered by scholars to be one of the oldest books of the sixty-six books within the Bible. So what can we conclude about how far back in history people 'connected the dots' to form pictures? Knowledge of constellations is very old!" This is a connecting activity that connects to a biblical view of the heavenly bodies with what they are learning in science class.

Later in the unit you will use the worldview issue that "the heavens declare the glory of God" (Ps 19:1) and they speak of God's power and glory to every language people group. This will also be a connecting activity toward the end of the unit. Later in the unit the difference between astronomy and astrology will also be addressed, and this will be a distinguishing or contrasting view to the Scriptures.

Also, later in the unit, there will be a student processing and distinguishing activity when the students study the human stories written about the constellations (myths) and discover that these are human-made stories, while the Bible is a special book of sixty-six books written over many years with many authors but providing one big story of God, his creation, and his specific relationship to humans. When the students research the difference between astronomy and astrology—in lesson elements 2 and 3—they discover which one of these, astronomy or astrology, is forbidden in the Bible and why (see Jer 8 and Deut 4). Which one, astronomy or astrology, might be a wonderful professional task of a Christian who is an astronomer-scientist? What additional processing activity would be appropriate for this first lesson in the unit? This depends on the objective of the lesson for the day.

ELEMENT THREE: PROCESSING ACTIVITIES FOR THE STUDENT

The students have already defined constellations using a processing activity in the activation part of the lesson. They have identified the constellations that are visible in their geographical area and have concluded that knowledge of constellations is very old from history books including the Bible. A closure-type processing activity might be to have the students, in pairs, write an article for the school newspaper explaining what they are learning about constellations.[11] The students can select a title: "Something

---

[11] *Closure* comes from a German word that means "to fit it in, make sense of it."

Visible Only at Night"; or "Something Old and Known for Thousands of Years"; or "Too Hot to Handle"; or "Connecting the Dots in the Sky." Or the teacher can let them create their own title. Limit the word count of the article depending on the age of the students.

Element 4: Assessment

How will the students find out whether they have learned well, and how will the teacher find out how well the students learned? Will you use test questions, an activity, a performance such as a speech about constellations, or what? In cognitive interactive learning, various methods are used in the assessment of learning. For example, based on their ending processing activity, you might have them write a speech on constellations that might be given to a lower-level class in the school. The speech should answer the question, "How are constellations like doing a dot-to-dot activity?" The student then puts his or her name on it and gives it to the teacher when they leave (we call this an exit slip), or it can be collected during class.

A Second Example of Cognitive Learning Using Shapes

ENGAGE: Read through this brief review of a lesson that includes the four elements of a cognitive interactive lesson and tell why each element fits with the concept of interactive learning related to how the mind works. Although the chapter on developing biblical worldview thinking is later in this book, we will address this practice specifically in this lesson.

Math for five- and six-year-olds

Lesson on basic shapes

What worldview questions might be answered by a simple math lesson?

About God: The visible and invisible speak of God (Col 1:16; Rom 1). His wisdom and glory are evident in mathematics and nature (see shapes in nature).

About humans: We are created in God's image—we have the ability to use shapes wisely (we see shapes in human-made structures).

About the external world: What of God's nature, his world, his work, is visible within the mathematics we are studying?

The Lesson:

Motivation: Have the children sort different shapes. Encourage them to do it different ways: first by color, then by size, finally by "something else" (shape).

Concept Development: "What makes these shapes in this sorted group the same?" Begin to develop the characteristics of the different shapes (three sides, four sides all the same, etc.). This is a beginning concept for later learning about scientific classification.

Processing Activity: Using pictures (or YouTube video) of nature (first) and human-made things (second), have the children find specific shapes (such as all the triangles, all the squares, etc.). Students will draw shapes and use cut-out shapes to make houses, boats, trees, and other images that fit the shapes.

Processing Continued—(worldview integration) "Who made the shapes in nature?"

"WHY do you think we see so many of the same shapes in nature?" (There is one creative Artist.) "WHO is the One who came up with the shapes? How do we know?"

"WHY do you think we see the SAME types of shapes in things we make as humans?" We are creative, made in God's image, and can use the shapes he designed. "Let's take the time to thank God for all the shapes he made."

Assessment: Have students draw or trace shapes and make figures such as houses or trees. When collected, thank God for the ability to re-create using shapes because we are made in his image!

"The Bible tells us who made the shapes of things we see in nature. Listen and tell me who that is." Show pictures of shapes in nature.

Read Gen 1:11: "Then God said, 'Let the land produce vegetation: seed-bearing plants and trees on the land that bear fruit with seed in it, according to their various kinds.' And it was so."

Refer back to the pictures of shapes in nature: triangle, circles etc. "Who made the shapes that we see in nature?"

Continued Student Processing:

The teacher reads on the internet that a person has written the following about shapes in nature. The students listen carefully to find out the answer to the question, to whom do they give thanks for shapes? The teacher emphasizes the bolded words in order to assist the students' thinking. "Have you ever thought about how **nature likes to arrange itself** in patterns in order to act efficiently? Nothing in nature happens without a reason, all of these patterns have an important reason to exist, and they also happen to be beautiful to watch. Check out examples of some of these patterns and you may be able to spot a few the next time you go for a walk."[12]

Nature is given credit, rather than the God who created nature. **Point this out and ask,** "But who made nature?"

Comment to the early childhood teacher: These concepts related to shapes are foundational for the golden ratio and Fibonacci sequence.

---

[12] "Math Patterns in Nature," Resources for Science Learning, The Franklin Institute, accessed January 21, 2022, https://www.fi.edu/math-patterns-nature.

In God's creation, there exists a "Divine Proportion" that is exhibited in a multitude of shapes, numbers, and patterns whose relationship can only be the result of the omnipotent, good, and all-wise God of Scripture. This Divine Proportion—existing in the smallest to the largest parts, in living and also in non-living things—reveals the awesome handiwork of God and His interest in beauty, function, and order.[13]

Additional information for mathematics at all levels: What does mathematics tell us about ourselves and the external world?

About ourselves. Humans, created in the image of God, can think quantitatively and spatially, discover patterns and relationships, and communicate and create with these.

About the external world. "How can it be that mathematics, being after all a product of human thought independent of experience, is so admirably adapted to the objects of reality?"[14]

God not only created all of the external world, the universe and the earth and all that is in it, but he created the human mind to be able to appreciate and use the patterns, shapes, and relationships to do a work for him.

Conclusion

It should be obvious to the reader that having a template for a model to use in lesson planning is a helpful tool. In this chapter we have presented a learning model informed by cognitive interactive learning. There are other templates that also fit interactive learning theory. Backward design, made popular by Jay McTighe and Grant Wiggins, is addressed in the next chapter, and the Five Es are addressed in the chapter on the structure of science as a discipline of study. The key elements addressed in this chapter are imbedded in each of these and others.

---

[13] Fred Willson, "Shapes, Numbers, Patterns, and the Divine Proportion in God's Creation," The Institute for Creation Research, December 1, 2002, https://www.icr.org/article /shapes-numbers-patterns-divine-proportion-gods-cre/.

[14] Albert Einstein gave an address on January 27, 1921, in Berlin, "Geometry and Experience." The lecture was published by Methuen in London, in 1922.

CHAPTER 6

Moving from the Teaching Model to Unit and Lesson Planning

Debbie MacCullough

Many teachers are taught to develop unit and lesson plans in colleges of education; however, the theory and teaching model behind the lesson template may not have been examined. This may cause one to revert to how he or she was taught through lecture/telling and testing—a passive model for learning. The goal of this chapter is to build a logical progression among three key issues:

1. the issue of the theory of learning (chapters 2–4)
2. the issue of the model or plan that emerges from theory (chapter 5)
3. the unit and lesson plans that emerge from this model

How Do I Plan?

To take the teaching model and use it to create units and lessons, we must examine the thinking necessary for good planning. Planning is simply the process of preparing ahead of time. Quality teaching requires quality planning. Even when given a curriculum, a set of outcomes, or objectives, a good teacher will still plan for the learning to take place.

In this chapter, we will examine how to plan a unit and a lesson using the cognitive interactive teaching model and the planning mechanism known as "backward design," developed by Wiggins and McTighe. In 1998, Grant Wiggins and Jay McTighe published a book entitled *Understanding by Design*.[1] The authors contended rightly that we must first know what we desire as an intended result for our students' learning. That is, what is our objective? What do we desire our students to know and be able to do? Once we have our aim in mind as we plan, we keep that in focus as we work *backward*[2] and plan for how we will help every student to arrive at that objective. This is the assessment element of the model.

Next, to plan our lesson (or our unit) we continue to work backward asking questions for each of the elements that were discussed in the prior chapter. What do my students need to process to be able to successfully show they have met the objective? What new information will my students need to learn? What prior knowledge do my students already have that I should activate? How might I motivate my students' minds toward the planned learning? The unit and the lesson are built upon the answers to these questions.

Most teachers will be provided a set of materials to use to teach their students. What is provided will depend upon several factors, including things such as whether your country has a national curriculum, whether your school has objectives or outcomes, local or national standards to be met, and whether you have textbooks available. No matter what materials a teacher is given, good planning will take place in similar ways starting with instructional objectives.

Start with Objectives

Every unit and every lesson must have a learning target in mind. To help in planning, objectives should be written to clearly express what the teacher desires each student to learn. Objectives should be written in singular, measurable, behavioral terms. Singular because each student should be able to meet the objective. Students are different and learn differently; however, the objective can be the same for each student. The objective should be written in measurable terms because it is used to assess whether students

---

[1] Grant Wiggins and Jay McTighe, *Understanding by Design*, exp. 2nd ed. (Alexandria, VA: ASCD, 2005).

[2] Thus, the name used for this type of planning is often called "backward design," and proponents of this way of planning refer to it by the initials of the book or UbD.

have met the learning target. Measurable does not simply mean that we must set a particular target in a percentage of answers on a test (i.e., 80 percent of the test) but rather that it is something that can be measured. I cannot measure "thinking" or "understanding" because there is no concrete way to measure the level. But I can measure the written or verbal explanation of a concept. I can measure how well a student "articulates" a concept. I can measure the completion of a task. Lastly, the objective should be written in behavioral terms (something the student does that is observable) because we can only see behavior. We cannot observe and measure something that is not a behavior.

ENGAGE: Read this list of objectives and decide if they are measurable and behavioral. Then, read the explanations for the provided answers.

- The student will understand multiplication.
- The student will be able to create an algorithm for division.
- The student will learn ten vocabulary words.
- The student will be able to learn 90 percent of the capital cities in the country.
- The student will be able to list the five largest cities in Spain.
- The student will be able to articulate the author's point of view in assigned readings.

EXPLANATIONS

- The student will understand multiplication: *This is not measurable. How do we know that a student "understands" the operation of multiplication? A better option is that the student will be able to draw a picture to illustrate the operation of multiplication.*
- The student will be able to create an algorithm for division: *This is both measurable (did the student create it?) and behavioral (the student has an algorithm or formula for division).*
- The student will learn ten vocabulary words: *This is not measurable. How does a teacher evaluate or measure the "learning" here? A better verb to use might be "define." The student will be able to define ten vocabulary words.*
- The student will be able to learn 90 percent of the capital cities in the country: *This is not measurable even though there is a percentage. The problem is with the verb "learn." A better word to use might be "to list" or be able "to correctly match capital cities with country."*
- The student will be able to list the five largest cities in Spain: *This is measurable and behavioral.*

- The student will be able to articulate the author's point of view in assigned readings. *Although harder to measure, this is also measurable. Did the student use words (in writing or orally) to describe and explain (articulate) the author's point of view? This can be observed and is therefore behavioral as well.*

Benjamin Bloom

Benjamin Bloom (1913–1999), an American educational psychologist whose work has been adopted all over the world, contributed to learning theory by designing an approach to mastery learning that included different levels of learning objectives with tiered levels of thinking. His taxonomy has three domains for objectives: cognitive, affective, and psychomotor. Learning at the higher levels is dependent on learning at the lower levels. Although his work was revised in 2001, it still remains a major contribution to teachers who use objectives to target higher and higher levels of thinking.

Bloom received a bachelor's and master's degree from Pennsylvania State University in 1935, and later, a PhD in education from the University of Chicago where he was employed until 1959.[3] He embraced the concept that home and school environments are crucial to learning and hard work and time are the keys to developing full potential. Effective learning is aided by using instructional objectives that can be measured. His taxonomy was one approach to help teachers design opportunities for mastery of information, attitudes, and skills that will push students toward excellence.

Bloom conducted research on early childhood education and working with gifted students. The Ford Foundation sent him to India to serve as an educational consultant. He also worked in Israel as well as in several other countries to help revise their education systems. He was well-known as an outstanding researcher in education and was elected president of the American Educational Research Association. His goal was clearly better student learning. He said in an interview for *Educational Leadership*, "We must keep searching for ways to ensure that every child learns well. . . . We can't solve all the problems of

---

[3] "Benjamin Bloom," *New World Encyclopedia*, accessed January 21, 2022, https://www .newworldencyclopedia.org/p/index.php?title=Benjamin_Bloom&oldid=1063221.

the world, but we can produce a generation of children who are interested in learning."[4]

Benjamin Bloom provided educators with a taxonomy that is often used to ensure that objectives encourage greater thinking. This taxonomy has been adapted and adjusted over the years but is useful for the creation of well-designed objectives. The taxonomy is usually shown as a triangle or stackable circles because a student must have the lower levels of a concept to be able to meet an objective written at one of the higher levels (see fig. 1).

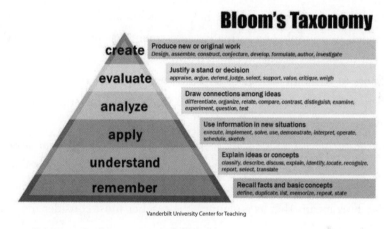

Fig. 1[5]

The student must be able to recall facts to be able to explain an idea. Therefore, ideas cannot be applied (higher level thinking) if they are not understood or remembered. In unit planning, a teacher may desire that by the end of the unit the student is able to create something related to the learning. Each lesson in the unit, however, will include objectives that build upon the taxonomy, moving student learning to higher levels of thinking essential for creative and critical thinking. We will return to this concept in our chapter on worldview integration.

---

[4] Ron Brandt, "A Conversation with Benjamin Bloom," *Educational Leadership* 37, no, 2 (November 1979): 157–61.

[5] Creative Commons Attribute License from Vanderbilt University Center for Teaching.

Assessment

Once objectives have been written, the next part of all Understanding by Design (UbD) planning—whether for an entire unit or for one lesson—is to determine the possible assessments that will be used to ensure that the students have met the objectives. There are two main types of assessments: formative and summative.

Formative assessments are those activities that the students will do as they are in the process of learning along the way in each lesson. They inform the teacher and the student about how well learning is occurring. They are often not graded but rather serve as ongoing feedback to the student and the teacher and require the teacher to provide feedback in comments, for example, or help in understanding. In the chapter on the teaching model, an example of a formative assessment was provided under the assessment element (4) of the lesson on constellations. The "exit slip" is a way for a teacher to ask students to write an answer to a question or issue for that day's lesson. This is collected before the class ends to "inform" the teacher and the students as to whether the objective for the day was met.

Summative assessments are typically assessment activities at the summation of learning and are usually graded. Both concepts of assessment are further explored in chapter 7.

When planning both units and lessons, the rest of the planning becomes an "iterative" process. This means that as a planner, the teacher must consider many factors to develop quality plans. The objectives and assessments will direct the teacher and keep the teacher "on target"; however, how to reach from objective to assessment is part of the "art" of teaching. Creativity and critical thinking about students, the content, the timing of the lessons, the other things students are currently learning, the current cultural situation, and a plethora of other factors will lead to developing quality units and lessons. Therefore, an effective teacher will never teach the exact same lesson every year. Quality teachers recognize that each year there are differences that lead to slight changes in learning plans.

An Example of Planning

Let us look at an example to see how this process of planning might work. Suppose that our next concept/skill in the curriculum is long division. This is an important skill for students to learn; however, it has several mathematical concepts that are critical for future mathematics as well. For those unfamiliar with the term "long division algorithm," this is when I take a large total amount and divide it into equal amounts that may or may not be large, to find out how many sets of the equal amounts are in the large total amount. The algorithm requires the use of place value, multiplication, and subtraction to find the correct answer. For example, I may wish to find how many groups of 24 can be made from 6144. The algorithm would examine how many groups of 24 can be made from 61 (using place value, really 6100) as you will see in the example below. The result is 2 (using place value, 200). The amount that can be "grouped" then is 200 × 24 or 4800. This amount is subtracted from the 6144 to leave 1344. We next examine how many groups of 24 can be made from the 1344 remaining. The entire process looks like figure 2:

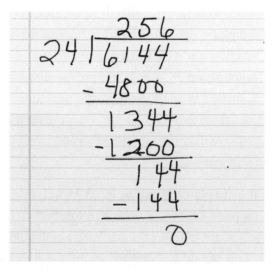

Fig. 2

How to Plan for This Long Division Lesson

Step One: The first step is to **write unit objectives**. The goal is that our students can correctly divide using the long division algorithm. Given our understanding of the structure of mathematics, we also want the students to understand the concepts that are used within the algorithm of long division. So, our unit objectives might be:

- The student will be able to explain the steps of the long division algorithm and connect those steps to the concept of division in the explanation.
- The student will be able to correctly use the long division algorithm.

Step Two: The objectives must then be connected to an **assessment**, first to a formative objective as they practice using the algorithm and then a summative assessment for the unit. This key step of backward design helps us keep the entire lesson and the unit on target. We may have the students fill out an "explanation guide" for each step of what they do in the long division algorithm. For the second objective, we may have several questions on a test in which the students are required to use the long division algorithm. The goal is to understand why the algorithm works.

Step Three: Now that we have our unit objectives and a possible assessment, we must begin to consider what is the **logical order** for students to learn the long division algorithm. Backward design[6] suggests an iterative process in which we examine what is known and what is to be learned. Answering this question for our lesson on long division requires us to consider what students already know about division. Most students, when learning the long division algorithm, have already studied the mathematical concept of division and have worked with small amounts. That is, they understand that they are taking a total amount and dividing it into groups of equal sizes to find out how many groups there are; or that they are dividing the total amount into a set number of groups and finding out the size of each group assuming they are of equal size. This unit is about how to do this with larger total amounts and larger numbers of groups (or group sizes) in a more efficient way.

Step Four: Now it is time to **plan the unit order**. A logical order for lessons might be to activate the students' prior knowledge with a lesson that reviews the operation of division. A second lesson might examine the challenges of dividing large total amounts into large group sizes. This second lesson is to "set up" the students to desire to find a "shortcut" as well as prepare them to understand the algorithm. It motivates them to want to know more. A third lesson would be examining possible "shortcuts" to use with the goal of getting to the standard algorithm for long division. A fourth lesson would be to practice the standard algorithm. In mathematics, this fourth lesson is a "student processing" element in our unit and lesson plans. It allows the students to work on understanding the algorithm, and it gives the teacher time to assist those students who need more information to make sense of the algorithm. A fifth lesson may be a formative assessment lesson in which the students work on using words to describe how their algorithm steps coordinate with the entire concept of division. Notice that the unit plans incorporate the elements of the teaching model. Each lesson within the unit

---

[6] "Backward Design" refers to the elements of Understanding by Design (UbD) that are part of the lesson planning.

will have all elements of the cognitive interactive teaching model as well. Both the unit plans and the individual lesson plans take into account how humans learn.

Step Five: After the unit has been planned, the **individual lessons must be planned**. A similar process is used for each lesson. First, the teacher will write objectives for that lesson. Next, the assessment (most likely, formative) for each lesson will be determined. The teacher will plan the delivery elements of each lesson. How will you activate the students' minds toward the concept to be learned? What new information will the student be given? What will you have the students do to process this new information? In the chapters on each content area, we will examine more closely how this is done in the content area of mathematics and other subjects as well.

ENGAGE: Locate a curriculum for the grade level you teach (or hope to teach) and a subject that you are comfortable teaching. Write two or three unit objectives. Next, decide on how you will assess these unit objectives. Once you have unit objectives and matching assessments, write out a logical lesson progression. Choose one lesson to plan as well.

CHAPTER 7

Formative and Summative Assessments

Ken Coley

Introduction

In his book *Transformative Assessment*, Popham provides a helpful definition of formative assessment: "Formative assessment is a process used by teachers and students during instruction that provides feedback to adjust ongoing teaching and learning to improve student's achievement of intended instructional outcomes."[1] Several key features are embedded in this definition. It is a process, as opposed to a particular test, and it influences the work of both instructors and students. In addition, it provides valuable data so that adjustments can be made to improve achievement.[2]

Marzano believes that formative assessment should be a part of an instructional unit from the very beginning and continue until the end of the unit. He cites a meta-analysis study of over 250 studies conducted by Black and William in 1998. The researchers determined that formative assessments produce a more powerful effect on student learning as opposed to summative evaluations. Marzano summarizes:

---

[1] W. James Popham, *Transformative Assessment* (Alexandria, VA: ASCD, 2008), 5.
[2] Popham, 5.

Research supports the conclusion that formative classroom assessment is one of the most powerful tools a classroom teacher might use. Formative assessments are defined as any activity that provides sound feedback on student learning. Characteristics of sound feedback include that it should be frequent, give students a clear picture of their progress and how they might improve, and provide encouragement.[3]

ENGAGE:

Scenario #1: Imagine a basketball practice leading up to a game with a crosstown rival. The coach emphasizes the importance of the game, reviews the strengths of the opponent, and the importance of shooting percentage. After rolling out a cart of basketballs, he tells the players to spend the remainder of practice shooting alone before he heads to the bleachers to read emails and catch up on unanswered texts.

Question: What is the likelihood of the players improving their shooting on Friday night?

Scenario #2: Your chorus teacher enthusiastically lists several new choral arrangements that she has selected for the group to sing at regional competition later that semester. Each day for the weeks leading up to competition she routinely has the full chorus sing through each piece, start to finish, without interruption or correction, repeatedly.

Question: How do you think the chorus will perform at regionals? Will the judges be impressed?

Scenario #3: The band director allows the band members to take out their instruments each afternoon and get tuned up in preparation for marching band rehearsal. He calls the group to order and shows a video of a college band performing a popular tune as it marches across a football field. Following the video, he picks up his own trumpet and plays the brass part, his own clarinet and plays the woodwind part, his own snare drum and plays the percussion rhythms, and so on. Meanwhile the band members sit motionless with their instruments in their laps.

Question: Will the band members flow across the field in synchronized formations that Friday night while playing in harmony?

---

[3] Robert J. Marzano, *Classroom Assessment and Grading That Work* (Alexandria, VA: ASCD, 2006), 9.

What is missing across each of these practices or rehearsals? Meaningful feedback from the coach or director. Targeted practice with focused coaching. Adjustments in the routine practice by both teacher and performer. Prediction: None of the leaders of these groups would be asked to return the next school year after students, administrators, and the community witnessed poor performances. Why is that? Because people pay to see and hear them perform and they keep score!

However, your memory may be filled with classrooms in which you were exposed to new ideas day after day by instructors who never paused to consider your progress until the final exam. Your individual progress was never evaluated. Your routine practice never varied. The teacher's rhythm of presentations day after day marched on without variation or interruption. You may recall instances of believing that you knew the material only to be ambushed by a test that told you otherwise. And even more tragically, did you continue to retrieve this information from your memory to be used in novel situations? I think not. Your loss of confidence and frustration with a low grade probably led to the brain dismissing those ideas.

Consider the root word in *formative*. Knowledge, skills, and dispositions are potentially being *form*ed throughout the class period and outside of class. Existing neural networks are strengthened, and new connections are constructed. What can change in addition to the new mental frameworks and neural networks that are being formed? The approaches to learning and the timing and methods of practice.

As teachers observe students missing the mark and failing to meet a standard, they adjust their approach in response to students' needs. This could mean slowing down or in some cases accelerating. It could mean scaffolding the skill development and thin slicing the steps in a process. Or it could mean chunking the material in smaller pieces. This chapter will explore a variety of teacher responses to data gathered by formative assessments.

But formative feedback is also vital for students. Often students need to adjust *their approach* to learning and practice. Notetaking may be ineffective. The amount of review on a daily or weekly basis may need to be increased. The methods for review may need to be adjusted or varied. But all of this takes place while learning is taking place and while there is still time for adjustments to be made prior to summative assessments, that is, a final exam or paper or end of grade testing (EOGs).

This chapter is divided into two sections related to formative and summative assessments. In the first part we will present the concepts related to formative assessments in three segments that routinely occur in a typical teaching episode: introduction, teaching of new concepts or skills, and conclusion. Often these subsections of a lesson run seamlessly together, and experienced instructors instinctively gather data about the comprehension of individual students and the class as a whole. These three subcategories created by this author require different approaches to data gathering. These will be referred to as *Readiness, Comprehension,* and *Application,* the R-C-As of formative assessments.

Assessments for Readiness

As you prepare to begin a new unit of instruction, you must consider where your learners are, what unique skills may be required to progress, and what unique needs exist in your class of students. The feedback you receive will be vital as you determine the starting point for instruction and consider if that will be the same spot for every student. In addition, how fast can you anticipate moving? Will certain levels of scaffolding be necessary in order to assure all the learners are where they need to be as you progress toward the stated outcomes?

REFLECT: Consider your reaction if your physical education teacher began the spring unit on track and field by inviting the entire class over to the high jump pit. Next, he set the bar at 5'0" and established that height as the beginning height for learning high jump techniques. Given your level of experience and overall athletic ability, how confident would you be that you could meet the instructor's expectations? What would be the likelihood of you learning anything about high jumping other than how difficult it is? Take this insight into the classroom you are preparing to lead . . . could your approach be just as daunting?

Tuttle refers to the first stage of formative assessment as pre-assessment and recommends a diagnostic test, particularly where state or national standards are concerned. He recommends sharing the learning standard and rewording the statement into student-friendly wording as needed. In addition, Tuttle encourages teachers to begin and end the class with an emphasis on the standard and related goals. Another popular practice is to share an "exemplar," a model example of the assignment. Students can review a standard example and begin to visualize what their own work needs to look like.[4]

---

[4] Harry Grover Tuttle, *Formative Assessment: Responding to Your Students* (Larchmont, NY: Eye on Education, 2009), 8–16.

Guskey defines *pre-assessments* as "any means used by teachers to gather information about students prior to instruction."[5] He divides these into three types of learning goals. First, *cognitive pre-assessments* measure academic goals and what students know and can do. Second, affective pre-assessments look for students' attitudes, interests, dispositions, and values. Third, behavioral pre-assessments try to measure observable skills such as body movements in athletics, dance, or music. His article entitled "Does Pre-Assessment Work?" includes lots of warnings about misuses of the strategy and the potential waste of time—the results merely confirm that students have not studied the content before. However, he concludes that pre-assessment has support in the research when the purpose and form are well planned.[6]

A simple and quick approach to assessing readiness is the *stoplight assessment*. Ask your students to view their level of readiness for the new ideas that are coming as if they are approaching a stoplight.

Red: If the new idea or vocabulary word is totally unfamiliar, it should be written on a red sticky note. This means "Stop. I'm not ready to move on."

Yellow: If the idea is somewhat familiar but they lack confidence, then it goes on a yellow sticky note.

Green: If they have confidence they can use the term and concept, then they are ready to move forward with new ideas.

Be sure to take note of the number of ideas or terms that students have listed on the red sheet. This will tell you whether to slow down or speed up. Do not forget to give them a chance at the end of the lesson to move items on the red sheet over to the yellow or green sheet if they feel more confident. The act of moving items builds confidence and means learning has taken place! (Look back at your notes and engagements in chapter 4 of this text for an example of this strategy.)[7]

Assessments for Comprehension

Fisher and Frey nuance the idea of formative assessment by calling the process "checking for understanding." Their discussion includes pointing out the value of looking for

---

[5] Thomas R. Guskey, "Does Pre-Assessment Work?" *Educational Leadership* 75, no. 5 (2018): 53.

[6] Guskey, "Does Pre-Assessment Work?" 52–57.

[7] Tuttle, *Formative Assessment*, 80.

nonverbal clues such as eye movements, facial expressions, and body language. Early in your career you may be concentrating on remembering the next step in your lesson plan and fail to notice eyes that are glazed over, blank stares, or slumping shoulders.[8]

College instructor Tim Howard challenges all educators not to be content with "civil attention." Howard argues that American educators are too often content to lecture and mistakenly believe they are impacting their students' thinking. Why? Because their class sits passively and cooperatively, not disturbing the presenter or distracting their classmates. They can even chuckle with the teacher on cue, while not understanding any of the concepts.[9] (We have found this to be true of international students as well.) We do not think you will be satisfied to be a teacher who has such low expectations.

Fisher and Frey recommend two active learning techniques that stimulate both thinking and movement while providing the teacher with valuable feedback. *Retelling* of a text or narrative requires that a student process and summarize new information. The teacher can listen for which concepts and details were included and which were not. Probing students about what was included as well as omitted will indicate their level of understanding.[10]

A second active learning technique recommended by Fisher and Frey is called *value lineups.* This approach not only provides data for a student's comprehension but also challenges students to listen to the interpretations of their classmates. Using a scale such as a five-point Likert scale that moves from *strongly agree* to *strongly disagree*, the teacher asks students to find a point on the spectrum that represents their value or perspective. For a unit on Shakespeare that includes the play *Macbeth*, students could respond to the statement, "The three witches are very powerful beings that manipulate Macbeth into killing the king." Pick your spot on the continuum and explain your position.[11]

Maxlow and Sanzo suggest another active learning approach that asks students to demonstrate their level of comprehension, make a value judgment, and explain their response. In the four corners strategy, teachers ask students to respond to a prompt that has four viable responses. Four responses, four corners. Each option is designated

---

[8] Douglas Fisher and Nancy Frey, *Checking for Understanding: Formative Assessment Techniques for Your Classroom* (Alexandria, VA: ASCD, 2007).

[9] Tim Howard, *Discussion in the College Classroom: Getting Your Students Engaged and Participating in Person and Online* (San Francisco: Jossey-Bass, 2015), 17.

[10] Fisher and Frey, *Checking for Understanding*, 26–28.

[11] Fisher and Frey, 25–26.

a corner of the room and the students move. Once there, students can pair up and develop a one-minute presentation on the perspective or facts that led them to that corner.[12]

Students Adjust Their Approach to Learning

At this point we suggest educators train students to monitor their own progress. Marzano points out, "One of the most powerful ways a teacher can provide feedback that encourages learning is to have students keep track of their own progress."[13] Teachers can provide a chart that serves as a visual representation of progress. Included in the handout can be space for students to state performance objectives and list specific ways they can improve.[14]

A second technique to enhance student learning is to provide coaching and time for them to reflect on their own progress. The standards/objectives can be written in student-friendly statements and distributed to the class. During this moment students score themselves on their perception of their progress toward the unit goals.[15]

Maxlow and Sanzo present a focused approach they term "forward feedback," meaning the strategies propel the student to evaluate his or her work with an eye on the unit goals. Here are three questions they propose incorporating into each instructional episode:

1. Where am I going? (goal-setting)
2. How am I doing compared to my goal? (self-assessment)
3. How am I progressing toward the goal? (self-monitoring)

The authors challenge educators to think about these questions in comparison to providing nonspecific feedback, such as "great work," "outstanding ideas," or "need to reread this." Forward feedback, on the other hand, presents a student with information that will allow him or her to recalibrate his work moving forward toward his or her goals.[16]

---

[12] Kate Wolfe Maxlow and Karen Sanzo, *20 Formative Assessment Strategies That Work* (New York: Routledge, 2018), 87–88.

[13] Marzano, *Classroom Assessment and Grading That Work*, 89.

[14] Marzano, 90.

[15] Marzano, 92.

[16] Maxlow and Sanzo, *20 Formative Assessment Strategies That Work*, 3.

REFLECT: Think about a classroom, mentoring, or extracurricular episode in which you received "forward feedback" as we just described. Next, consider your event through the lens of this quote from educator Susan Brookhart:

> Feedback can be very powerful if done well. The power of formative feedback lies in its double-barreled approach, addressing both cognitive and motivational factors at the same time. Good feedback gives students information they need so they can understand where they are in their learning and what to do next—the cognitive factor. Once they feel they understand what to do and why, most students develop a feeling that they have control over their own learning—the motivational factor.[17]

Polling

Some teachers may be concerned that formative assessments take too much time away from the presentation of new material. Setting aside for a moment the data that supports strong academic results related to formative assessments, the use of a variety of polling techniques as new concepts presented can be done quickly and efficiently. Here are a few examples:

Thumbs Up: Ask for a quick class response by challenging students to react to a statement by voting it up or down.

Hands Up: Ask students to simply raise their hands if they are aware of a new store in town, a particular website, or a popular song that fits as an illustration of a point you are making. (If no hands go up, pick another illustration!)

Are You Getting This? Ask students to rate their level of understanding to that point in the presentation using three fingers: 3 for catching on; 2 for somewhat; and 1 for unsure.

Likert Scale Response: If you want to ask about a perception or attitude, the familiar *strongly agree* can be shown by four fingers and thumb (four fingers *agree*, and so on).

---

[17] Susan M. Brookhart, *How to Give Effective Feedback to Your Students* (Alexandria, VA: ASCD, 2008), 2.

Multiple Choice Practice: Students each have a pack of five cards with letters A-E printed one per card. (This technique can include future exam questions.)

Audience Response Systems (ARS): A variety of free web-based tools allow teachers a digital way for students to respond to both multiple choice questions and open-ended questions that are qualitative in nature.

Following any of these, particularly if the activity involved questions for which there were correct answers, can trigger discussions about the students' level of confidence in their responses, next steps for learning the material, and insights into progress towards the unit goals.

Pepper

A familiar pregame warm up for baseball players of all ages is Pepper. One player holds a bat while players take turns tossing the ball to him and each participant must stay ready for a dribbler hit his way. In the classroom version, students are chosen to stand, and the teacher calls a name and asks a factual review question. The student responds, and the teacher goes to another student in random order. For example, a review of American authors may sound this way:

Name the author—*The Raven*	response—Poe
Name the author—*The Scarlet Letter*	response—Hawthorne
Name the author—*Huckleberry Finn*	response—Twain

With repeated success, the teacher can replace participants or can gradually include tougher questions for players who are ready. This formative assessment can bring new energy to a class review and get the attention of students who need more practice.[18]

Online Formative Assessments

For a variety of reasons, online learning has mushroomed and is here to stay. The COVID pandemic disrupted in-person instruction in most schools in the US and worldwide for much of 2020 and 2021. Before that major factor the popularity of "flipped classroom" techniques inspired increases in online learning. And in this decade

---

[18] Doug Lemov, *Teach Like a Champion: 49 Techniques That Put Students on the Path to College* (San Francisco: Jossey-Bass, 2010), 131.

many localities, both public and private, are offering K–12 online instruction as a full-time alternative.

Several challenges have arisen with these trends and interruptions. First, the need to establish community among the instructors and learners. Second, to establish effective and frequent assessments that provide teachers with daily data about student progress, especially absent the in-person nonverbal clues such as attentive expressions, enthusiastic reactions, and eyes that track with class activities. Third, the need to experience positive collaborative interaction that is so important for social-emotional learning. Here are five recommendations that speak to these challenges and provide active engagement for all ability groups of learners for grades 4–12:

1. *Summarizing readings*: Students can be asked to briefly summarize a common reading assignment or select some facet each student finds most interesting. Additionally, students can be required to read the posts of a given number of classmates and leave a short response. At a glance the teacher can see which students are tracking with the unit concepts.

2. *Jigsaw:* A popular activity is to make specific assignments of "a piece of the material or research" and then each student or group brings back a summary of information to assist the others. Each piece snaps into place to form the full picture.

3. *Team practice*: For skill development objectives, students can approach an assignment as practicing for a big game. Each should be challenged to do his or her best, just like in athletic practice, but these assignments are only scored for effort. For example, each student posts his or her response to a brief article following a prescribed rubric. Once again, classmates evaluate each other's posts, giving positive comments and suggestions for improvement.

4. *Case study*: For high school students, learning to apply new concepts to a real-life situation is exceptionally valuable. Students can be given a case study related to the current unit of study followed by a series of questions that direct them to evaluate the case study. After posting their responses, students post responses to a given number of group members.

5. *Ask the expert*: Depending on the complexity of the unit concepts and availability of resources, students in the group can become "the expert" on a designated topic, or outside community leaders can be asked to provide their experience and training. One option is to pair this activity with the case study assignment,

with the acknowledged expert posting a response to the case study following the responses from all the students.

Assessments for Application

At the conclusion of any lesson, the teacher can distribute half sheets of paper or a notecard and say, "This is your *exit ticket*. Write down the most important idea in the material today. Hand it to me at the door." And that is what is required to leave. The teacher then has immediate feedback from each student and can use these insights as he or she prepares for the next day. I did a variation of this ALT (Active Learning Technique) while teaching in Haiti—my students were asked, "What was the muddiest point today?" My French is still good enough to identify one concept that several students listed. Honestly, I had really messed it up and retaught the concept the first ten minutes the following day.

Peer review and celebration can provide powerful assessments. A well-known interaction involving cooperative learning products and peer assessments is ***gallery walk***. Once your students have their collaborative skills and relationship chemistry established, they can cooperate on a major project that takes one or more full periods. Having completed the project, each group places its work on display and selects a member to serve as a docent. All the groups stroll around the room reviewing the others, with the docent remaining behind to answer questions.

In *Grading Smarter, Not Harder*, Dueck describes an assessment related to the preceding ALT. Following the display of individual student projects, classmates move from one project to another leaving behind sticky notes with comments and questions. Dueck calls this formative assessment ***sticky walks*** and finds they are particularly useful for work products such as paintings and other artworks.[19]

1. *One-Word Summary:* Conclude your class with a quick, but cognitively challenging activity. Present these instructions: "Give me a one-word summary of today's lesson and explain in one sentence why you chose that word." The word could be written on a sticky note and placed below the objective for that lesson.

---

[19] Myron Dueck, *Grading Smarter, Not Harder: Assessment Strategies That Motivate Kids and Help Them Learn* (Alexandria, VA: ASCD, 2014), 84–85.

2. *WWWWW in One Sentence:* Working alone or in small groups, challenge students to use this strategy as a final application activity to summarize a history lesson, a Bible passage, or a discussion of a novel in one sentence that includes *who, what, where, when,* and *why.*

Jesus Modeled Formative Assessments

As we have pointed out throughout this text, Jesus is the consummate example of great teaching, and his modeling includes examples of formative assessments. In Luke 5 Jesus begins to recruit his disciples, and he includes a test for **readiness**. Following a period of teaching, Jesus said to Peter, "Put out into deep water and let down your nets for a catch" (v. 4). Jesus had observed the fishermen returning from a futile day of fishing followed by cleaning their nets. Jesus was testing His potential recruit to find out if Simon would follow his lead. After a shocking result, Simon returned and fell at Jesus's feet. The Lord responded by stating the **objective** of the mission: "Don't be afraid. . . . From now on you will be catching people" (v. 10).

The Gospels are filled with the disciples being given formative assessments to measure their **comprehension**. In Luke 9 they were sent out in pairs to practice what Jesus had been modeling for them. When they returned, the disciples were filled with exhilarating stories of preaching, healing, and casting out demons. But soon they had another test when faced with 5,000-plus hungry people. They suggested that Jesus send the crowd away. He said, "You give them something to eat" (v. 13). More snapshots of assessments include:

Luke 9:18, 20: "Who do the crowds say that I am?" "But who do you say that I am?"

Luke 9:23: "If anyone wants to follow after me, let him deny himself, take up his cross daily, and follow me."

Luke 9:44–45: "'Let these words sink in: The Son of Man is about to be betrayed into the hands of men.' . . . But they did not understand this statement; it was concealed from them so that they could not grasp it, and they were afraid to ask him about it."

Luke 22:54–60: Peter was approached three times about being a follower of Jesus. Finally, he stated, "Man, I don't know what you're talking about!" (v. 60).

Fortunately, the story doesn't end at that point. Following his crucifixion and his resurrection, Jesus gives Peter the opportunity to be restored and to apply what he had learned. In John 21 Jesus gave him a test for *application*: "Simon, do you love me? . . . Shepherd my sheep" (v. 16).

Class Discussions as Formative Assessments

All too often we hear, "Does anyone have any questions?" And the teacher believes this to be a legitimate way to check for understanding. The result is usually no comments or questions, or the same students rescue the teacher who is standing alone up front. I call this group of students the "varsity volleyball team." This group consists of students who process new concepts quickly and are generally enthusiastic about batting their ideas or interpretations around while other students simply listen or tune out. Soon those who are not a part of this team tragically stop considering questions or cease to put the new material in their own words. They become spectators.

Authors Persida Himmele and William Himmele describe the Ripple, an approach that begins with challenging each student to formulate a response to a question that requires comprehension of new material (a prompt that serves as a pebble dropped into your classroom). Once an appropriate amount of time is allowed (usually no more than 60 seconds), students turn to a shoulder/elbow partner and verbalize their responses. The teacher then selects different pairs to share one or both responses. This is called Think-Pair-Share. The crucial aspects of this approach are that every student is given a brief moment to process the question or prompt and consider how to best articulate the answer. In addition, every student is engaged even if he or she is speaking to only one classmate.[20]

After students become accustomed to these expectations, the teacher asks pairs to join another pair, and the formative assessment becomes Think-Pair-Square-Share, which concludes with some groups sharing with the entire class. I have used these instructional techniques in many international contexts with great success.

Summative Evaluations

Popham views "formative assessments as a way to improve the caliber of still-underway instructional activities and summative assessments as a way to determine the

---

[20] Persida Himmele and William Himmele, *Total Participation Techniques: Making Every Student an Active Learner* (Alexandria, VA: ASCD, 2017), 19–20.

effectiveness of already-completed instructional activities."[21] Summative assessments most often come at the conclusion of a unit of instruction or at a midpoint, at which time progress needs to be measured. Whether these are done at various mile markers, semester exams, or end of grade testing (EOGs), the assessment often results in a final grade, important data for promotion to the next grade, or decisions related to changing instructional grouping or curriculum track. In most cases, but not all, the data is also valuable for instructors and administrators to evaluate the objectives, resources given to students, and instructional activities. This section includes perspectives regarding the makeup and validity of the test itself, the potential for differentiation, and the use of assessment results as formative in future classes.

REFLECT: As a student preparing to lead instructional activities and give summative examinations, do you recall taking an exam for which you honestly thought you were prepared but the test results said otherwise? Did you try to solve the mystery? Here are some possible factors that will be explored in more detail in the remaining section:

1. Did you review the correct material?
2. Did you prepare for the right type of questions? (Objective or essay)
3. Had previous discussions and assignments prepared you for the correct level of the exam questions? (Emphasis on remembering details versus ability to respond to higher order thinking)
4. Did the exam questions actually mesh with the stated objectives of the unit? (Sometimes old exams are used that haven't been updated.)
5. Was there an effort by the instructor to establish a "normal curve" in final grades? (Were exceptionally difficult questions included to create distinctions in the group's grades?)
6. Were there any opportunities in the exam to allow for your individual strengths to assist you in demonstrating mastery?
7. Had the teacher already assessed your learning on the topics through formative assessments or was this the only assessment your received?

Conditions for Summative Tests

Vatterott challenges teachers to consider the conditions surrounding their tests. She compares feedback, formative assessments, and summative evaluations to theater

---

[21] Popham, *Transformative Assessment*, 4.

practices. *Feedback* occurs when the actors are rehearsing with no one present. A *dress rehearsal* (formative assessment) allows the performers to see how close they are to being ready. The summative assessment occurs at the *actual performance* in front of paying patrons and critics. It's important to note that she coaches teachers not to count formative assessment grades in the final score. "Students who achieve mastery should not be penalized for earlier struggles." We think that the prior, formative assessments should have some modest influence on the final grade. More important than a point total, however, is the opportunity for teachers to see the clear indication of progress and needed course corrections for each student as he or she pursues the unit objectives.

Here are some of Vatterott's points related to conditions under which the final assessment occurs:

- Do students know in advance the skills and knowledge being assessed?
- Do they have adequate time to prepare?
- Is enough time allotted to complete the assessment?
- What resources can the students use during the exam?
- What is being assessed—rote memory or deeper comprehension?
- Can a different type of task reflect mastery, such as a verbal test or project?[22]

Tomlinson and Moon give educators a list of crisp, precise indicators that summative assessments are meaningful and accurate. We cite the author's statements below followed by brief explanations:

Indicator #1: The assessment mirrors the learning goals. Educators must be careful to ensure integrity in their evaluations. These must be in alignment with both the goals/standards and the instructional episodes leading up to testing for proficiency.

Indicator #2: The content of the assessment reflects the relative importance of each learning goal. We have previously discussed the process of backwards design. With the end in mind, educators must plan out the most critical outcomes related to knowledge, skills, and dispositions. The assignments and activities need to be equal to the weight each competency is given in the evaluations. Tomlinson argues that the summative assessments need to be developed in advance of the instructional activities.

Indicator #3: The format of the assessment is aligned with the cognitive level of the learning goal. If the learning goals expect learners to simply identify certain facts, then test items such as matching or fill in the blank are appropriate. However, if higher

---

[22] Cathy Vatterott, *Rethinking Grading: Meaningful Assessment for Standards-Based Learning* (Alexandria, VA: ASCD, 2015), 66–68.

order cognitive skills are required (synthesis or evaluation, for example), then test items requiring responses to novel problems are in order.

Indicator #4: The range of knowledge indicated by the learning goals is the range of knowledge reflected in instruction, which, in turn, is the range of knowledge needed to respond to assessment items. Once again, the importance of the alignment of the stated goals, the instructional activities, and the assessments are crucial. For example, if the expectation is for learners to evaluate and critique arguments, but the class activities emphasize summarizing other positions, then the two are out of alignment.

Indicator #5: An assessment should not require students to have specialized knowledge, understanding, skill, or resources beyond what is targeted by the learning goals and is taught in class. Here's where Tomlinson's theme of differentiation is evident. She argues that an ESL learner could be offered the opportunity to communicate proficiency in his or her first language and then have someone translate it. In addition, some outside projects may require specialized resources that put some students at a disadvantage.[23]

For Christian educators who are motivated to develop a testing philosophy from a biblical perspective, two verses in Proverbs provide the standard for excellence. In Prov 11:1, Solomon wrote, "Dishonest scales are detestable to the LORD, but an accurate weight is his delight." In Prov 20:23, he stated, "Differing weights are detestable to the Lord, and dishonest scales are unfair." Keep in mind the statistical term *validity*: Do our summative assessments measure what we say they measure? And the word *reliability*: Do our instruments measure learning consistently over time? We must commit to being diligent in our design and administration of assessments so that each student is fairly and accurately evaluated.

As a high school English teacher, I established an overarching outcome that I wanted to see my students embrace, a type of disposition related to the often-overwhelming study of a Shakespearean drama—given the opportunity to attend a play in the future, the students would choose to do so. (How many adults do you know who run the other way?) So early in the unit I announced the capstone or final evaluation for our study of *Romeo and Juliet.* Each student would propose a final project to be presented to the class that would portray that student's level of understanding of the themes and characters in the play, including staging, costumes, and props. The added bonus was that the presentations would collectively enhance each student's understanding as he or she learned from classmates. No final test about quotes, characters, or event sequences.

---

[23] Carol Ann Tomlinson and Tonya R. Moon, *Assessment and Student Success in a Differentiated Classroom* (Alexandria, VA: ASCD, 2013), 93–97.

No tortuous memorizing of lines, unless a student chose that as his or her presentation. Some designed elaborate costumes and explained the scene and characters who would wear them. Other students recruited friends and blocked out entire scenes and became the director of a performance. Some were fascinated with all the sword play and chose to present sketches of various weapons used in Elizabethan theater. A few built an entire Globe Theatre and pointed out production challenges and solutions. A few preferred library research, so we went in search of how this play has been interpreted over the years since its early performances in London. Interestingly enough, I never had a student request a paper/pencil exam as a replacement for a personalized presentation. And the learning experiences continued as the research and projects were presented. Tomlinson and Moon point out, "Summative assessments that are performance oriented (performance tasks, constructed response, and products) almost inevitably include room for differentiation in response to students' readiness, interest, and learning profile."[24]

Norm-Based or Criterion-Based Grading

Most grade levels, schools, and districts have established procedures for totaling grades and using summative assessments. On this point we would urge you to base your unit and semester grades on the comparison of each student's achievement to the established criteria for the learning outcomes. An alternative approach would be to compare an individual's performance to the other students in his or her class or grade level. Tomlinson and Moon argue that this second approach, the normative approach, weakens the validity and reliability of the assessments by introducing other variables—that is, the abilities of a unique group of learners. Secondly, it creates a sense of competition among students for receiving the higher grades as opposed to challenging a student to compete against himself or herself.[25]

Summative Becomes Formative

Contrary to perception and practice, the final grade on the project or unit test doesn't have to be the final chapter in learning. Brookhart maintains that excellent opportunities for continued growth follow a summative assessment. Some teachers allow students to resubmit another draft that builds on the instructor's feedback. Acknowledging that

---

[24] Tomlinson and Moon, 101.
[25] Tomlinson and Moon, 129–30.

some students would take advantage of this approach, Brookhart encourages educators to coach students to build on the recent feedback and apply what they learned in the next unit, particularly when course-specific skills are involved. This requires that the teacher plan and scaffold these skills in advance.[26]

Conclusion

Think of solitary moments during which you tried to polish a skill that was valuable to you . . . a private rehearsal room, a batting cage or empty gym, a library carrel where you crafted a passionate argument, a prayer closet where you asked the Lord's guidance. Reflect on the motivation that propelled you, the coaching tips that were woven into your thinking, and the words of encouragement that you had received along the way. Strikeouts, missed shots, tryouts ending in eliminations. These snapshots mesh with applause, awards, accomplishments. All these moments coalesce to make you an educator who will guide students as learners and achievers. But many of them will come to you lacking the intellectual and emotional resources you possess. Refining the tools of assessment will provide you with exceptional opportunities to impact their lives in ways you will only understand in eternity.

---

[26] Brookhart, *How to Give Effective Feedback to Your Students*, 45.

SECTION 3

Developing a
Learning Community

Building a Learning Community

Ken Coley

In this book, the authors have shared some of their own experiences in teaching in various settings, various levels, and various places around the world. Some of what has been shared has related to the topic of this next section, building a community of learners. So, what is a "community" of learners? Before we address this key component to a truly Christian philosophy of education, take a few minutes to complete the engagement activity.

ENGAGE: Jot down the different communities you have been a part of prior to or during college, including your current context. For example, athletic teams, Scouting, and church groups, school classes, musical groups, etc. What do they have in common? In what ways were/are they different? In what settings did you grow the most—intellectually, emotionally, and spiritually? What were the characteristics of the group that helped you to grow as a person? Keep these concepts in mind as you work through these chapters. Ask yourself, "How can I establish a community in which each learner flourishes?"

A Biblical Perspective on Community Building

The Lord inspired the crafting of Psalm 78, and in doing so gave his community of believers a clear mission to educate their children to know and follow their Creator:

2 ¶ I will declare wise sayings; I will speak mysteries from the past—

3 ¶ things we have heard and known and that our ancestors have passed down to us.

4 ¶ We will not hide them from their children but will tell a future generation the praiseworthy acts of the LORD, his might, and the wondrous works he has performed.

5 ¶ He established a testimony in Jacob and set up a law in Israel, which he commanded our ancestors to teach to their children

6 ¶ so that a future generation—children yet to be born—might know. They were to rise and tell their children

7 ¶ so that they might put their confidence in God and not forget God's works, but keep his commands.

The authors of the text embrace this passion to train future generations and have been privileged to train and learn from Christian educators from almost fifty states in the US and more than thirty-five countries all over the world.

Creating Community in Your Classroom

Let's take a moment to examine what we mean by the concept of community. Well-known educator Thomas Sergiovanni wrote, "Communities are collections of individuals who are bonded together by natural will and who are together bound to a set of shared ideas and ideals."[1] In a chapter entitled "Schools as Communities of Grace," Heckman paints a compelling picture for Christian educators:

Caring relationships within a confessional community provide an important key to effective schooling. A school as a community provides students with the moral, intellectual, social, and spiritual resources to live and serve

---

[1] Thomas Sergiovanni, *Leadership for the Schoolhouse: How Is It Different, Why Is It Important?* (San Francisco: Jossey-Bass, 1996), 48.

fully wherever God directs their pilgrim paths. The context of schooling is an important part of the content of schooling. Furthermore, Christian school communities should be characterized by grace so that the world sees that God is at work within them.[2]

William Purkey has spent his professional career designing what he calls the Invitational Theory of schooling. He selected this word because it brings to mind encouragement to receive something beneficial, as opposed to being pushed away. He describes the characteristics of his model:

- People are able, valuable, and responsible, and should be treated accordingly.
- Educating should be a collaborative, cooperative activity.
- The process is the product in the making.
- People possess untapped potential in all areas of worthwhile human endeavor.
- This potential can best be realized by places, policies, programs, and processes specifically designed to invite development and by people who are intentionally inviting with themselves and others, personally and professionally.[3]

As you read through this introduction and the following chapters, we challenge you to consider Purkey's five assumptions about invitational teaching. The authors of this text have brought this compassion and enthusiasm to their interactions with various audiences including many international audiences.

As a result of the extraordinary advances in technology and distance-learning options, more and more virtual classrooms in new countries are added to our teaching experiences each semester, and we experience the delight of interacting with new and diverse cultures. In a recent synchronous presentation, I noticed one moment in class during which doctoral students from the Dominican Republic, Rwanda, and Uganda were all speaking to each other during the discussion. Each in his/her context was wrestling with hindrances to theological higher education. The rest of the cohort just sat back and listened. So how do you bring all students into the conversation when in a virtual setting? These present new challenges to building community.

---

[2] Bruce Heckman, "Schools as Communities of Grace," in James L. Drexler, ed., *Educational Leadership, Relationships, and the Eternal Value of Christian Schooling* (Colorado Springs: Purposeful Design, 2007), 9.

[3] William Watson Purkey and John Michael Novak, "An Introduction to Invitational Theory," *Journal of Invitational Theory and Practice* (September 2015): 1.

Our experiences tell us that Christian educators share many qualities in common: joy in teaching, compassion, willingness to sacrifice for others and carry others' burdens, encouragement, desire to glorify the Lord, and the list could go on. In short, the similarities among Christian educators are more numerous than the differences. As creatures, created in the image of God as social beings, we can build community better when we are manifesting Christlike characteristics. Better results should occur in a Christian setting than in any other.

And on every continent the Lord is using his educators to build communities of learners to grow spiritually, intellectually, physically, emotionally, and socially. If you look up the definition of *community*, you will observe that there is a theme repeated throughout the half dozen different definitions—the root word *common*. People from the same neighborhood, school, and church share many things "in common." They usually include things like dress, accents, and gestures. Acts of hospitality and manners are some of the behaviors that are shared.

It does not take long to discover the values, attitudes, and beliefs that are generally shared. For example, my conferences and classes that I taught in the United States, Canada, and Ukraine always started on time and the students were punctual and time conscious, especially when the schedule and the clock said it was time to end. In cities like Port-au-Prince, Santiago, Kinshasa, and Jinja, students were less likely to be stressed about starting on time. However, in the latter contexts, connecting with others and building community were given a higher priority than in the other three contexts.

Being an Educator or Learner in a New Culture

Fisher, Frey, and Almarode maintain that many of the characteristics of a successful Professional Learning Community (higher education or professional development beyond basic PreK–12 education) are also present in Student Learning Communities (PreK–12). They see structures that allow for and encourage collaboration as vital. Second, the presence of supportive, positive relationships is found in both. Third, agreed upon values and vision are essential. Fourth, the intentional practice of learning together leads to necessary teamwork skills.[4]

My middle schoolers invited me into their community and changed me forever with just one question: "Mr. Coley, where do you stay?" As a rookie teacher in a new

---

[4] Douglas Fisher, Nancy Frey, and John Almarode, *Student Learning Communities: A Springboard for Academic and Social-Emotional Development* (Alexandria, VA: ASCD, 2021), 5.

state, I had never considered a person's home location in this way. Fortunately, I caught on quickly and described the nearby town and apartment where I "stayed" when I was not at school. One word opened a deeper understanding of the students in my class, their life experiences, and the vocabulary that expressed their community's shared experience. This was a cultural experience, the first of countless encounters that make me who I am today. Craig Ott, author of *Teaching and Learning across Cultures*, provides insights into our challenges as educators in new worlds:

> Teachers tend to teach others in the same manner by which they were taught, and if they do change their teaching methods, it will be in ways that are most naturally them. Teaching methods, expectations about relationships between teachers and learners, the institutional parameters of teaching, and even the physical conditions of teaching are all influenced by culture. Thus, teaching that comes naturally and is effective in one's home culture can become like the proverbial square peg trying to fit in a round hole when it is attempted in another culture.[5]

Two US public school educators, Laurie Barron and Patti Kinney, simplify the discussion with one profound word, *belonging*. To what extent do learners recognize that they are accepted and valued on the school campus and in your classroom? Barron and Kinney state, "Schools offer multiple and unique social situations for young people to develop a sense of belonging—or, conversely, to have their sense of belonging thwarted. Thus, schools are critical settings for attending to the need to belong."[6] This theme is at the heart of this third section and should be woven into your philosophy of Christian Education. For example, even discipline, when done for the right purposes, indicates belonging. "The Lord disciplines the one he loves" (Heb 12:6). Certainly, our attitudes, investment of extra time and patience, and loving care for diverse and English language learners, is also a manifestation of inviting to belong. Effective assessment practices that include both formative (as the students are learning a new skill or concept) and summative (more formal and final evaluation of learning) should show grace and encouragement that creates a wonderful family-like belonging.

---

[5] Craig Ott, *Teaching and Learning Across Cultures: A Guide to Theory and Practice* (Grand Rapids: Baker Academic, 2021), 4.

[6] Laurie Barron and Patti Kinney, *We Belong: 50 Strategies to Create Community and Revolutionize Classroom Management* (Alexandria, VA: ASCD, 2021), 2.

Building a learning community has been woven into the fabric of our faith community from the earliest records. In Deuteronomy 6 parents and teachers are charged with the responsibility to "teach these things to your children." The value of children is referred to in Ps 127:3 (NLT), "Children are a gift from the Lord, they are a reward from him." Years later Solomon would write, "Train up a child in the way he should go; even when he is old he will not depart from it" (Prov 22:6 ESV). Jesus likewise points to the value of children and exhorts us to teach well. In Matt 19:14 (NIV), Jesus said, "Let the little children come to me, and do not hinder them, for the kingdom of heaven belongs to such as these." Paul also adds his voice when he instructs, "Fathers, don't stir up anger in your children, but bring them up in the training and instruction of the Lord" (Eph 6:4). The next generation and those that follow depend on the faithful and accurate transmission of our faith to them. Many related skills involving reading, writing, speaking, critical thinking, and problem-solving are closely related to teaching God's Word.

At first glance it may not be obvious how the chapters clustered in this section fit together. Consider some of the following values that you may plan to incorporate into your philosophy of teaching: the dignity inherent in each student; the importance of equality of opportunity that should be present in your classroom and school; the celebration of differences as a response to the diversity throughout your school community. These examples illustrate how children, teens, and adults can work together to build a productive learning community.

Most educators are familiar with the authors Wiggins and McTighe's phrase, "Start with the end in mind."[7] In their text, *Understanding by Design*, they coach curriculum planners to carry out "backwards design," as was addressed in chapter 6. This three-step process begins with a strategic decision:

1. What results do I want to achieve in the lives of my students?
2. What data do I need to determine if I am successful?
3. What educational experiences do students need to achieve these results?

No matter the locale, parents, educators, and community leaders must accept the challenge to chart a course and navigate treacherous waters to arrive at a predetermined destination.[8] This is true, as well, for building a community of learners. What is the

---

[7] Grant Wiggins and Jay McTighe, *Understanding by Design* (Alexandria, VA: ASCD, 2005).

[8] Wiggins and McTighe, 7–19.

target or aim, how will I know how or if the aim has been accomplished, and what will I do as a teacher to work toward that aim with my students?

Here's how the Center for the Developing Child (Harvard University) puts this:

> Learning communities provide a space and a structure for people to align around a shared goal. Effective communities are both aspirational and practical. They connect people, organizations, and systems that are eager to learn and work across boundaries, all the while holding members accountable to a common agenda, metrics, and outcomes. These communities enable participants to share results and learn from each other, thereby improving their ability to achieve rapid yet significant progress.[9]

ENGAGE: Using the three UbD questions in the preceding paragraph, select one potential goal for your classroom and think through how you will use instructional goals to strengthen your classroom community.

1. What is the target or aim?
2. How will I know when the students have accomplished them?
3. What instructional activities will I use to assist them along the way?

I met such a leader in Orlando, Florida, at a Christian school conference. When I inquired about his school, he explained with great joy that he was a pastor who led a church to sponsor a Christian school. The K–12 program had exploded, and there were plans underway to add a two-year postgraduate degree, similar to a community college. With clarity and passion, he described one of the goals they had in mind— every student would possess some type of trade certification at the time of his or her graduation (electrician, plumber, cosmetologist, etc.). All their planning was based upon this result. His leadership and vision were truly inspiring. What is your vision for your class or school?

The chapters in section 3 will present principles related to building a learning community while valuing each individual. For example, the exceptional value of each student as being "God's workmanship" is acknowledged in classroom procedures that require respect for each class member, both his or her physical safety and emotional well-being as cooperative learning takes place. A student's dignity is acknowledged as respectful discipline policies are carried out in ways that demonstrate fairness across

---

[9] "Learning Communities," Center on the Developing Child, Harvard University, 2021, https://developingchild.harvard.edu/collective-change/key-concepts/learning-communities.

the school. Empathy is modeled by teachers as they carry out management and discipline policies and classmates learn to show compassion for others who are different in backgrounds and talents. As students are taught these skills, each earns a sense of success, and classmates learn from his or her contributions. Assessment procedures are designed to acknowledge that students have different readiness, skills, and aptitudes but celebrate all students' potential and ability to achieve academic successes.

ENGAGE: Following the model of the previous paragraph, select an attitude or value that you plan to emphasize in this aspect of your philosophy of Christian education, building a community of learners. Identify in what ways that value/attitude enhances the overall community spirit of your classroom and school. Put another way, as that value permeates the culture, how does the school become a stronger learning community? Then trace that quality through the chapters in this section. Begin to jot down ideas now and craft your response as you read each chapter.

CHAPTER 8

Classroom Management

Marti MacCullough

What Do the Polls Say?

National polls taken in the USA report parental concerns and even frustration about discipline and classroom management in schools. Every few years one or more educational research associations conduct surveys on school effectiveness. Usually there are questions related to discipline in schools as a part of the survey. Phi Delta Kappa, a US professional organization for educators, reported that just 14 percent of all parents express "a lot" of trust in their school to handle discipline. Among teachers, moreover, just a narrow majority (53 percent) trust the school where they teach to handle discipline fairly.[1]

Another organization addressed the topic of school discipline and urged parents to ask questions about this topic when they are planning to enroll their child in an international school. The organization provides tips for inquiring into the effectiveness of the school. Parents who are deciding about specific internationals schools (of the more than 2,000 listed on their website) are encouraged to ask the question, "How is the student's behavior in your international school?" Tip #9 asks the following: "Does

---

[1] Phi Delta Kappa, *Frustration in the Schools, PDK 2019 of Public Attitudes Toward the Public Schools*, PDKPoll, accessed January 2021, https://pdkpoll.org/wp-content/uploads/2020/05/pdkpoll51-2019.pdf.

the school properly deal with disciplinary problems? Some international schools, unfortunately, are lax on discipline, and problem children and their disruptive behavior can adversely affect other children's learning."[2]

A study conducted on schools in forty-one countries by Chiu and Chow concluded that school discipline is associated with the values of a culture and does affect learning.[3] Addressing discipline in schools is a worldwide task in the twenty-first century. While the concept of discipline is embedded in cultural values and norms, we will address it from a biblical perspective that crosses all cultures.

While polls and research do not tell the whole story, they do represent attitudes and concerns of the general public. The Phi Delta Kappa quote earlier was from the 2019 poll of public attitudes about public schools in America, *Frustration in the Schools*. Note the title of the poll includes the term *frustration*. Year after year, the annual Gallup Poll has shown the need for increased teacher understanding and skills for classroom management and discipline. Responses reported in the 2019 *Communities in Schools/ Gallup: Discipline in School* survey reflect these concerns. To the question on prepared-ness of "most" teachers "to handle discipline issues in the classroom," 54 percent of those polled, questioned teacher preparation indicating that most teachers are "very unprepared" (18 percent) or "unprepared" (36 percent). The poll offered several options for improvement. The two options selected with 90 percent agreement were "more training for school administrators and teachers on appropriate discipline practices," and "increased efforts to foster a positive school environment."[4] These two options for training will be addressed in this chapter and the next.

Private schools have been included in the samples of polls as well. One such poll was conducted by Education Next in 2016. The poll indicated that private school parents are the most satisfied with their choice of schools for their children includ-ing school discipline (46 percent) compared to public school parents (17 percent) or

---

[2] "How is the students' behavior at your international school?" International School Community, March 11, 2019, https://internationalschoolcommunity.com/blog/tag/classroom -discipline/.

[3] See Ming Ming Chiu and Bonnie Wing Yin Chow, "Classroom Discipline Across Forty-One Countries: School, Economic, and Cultural Differences," *Journal of Cross-Cultural Psychology* 42, no. 3 (2011).

[4] "Gallup Poll Discipline in the Schools," Communities in Schools, accessed January 2021, https://www.communitiesinschools.org/our-data/publications/publication/gallup-poll -discipline-schools.

charter school parents (34 percent). Percentages include the response of very satisfied and satisfied.[5]

From a very small sampling of American research surveys, it appears that, overall, there are major concerns about discipline policies, practices, and teacher preparation. The problems identified are also seen in schools around the world to some extent for varied reasons. Even though one cannot draw conclusions from one survey nor generalize to other private schools not in the sample, it is worth noting that parents in private schools in this survey seem to be more satisfied with teachers and the disciplinary procedures and practices of their schools than are parents in public (non-charter) schools in the United States. You may already have some answers as to why this might be so.

Why write about classroom management and student discipline; aren't they the same? You may be wondering why the title of this chapter includes classroom management *and* student discipline and why both are in a book on instructional design for effective teaching and learning, specifically in the section on building a community of learners. There are at least three key answers: (1) Classroom management and student discipline, although related, are different in character, and teachers must understand the differences to be effective educators. (2) Instructional design must include principles and practices for effective management of the classroom if the design is to work well. (3) Both class management and student discipline are essential to building a caring and effective community of learners. In this chapter we introduce the tandem pair by addressing classroom management followed by two chapters on student discipline.

What Is Classroom Management?

Harry and Rosemary Wong have been influential in helping teachers develop sound classroom management practices. When I taught the Discipline Seminar at the university level, my teacher education students used the Wongs' book *The First Days of School* to develop effective procedures and practices for classroom management. Our pre-service teachers interviewed several teachers to compare their practices to those in the book. Wong and Wong describe classroom management by stating that it is "the

---

[5] Samuel Barrows, Paul E. Peterson, and Martin R. West, "What Do Parents Think of Their Children's Schools?" *Education Next* 17, no. 2 (2017), https://www.educationnext.org /what-do-parents-think-of-childrens-schools-ednext-private-district-charter/.

practices and procedures a teacher uses to maintain the environment in which instruction and learning can occur."[6]

Harry Wong uses a study conducted by Julie Sanford many years ago to describe a
well-managed classroom. According to the study, there are several key characteristics of
a well-managed classroom: (1) students are deeply involved with their work, especially
with academic, teacher-led instruction; (2) students know what is expected of them and
are generally successful; (3) there is relatively little wasted time, confusion, or disrup-
tion; and (4) the climate of the classroom is work-oriented but relaxed and pleasant.[7]

The Classroom Teaching Skills, edited by James M. Cooper, Carol Weinstein, and
Wilford Weber describes *classroom management* as "the actions teachers take to create
an environment that is respectful, caring, orderly, and productive."[8] I appreciate the
addition of *social skill development* described by Weinstein and Weber. The definitions
above for classroom management focus on what the teacher does. Keep this in mind
as we explore the difference between classroom management and student discipline.

My Own Operating Definition

*Classroom management includes all of the planned procedures and practices necessary to main-
tain an effective group environment in which learning and social development can occur.* The
focus of classroom management is (1) on the class as a group, (2) on the teacher and
the teacher's expectations, and (3) on the total environment for learning. The focus
of student discipline, however, is different and will be addressed later. My personal
label for the ideal classroom atmosphere is "relaxed structure." This book addresses
the development of an effective community of learners, and this, of course, includes
classroom management.

A First-Year Teacher's Journey

Several years ago I conducted a seminar on classroom management and discipline.
When our time had come to an end, a young teacher in her first year out of college

---

[6] Harry Wong and Rosemary Wong, *The Classroom Management Book* (Mountain View,
CA: Harry K. Wong, 2014), 2.

[7] Julie Sandford et al., "Improving Classroom Management," *Educational Leadership* 40,
no 7 (April 1983) in Harry Wong, *The Well-Managed Classroom* (Professional References for
Teachers, Holt, Rinehart and Winston), 1; accessed April 2021, https://www.wtc.ie/images/pdf
/Classroom_Management/cm6.PDF.

[8] Carol Weinstein and Wilford Weber, *The Classroom Teaching Skills*, ed. James M. Cooper
(Belmont, CA: Cengage, 2011), 230.

came up to me in tears. She was considering leaving the profession she loved because of the inability to handle a classroom full of students. As we chatted, there were two things that impressed me. First, she admitted that she had used a weak set of classroom procedures to organize the class beginning on day one of the school year. Second, she had asked for help from more seasoned and successful teachers and was trying to undo early bad habits of her students by using some of their ideas. This was good news. I knew she was a learner!

Through tears, however, she shared what she had learned in her teacher education program at a state university: if she had discipline problems it was *all* her fault. This indeed was bad news; her tears after the seminar, however, were tears of relief. Through the seminar, she was given hope by beginning to understand the difference between classroom management and the much bigger and more complex concept of student discipline. She began to understand human nature as involving will (choice), thinking and reflecting, emotions, and a flawed nature because of the fall of humanity resulting in a sin nature that needs outside intervention. She realized that effective classroom management strategies and procedures would prevent some discipline situations but certainly not all. She was willing to learn.

You may be a first-year or a seasoned teacher reading this book. This chapter on classroom management may not be needed by you if your procedures and practices for managing a classroom are already sound. A good set of procedures will reduce the number and severity of student discipline problems but will not erase all of these. It is helpful to know the difference between discipline and classroom management, whether you are new to the profession or one who has taught for many years.

How Is Student Discipline Different from Classroom Management?

While classroom management is about classroom organization and procedures to foster *group* functioning for the sake of learning, discipline is different. In fact, the term *classroom discipline* is a misnomer. Discipline is individual. In this book we use the term *student discipline* (singular) to refer to the process that involves changes in thinking and acting on the part of a student.

Some educators today use the term *behavior management* to describe discipline. However, that term connotes a "management of the student" or what the teacher does rather than what the student thinks, learns, and does. I do not use the term *behavior "management"* as a synonym for discipline. Some current books on discipline confuse the two terms—classroom management and discipline—and in many cases view discipline as equal to punishment. To those authors who hold this view, discipline is a negative concept. But this is not an accurate use of the term *discipline*, especially when viewing it from a biblical perspective. Below are two definitions of discipline that focus on far more than classroom management and are not negative but rather positive in focus.

ENGAGE: As you read the definitions below, select the elements of discipline that are positive. Discipline is:

> "training that corrects, molds or perfects the mental faculties or moral character."[9]

> "training expected to produce a specific character or pattern of behavior, especially training that produces moral or mental improvement"[10]

Did you find the key targets for discipline according to these definitions? At least two are provided: moral and mental improvement. Discipline is education or learning that produces *moral* and *mental* improvement. It is a learning event that impacts the character and the thinking of an individual and ultimately the behaviors as well. I personally do not use the term *training*, as used in these two definitions, because it connotes a certain type of learning that is rather automatic and not thoughtful. So, I prefer to use the broader term *education* that includes training but much more. "Discipline is *education or learning* that produces moral and mental improvement." If discipline is a learning event, then our understanding and practices should fit with our accepted theory of learning (see chapter 3).

Other Views about Discipline

Many books written on the topic of discipline use behavioristic principles and strategies even though the authors are advocates for cognitive interactive instructional strategies for their general classroom teaching. This may create a problem for teachers that will be addressed in the next chapter.

While Wong and Wong contribute significantly to the development of classroom management procedures, they miss the purpose and effects of discipline, in my view. According to the Wongs, "Discipline, although necessary, does not lead to learning. It only stops deviant behavior. In most cases, getting students to behave entails nothing

---

[9] *Merriam-Webster*, s.v. "discipline," third entry, accessed June 2021, https://www.merriam-webster.com/dictionary/discipline.

[10] Farlex, The Free Dictionary, s.v. "discipline," accessed June 2021, https://www.thefreedictionary.com/discipline.

more than coercing students to comply."[11] This statement seems to reflect the understanding that discipline is equal to punishment (negative), and does not involve learning. This view will be challenged by addressing discipline from a biblical perspective. Likewise, in *Classroom Teaching Skills*, chapter 8, contributors Weinstein and Weber view classroom management as the universal set and discipline as a small subset that must be addressed in unique ways. In their book, behavioristic approaches (discipline is not a learning experience but simply stops a bad behavior) are used for discipline problems while so much of the book champions interactive learning for overall classroom instruction.[12]

Some educators view discipline as "what we do *to* an individual after misbehavior occurs" while viewing classroom management as preventative. It is true that there will be fewer discipline situations in classrooms that practice effective organizational procedures; however, there is much more to discipline than many educators seem to understand. As we address student discipline in the next chapter, we will use a far more robust understanding of discipline as a *learning* event.

Classroom management expectations and procedures are preferences of the teacher, and while they may be related in some way to one's philosophy of education or theory of learning, they are simply organizational and functional in character. On the other hand, discipline is directly related to one's philosophy of education and theory of human learning, as you will see in the next chapter.

Developing a Set of Procedures for Classroom Management

When does a teacher begin to plan for classroom management? Planning must begin prior to the opening of the school year and be available to initiate on the very first day. The teacher must consider several things in planning:

- the physical space available and the potential number of students
- the grade level of the students
- the preferred instructional approach, strategies, and methods that are to be used
- the cultural makeup of the class in general

This is a major task for first-year teachers.

---

[11] Wong and Wong, *The Classroom Management Book*, 9.
[12] See Weinstein and Weber in *Classroom Teaching Skills*, chap. 8.

Seasoned teachers may evaluate the previous year's effectiveness and simply tweak or modify procedures for the new year. Procedures and expectations should help to build a learning community in which all students can grow academically, socially, and personally. Developing an effective learning community is integral to a well-functioning classroom and is the subject of section 3. These chapters should be linked together for implementation.

What are the categories of procedures that require careful planning? Below is a chart of potential categories, adapted from my book *Flourishing in the Classroom: A Guide for Classroom Management and Student Discipline*.[13] However, these are found variously in many books on the topic.

I. Materials and Equipment	IV. Instructional Routines
Distribution of materials	Question and answer
Collection of materials	Learning activities
Storing location of personal things	Noise control
	Paying attention to the teacher
II. Entrances/Exits	Getting help from others
Entering the room	Free time
Taking attendance	Talking
Leaving the room	Ending lesson (secondary)
Bathroom and water needs	Ending of day (elementary)
Taking attendance	
III. Movement within the Classroom	
Seating arrangement	
Wastebasket	
Pencil sharpener	
Movement to groups	
Safety drills	

The teacher must ask, "What will I have the students do for each of the areas listed above and possibly others depending on the school and its environment?" Selected procedures must be taught. It must be noted, however, that procedures are not the same as rules. We address rules under discipline in the next chapter. Patience and repetition are important as procedures are learned and habituated. When a student consistently and defiantly will not follow the procedures, the behavior becomes a discipline issue.

---

[13] See Martha MacCullough, *Flourishing in the Classroom: A Guide for Classroom Management and Student Discipline Informed by a Christ-Centered Worldview* (Wheaton, IL: Wheaton Press, 2019).

ENGAGE: Identify one age-appropriate procedure for your future classroom (see list in chart above) and describe how you would explain and rehearse that procedure.

Considering the Physical Environment

Before teachers address possible procedures, they must consider their physical environment. What kind of seating arrangement do you prefer? This will depend on several things: the age level of the students, the number of students in the class, the available space, and adopted learning approach. For example, do you want the students to work in quads, cooperative groups, or clusters? Do you want to have them seated in a circle or horseshoe (providing there is enough room)? Do you prefer rows and columns but allow for movement of chairs into circles or to work in pairs? Do you have seats that cannot be moved (fixed to the floor) and you cannot change this situation? If you were assigned a classroom filled with large, multi-student desks and long benches, how would you proceed? What are some obstacles or challenges that may confront you? Does your early childhood classroom have kidney-shaped tables to be used for some activities and corners or rugs for others? Make a visual assessment of your space.

Deciding the preferred physical arrangement of seats or desks is usually up to the teacher and can be changed for certain teaching situations as needed. Always have the seating arrangement determined for the first day and decide how you will tell the students where to sit. Changes can be made later if necessary.

ENGAGE: Use the grid below or graph paper to draw the physical arrangement of door/s, tables, desks, rug space for instruction, your desk, location for teaching supplies, location for storing student backpacks or bags, and other special things for your classroom: bathroom (if there is one in the room), science equipment, music stands and equipment, layout of the gym for PE teachers, standard objects such as an aquarium, etc. If you are not yet teaching, create an ideal room. Multiple free classroom planning apps are available on the internet for teachers, or you may use graph paper to lay out your room. See footnote for one example of a free floor plan site.[14]

---

[14] "Editable Classroom Floor-Plan, Set-Up, Design, & Seating Chart," Teachers Pay Teachers, accessed January 13, 2022, https://www.teacherspayteachers.com/Product/Editable -Classroom-Floor-Plan-Set-Up-Design-Seating-Chart-2619874?gclid=Cj0KCQiAuP -OBhDqARIsAD4XHpcEwUMztCbvMEjj24F4IjJZ2joZbYI3f7lrmQpwv.

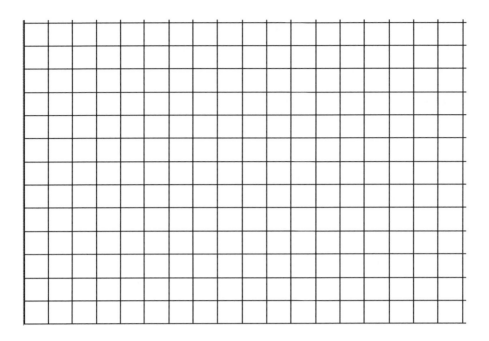

Take the grid and troubleshoot for accessibility, practicality, and effectiveness. How will this arrangement help to maintain order, prevent chaos, and enhance learning? Will this serve the learning community well? You may wish to discuss this with other teachers or prospective teachers.

Seating on the First Day

For early childhood classrooms, it is suggested that the names of each student be placed on the desk or table as assigned. When the children enter the classroom, the teacher will escort each one, in turn, to the prearranged seat and show the student his or her name, thus personalizing the space. The teacher may have something special for students to look at or do at their desks or table while they wait.

For elementary classrooms, name placards may also be placed on the assigned desk or table. At this level, there is little need to escort students to the desk or table where their name appears (for most students). You may allow older elementary level students to select their own seat on the first day and then use their choices to create a seating chart. Be aware that this may cause some uncomfortable situations. For example, a student may not wish to sit next to a certain person, however that seat is the only one left. This situation is less uncomfortable if the teacher has selected the seats. In addition, even if you wish to allow students (at a later day) to choose their seats, assigned seats for the first week will aid the teacher in learning the names and faces of their students. Be aware of various heights and size of students as you evaluate the seat assigned for comfort.

For secondary level, some teachers prefer assigned seats for the first week or two while they are learning names, a task significantly more complex than the task of elementary teachers because of the number of students they see each day. After the initial weeks, teachers at this level may use free seating. They will announce, "Sit wherever you wish on Monday," for example. This is a privilege, and students will be held accountable for behaviors that hinder learning such as too much talking at the wrong time to a friend. The privilege can be taken away. To take away a privilege, you must have privileges in your class. Allowing students to choose where they sit can be instrumental, as well, in having them show up on time for fear of missing the opportunity to sit by a friend.

ENGAGE: If you are a seasoned teacher, take a minute to evaluate your practices related to seating. If you are a new teacher, take time to write out what you intend to plan for seating students on the first day.

Principles for Managing a Class Effectively

Principle #1: Knowing names *before* students arrive is vital in building community and in sharing expectations for the class. Rehearse names and faces ahead of time. Available technology assists in providing pictures with names. If this is not available, in-class pictures on the first day may be taken using a cellphone or smartphone. This will provide opportunity for teachers to rehearse names with faces before day two.

In my graduate classes, I prepare a PowerPoint slide with pictures of class members that I have collected from the university electronic files. I practice names as I view their faces before the first class. Some of the students are surprised when I know first names on day one. I have to admit that graduate classes are usually smaller in number than the 35–40 students in some undergrad classes and in many high school classes as well. A smaller number of students makes the task much easier. Pictures, with names, will help no matter the size of the class! Community building begins on the first day with a personal touch of knowing names.

Principle #2: Teach the expectations for class decorum *as needed*. Not all will be needed on the first day. Learning is more effective if procedures are taught in the context in which they are needed at the time.

Principle #3: On the first day get acquainted *and* get started! Some teachers do not include both getting acquainted and getting academically started on the first day and miss opportunities to set the stage for classroom decorum.

What Procedures Will Be Needed on the First Day?

Each state or school district in the USA selects the organizational model for school years. In general, school education covers prekindergarten or kindergarten through high school; however, the divisions vary. Countries around the world vary in the number of years of education and the divisions. The labels for grade levels used for suggestions below are arbitrary, and readers will need to determine where their class might fit. Because entrance into the classroom is needed first, we begin here.

Entrance Procedures

Entrance into the school building is usually an all-school procedure that all students must follow. Entrance procedures into a classroom are usually the responsibility of the teacher. What are your expectations for *entrance* into your classroom? Is there more than one door to enter the room? If so, how will you handle entrance into the room? Your expectations will, of course, vary with age level. Below are suggestions to consider.

Early Childhood: Prekindergarten through 1st grade (approximate ages 4–6)

Some schools have the children line up outside or in a hallway when they arrive. Each class is led inside by the classroom teacher or aide. Some schools allow the parents to deliver their child to the classroom. Usually, the school has entrance procedures for young children designed for safety and order. New teachers should make sure they are aware of all-school procedures before day one.

Effective and caring teachers will greet each child by name with a warm smile and perhaps say, "I am so glad you are here" or offer a fist bump or high five to each one. They will also make sure each child knows where to sit. But what do the students do next? Do they hang their jackets or coats at an assigned place? Do they place their personal materials and perhaps lunch containers in an assigned location? Or do they go directly to their desks or table, and when instructed, hang up their jackets and store their personal items in predetermined places? On the first day it is best to have them take a seat and then learn where to place their personal items. This is a procedural lesson for the first day. On day two this might be repeated, and on day three remind them where to hang their jackets and place other items *before* they take their seats and see how they do. Some will need help, others not.

ELEMENTARY/PRIMARY: 2ND THROUGH 5TH GRADE (APPROXIMATE AGES 7–10)

Use the school's procedures for entrance into the building. Lower levels may have the classroom teacher escort the students to the room for the first few days or as a regular practice. Is there a bell to indicate when to enter? Are there different procedures in cold or extreme hot weather? These are things an administrator or head of school will need to determine. Teachers decide what the students will do after they enter the room. It is wise to meet and greet students warmly at the door each day and, on the first day, have them find their name placard located where they will be seated. Help them as needed.

Instructions for hanging jackets and storing personal items will be necessary on the first day. It is prudent to have backpacks stored in a location other than on the floor where children could trip. One possibility is that school bags could be placed under the hooks on which coats or jackets are hung. There should be a procedure for taking out needed materials *before* placing their bags at the assigned place. "Take a seat, remove materials from your bag, and quietly walk to the back or side of the room and place your bag in the assigned place."

When homework has been assigned, sometime after day one, students will be instructed to take out needed materials such as paper, notebooks, and pencils or pens, and take out their homework to have ready for use in class or ready to place in a bin that will be passed around at the beginning of class. Then students are to carefully place their school bags and perhaps lunch bag or box (if they bring lunch) in the assigned place and return to their seats. To avoid chaos, you might wish to call on sections of your seating arrangement one at a time. This will avoid having too many students up at the same time. Eventually, however, the students should learn how to do this in an orderly fashion as they enter the room each day.

MIDDLE SCHOOL: 6TH THROUGH 8TH GRADE (APPROXIMATE AGES 11–14)

Entrance into the school building is an all-school procedure. Some middle schools, especially if they begin at the 5th grade level, use the model for entrance that most elementary schools use. Students are assigned a main teacher for each grade level, one who may teach most or several subjects. Perhaps these same students will move to one or two other rooms for instruction by other teachers during the school day. Movement, however, is limited.

Another model has the teachers moving from classroom to classroom rather than the students. Students begin the day with a main or homeroom teacher who is responsible for several clerical activities such as taking roll, reporting absentees, encouraging social interaction that is positive community-building, and listening to any all-school announcements. Students stay in the same room for most of the day. The next period may be taught by the homeroom teacher or another teacher who comes to the room. If this model is used, the practices addressed under elementary, above, can be used and modified for the age level. However, the team of teachers, whether just two or more, must work together on classroom procedures to allow for continuity.

Many middle schools are organized to move the students from room to room for each subject area after they have begun the day in their homeroom or advisory room. When students arrive at their "homeroom," the assigned teacher will set up the procedures for seating and select either free seating or assigned seating. There are additional functional issues that must be addressed before students move to period one; for example, attendance, announcements given by the main office through the school sound system, taking orders for lunch or storing lunch bags, and other clerical tasks. Establish procedures for these as well. How will you take attendance? What may the students do during this time and during announcements, etc.? If you are a homeroom/advisory teacher, procedures for the start of the day are vital and should be consistent.

HIGH SCHOOL: 9TH THROUGH 12TH GRADE (APPROXIMATE AGES 15–18)

Most high schools utilize departmental organization for their classes in which students move from room to room to a specific department for their next subject. Students are assigned a "homeroom" teacher to take care of clerical issues and to form a common community of students that will provide an opportunity for social development. Each department teacher will receive approximately 15 to 30 students for each of the four or five classes they teach. Learning the names of 75 to 150 students is not an easy task, but it is important; so too are entrance expectations.

Procedures for entering the classroom must be taught and retaught. Individual teachers develop their own set of management procedures and these may be different from yours; it will be necessary to remind your students of *your* expectations, especially during the first weeks of the school year. Are they to take a seat immediately when they enter? Where will they place their jackets or sweaters and when? What essential materials will they take out of their school bags or backpacks immediately before storing them for the class period? Will you have a "problem of the day" for mathematics, or a sentence to "fix" for English, projected or written on a white- or chalkboard for them to begin working on immediately after they have stored their school bags? May they talk quietly until you are ready to begin? I allowed quiet talking during this time, and it worked well. The students will talk anyway! However, permission to talk quietly will let them know that you are in charge of classroom decorum and understand their desire to talk with one another. Permission may sound something like this: "You may talk quietly while we take care of some clerical issues and while you are removing things from your school bags for storage. When we are ready to begin, I will move to the front of the room and ask for your attention. Thank you!"

Where will they place their school bags? This is a huge decision, as you will discover in the chapter on discipline. The teacher, as well as the students, must be able to walk safely around the room without tripping over obstacles. Bags or backpacks should be placed, for example, in the back of the room or in a student's assigned place after they have removed their materials for the day.

ENGAGE: What other classroom procedures and expectations must be addressed on the first day? Think of the grade level you teach or will teach in the future and determine what other procedures will need to be taught that first day.

List these here: _____

_____

_____

_____

_____

Exit Procedures

Instructions for how to *exit* the classroom will be needed. How will you dismiss the class at the end of the class period or at the end of the day? What are some possibilities that will enhance classroom order rather than promote chaos?

LOWER LEVELS

PreK–K students may be escorted to the exit door at the end of the day and wait there for a parent to pick them up. Care must be taken to assure they are not taken by a stranger or by a person not identified by the family (school procedures should be developed to prevent this). Other arrangements include having a parent come to the classroom for pickup. In some schools, a school bus is designated for this level and the teacher escorts the students to the bus or busses. Usually, students have a tag pinned on their blouse or shirt to indicate the bus on which they should ride. Many of these procedures are determined by the school leadership; however, the classroom teacher will be involved in carrying them out.

Elementary level teachers will dismiss their classes for such subjects as music, physical education, lunch, and special events. On the first day, perhaps the only class dismissal will be at lunch or at the end of the day. At that time, you will begin to teach your expectations for exiting the room. Will you have students line up at the door as you dismiss them by groups or tables or rows, or by alphabet of last name? Will you wait until all are in line to dismiss the class with instructions for hallway decorum (usually set by the school administration). You may be required by your school leaders to escort the class to the next location. The school in which I taught middle level grades dismissed students at the end of the day by transportation: bussed, car pickup, or walkers. If this is so, how will you organize this? Or is this the task of the school leadership and you just institute the procedures? Ask, or read the school manual carefully.

End-of-the-day expectations are more than how to exit. What will be your expectations for the physical appearance of the room before the students pack up and exit? At the end of the day, and before dismissal, will you require a clean desk and waste papers around the desks placed in a trash basket that is carried around the room by a class helper? (Note: to have each student take trash to the trash basket right at the end of the day could create chaos!)

In the school in which I worked for several years, students were required to clean around their desks and put their chairs upside down on top of their desks to assist those who swept the floor each night. This was an all-school regulation and saved time and money for the school. Decide on procedures for preparing for exiting the class and leaving it as neat as possible.

Middle School and High School

Each period of the day requires exits. Multiple teachers will be seen by the students each day and each will have his or her own expectations. Reminders of *your* expectations will be more frequent during the first few weeks. How do you want the class to exit? Do you have a school bell that rings to change classes? Do you dismiss by the clock at a specified time? A bell or intercom announcement makes the dismissal time uniform. Do you require the students to wait for your word of dismissal even when there is a bell or clock or intercom notification? Or do you allow them to get their bags, pack up, and leave when they are ready? You decide the best approach for you and your classes. But make sure that your students know and understand your expectations. Do not leave it to chance! It is a good idea to discuss your practices with other teachers on your team and perhaps agree on exit requirements. This is helpful to the students and teachers.

Note on intercom systems: Schools that utilize intercoms for communication use these for emergency information, announcements, paging teachers and students, and room-to-room communication. Teachers are often provided distress codes for medical emergencies, unruly students, safety threats, or missing student communications. Some schools that do not have access to intercoms use smartphones with emergency connections to the office.

Other Procedures Taught on the First Day as the Need Arises

- Use of bathroom and drinking water passes
- Getting attention of the class by the teacher
- How to listen and respond when others speak
- Asking questions
- Distributing and collecting papers, if necessary, on day one
- How to label papers with name, class period, name of subject, and date (middle and secondary level). Teach them where you want them to write that information, upper right corner or left; this is your preference.
- Group or pairs work expectations (if you have groups or pairs on the first day)
- Discarding waste materials and pencil sharpening, etc.
- Safety issues (This is where a procedure will be combined with a rule that sounds something like this: "Do what the teacher asks you to do when you are asked." This should be on every short list of rules and will be addressed in the next chapter.) The procedure is what the students are expected to do when the fire alarm or emergency alarm rings, the intercom indicates an emergency, or the teacher tells them directly of an emergency or safety issue.

What Procedures Do You Save for Another Day?

Any that are not needed on the first day. All that are taught on the first day will be repeated at the appropriate time for the next few days until the class members begin to operate within your stated and *taught* boundaries. Expectations and procedures must be taught. Visuals and illustrations help. You cannot assume that students know *your* specific preferences automatically.

When I taught kindergarten my first year out of college, I taught my students to move to our rug corner for instruction for a subject such as mathematics. When they were dismissed by table, each one picked up a slate, chalk, and an eraser from the piano bench. They took a seat on the floor on the carpet of the "rug corner" and put their slate to the side of their legs with the chalk and eraser on top ready to use. One day I had a visitor from a local college come to observe my class. We had a "numbers" lesson on the rug carpet that day. When dismissed from their table, the students did as they had learned, picked up supplies and went to the rug ready for the day's lesson. Later the visitor commented on the orderliness of the students, to which I replied, "You should have seen them on the first day and next few days when instructed to do this. It didn't look like this!" It takes time. However, consistent reminders over time can lead to more orderly procedures that allow for more teaching and learning time. Practice of a procedure *in context* with praise as feedback to the students yields better productivity.

Modifying Procedures

Which of the procedures will be modified after the first day? There is no need to modify what is working well, even though it may take time for students to learn your expectations. While it is a good management procedure for elementary and secondary students to learn a routine for entering the classroom each day, it may be that you find a glitch in the process. If so, do not be afraid to make adjustments and be honest as to why you are doing so. Is the glitch associated with a procedure such as hanging coats or jackets, taking materials from their school bags or backpacks to be used in class and placing them on their desk, putting homework in the homework bin or on their desk to be used later, taking their school bags to the assigned place in the room, or whatever the ineffective procedure might be? Do not be afraid to make a change if necessary.

Sometimes a procedure may not be working because the students do not know what to do next. For example, effective teachers will have an activity for students to complete located on the desk of each student, on PowerPoint, or on the white- or chalkboard after they have completed the first tasks of the day and settled at their desk. It could be a practice problem or a review of some kind or it could be a motivation/engagement activity for the lesson of the day. You may think of other "what next" times that may need a follow-up procedure as well.

Getting Acquainted!

The most important thing to plan for the first day is how you will get acquainted and get started! During these tandem plans, there will be opportunities to give instructions concerning procedures in context. Seasoned teachers may have great ideas for get-acquainted activities. Do not be afraid to ask. Search the internet for other ideas.

If you play a get-acquainted game that requires movement around the room and talking, this is a time to let your students know your expectations for this type of activity: walk carefully and talk quietly. When you are ready for the students to take a seat, let them know what your signal will be to finish the last thing they are writing or discussing and have a seat.

At the middle school or high school level, each class might experience a get-acquainted activity as students move from class to class. The fun activity you devise may be primarily for the you, the teacher. The students, who may have moved from subject to subject as a group, may have already experienced several activities to get to know each other prior to coming to your class. These activities are opportunities, however, to share your expectations and should not be omitted.

If you have students complete a questionnaire about themselves, this is the time to tell them where you want them to write their name and class period or subject area (middle and high school) before handing it in. When collecting the questionnaires, teach students how you want papers to be collected, across the rows or down the column. When my college classes were in rows, I always had the students pass papers to their left across the rows rather than down the column starting from the back. Why? It is easier to get the attention of the next person to receive the papers when you can see his or her face. I then collected each row's set of papers. Across the rows rather than down the column prevents students from smacking the persons in front of them with papers to get their attention (not that college students would do this). Procedures are preferences, and if they do not work well, try something else.

Get Started!

When you "get started" academically on the first day and require students to discuss a question in their quads or in pairs, this is the time to provide expectations for voice level talking that cannot be heard distinctly by another group or by the teacher. When a student oversteps your expectations, go directly to the student with a reminder repeating your expectation of noise level. "Please, your voice should not be heard distinctly above others in the classroom; if it is, your voice level is too loud." Do not ask students to whisper; this is not using a natural conversation voice. However, they can learn to project their voice when speaking to the whole class and to moderate their volume when in pairs or small groups. This is a social skill.

The first day is a good time to introduce your subject and some of the topics you will be addressing during the semester or term. If you have students work in groups or pairs on the first day, use this time to share your group or pair-share expectations for work and oral contributions.

Of Most Concern: Getting Their Attention

One of the procedural issues that most concerns new teachers is how to get the attention of students to begin class or to call students back together after a group activity. All kinds of signals may be used. Some use a bell; some use a raised hand and expect the students to see it and settle down; some use a clapping approach. In this latter approach, the teacher claps once and gets the attention of one or two, then asks the one or two to join in the clap, hoping that the entire class will be drawn to clapping. This can be a fun approach, especially the first time it is used. The teacher announces that when students are working with others and it is time to come back together, she or he will use the clapping signal. Instruction: "You are expected to begin clapping as soon as you hear my clap and then move back together. You will look at my arms and clap once each time my arms cross one another." This gets the students looking at the teacher and doing something together. This can be fun. For example, you can say to the first ones to see you clap once: "Just clap once for every time I cross or uncross my arms." As more and more students join in, you cross and uncross your arms more rapidly and it sounds like applause. When all are together and clapping, simply say, "Thank you for the applause; I love your attention." For what age level might you use this strategy? I have used it on women's retreats with adults as well as with 6th graders and high school and college students after group work.

At times other than after group work, your presence at the front of the class (after walking around to greet or help students) and a simple, "May I please have your attention?" may be sufficient. But not always!

Bathroom and Water Breaks

What will you do when students ask to go to the bathroom or need to get a drink of water? How will you prepare them ahead of time so they are not overly concerned?

Early childhood and some elementary classrooms may have a bathroom located in the room. This certainly makes bathroom needs easier to handle. This was true of the kindergarten room in the schools in which I taught during college and my first year after graduation from college. But this is not always the case. What will your procedure be for young children who will need an escort in the hall when they need to use the bathroom? You may have a "group" break, but even after you have provided for the entire class, a need may arise. Do not ignore it or you may be cleaning the floor and helping a sobbing child who is embarrassed.

Elementary and secondary levels use bathroom passes that are arranged for boys and girls. Determine how you wish to use the passes. Tell them on the very first day. Will you require a "sign out-sign in" process for older students with the time they left class and the time they came back? If so, provide a clock and a sheet to write name and time with a pen or pencil. Will you give each student a week's supply of passes to use judicially for bathroom breaks and then allow them to redeem any leftover passes for a chosen privilege at the end of the week? This is a popular procedure for older students but not younger ones who might choose to "hold it" rather than to relieve themselves because they want leftover passes to buy certain privileges. I am not personally fond of this weekly privilege-passes procedure, but it may work in some situations. In other words, I do not recommend it although it is popular, and I see it in schools today as I visit them!

Will you control the bathroom passes at your desk or place them at an accessible location that will avoid interference with learning activities? How do you want students to let you know they need to be excused to go to the bathroom? Will you use a signal or raised hand? It is wise to ask seasoned teachers in your school for their suggestions.

In some schools, the procedures for meeting bathroom needs are determined by the head of school or school leaders who are immediately over teachers at your grade level. These regulations are usually considered as regulations for movement in the school hallway. It is always wise to ask before instituting your own plan when it involves leaving your room.

Water breaks require less organization than bathroom breaks. At many schools in the United States and around the world today, students are encouraged to have water bottles at their desks. These can be refilled at lunchtime. If there is a water fountain or water dispenser near the classroom, the teacher can permit students who are too thirsty to wait to either use a pass or go quickly refill their bottle or take a drink at a fountain and return.

Procedures for Use of Technology in the Classroom

Today's student population has access to cellphones, iPads, and computers. Procedures for in-class use must be established on the first day. Some teachers have students place their turned-off phones in a sleeve much like an old hanging shoe holder, with their name on a specific pocket. Phones are placed in each student's pocket or slot at the beginning of class. Computer use may be limited to certain times or may be used at any time on student desks depending on how you are using computers in the lesson of the day. Age level and teaching approaches of the teacher usually determine computer use in the classroom. Write your own expectation procedures such as "Laptops are closed until you are asked to open them for a specific lesson." When you are using open computers, it is wise to walk around the room and take a look at what the students are viewing.

Selecting and Assigning Classroom Tasks

There are numerous tasks that are assigned to students for the care of the classroom and for keeping an effective, clean, and attractive learning environment. You decide what the students can do to help and then assign each one a job. Rotate these periodically. Classroom tasks are more often used in elementary classrooms than secondary. How to do one's job is taught by the teacher the first time. On the weekly rotation of jobs, the previous holder of the position teaches the next selected person how to do that job. This can be a learning experience for each one. For additional classroom procedures, see Wong and Wong's *The Classroom Management Book*.

How to Teach Your Expectations and Procedures

Wong and Wong suggest a three-pronged plan: Explain, Rehearse, and Reinforce.[15] Starting as needed on the first day, the teacher *explains* a procedure—for example, use

---

[15] See Wong and Wong, *The Classroom Management Book*, 48.

of the bathroom pass—and demonstrates how to get the teacher's attention and what to do when recognized by the teacher. "Pick up the pass (show location), leave the room quietly without interrupting others, and return as quickly as possible. Replace the pass at its designated location." This process will need to be *rehearsed* several times and *reinforced** until it becomes routine. It will take a week or so for all class members to learn the procedure. Not all will need to be excused for a bathroom break on day one, especially those in middle and high school levels who may be in your class for less than an hour and have time to use the facility between classes.

*Note: Reinforcement in cognitive interactive learning theory is feedback information to the students that they "did it right." This helps them to process and decide to continue to use the procedure as you intended. A nod of the head indicating that the pass was put in the proper place or a comment after the whole class has given you attention at your request or signal are considered feedback information that communicates "Well done; keep it up." If the student abuses the time allowed out of class, the teacher must give negative feedback that says, "This is not how we do it and your privilege will be stopped if you cannot return in a reasonable time."

Maintain a Management Plan

Now that we have addressed how to begin to implement your classroom management plan, how is it maintained? First, do not be afraid to change a procedure if it is not working well. Tell your students that because this procedure is not working for this class, we are going to do the following. Then share with them the new procedure and ask them for feedback as to how they think this might work better, allowing partner-ownership with you in making a procedure better. The need to change a procedure should be rare as teachers grow professionally. However, there may be a need to do so occasionally.

Be Consistent

Consistency in following your procedures is vital. Reminders to individuals who do not follow a procedure are important. Routines learned and executed each day enhance learning time; they are not an end in themselves. All classroom procedures and expectations should be carried out in a loving and caring and yet firm way. The goal is to build a productive, caring community in which all students grow and develop and flourish as God intended. The best classroom management procedures carried out in a mechanical way without a developing love for one another are just that, mechanical. Our goal in

Christian education is to learn to function as a community and to care for and respect one another as human beings.

In the next chapter, we address student discipline. This, of course, is related to classroom expectations for living and working as a group, but also different as we saw earlier in the definitions of the two concepts. A student who deliberately ignores classroom procedures and expectations after the initial learning period may be considered a candidate for student discipline. However, teachers who build relationships with students and show care, understanding, and patience while holding to consistent high expectations have fewer discipline problems to handle.

Reflect and Create a Classroom Management Plan

Think about your classroom. Create a classroom management plan by listing the routine expectations that will promote effective learning. Write your procedures and think about how you will teach them. Make sure you are aware of all-school policies and procedures. These must also be addressed. It is wise to write out a plan in detail for the first day of class beginning with greeting each student all the way to exiting the room for the next class or the end of the day.

Extended Research and Reflection: If you or your school are using the InTASC Standards, how does this chapter on managing a classroom of students address Standard #3?

> Standard #3: Learning Environments. The teacher works with others to create environments that support individual and collaborative learning, and that encourage positive social interaction, active engagement in learning, and self-motivation.[16]

---

[16] "Interstate Assessment and Support Consortium," Council of Chief State School Officers 2013 (Washington, DC).

CHAPTER 9

Student Discipline

Marti MacCullough

S tudent discipline is often considered a necessary evil rather than a loving, caring, learning process. The "necessary evil view" is not biblical! In the previous chapter, there were several quotes from authors on the topic of discipline that would lead to confusion rather than help for teachers. Here is another quote describing discipline from the book *Ace Your First Year Teaching*. The author writes, "You may have noticed that in this chapter, as well as the two preceding chapters, I have not used the word *discipline*. That has been intentional. That is because 'a well-managed classroom does not have to resort to discipline.'"[1]

The author seems to consider discipline as a last resort or inappropriate altogether if you are a good classroom manager. You may recall from the last chapter that Drs. Wong and Wong declared that, while necessary, discipline is *not* a learning event. So discipline is seen by some as not necessary if you are a good manager, and not really a learning event by others. It is no wonder that teachers, Christian or not, have difficulty determining the differences between classroom management and student discipline and are led to believe that if they manage a classroom well, there will be little or no

---

[1] Anthony D. Fredericks, *Ace Your First Year Teaching* (Indianapolis: Blue River Press, 2017), 174.

discipline problems. This thinking may have disastrous consequences in my view and lead to missed opportunities for student development.

How Is Discipline Addressed from a Biblical Perspective?

One of the best passages in Scripture that addresses discipline as God views it is found in Hebrews 12:

> For they [fathers] disciplined us for a short time based on what seemed good to them, but he does it for our benefit, so that we can share his holiness. No discipline seems enjoyable at the time, but painful. Later on, however, it yields the peaceful fruit of righteousness to those who have been trained by it. (vv. 10–11)

ENGAGE: Before you continue reading, please pause. Read the verses above and select the qualities or characteristics of discipline as viewed by God. Write these here:

_____

_____

_____

Characteristics of Godly Discipline

1. Discipline Is for Our Good

Keep this in mind as you think of discipline in your classroom. Discipline is for the good of the one being disciplined. Some authors of books on discipline focus on the teacher, declaring that discipline is for a teacher's right to teach and be respected without barriers and for the right of other students to learn.[2] This view, while focusing on classroom teaching and learning (a good thing), contrasts with God's view of the ultimate purpose for discipline. This shortsighted perspective was the view of Lee and Marlene Canter in their early presentation of a program called Assertive Discipline that became popular in the late 1970s. The Canters were addressing severely inadequate practices in school discipline popular in the "romantic" days of permissive education in the 1960s and '70s.

---

[2] For an overview of the early work of a take-charge approach to discipline, see "Types of Classroom Management: Assertive Discipline," Universal Class, accessed January 13, 2022, https://www.universalclass.com/articles/self-help/types-of-classroom-management-assertive-discipline.htm.

Behaviorism as a theory was the option to consider if the "active self" psychology—the autonomously active and morally good approach—was not adopted. Cognitive theories were relatively new at the time.[3]

Assertive discipline was a popular "behavior management" program used by school districts in Pennsylvania (the state in which I taught) in the '80s and '90s, and still today around the world. The program has gone through several iterations that focus on increased positive reinforcement rather than negative consequences that seemed to dominate the early views. In an article written for *Phi Delta Kappan International* titled, "Assertive Discipline Is More than Names on the Board and Marbles in a Jar," Lee Canter writes, "Assertive Discipline is catching students being good: recognizing and supporting them when they behave appropriately and letting them know you like it, day in and day out."[4]

In the same article, Canter also advised teachers to make sure they positively reinforce at least two students for correct behavior before administering discipline for a bad behavior of the same kind. While I agree that students need positive feedback to process the results of their behaviors and learn acceptable behaviors, I do not agree that the time to do this is at the moment when you must discipline another student for inappropriate behavior.

The focus of the Canter program seems to be on the teacher managing a student rather than on the student learning and internalizing good behavior. While the views inherent in the program have some merit, the system was designed, primarily, to change behavior rather than to target a change in mind, motives, *and* behaviors of the student that will contribute to character development. God's view of the purpose of discipline differs greatly from the stated purpose of Assertive Discipline and other similar programs. A biblical goal is character development for the good of the one disciplined. Discipline, rightly understood, is a good thing!

2. Discipline Allows Us to Share in His Holiness (His Character)

Keep this in mind as you think of *why* you do *what* you do in discipline situations. Discipline is a moral process. It is more than stopping a behavior at the moment or to help teachers feel vindicated.

---

[3] See Lee Canter and Marlene Canter, *Assertive Discipline: A Take-Charge Approach for Today's Educator* (Seal Beach, CA: Lee Canter, 1976).

[4] Lee Canter, "Assertive Discipline Is More Than Names on the Board and Marbles in a Jar," *Phi Delta Kappan International* 71, no. 1 (September 1989): 58.

Is character education/development dead in today's schools? Two decades ago, James Davison Hunter wrote, "Character is dead. Attempts to revive it will yield little."[5] Since the time of Hunter's postmortem comments, there have been calls for reestablishing character in our culture. The need is evident; humans are very flawed in character as judged particularly by their treatment of fellow human beings. Discipline contributes to character development and addresses these flaws. The "death" of sound disciplinary practices in schools may have contributed to the death of character in modern culture, but this negative view of discipline should not be the practice in Christian education that fosters biblical worldview thinking.

For those who have enthroned the human *self* as the foundation of their worldview and have dismissed the living, loving, sovereign God, there is no absolute standard for "good character." This may be one reason why there are many issues related to character education in schools today. For the Christian, however, the standard for character is God himself, and that standard is unchanging because he is unchanging. No wonder those who study our culture have announced that character is dead! Worldview beliefs do have consequences.

The Humanitas Forum on Christianity and Culture reported in an essay, "The Death of Character—Ideas Do Have Consequences," that "moral character ceased to be possible as our culture increasingly refused to accept objective good and evil."[6] One of the issues addressed concerning moral character was whether there is a source higher than, and independent of, humans. This is a question posed by others who write about character education as well.

Les T. Csorba, former White House advisor and author of *Trust: The One Thing That Makes or Breaks a Leader*, wrote, "Just as character requires a bigger reality than oneself, we require a reality impinging upon us that is immune from our manipulation and one that dictates the structure and boundaries of leadership."[7] And that reality, according to Csorba, who professes to be a Christian, is the God of the Bible.

In our postmodern and post-Christian culture, can we expect to view discipline as a part of character education? I believe we can, because our biblical belief system is grounded in a reality bigger than us—that is, in the living God who has chosen

---

[5] See James Davison Hunter, *The Death of Character: Moral Education in an Age Without Good or Evil* (New York: Basic Books, 2000), Postmortem section 1.

[6] "The Death of Character—Ideas Do Have Consequences," The Humanitas Forum on Christianity and Culture, April 11, 2014, https://humanitas.org/?p=2883.

[7] See Les T. Csorba, *Trust: The One Thing That Makes or Breaks a Leader* (Nashville: Thomas Nelson, 2004), 248.

to reveal himself to humanity. Christian families and schools that utilize principles and practices of discipline informed by their biblical worldview may find success in promoting character education and personal growth. Discipline is God's idea, and his purpose for discipline is development that moves us toward reflecting his unchanging character. His motive is love, for he is love. Christlike character traits do not change with a changing culture! We have an unchanging standard, a reality, that exists outside ourselves and is "bigger than we." This is good news. There is no moving target that confuses the issue for biblical Christians. So, here is a simple principle that emerges from Scripture: Loving God and loving others—a mandate of Scripture—demands character education, and character education requires discipline.

3. Discipline Is Not Pleasant at the Time and May Be Painful

Keep this in mind: discipline is not pleasant for the student or the teacher; it is uncomfortable, complex, and can be difficult to deliver. In some parts of the world, discipline is harsh and involves beatings and shaming that seldom work to develop Christlike character. It serves more to turn students away from a loving God than to draw them nearer. It is important to deliver consequences with grace and an attitude that says, "This is not comfortable for the moment, but I love you and want the best for you." Biblical discipline builds up rather than tears down.

Many years ago, when I taught sixth grade, I received into my class in the fall a student for whom records from his previous school had not yet arrived. Our middle school was partially departmentalized with two or three colleagues teaching subjects to each of the sixth, seventh, and eighth grade classes. I was the sixth-grade homeroom teacher.

The new student manifested poor choices in behavior and had to be dealt with by all of his teachers. Some did better than others, but all had serious questions about the student's behavior. We shared ideas to help each other, and we conferenced with his parents. However, his misbehavior persisted.

We found out a month or so later, when his prior records finally arrived, that he'd had many previous problems in former schools. He was also seeing a psychologist. That scared the three of us who taught him and made us fearful in knowing what to do. Discipline became more complex because of the knowledge gained from his records. I finally asked our head of school if we could have a conference with his psychologist with permission from his parents. Among other things, the psychologist told us that the student needed stern discipline and firm boundaries, which he was not receiving at home. This was a shock to us. We had assumed that he needed to feel accepted and to be loved, and we tempered our discipline practices based on that assumption. This whole experience was not pleasant.

Our school had accepted the student, and we were obligated and committed to try to help him develop acceptable behaviors for his own good. In addition, we wanted to maximize his learning while doing the same for his classmates. However, this was not easy, and it took a lot of time and effort from the team of teachers. The consequences for his behaviors were not pleasant for the student either. This event was a good reminder to me that discipline is for the good of the student even though it may be unpleasant "at the moment." Although it is not the easiest part of our job as teachers, it may contribute to the changing of lives for good. Change may take time, and much prayer.

4. Godly Discipline Produces a Harvest of Righteousness and Peace

If learning occurs, discipline yields positive results. Keep in mind that discipline is a learning event that targets changes in behaviors and better choices by the student as well as peace in your classroom. Sometimes the products are not seen immediately. Some ten or so years after my last year teaching in K–12 education, a parent of one of my former sixth grade students came to visit me at the university where I had taken a position. She had heard that I was back in the area and wanted to tell me about the positive changes that had occurred in her son during his year in my class, some of which I was totally unaware of. What a joy to hear! Her son was my number one challenge in that class in his behaviors, his responses to discipline, and in the amount of time it took to learn acceptable behaviors. But he learned! Ten years later, I thanked the Lord for the result.

5. Discipline Is an Act of Love

Hebrews 12:6 reads, "The Lord disciplines the one he loves." Above all, discipline should be done out of love for the student; that is, out of motives and actions that are reflective of one desiring God's best for the student. Discipline should be delivered in a loving, caring, but firm way.

Research on student discipline will provide suggestions for the reader to consider. When you have a biblical framework out of which to think about these suggestions, it is more likely that you will benefit from the research and be able to accept that which agrees with a biblical worldview and reject that which does not. One who has a well-grounded worldview can theoretically be more open-minded and benefit from others more than one who does not.

Discipline and Your Philosophy of Education

Chapter 1 provided a framework for developing a philosophy of education. A philosophy of discipline is a subset of an educational philosophy. Questions about discipline fall under each section of one's philosophy.

What is the aim of education?

What is the aim or purpose for discipline?

What is the role of the teacher in education?

What is the role of the teacher in discipline?

What is the nature of the student and learning?

What is the nature of the student that affects the learning event we categorize as discipline?

What is the nature and purpose of the curriculum?

What is the nature and purpose of discipline in a classroom setting, and how does it affect the curriculum and community of learners?

In this chapter we briefly address these key areas and then develop principles and practices for student discipline.

The Aim of Discipline

Human Flourishing

Chapter 1 developed a biblically informed aim of education as *human flourishing*—that is, the goal of promoting the full development of the student in every area: socially, physically, emotionally, mentally, and spiritually as God intends. You may wish to refer to the discussion on human flourishing in chapter 1 before continuing.

ENGAGE: How might discipline, patterned after God's view, fit with human flourishing? Review the characteristics of God's view of discipline (above) and determine how the right kind of discipline might lead to a student's flourishing. Write your thoughts here. _____

_____

_____

_____

_____

Flourish is defined by the *Oxford Dictionary* as to "grow or develop in a healthy or vigorous way, especially as the result of a particularly congenial environment." I like the example Oxford provides: "wild plants flourish on the banks of a lake."[8] What is a congenial environment? It includes the nourishment of water as a source of life.

Our sometimes "wild" students need to be nurtured by providing information from the source of life. Jesus said, "I am the way, the truth, and the life" (John 14:6). Recorded in John 10:10, Jesus also said that he came to give life to the full (human flourishing to the max). Discipline, understood biblically, includes learning by which students grow and flourish. Human flourishing is, therefore, the aim of discipline as well as the aim of education with the focus on character development. Discipline is not a "last resort" or an "unnecessary evil," or "just to stop a behavior at the moment." It is for the good of the person as a part of life.

Role of the Teacher in Discipline

In the chapter on philosophy of education, several roles of the teacher were identified and reviewed. Several Scripture passages were used to read and determine key roles for educators. These four were suggested as keys to understanding what we are to do and be as teachers:

To teach

To serve

To be in charge

To be a role model

ENGAGE: Which of the general roles (above) do you think apply to student discipline? With your class or another teacher in your school, discuss how these roles might apply to discipline.

If you selected all four as applying to discipline, you are correct.

To Teach

Since discipline is a learning event, teaching is involved. The English word *discipline* comes from the Latin word *disciplina*, meaning "instruction given, teaching, learning,

---

[8] *Oxford English Dictionary*, s.v. "flourish" (first entry), accessed June 21, 2022, https://www.lexico.com/definition/flourish.

and knowledge." Discipline requires instruction; there must be information provided to the one disciplined. The word itself indicates that it is a learning event. Disciplining is what the teacher does in the process of instructing the student so that learning can occur. Since humans, communicators by nature, process information and can choose to behave accordingly, the teacher, first and foremost, must tell students what they are doing wrong and what they must start doing immediately. This is communication! This is information!

Clearing your throat, snapping your fingers, or the like that might be used for animal training are not sufficient for humans. Speak to the student; provide information for the student to process and respond to by obeying or not obeying. Discipline centers on the person (student) who chooses to learn from the experience and thus begins to develop better patterns of behavior.

The theory of learning adopted in this book is based upon the cognitive interactive human for whom inside and outside factors are both important. (See chapters 2–3.) A teacher is an external factor; student motives are internal factors. The student is motivated to misbehave for a variety of reasons. How the teacher decides to initiate a discipline event depends on the understanding of both the motive and the behavior. When educators say that discipline or punishment simply stops a behavior and changes nothing inside, their views do not reflect a biblical view. Change that is inside and outside is the goal.

To Serve

The same root word for discipline is also the root word for *disciple*. A disciple is simply a student of someone. Teachers who are viewing their role as a Christ-centered servant will consider their students as disciples and use principles of discipleship as Jesus did with his followers.

Discipline is difficult and complex, and students can get under your skin. Situations can get out of hand and prompt teachers to yell or use sarcasm or ridicule, none of which help in the process of discipline. Unless we view our teaching as a ministry and have the attitude that Jesus did as he served his disciples, we will find it stressful rather than joyful in seeing students grow. As we serve students, we are serving the Lord.

To Be in Charge

This role is often abdicated by teachers who do not understand the purpose for discipline or authority. If the teacher does not take charge of the class, the students will take charge and chaos may emerge. Refer to chapter 1 to see the biblical view of authority as "delegated." All authority in the universe is delegated by God, whether parents, governors, presidents, school boards, heads of school, or teachers.

Beginning from day one, it is important that students see you as in charge of the classroom. This does not mean that you are the "boss." However, it does mean that you set the classroom expectations, provide the rules, and carry through on instruction and discipline as needed. It also means that you are responsible for the safe care of your students. Being in charge does not mean that students are not involved in modifying procedures as needed or even creating rules for class members. It does mean that even your physical presence is important. I tell my students who are ready for their first clinical teaching experiences to enter the room with confidence (in the Lord) rather than manifesting in their body language fear and trepidation. When they are to take over the class, at the classroom teacher's direction, I remind them to make sure they continue to present as one who is in charge just as the classroom teacher has modeled. Body language matters in teaching!

The Canters, who developed Assertive Discipline, were right to emphasize the in-charge role of the teacher; however, they did not underscore the source of all authority as delegated by God, and this led many teachers to assume that the authority resided in themselves; they were the "boss." This is not a biblical view. As well, a biblical view combines authority, love, and servanthood all in one person.

To Be a Role Model

It seems logical that if you expect certain attitudes and behaviors from members of the class community, you too must model these social behaviors and more. Our discussion in chapter 1 provides the source of our pattern for being a role model. That model or pattern is Jesus Christ. If we are allowing God's Spirit to work in our own lives so that more and more we are manifesting Christlike characteristics of love, care, forgiveness, and compassion, we will continue to be a role model even when we are disciplining a student. That often means a quick SOS to the Lord, asking him to help us with the discipline situation in front of us and asking him for wisdom. While disciplining students may be difficult for any teacher, when it is done out of biblical understandings, it should not be destructive to the teacher or student.

Resilience in managing a classroom and in student discipline: "Will I survive as a classroom teacher? A common research conclusion is that many teachers leave the profession within five years and the number one reason is failure at managing a class-room filled with today's students.

I am fascinated by literature that affirms what I believe and yet approaches an issue from a secular viewpoint. One such issue is resilience of teachers. In the June 2015 issue of *Time* magazine, Mandy Oaklander presents his findings about why some people "bounce back" more quickly than others after hardships. In the article "The Art of Resilience," he lists ten "Expert Tips for Resilience." The very first tip is "Develop a core set of beliefs that nothing can shake."[9] I agree. Christian teachers can remain resilient even when disciplining their students because of our core beliefs. For the Christian teacher, that core set of beliefs includes a biblical view of the human and learning and a biblical view of the teacher's role in the learning event. Sound biblical discipline is based upon this set of core beliefs and can serve to help Christian teachers thrive.

ENGAGE: You may wish to pause and describe a teacher who serves with confidence in her beliefs and in the One who informs those beliefs. What might that person look like or sound like when exercising necessary student discipline?

Nature of the Student and Learning

In the book *The Hunger Games* by Suzanne Collins, the issue of human nature and worth is clearly addressed through the characters' words and actions. The setting is the futuristic country of Panem that consists of twelve districts that surround the tyrannical Capitol. Each year the Capitol forces the districts to send a boy and girl, 12–18 years in age, to fight to the death. The Gamemakers hired by the Capitol produce this war of the tributes (kids) as a live reality show to "thrill" its citizens. Only one representative from the districts can win; all others must be killed.

Gale, one of the district tributes, advises Katniss, the protagonist in the story, to forget that her fellow fighters are people and to think of them as animals. He knew that she was an excellent hunter and could kill animals without guilt. However, if she thinks of the other tributes as "humans," her heart will go out to them, and she will not be able to kill them.

The Hunger Games portrays a view of human beings by the Gamemakers that is frightening! However, it is a great book for an eleventh or twelfth grade literature unit that is designed to develop biblical worldview thinking. It addresses the worldview

---

[9] Mandy Oaklander, "The Art of Resilience," *Time* magazine, June 2015.

questions: What is a human being by nature (birth)—animal, angel, machine, or what? There are major consequences connected to our answer to these questions—What is a human being and how do we learn?—that impact how we teach *and* how we discipline. How do these answers filter through views of human learning and, specifically, discipline?

Psychologically Passive Views (outside factors are the focus)

Behavioristic approaches that follow the underlying beliefs of B. F. Skinner present the students as animals, higher in development, but *not qualitatively* different. They can be trained (conditioned) much like a dog, and since they are morally neutral (neither good nor bad by nature), they can be made "good" by reinforcing the behavior you want.

Behavioristic views have led to the process of conditioning good behavior or simply stopping a bad behavior without a view toward any change inside. Remember that learning, by definition, is a relatively permanent change in *thinking* and *acting*. The mind is involved. This was not a concession that B. F. Skinner would make. In an interview with Daniel Goleman in 1987, he said, "The cognitive revolution is a search for something inside that is not there."[10] His theory omitted the mind and especially motives for behavior. He declared that behavior is changed through reinforcement of the behaviors you want. Finding a good behavior that allows the teacher to issue a reinforcement is the key to discipline in this view. This led to the "catch them being good" practice used by Lee Canter and many elementary teachers today.

Early in Skinner's research, he told teachers and parents to ignore bad behaviors and they will diminish or go away. But often, they did not! This was a major problem in his theory. Toward the end of his years, he admitted that punishment, something that his original theory did not allow, may be needed to stop a behavior at the moment. Most neo-behaviorists today agree with his change in thinking and do include punishment as a "last resort" in their theories to stop an immediate behavior that is unacceptable. You will see this influence in articles you may read on discipline in schools today.

Autonomously Active and Morally Good Views (inside factors are the focus)

These views have led to permissive practices in discipline. If the child is morally good and everything comes from inside naturally, then restraint is bad. Natural always means

---

[10] Daniel Goleman, "Embattled Giant of Psychology Speaks His Mind," *New York Times*, August 25, 1987.

good to those who hold this view. It was the view of Alexander Sutherland Neill, head of Summerhill, a school that began in 1921 in England, and was documented by Neill in his 1960 book, *Summerhill: A Radical Approach to Child Rearing*. It was required reading in many education programs in the USA and influenced educational philosophy and especially discipline for a time.

Neill substituted freedom for authority and wrote that the child is the "boss," not the teacher. He abandoned discipline completely. He believed that if a child is left on his own, goodness will emerge. Restraint is bad. "Children do not need teaching as much as they need love and understanding. They need approval and freedom to be naturally good."[11] Neill also said that "Summerhill runs along without any authority."[12] His goal was to abolish authority and let children be themselves. To Neill, love and authority are antithetical.

Those who held to the autonomous, morally good child belief adopted his permissive views. This led to many discipline problems in schools and confusion on the part of teachers about their role in developing an orderly class. Christian teachers who disliked the behavioristic approaches to discipline were very tempted to adopt Neill's views. The two views about discipline—behavioristic and romantic—have vied for the minds of educators for more than one hundred years and are still alive today.

How do **you** view the human being? How will that affect your discipline?

ENGAGE: How might the two views about human nature above (simply higher developed animals to be conditioned to be good or basically good and can do no wrong) impact a teacher's responses in discipline situations? Write and share your ideas.

_____

_____

_____

_____

_____

_____

In chapter 2 I addressed the value and worth of students as special creatures created in a separate category of living things, not in the animal or angel categories. Humans

---

[11] Alexander Sutherland Neill, *Summerhill: A Radical Approach to Childrearing* (New York: Hart, 1960), 82.

[12] Neill, 104.

are created in the image of God and are the only category of living things of which this is said. This truth gives us great worth. We bear God's image. Truly believing this will change our perspective toward discipline when individuals blatantly make wrong choices. And they will do wrong because the image-bearing capacity was marred when sin entered the world. Humans "naturally" manifest a sin nature that needs God's intervention. Humans are still image-bearers and of great worth, and their unacceptable behavior does not change this truth. Our goal is to help them change and develop as we work with them each day to become more and more like Christ in character.

Chapter 3 provided information on the nature of the learner and how educators can develop a theory of learning based upon that information. The conclusions drawn were that psychologically *passive* understandings of the nature of the student and autonomously *active* understandings do not fit well with a biblical view. We suggested that understanding the human as an information processor who is cognitively *interactive* in the learning event fits best with a biblical view of human learning. Views of human learning impact how we view discipline. Both teacher and student must be actively involved in any discipline event as inside and outside factors are considered.

Cognitively Interactive Views (inside and outside factors working together)

These views challenged the other two views for learning in general, and for discipline as well. We address this view as we look at principles and practices and describe both inside factors and outside factors.

Learning Theory and Discipline

When describing student learning, many teachers today take a broad, interactive view and develop lesson plans filled with student interaction and student processing activities. However, it is common for those same teachers to switch from a broadly interactive view to a purely behavioristic view when it comes to discipline. This may be true because so many authors of books on discipline view discipline practices from a behavioristic viewpoint that champions the idea, "change the behavior or stop the behavior" using reinforcement or punishment. Many do not view discipline as a learning and growing experience, but rather a necessity for the students and the teacher to survive. This leads, in my view, to inconsistency in an overall approach to learning. If you adopt a cognitive interactive position for student learning, you should also take a cognitive interactive position for discipline. What will that look like? Here are two key principles for student discipline that emerge from a cognitive interactive theory of learning.

(1) **Motives *and* behaviors matter**! Behavior is always in a context. Motives are simply reasons for acting or behaving in a certain way. Behaviorists do not seek to determine the motives and simply deal with the behavior, and humanistic (active) theories hold that any negative motives are not rooted in the child since the human is basically good. Bad behavior is the "fault" of the environment and not the child. However, cognitive interactive theories suggest that both motives and behaviors should be viewed as a whole in the discipline event!

(2) **One's view of human beings as communicators by nature matters**! Humans are thinkers, feelers, doers. We are communicators by nature, and we process information using our God-given capacity. The mind and emotions impact actions. A cognitive interactive approach will include talking to students and listening—let them talk. This approach also requires the teacher to provide information to students that tells them what they are doing wrong, what rule has been broken, and what the expectations are for changed behavior. Communication matters! As well, a cognitive interactive approach requires the teacher to try to discern motives, feelings, and emotions in the situation and not just focus on the behavior alone. Yes, this takes discernment. However, it is not as hard as it may seem.

What Are Some Possible Motives for Misbehaviors?

I use several D's that represent the first letter of specific human characteristics to highlight possible motives for behaviors. They are derived from an understanding of human nature informed by Scripture. (1) Humans are developmental by nature (not miniature adults); (2) Humans are created in the image of God (not robotic or machine-like); (3) Humans are sinners by nature, want to be in charge, and find it is hard to submit to authority (born with the fundamental flaw of humanity, the result of the fall); (4) Humans are diverse and have diverse needs (born into different cultures, born with different proclivities in various areas of experience, and some possess specific disabilities); and (5) Humans have great worth (born into the human family and created in the image of God). We will look at these individually.

DEVELOPMENTALLY TRIGGERED BEHAVIORS

Because humans are developmental by nature, some behaviors at every age level may be attributed to developmental characteristics. Consider the fact that many preschoolers cannot sit still for a long period of time without fidgeting or getting up. Or consider the second grader who comes in hot and excited from recess and plops in his or her chair causing it to turn over but then picks it up quickly and sits down. Or consider middle school girls who giggle together about something they think is funny, and when told to stop have a hard time not laughing when they have eye contact with each other. Or consider the high school boy who carries a comb in his back pocket and several times during class takes it out to groom himself, often drawing comments from his peers. While these developmental behaviors may lead to disciplinary attention, they are not motivated at first glance by deliberate disobedience and should not be handled in the same manner as disobedience.

DESIRES AND NEED-MOTIVATED BEHAVIORS

These behaviors are common in school classrooms. In fact, bullying may come under this category. Because humans have personhood; that is, they think, communicate as social beings, and need attention and acceptance, they may seek attention in unacceptable ways. Attention-seeking behaviors are probably the most common misbehaviors observed in schools, but they are not always motivated by defiance or rebellion and should not be treated as such.

DELIBERATE DISOBEDIENCE AND DEFIANCE

Because humans are flawed by nature, deliberate disobedience and defiance are not illusions. They are real. Humans need direction and intervention. It was the intervention of God in sending his Son, Jesus, to die for our sin that made possible a restored relationship with God and hope for a changed life. Remember that sin entered the world through the disobedience of Adam and Eve to God's one command in the garden of Eden. It is his model of loving intervention that teachers must use when a student manifests deliberate disobedience. While it is the hardest motive to address, it is out of love for the student and desire for the student's best that teachers do what is necessary to identify and address defiance or disobedience.

DIFFERENCES AND DIVERSITY

Not only are differences in personal motives important to consider, but also group expectations that are social, emotional, and cultural in nature. Teachers must know the general culture in which they teach and the backgrounds of each of their students as much as possible. Expectations for behaviors vary from culture to culture, and these expectations make a difference in the total context of the misbehavior. Discerning motives and reasons for certain behaviors includes understanding these differences.

Disabilities

Disabilities can also be considered under the label "differences and diversity." They cross every socioeconomic and cultural difference and may contribute to developmental and attention-seeking behaviors as well. They require additional professional consideration. There are multiple disabilities represented in classrooms today of which teachers must be aware. Discerning motives for misbehavior can be more complex when a child has a clinically determined disability. However, teachers must discipline when needed regardless of disabilities such as cognitive processing capacities or other learning disabilities, clinically designated behavioral issues, prior trauma issues, autism, or other specific disabilities. It is possible that a misbehavior may be motivated because of one of the above issues. Disciplinary intervention may need to be modified in special cases.

Definite Worth and Value

This is the primary motive for the teacher who desires to handle student discipline from God's perspective, out of his love "shed abroad in our hearts" (Rom 5:5 KJV). As we intervene when students have behaved in unacceptable ways, we must reason that what we do is for the good of the student and it may be uncomfortable for both student and teacher "for a moment." However, if the student learns and changes, it will lead to human flourishing in the long run and peace in the classroom. Applications that address these various motives is the subject of the next chapter.

CHAPTER 10

Strategies for Student Discipline

Marti MacCullough

Three Categories of Misbehavior

Teacher beliefs alone, while necessary, are not sufficient for effective student discipline. Teachers must understand that various motives may operate to "cause" certain behaviors that are unacceptable in a school setting. This chapter addresses some of the possible motives for misbehavior and offers helpful suggestions for handling the discipline event. These suggestions are provided in numbered format for quick reference.

Category One: Developmentally "Caused" Behaviors

1. Know your students' development limits—socially, emotionally, physically, and mentally—so that you can plan developmentally appropriate activities and procedures and hold developmentally informed expectations.
2. Set guidelines and boundaries for each new activity and "nip in the bud" any overstepping of the boundaries or stated expectations. Be consistent from the very beginning of the year and good habits will be formed.
3. Set reasonable limits for classroom procedures such as breaks and bathroom procedures or passes.

a. Breaks: Be aware that young children need breaks more frequently than older children because of their developing central nervous system. However, all students need breaks from focused attention in learning so that their central nervous systems may relax a bit.

b. Bathroom: Bathroom passes/procedures must be thought through carefully for each developmental level. For example, it is not a good idea to tell a first grade student to "just hold it; you were supposed to go when we came in from recess." Why? You may have to clean up the child and the floor sometime after this statement and then deal with the emotions of the embarrassed child.

4. Counsel concerning "growing up" behaviors. When a student at any level consistently manifests immature behaviors, the teacher must counsel privately, determine with the student a plan to improve behavior, and write the plan. The written plan will be available to show parents if this behavior continues. Indicate to the student that the next time this behavior is observed, there will be a consequence beyond a warning. The consequence might be to place a call to the parents to let them know what has been going on and to ask them if they have observed this behavior at home. When a parent is called, and they agree that this behavior is seen at home, ask what they do to help their child. It is important to let the parents know that you understand that they know their son or daughter better than you and you value their input. "We are in this together as we work for the good of your child and learning." Teachers should never be considered an adversary but rather a caring person wanting the best for the child. This attitude breaks down barriers between teacher and parents.

5. Expect a positive response. Avoid saying things like, "It's about time you did this or that!" Or, "It is about time you grew up!" Be matter-of-fact and expect the students to respond to your request but do not use sarcasm. When they do not respond positively, the matter becomes a more serious discipline issue.

6. Praise positive signs of maturity, good habits, and consistent following of classroom procedures. Do not be afraid to make positive comments to the *class* when they have worked well in groups or completed a class project, for example. Praise *individuals* privately. Individuals who have responded to your counsel in certain areas and who are improving each day need feedback that helps them process "I am doing this right." Do not omit positive feedback. This helps the

student to process and choose to continue to grow. For example, if you have had to speak to a student about blurting out negative comments about the contributions of others in a class discussion, make sure that when this has not occurred for a day or two after your warning, you simply pass by the student's desk and quietly acknowledge that the improved behavior is noticed. Avoid praise if this has been an attention-seeking behavior (see below). If the behavior seems to be immature or impulsive but not really attention-seeking, do not omit the feedback necessary for growth.

Reasons for behaviors are important in discipline even if the behavior seems to be a developmental issue rather than attention-seeking or deliberate disobedience. If a rule has been broken, there must be a consequence even for developmentally triggered behaviors (more on this principle later). Many of the infractions in this first category may be related to classroom management procedures. Patience and reminders will be multiple when teaching your classroom procedural expectations. Following through consistently with your stated procedures and expectations for class decorum will help to prevent behaviors in this category from becoming more serious issues.

Category Two: "Desires and Needs" Misbehaviors, Such as Attention-Seeking

In general, stand to teach. I know it is not possible for some to stand for a long period of time; however, if you can, it makes classroom management and especially student discipline more effective. If you are standing and moving as you teach, it is easier to use physical proximity and "nip in the bud" (handle quickly) any infractions that occur by speaking directly and quietly to a student who is misbehaving. It is not a good practice to try to discipline from the front of the classroom. Try the following for this category of motives.

1. Do not ignore attention-seeking behavior (it will not go away if the behavior is getting the attention of others in the room).
2. Do not feed the attention-seeking behavior by making the offending student a helper. While this may work to get the student out of sight, it usually promotes rather than inhibits the attention-seeking behavior. This is usually done by giving the offender a "special privilege" such as taking a note to another teacher or doing a task for you just to get the student out of the classroom. If the misbehavior is rewarded, the student will do it again to get more attention

from you and to receive some special task. In fact, other students may also pick up on this idea and misbehave to get your attention and get to leave the class. Teachers should not be guilty of this practice.

3. Do not try to discipline the offender through the rest of the class by saying, "I'll not start until *someone* stops talking." The students know who is acting out, so why not speak directly using the name of the offender. Move to the student and tell the student in a matter-of-fact tone what he or she is doing, that he or she should stop, and what the student should start doing immediately. It might sound like this: "Harry, stop talking to your neighbor and take out your silent-reading book and begin to read." Communication of immediate expectations is vital. Snapping fingers or shouting are not the best procedures.

4. Do not interrupt your lesson (if possible) but keep walking toward the offending student, and then pause briefly to speak with the student as quietly as possible. Expect the student to respond positively and then return to your teaching position walking backward still facing the student. This is a good reason to place school bags or other items at a designated place in the room away from walking paths where students and teacher must walk. Physical proximity, high expectations, and firmness are essential. Interrupting your teaching gives the offending student more attention and a feeling of being in charge. Try not to interrupt the lesson more than a brief pause.

5. Do "nip it in the bud." Do not delay your response. Use the student's name, physical proximity (move quickly to the student), your eyes and voice, and expect a positive response. Do not allow an incident to escalate, especially if the motive is attention-seeking. If the student is receiving attention from peers, the behavior may continue and increase in intensity if not handled immediately.

6. Counsel privately, at a later time, if the student responds immediately. The student must know that his or her behavior broke a rule. If this is a first incident, a warning is sufficient; if not, there must be another consequence. If the student does not respond, the situation must be handled immediately because it will have become deliberate disobedience and maybe even defiance.

7. Be cautious in the use of demerits for attention-seeking behaviors. These usually allow the student to repeat the misbehavior three times or more, gaining more attention without a consequence.

8. Determine a point and a technique to recognize when an attention-seeking behavior has become deliberate disobedience or defiance.

Category Three: Deliberate Disobedience and Defiance

1. Do not lose your cool. When a student defies you, it may trigger a very human defensive response that could lead to unhealthy and ineffective teacher-behaviors that most of us would not want to manifest. It is important to keep in mind the purpose for discipline and the target goal of human flourishing. An SOS to the Lord is in order. "Help me, Lord, to handle this situation as you want me to."

2. Do not take personal offense and resort to ridicule or use sarcasm. I have observed many different classrooms at all grade levels in my roles at the university. I have occasionally observed some very poor teacher-behaviors in discipline situations. In one middle school, a teacher of seventh graders used ridicule to try to stop a behavior of a student. He called the student "Shrimp," "Pee wee," and a few other derogatory names because the boy was small for his age.

   I have heard attempts to control a misbehaving student by using sarcasm as well. Teachers may resort to this kind of communication because they are taking the misbehavior of the offender personally and not focusing on the need for change in the student. While it may be a rather human response to take personal offense, it should not lead to unprofessional responses. We need help from the Lord to focus on the student and not on ourselves.

3. Do not openly, verbally challenge the student in front of the class. Do move quickly and confidently to the student (praying) and firmly escort him or her to the hall or to a private place in the room. The need to get information is important. You can ask the student questions about the behavior, but he or she may respond by hanging his or her head and saying nothing. Be assured, he or she can hear.

   When you stop the class instruction to speak individually with the student in as private a place as possible, give the rest of the class permission to talk quietly. They will talk anyway in this situation. If you can, give them something to talk about from the lesson.

   The first thing I suggest asking the offender is "Did I or someone else say or do something that contributed to having you act as you did?" This allows him or her to relax a bit. Allow the student to talk. Sometimes the student will tell you about a bullying event, or a breakup with a boy or girlfriend, or numerous other triggers for hurt and anger. Sometimes he or she may say nothing. No matter the "cause," the teacher must say, "The behavior you manifested (specifically what they did) is totally unacceptable in this classroom." The student must know this no matter what the triggers might have been. These triggers may be addressed quickly during this communication or later. They should be addressed.

4. Do speak to him or her and decide on a consequence. If this is a first-time behavior of this type and the student shows remorse, you might just give a strong warning. If this is the case, you should prepare the student to reenter the classroom and not pretend that the meeting with the teacher was not a big deal, "I got by with no consequence." Before dismissing the student, tell him or her what the consequence will be if this happens again and write it down. Usually, a next step is to call the parents, explain the behavior, and ask them to speak with their child about it. Tell the student that if he or she does not go immediately to their seat in remorse, the next determined consequence will follow today. This will prevent a cavalier response on the part of the offending student to act as though he or she did not receive a consequence for the behavior to save face with his or her peers.

    If this is a second or third offense or more, possible consequences include a parental conference, an in-school suspension, an out-of-school suspension, or an expulsion from the school for the semester with the hope of returning if attitudes and behaviors change. Deliberate disobedience and defiance are very serious!

    When should the head of school be brought into the situation? After the phone conference with parents or after the teacher-student-parent conference. These are usually teacher-led, and there is little need to contact the head of school. However, contact with the administration should occur before an in-school suspension, and always before an out-of-school suspension or expulsion. This reporting procedure varies with schools or school districts, and each teacher must be fully aware of school regulations. The teacher usually does not expel; the administrator does. Keep the head of school informed along the way for any potential suspensions.

    Write an account of the situation and consequence, and for older students, have them sign it making sure they understand what will follow if the behavior occurs again. Keep parents informed as needed.

Motives and behaviors should be viewed as a unit in student discipline when operating under the cognitive interactive theory of learning. Thinking and doing, inside and outside factors, must be considered. Of course, behaviors are obvious. Discernment of motives requires a growing knowledge of each student and wisdom from the Lord. It is worth the effort to discern motives and it is a fairer approach to discipline. Each of the various motives is addressed more fully in my book *Flourishing in the Classroom*.[1] For more information, consider reading and researching the topic more extensively.

Rules

Behaviors That Demand Student Discipline Are Related to Classroom Rules

Almost every classroom today has a set of rules that when broken require a consequence. While classroom procedures are usually the preferences of the teachers in how they wish to organize the functions of the class, major rules are related more to character responses to "instructions that tell you what you are allowed to do and what you are not allowed to do."[2] This may seem like one is saying the same thing: the teacher's personal preferences in organization and functioning on the one hand, and rules that tell what may or may not be done without a consequence on the other. The key differences are (1) the weight of the rule versus a classroom procedure; (2) the fact that a broken rule always leads to a consequence, while classroom procedures take time to habituate; and (3) the goal of student discipline is as a learning event for individual character development, while procedures are simply tools to manage a group of individual so that learning can be maximized.

Most Students Understand the Label "Rule"

There are rules to games such as basketball. Breaking of a rule always leads to a consequence of some kind. In basketball, if a player has the ball and stops dribbling and then moves both feet before passing the ball, the referee calls this broken rule "traveling." What is the consequence? You lose the ball to the opponent. Sure, the referee may not see the act, or it may be missed, because they, like teachers, are human. However, if they see it and call it, there is an immediate consequence. We are all acquainted with rules. There are rules for driving a car, rules for paying taxes, etc., and these are not

---

[1] Martha MacCullough, *Flourishing in the Classroom: A Guide for Classroom Management and Student Discipline Informed by a Christ-Centered Worldview* (Wheaton, IL: Wheaton Press, 2019).

[2] *Collins Dictionary*, s.v. "rules," first entry, accessed April 16, 2021, https://www .collinsdictionary.com/us/dictionary/english/rule.

suggestions. There are a variety of possible consequences for breaking these rules, some of which may take into consideration the situation under which the rule was broken. However, there are consequences for breaking a rule even if it just a severe warning. So, the key principle related to rules in a classroom is this: **If you have rules, there must also be consequences!** Put another way, if you have rules and do not deliver consequences for breaking them, you might as well not have rules.

Comparing Theories of Learning and Rules

Those who seriously hold to the autonomously active and morally good human view usually do not have rules or stated consequences. However, behavioristic theories always suggest a set of stated rules and the specific consequence for breaking a rule in a one-to-one correspondence (rule to matching consequence). It will appear like this on a chart: "If you break the rule of _____, you will receive this consequence: _____." (For example: If you talk out of turn, you will receive one checkmark on the white board.) Both of these views—(1) no stated rules or (2) rules for which there is a specific stated matching consequence—are challenged by the cognitive interactive theory of learning because motives and behaviors are always considered, and discernment of the teacher encourages an informed professional response.

The cognitive theorists, who consider both inside and outside factors in the learning event, will suggest a list of rules and a series of *possible* consequences from which the teacher may choose. The choice of consequence depends on the complete context of the behavior, possible motivation for breaking the rule, and number of times the rule has been broken. For example: If you have a rule that homework must be completed and turned in the following school day, the consequence for the same behavior might be different for two individuals in the same class on the same day. How so?

ENGAGE: Scenario to consider:
Rule: Homework must be completed and handed in the day it is assigned to be collected.

Two students do not turn in their homework that is due on Tuesday. When asked, Student #1 tells the teacher that the homework was just busywork and "I had more important things to do than to do it!" The tone of the reply was belligerent. Student #2 explains to the teacher that when she arrived home on Monday, she was not feeling well, and her mother sent her to bed early. She was unable to complete her homework. However, she was better in the morning and her mom sent her to school. The *behaviors* in breaking the rule are the same. Neither student turned in homework. The rule is broken, but for different *reasons* or motivation. Would you agree? However, even if one motive is more acceptable and understandable than the other, both must receive a consequence. If you have rules, there must be consequences for breaking one.

A teacher using a matching rule to matching consequence approach, as suggested by behaviorists, might deliver the paired consequence to both students. Each would receive the exact same consequence. Does this really seem fair? Teachers who use this behavioristic approach can be just as compassionate as others. They might say to the student who was ill the night before, "I am sorry you didn't feel well," and then drop the issue without a consequence. This practice leads to much more inconsistency than does the approach I am sharing. For every broken rule, there must be a consequence, and the consequence must be related to the behavior and the motive.

We will come back to this scenario shortly, but first let us look at classroom rules and consequences as viewed by consistent cognitive interactive theorists. Rules should be limited to four or five simple, easy-to-understand rules, written in positive language as do's rather than don'ts. There should be a list of at least seven or eight consequences for choosing to break a rule. A title on the posted list of consequences should be similar to this one: *If you choose to break a rule, you will receive one of the following consequences.* Students can assist in writing the rules if a teacher so desires. I have found, however, that when students create consequences, they suggest much more complex and severe consequences than those provided by the teacher and often their suggestions need to be modified. Some teachers prefer to write their own set of rules and consequences.

One rule that must be on every list of rules: *Do what the teacher asks you to do when asked.* This covers many behaviors in the classroom and is a safety issue as well as a broad rule that encompasses the classroom procedures. Therefore, if a student habitually fails to follow a classroom management procedure, the behavior may become a discipline event. The teacher will communicate, "You have broken the rule that says that you are to do what the teacher asks, when asked. You know our classroom procedures but have chosen not to abide by them repeatedly. I am giving you a one-time reminder; after this, if you continue to ignore classroom procedures, you will receive another one of the listed consequences that is appropriate."

One consequence that must be on every list of consequences: *You will be given a one-time reminder or warning.* This is not only a matter of grace, but this provides an opportunity to counsel and instruct toward improvement. You will record this first consequence and note that the next time the student refuses to follow a particular classroom rule, the student will again receive a consequence, but it will be one beyond a "reminder."

The reason I write that a warning or reminder for a particular behavior that breaks a rule should be singular (one time), is that too many approaches allow the student to have three events presenting the same rule-breaking behavior before there is a consequence; it is a "three strikes and you are out" policy. Three checks by the name of the offender on the board is an example of this approach. I view this as inviting the student to misbehave two more times before there is a consequence. It is easy to use a checkmark system because there is little communication, counsel, or instruction. However, allowing three misdeeds may defeat the purpose of discipline to develop character and self-discipline.

Back to the scenario on breaking a rule: Let us return to the scenario of the two students who did not complete the homework assignment. Does the girl who was ill deserve a consequence? She certainly deserves respect, compassion, and understanding. However, the principle that a broken rule creates a consequence comes into play. If the rule was broken, the answer is yes, there must be a consequence.

In this scenario, the girl will be given *a reminder* that in the future she should bring a note from home telling why she did not do her homework. Since she did not complete the homework that was vital to the learning for the day, the teacher will allow her to work on and complete the assignment during the day, if possible, and offer to help her complete it during lunch break or free time, or have another student in class help her complete it. This is not punishment but rather caring and compassionate help to prepare her for the day's lesson. It is an inconvenience for the teacher and may be for another student as well! It is the practice of servanthood, however. A gentle reminder that the next time she is ill, or something comes up that deters her from doing her homework, a note from home is appropriate. This latter statement is instruction. Remember, discipline involves instruction. Did she receive a consequence? Yes. She was warned and instructed to bring a note the next time something occurs that is similar to this time.

The second student was belligerent and disrespectful. While his *behavior* was identical to the student above, his reasons and motives were quite different. What will be his consequence?

As with all discipline situations, communication is the first step. I would ask the student if he understood the assignment and needed help to complete it. Let the student talk. Then share that he will need the homework for the lesson today and you will help him if needed. You may wish to have him miss a free time to do the work and tell him you will be available to help if needed. Some very rude responses to teachers are because of frustration and not knowing how to proceed. Some rude behaviors are to save face with the group. But what is his consequence?

The first thing a teacher should ask when dealing with a belligerent child is "Did I or some other person say or do something that triggered this response?" Let the student talk. But then the teacher must say, "The behavior and attitude you just manifested when you were approached about breaking the homework rule is totally unacceptable; do you understand? The next time this occurs, your parents will be called to discuss the behavior and the attitude you presented." The teacher should write it down. I used a clipboard for this kind of note reminder. If the student is middle school or above, I would have him or her sign it. This indicates that you are serious about the rude or belligerent attitude, and this (next consequence) will happen if this occurs again.

I selected as a scenario, homework, because so many teachers have a rule that homework must be turned in the day following the assignment. When I taught middle school, I did not have homework on my list of rules. Homework was either to practice what was learned that day or to prepare for learning the next day in some interesting way, such as a survey question to have three people answer. Among the rules I used when homework was not completed was the one listed above as a must. Homework could be considered under the rule to "do what the teacher asks when asked." If homework is not completed and turned in, the teacher has the professional responsibility to find out why. Depending on the circumstances, a consequence and instruction should follow.

The grade level to some extent guides in the establishing of rules. Even for the high school level, the first rule may be worded, "Do what the teacher asks you to do when asked." When instructing about rules, it is wise to say that you will never ask students to do anything that will harm them or that is morally wrong.

Examples of Classroom Rules

Here are some examples of rules written by teachers, posted in their classrooms, and used daily. The meaning of each rule must be discussed and taught. Some of the rules listed below are a crossover between a classroom management procedure and a weightier rule. They could be placed on the rule chart because they are an absolute must for decorum in learning. Take note of the rules in bold. This is the one I think is essential on every list and covers a multitude of infractions. The following examples were taken from education majors' observations in actual classrooms.

Elementary Level: 5 Rules

1. **Listen carefully to what the teacher says and do what the teacher asks you to do when asked.**
2. Take care of all the things that belong to you, the school, and the classroom.
3. Follow all classroom and school procedures to provide a community in which we can learn.
4. Raise your hand and ask for permission to leave your seat.
5. Be kind and respectful to others at all times.

Middle School: 4 Rules

1. **Listen to and follow directions the first time they are given by the teacher.**
2. Speak appropriately by not using vulgar or offensive language.
3. Move from one activity to another quietly and follow all other classroom procedures.
4. Respect yourself, other classmates, and the teacher by keeping your hands and your things to yourself and not using the property of others without permission.

High School: 4 Rules

1. **Do what the teacher asks you to do when asked**.
2. Raise your hand and wait to be acknowledged when you wish to speak or want to leave your seat.
3. Keep your hands to yourself; only with permission may you touch another person or their things.
4. When someone is talking in front of the group, look at him or her and listen respectfully.
5. Be an encourager by not putting people down with talk or actions.

You can see in these brief lists why the very first rule should be all-encompassing. The other rules are more specific, while the "required rule" covers a multitude of misbehaviors.

ENGAGE: Pause and take a few minutes to (1) evaluate each of the rules above at the grade level you teach and determine potential problems or possibilities that each one might bring; (2) write a set of four or five rules worded as you would like to have them worded for your class and grade level.

Examples of Consequences

Below are some possible consequences for your list. Select the ones you would like to post and add others that fit your situation.

If you choose to break a rule, one of the following will happen:

You will receive a one-time warning.

You will be assigned a different seat.

You will lose a privilege.

You will be given a written reflection assignment about what you did.

You will not have the choice to use certain materials.

You will be sent to the school office for discipline. (This should be rare.)

You will be required to have a conference with the teacher and principal.

Your parents may be called.

Your parents may be called to the school for a conference.

You will receive a detention.

You will receive an in-school suspension.

You will be referred to the head of school for out-of-school suspension.

You may be referred to the police if a law is broken. (This is always done by the chief or head administrator.)

ENGAGE: You may think of other possible consequences for your school. Add these. Evaluate both the rules and the consequences for practicality and effectiveness.

Rules and consequences must be understood by the students. For example, if you have a rule that forbids unkind or vulgar language in the classroom, students must be aware of what you consider unkind or vulgar speech. Even before such words come from students' mouths, the teacher should teach the rule and encourage class members to "put on" edifying or building-up speech and "put off" unwholesome talk. Ephesians 4 is a great passage to use. Paul, the author, speaks of putting off unwholesome talk and "putting on" speech that builds up. Discuss what building up others means. James 3 is another good passage that speaks of what comes out of our mouths and what it can do to others. Foul language is often a habit that must be broken. It takes not only patience but also a willingness to persevere consistently on the part of the teacher. Consequences should be couched in the language of: "I know that this word is a habit and I want to help you break the habit for the good of yourself and others."

When you teach the rule about listening to and doing what the teacher asks when asked, it is important to give several situations that will include: instructions for getting attention, instructions for an activity, instructions for lining up to leave the room, instructions to follow if or when the school office communicates an emergency, etc. Many of these examples fall under your classroom management procedures that may become discipline situations if a student habitually fails to follow decorum. When students have examples to connect with rules, they will understand the nature of the rule and be less inclined to make excuses for their behavior.

Summary of Principles for Student Discipline

1. Motives and behaviors are important. Look at the breaking of a rule in context. The behavior alone is never the total issue.

2. For every broken rule there must be a consequence, and the consequence should be determined by teachers as they discern the whole situation including the number of times the rule has been broken (first time or fifth, for example) and whether or not the broken rule was something purely developmental, for attention, or out of deliberate disobedience.

3. Teachers should fit the consequence to the motives/reason for the behavior as best they can determine. Give the student the benefit of the doubt. Two-way communication is vital. Let the student talk. However, do not let him or her talk you out of a consequence.

4. Teachers must have a range of consequences from which to choose as they professionally use their knowledge of the situation. (This is a professional skill.)

5. Discipline involves communication. When there is a need to discipline a student, ask yourself, "What should I do?" (action) and "What should I say?" (communication).

Communicate with clarity. "This is what you are doing wrong, and this is what you should begin to do now!" This is a major key to discipline and gives the student the opportunity to immediately choose to follow the rule or choose to break the rule and suffer the consequence. Remember, humans have a mind to think about the situation and a will to choose right over wrong. Sometimes their immediate actions are simply developmental, and a reminder is in order with information concerning the incident to help them grow and avoid it another time. Some misdeeds are attention-seeking misbehaviors and if stopped immediately may be discussed at a later time in the day with a warning. (But do not forget to address it.) If it is a repeated behavior, another consequence is issued. Some misbehaviors are deliberate disobedience or defiance and must be handled immediately.

Movement. In handling most discipline situations, it is important to go directly toward the student. **Physical proximity** is vital. It is easier to discipline if you are off your seat and on your feet as you teach. Movement around the classroom as you teach provides a visual advantage that standing behind a podium or sitting at a desk does not afford. When you are within three feet of a student, your comments or questions can be directed toward the offending student quietly addressing the situation. This is far better than yelling across the room.

On task. To avoid discipline situations, use effective classroom management practices, one of which is to get the students on task immediately as they enter the classroom. When they are working on something either individually or in pairs with or without allowed talking, there will be less occasion for fooling around that may cause trouble. Some class-starters require talking and are motivation or engagement activities for the lesson of the day. During this time, it is important to be alert to all that is going on even when you might be taking roll for a middle school or high school class.

"With-it-ness," a term coined by Jacob Kounin in the 1970s, refers to the ability of teachers to be aware of "what is going on in their classrooms at all times."[3] It includes not only awareness but sensitivity to the needs of their students. It is one of the chief characteristics of a good teacher and is essential for effective classroom management and student discipline.

Conclusion

Teachers who wish to be Christ-centered in their approach to discipline and consistent with their theory of human learning will understand that discipline of a student never stops with the consequence. To be effective in promoting the aim of life, the aim of education, and the aim of discipline, there must be a demonstration of compassion,

---

[3] Anita Woolfolk, *Educational Psychology*, 11th ed. (Columbus, OH: Merrill, 2010), 432, 433.

forgiveness, and restoration that promotes growth. Discipline is always motivated by love. And love is described in 1 Corinthians 13 this way:

> Love is patient, love is kind. It does not envy, it does not boast, it is not proud. It does not dishonor others, it is not self-seeking, it is not easily angered, it keeps no record of wrongs. Love does not delight in evil but rejoices with the truth. It always protects, always trusts, always hopes, always perseveres. Love never fails. . . . And now these three remain: faith, hope and love. But the greatest of these is love. (vv. 4–8, 13 NIV)

REFLECT: Think through the keys to a cognitive interactive approach to discipline that includes taking into consideration the behavior and the motive in context. How might this approach deliver a fairer and more consistent pattern for discipline? Why might this be so?

Now think about your current practices or past experiences. Contrast the approach suggested in this and the previous chapter and 1 Corinthians' character of love to what you have done or experienced in the past.

ENGAGE: Write your philosophy of discipline using the four key components:

1. Aim of discipline
2. Nature of the learner (discipline is a learning event)
3. Role of the teacher in discipline
4. Nature and purpose of the curriculum as it relates to a caring learning community

Extended Research and Reflection: In what ways has the content of this and the previous chapter addressed these InTASC standards?

> Standard #2: Learning Differences. The teacher uses understanding of individual differences and diverse cultures and communities to ensure inclusive learning environments that enable each learner to meet high standards.

> Standard #3: Learning Environments. The teacher works with others to create environments that support individual and collaborative learning, and that encourage positive social interaction, active engagement in learning, and self-motivation.[4]

---

[4] "Interstate Assessment and Support Consortium," Council of Chief State School Officers 2013 (Washington, DC).

CHAPTER 11

Social and Emotional Learning

Ken Coley

Introduction

Few topics of concern in our profession have received the attention that Social and Emotional Learning (SEL) has received in the past decade. In this chapter we will present an overview of the research related to the impact, both positive and negative, that social environment and relationships have on a student's academic progress and overall well-being. Closely connected to these external influences are a student's emotions that have an overwhelming influence on an individual's ability to focus, comprehend, and remember new information. In addition, educators are increasingly aware of life skills related to both dimensions that we need to guide young people to develop. The days of viewing learning as a purely cognitive activity are in the rearview mirror, along with the notion that much needed interpersonal and intrapersonal skills are to be taught at home. Our students of all ages need our support and coaching to be successful as scholars and as future leaders and citizens.

As you have been challenged to think biblically in each facet of your educational philosophy throughout this text, you will need to process the presentation of educational research through the lens of Scripture. Frequently in academic discussions on social-emotional learning the notion of *self* is presented as a focus of concern, even one's ultimate concern. Our Christian commitment compels us to place our Creator God above all else, even our own personhood. And second, to love our neighbor as ourselves. We order our values, attitudes, and behaviors from these perspectives. As this chapter unfolds, we trust that our readers will begin to integrate biblical principles into this dialogue. *Our faith based on the reality of grace and mercy available to us through our Savior must be the foundation of all our social interaction.*

A young educator does not have to spend years or even days in a classroom to make meaningful observations about the powerful impact that social relationships and personal emotions have on learning. Early in my career I gathered my class of seventh graders around a cassette player to listen to a narrator with a deep bass voice read one of Edgar Allen Poe's short stories. To enhance the experience, I turned the lights down and lit a single candle. The tension built until the dramatic climax of frightening events for which Poe is famous. One student was so involved in the story that she let out a spontaneous scream. I believe everyone in the room at that moment jumped from their seats including the teacher. We all had a great laugh and settled in for the denouement of the story. Just to be clear, scaring my class was not part of my lesson plan, but no one has forgotten Poe and his ability to captivate his readers. That twenty-two-year-old English teacher had no insight into the neuroscience behind that instructional episode, that is, what brain activity brought about durable learning in those moments. He had never heard of cortisol or dopamine, chemicals the brain releases as we focus on a mysterious story. He just knew middle schoolers love a good story. That is just one snapshot of an exciting first year of teaching during which I believe I learned far more than my students, and I am excited to share the current research on social-emotional learning, almost fifty years later, with the readers of this text.

Permit me one additional snapshot of a high school teaching experience before we progress to the research. I moved to a new area and school where I was a total stranger. I invested time getting to know my students' names and began to connect with each class. I also quickly discovered there was a young man who had a noticeable birth defect that had earned him a cruel nickname. I observed he was exceptionally quiet and withdrawn. He would enter the room, drop his bookbag, and immediately dive into a science fiction novel. I recall praying for a day when he would be absent. A day of reckoning for his classmates. Finally, that day came. To say I had a serious talk with those who used that demeaning nickname doesn't accurately characterize my ire. But the name was never spoken again in my room for the remainder of the year. I had three simple goals that day of reckoning: protect the emotional well-being of their classmate, establish my classroom as an oasis for all students to be secure and safe, and start the group of insensitive students on a journey of learning empathy for others.

CASEL and SEL

Two other acronyms that you may have already encountered occur frequently in the literature. The Collaborative for Academic, Social, and Emotional Learning (CASEL) is a trusted source for knowledge about high-quality, evidence-based social and emotional learning (SEL). CASEL supports educators and policy leaders and enhances the experiences and outcomes for all PreK–12 students. "CASEL's mission is to help make evidence-based social and emotional learning (SEL) an integral part of education from preschool through high school." Previously, their website also stated, "Our work is critical at a time when educators, parents, students, and employers increasingly recognize the value of SEL. Together, we are united in our call for schools to educate the whole child, equipping students for success in school and in life."[1] Many educators reference the five interrelated cognitive, affective, and behavioral competencies, for which CASEL (2005) is given credit, for developing: self-awareness, social awareness, relationship skills, self-management, and responsible decision-making.[2]

The Five Cognitive, Affective, and Behavioral Competencies

ENGAGE: Make a list of the five competencies from CASEL described below and reflect on your initial impressions. To what extent did you receive coaching and encouragement in these areas? Which ones do you believe you are strong in and are prepared to mentor your students in that area? Is there a corresponding category that you feel you need to improve in before you are ready to model this skill to students? Having considered all five categories, is there something missing? Review your philosophy that you designed, and we'll come back to this last question later in this chapter.

---

[1] CASEL, Our Mission and Work, "Our Mission," CASEL website, https://casel.org /about-us/our-mission-work/; "Collaborative for Academic, Social, and Emotional Learning (CASEL) (SEL Resources During COVID-19 and Infographics)" TTAC Online, https://ttac online.org/Resource/JWHaEa5BS75Su6aQC1Lg9w/Resource-collaborative-for-academic -social-and-emotional-learning-casel-sel-resources-during-covid-19.

[2] Nancy Boyles, "Learning Character from Characters," *Educational Leadership* 76, no. 2 (October 2018): 70; Nancy Frey, Douglas Fisher, and Dominique Smith, *All Learning Is Social and Emotional: Helping Students Develop Essential Skills for the Classroom and Beyond* (Alexandria, VA: ASCD, 2019), 3–4; Marilee Sprenger, *Social Emotional Learning and the Brain: Strategies to Help Your Students Thrive* (Alexandria, VA: ASCD, 2020), 3.

1. **Self-awareness**: The ability to understand one's own emotions, thoughts, and values and how they influence behavior across contexts. This includes the capacity to recognize one's strengths and limitations with a well-grounded sense of confidence and purpose.

2. **Self-management**: The ability to manage one's emotions, thoughts, and behaviors effectively in different situations and to achieve goals and aspirations. This includes the capacity to delay gratification, manage stress, and feel motivation and agency to accomplish personal and collective goals.

3. **Responsible decision-making**: The ability to make caring and constructive choices about personal behavior and social interactions across diverse situations. This includes the capacity to consider ethical standards and safety concerns, and to evaluate the benefits and consequences of various actions for personal, social, and collective well-being.

4. **Relationship skills**: The ability to establish and maintain healthy and supportive relationships and to effectively navigate settings with diverse individuals and groups. This includes the capacity to communicate clearly, listen actively, cooperate, work collaboratively to problem solve and negotiate conflict constructively, navigate settings with differing social and cultural demands and opportunities, provide leadership, and seek or offer help when needed.

5. **Social awareness**: The ability to understand the perspectives of and empathize with others, including those from diverse backgrounds, cultures, and contexts. This includes the capacity to feel compassion for others, understand broader historical and social norms for behavior in different settings, and recognize family, school, and community resources and supports.[3]

Another important term is **adverse childhood experiences** (ACEs), traumatic events that prevent or decrease learning. Benson points out that many schools collect data on their students including physical and emotional abuse, domestic violence, and household mental illness.[4] Sprenger points out that "positive childhood experiences can counteract some of the resulting trauma. Social emotional learning has the power to create some of these positive experiences."[5] In her book *Fostering Resilient Learners:*

---

[3] "CASEL's SEL Framework: What Are the Core Competence Areas and Where Are They Promoted?" October 1, 2020, https://casel.org/casel-sel-framework-11-2020/.

[4] Jeffrey Benson, *Improve Every Lesson Plan with SEL* (Alexandria, VA: ASCD, 2021), 5.

[5] Sprenger, *Social Emotional Learning and the Brain*, 1.

Strategies for Creating a Trauma-Sensitive Classroom, Kristin Souers cites research from Anda and Felitti's study on the prevalence of the following ACEs:

- Substance abuse in the home
- Parental separation or divorce
- Mental illness in the home
- Witnessing domestic violence
- Suicidal household member
- Death of a parent or another loved one
- Parental incarceration
- Experiences of abuse (psychological, physical, or sexual) or neglect (emotional or physical)[6]

The presence of ACEs in so many students' lives compels Souers to argue that in addition to the traditional three Rs in academics, educators must prepare themselves to assist students in learning the Rs of *Responsibility*, *Respect*, *Resilience*, and *Relationship*.[7] Throughout her book she stresses the need for a classroom where each student experiences an environment in which he or she is healthy, safe, engaged, supported, and challenged.[8] Gregory and Chapman concur with this concern. They state the issue succinctly: "Students living in fear cannot learn. Students will not attend to learning if their major concern is safety. The higher the level of stress, the less access to higher levels of thinking and the greater the feeling of flight or fight, a basic survival response."[9]

ENGAGE: Review the list of terms below associated with SEL. Rate your understanding of each on a scale of 1–3 (like a stoplight).

1–no understanding (red: *stop!*) **2**–somewhat familiar (yellow: *move slowly*) **3**–I got this! (green: *go!*)

Self-efficacy	Grit	Empathy
Growth mindset	Resiliency	Mindfulness

---

[6] Kristin Souers, *Fostering Resilient Learners: Strategies for Creating a Trauma-Sensitive Classroom* (Alexandria, VA: ASCD, 2016), 17.

[7] Souers, 1.

[8] Souers, 3.

[9] Gayle H. Gregory and Carolyn Chapman, *Differentiated Instructional Strategies: One Size Doesn't Fit All* (Thousand Oaks, CA: Corwin, 2013), 17.

Self-Efficacy

Educators Nancy Frey, Douglas Fisher, and Dominique Smith present the six key words in the previous engagement in their discussion of SEL. First, consider a term related to self-belief. *Self-efficacy* has to do with a student's perception of his ability to take action, solve problems, and accomplish a task. Frey, Fisher, and Smith challenge educators to "consider that an important factor in self-efficacy is believing that the task is within your capacity, and a step toward that belief is seeing someone else complete the task successfully—particularly someone like you."[10] They suggest using videos or pictures of previous classes achieving the outcomes of the lessons. Our discussion in chapter 4 about scaffolding is crucial in developing your students' self-belief. Incremental improvements toward curriculum goals encourage students' momentum to achieve new skills.

A related topic to this discussion on self-efficacy is an individual's ability to cheer for his or her own achievements. Souers reminds educators that "students who have experienced trauma have a significantly compromised capacity to *self-acknowledge*— that is, to recognize and validate themselves, their feelings, or their efforts."[11] Students who have experienced trauma often rely on external cues from their environment to make decisions about what they should or should not attempt. As each student is able to strengthen his or her own capacity to applaud his or her own effort and be less reliant on the praise of others, each will grow in self-efficacy.

In another publication Frey, Fisher, and Almarode recommend that teachers develop tools for self-assessment that allow their students to evaluate their own progress toward curriculum goals. One such approach is for teachers to list the success criteria for a unit of study early in the unit and have each student rank the level of challenge (1=easy, 5=hard) that goal presents. They argue that such skills are crucial as students progress toward careers that require employees to set goals and assess their own progress.[12]

Here are other strategies to assist students in this important area of development:

- Praise students' effort, not just goal achievement.
- Present models of success and corresponding rubrics.

---

[10] Frey, Fisher, and Smith, *All Learning Is Social and Emotional*, 29.

[11] Souers, *Fostering Resilient Learners*, 184.

[12] Douglas Fisher, Nancy Frey, and John Almarode, *Student Learning Communities: A Springboard for Academic and Social-Emotional Development* (Alexandria, VA: ASCD, 2021), 69–71.

- Present poor models and challenge groups of students to collaborate on evaluating them.
- Differentiate all aspects of instruction: content, process, product evaluation.

REFLECT: Think about areas of your professional and personal life that you lacked opportunity to explore, failed to receive any basic guidance or coaching, or even worse, were discouraged by adults to attempt. Any regrets? I frequently regret dropping my physics class in high school. I often have curiosity about the way things work but lack any understanding of rudimentary properties such as speed, friction, force, mass, etc. How can your experiences of regret fuel your desire to inspire others?

One day I received a package containing a book that I didn't order nor was I familiar with. It was a children's book. With curiosity I opened the cover to find the following handwritten note:

> *Dr. Coley,*
> *Your encouraging words over 20 years ago took root—growth was slow, but it did come.*
> *Thank you! Happy reading!*

Over two decades after one of my creative writing students graduated from high school, this author included my name on the acknowledgments page and followed up with a personal letter enclosed. I cannot recall a more succinct and moving example of growing self-efficacy. It read in part:

> *I'm sure you don't remember me in your high school English and Creative Writing classes. I was a skinny, shy, rather awkward young lady. Not memorable really in any way. When other folks describe their senior year as "the best of their lives," I just shake my head in wonder. . . . But the year had two good things going for it. I made a few close friends, and I took Creative Writing from Mr. Coley. You always had some encouraging words on each assignment I did. I doubt I deserved that, but in your enthusiastic and encouraging way you'd write a phrase, and it always ended in an exclamation point! I thought to myself, "Someday when I write a book, I've just got to thank him!"*

REFLECT: Unfortunately, many adults grew up in home, school, and athletic environments in which words of encouragement were in short supply. I often ask educators attending my workshops to spontaneously make a list of words of praise that they write on student papers. It's remarkable how often I encounter teachers who have been in classrooms for many years who can't come up with more than four or five words. How about you?

Teacher-Student Relationships

"Classroom teachers probably spend more time with students than any other adults. This is an opportunity to model appropriate social interactions, show students that we care for them, and support them in their endeavors."[13] Jesus pointed out in Luke 6:40, "A [student/]disciple is not above his teacher, but everyone who is fully trained will be like his teacher." Hudgins refers to this as "likeness education."[14] Sprenger urges us to consider, "Before we can teach students how to handle relationships with their peers, we, as educators, need to model relationship building."[15] "If you ask adults how many teachers they had meaningful relationships with—that is, how many teachers they trusted and knew cared about them—most respondents would probably come up with only one or two from grades K–12 and most likely none at the university level."[16] I have posed the same question in countless workshops and conferences and gotten the same answer—one or two, but many adults report zero.

When I was the head of a Christian school, I instinctively understood the impact just one adult could have on a student's life. As a faculty we systematically combed our class rosters and made sure every student had at minimum one teacher or coach who interacted with him or her as an individual. We challenge you and your colleagues to do your own research. Ask adults whom you interact with to respond to this question:

"Beyond conversations about discipline issues, do you have mental snapshots of a teacher, coach, or administrator talking to you as an individual? If so, what was the impact of that conversation on your life and relationships at school?"

Growth Mindset

A second term of major importance in SEL involves the attitude you bring to a new task or learning episode. Carol Dweck was one of the first educators to discuss the powerful impact a student's mindset has on learning. She maintains that there are two prevalent

---

[13] Sprenger, *Social Emotional Learning and the Brain*, 19.

[14] Thomas W. Hudgins, *Luke 6:40 and the Theme of Likeness Education in the New Testament* (Eugene, OR: Wipf & Stock, 2014).

[15] Sprenger, *Social Emotional Learning and the Brain*, 13.

[16] Sprenger, 15.

mindsets: *fixed* and *growth*. Students with a fixed mindset believe their chances of success are restricted by their natural talents and abilities and their effort has little to no impact on the results. Because of this perspective, many students will take one shot at achieving a goal. If they are not successful, their mindset causes them to stop trying.[17] Students often think, "Nothing is going to change. I'm not smart enough to get this."

On the other hand, students with a growth mindset believe their current abilities can be expanded through hard work and dedication. Marilee Sprenger encourages educators to actively teach students about how their brain works—that their brain changes as they learn new information and reinforce prior learning. As a classroom teacher, Sprenger refers to herself as a "brain-changer" and explains that their brains are like muscles—working out yields stronger muscles in the gym. So, too, tackling new information in the classroom builds stronger networks and connections.[18]

As a first-semester senior, just prior to my semester of student teaching, I spent that fall at the University of London studying literature. One afternoon, it was my turn to present my paper on the Russian novel *Crime and Punishment* by Fyodor Dostoevsky. Despite my enthusiasm for the book and my diligent preparation, I was humiliated by my professor who dismantled my argument and embarrassed me in front of the class. What made the lasting impression on me that evening as I rode the London subway and stared into the darkness was the nagging doubt that I couldn't achieve my goal to become a teacher. That afternoon's failure had created that uncertainty. However, I came to realize in the days that followed that I had indeed been called to teach by God and that I could learn from the stinging experience and grow in my pursuit of my calling. Long before the recent discussion on growth mindset, I was an educator who believed students could grow from their experiences, myself included.

Marc Brackett, director of the Yale Center for Emotional Intelligence, gives educators helpful insights from his research in this area.

> By unlocking the wisdom of the emotions, we can develop young people who are kind, caring, and resilient as well as academically successful. We can teach our students to collaborate, take risks, and get up when they're knocked down. Emotion skills are especially important for students facing adverse childhood experiences because the psychological and biological stress responses that accompany trauma impact motivation and executive functioning. If children

---

[17] Carol Dweck, *Mindset: The New Psychology of Success: How We Can Learn to Fulfill Our Potential* (New York: Ballantine Books, 2006), 6–7.

[18] Sprenger, *Social Emotional Learning and the Brain*, 82.

facing trauma have tools for dealing with their hurt, frustration, and stress, they too will have opportunities to learn and thrive.[19]

Grit

A third key term in this discussion, which is closely related to growth mindset is the notion of *grit*. Well-known educational researcher Dr. Angela Duckworth spent years tracking data from multiple sectors like US Military Academies, National Spelling Bee competitors, and average students in inner-city schools. She asked a compelling question: What factor is the single best predictor for success? Her answer: *grit*. In a recent interview, Duckworth described the concept as "one-part passion and one-part perseverance."[20] She describes it this way: "Grit really starts with passion. . . . Usually it starts as interest, curiosity." And what does a gritty school look like? "I think that's what a gritty school and a gritty classroom look like. It's really demanding. It asks for things you don't think you can do, but then you have a person with unconditional support, that you surprise yourself with what you can accomplish."[21]

Frey, Fisher, and Smith link grit and perseverance in their discussion of a student's willingness to stick with a challenge. They point out that schooling is filled with opportunities to establish goals (some long-term) and work hard over an extended period to achieve these goals. In addition, they maintain that these qualities should be invested in pursuits that better the lives of others.[22] Many schools and churches offer children and teens challenging events like food drives or home renovation projects that provide both significant challenges and meaningful contributions to the lives of others.

Hoerr presents an interesting and valuable nuance to this discussion—coaching "smart grit," teaching students "to recognize those times that when stopping the pursuit of a goal is wise because the gain is not worth the cost."[23] I recall endlessly practicing the game of basketball to make the varsity team. After failing to do so my junior year, I thought it a better use of my time to switch to track. The decision paid off my

---

[19] Marc Brackett, "Intelligence We Owe Students and Educators," *Educational Leadership* 76, no. 2 (October 2018):18.

[20] Sarah McKibben, "Grit and the Greater Good: A Conversation with Angela Duckworth," *Educational Leadership* 76, no. 2 (October 2018): 44.

[21] McKibben, "Grit and the Greater Good," 44–45.

[22] Frey, Fisher, and Smith, *All Learning Is Social and Emotional*, 34.

[23] Thomas R. Hoerr, *The Formative Five: Fostering Grit, Empathy, and Other Success Skills Every Student Needs* (Alexandria, VA: ASCD, 2017), 120.

senior year when I earned a letter and graduated with the school record in the two-mile event. But it wasn't lost on me that the tenacity and discipline I learned from one transferred to the other.

Here's how educators can develop a gritty culture in their classrooms:

1. Establish the environment: What do you praise, applaud, and reward?
2. Setting expectations: Faculty must model for students adapting to frustration and failure.
3. Teaching the vocabulary: Ideas such as "good failures" strengthen understanding.
4. Creating frustration: Announce to students that some days or events are meant to be difficult.
5. Monitor the experience: Teachers must be aware of students' attitudes and struggles.
6. Reflecting and learning: Lead students in discussions on challenging situations.[24]

ENGAGE: Imagine ways that you can create a classroom environment that inspires the courage and risk-taking that accompany grit. Will you have to change how you grade? What do you applaud and praise? Reflect on the quote below and discuss with other educators a new rubric that includes attitudes like this one:

> Grit gives us the courage to take risks and to fail because we know that failure is a necessary ingredient in ultimate success.[25]

Trauma

Blodgett and his team of researchers from Washington State conducted a study of elementary-aged children in Spokane County to gauge the frequency of the eight ACEs listed previously. The results confirmed the prevalence of ACEs:

- 45 percent had at least one ACE.
- 22 percent of students had multiple ACEs.
- 1 in 16 students had an ACE score of 4 or higher.[26]

---

[24] Hoerr, 123–26.
[25] Hoerr, 119.
[26] Souers, *Fostering Resilient Learners*, 20.

In the midst of extreme stress, our bodies are forced to respond via a heightened state of alert known as the flight, fight, or freeze response. Our bodies are designed to be in that state only for brief periods, and only in the face of extreme danger. But when children are exposed to complex or acute trauma, the brain shifts its operation from development to stress response, which can have lasting repercussions.[27]

The Old Testament has three remarkable portraits of teens experiencing trauma and responding with a godly response and their own brand of grit. Though we do not know all the details in each case, their character, speech, and behavior under extreme pressure reveal a foundation of belief that can inspire all of us, especially teachers of teens. As you review these familiar characters, consider adding a fourth option to our list of classic responses: *fight, flight, freeze*, or ***faith***.

Trauma #1: Joseph was cherished by his father Jacob but despised by his brothers. He was attacked, thrown in a pit, and sold into slavery. When he arrived in Egypt, he became a servant in a strange world. But when confronted with the opportunity to betray his master by sleeping with the man's wife, his character and spiritual training overrode his emotions. Thinking clearly, he acted bravely and decisively (Genesis 39).

Trauma #2: Daniel and his teenage companions were rounded up by the conquering Babylonians and taken to the capital of a foreign land. The young men were enrolled in a training program that would challenge everything they had ever been taught, even the food they were to eat. When confronted with the opportunity to set aside their training regarding food and drinks that Jewish men were not to accept, they requested in faith for a period of time to prove themselves to their captors. The result: None better (Daniel 1)!

Trauma #3: Esther was an orphan who lived with her relative in a foreign land. Because of her beauty, she was selected to be queen and marry the king of Persia, a harsh man who had banished the previous queen. In addition, he did not care anything about her Jewish faith and worship of God. He didn't even know she was Jewish. When all Jewish people under the king's rule were threatened, she set aside her own safety and acted in faith so that all her people were saved (Esther 8).

---

[27] Souers, 21.

REFLECT: Perhaps you, like many members of your generation, have experienced one or more of the ACEs described in this chapter. Before you turn your attention to helping others heal, have you taken the necessary steps for your own healing? I have shared the above biblical portraits so that you may be strengthened in your faith and encouraged as you move forward in your career. As was stated by Joseph in Gen 50:20, "You planned evil against me; God planned it for good."

Resiliency

Many athletes of all ages have written Scripture on the bill inside their baseball hat or on some athletic tape or wristband or had it printed on a T-shirt worn underneath a uniform. One of my favorites is Phil 4:13: "I am able to do all things through him who strengthens me." This speaks to the term *resiliency*, the ability to overcome challenges.[28] Souers defines *resilience* as "our capacity to acknowledge and attend to personal difficulties while still working toward expectations."[29] All members of a school community, adults included, face adversity and react in a variety of ways. Many have personal and/or internal resources that allow them to bounce back and even learn from difficulties. All too often, some students are left struggling or emotionally paralyzed. Frey, Fisher, and Smith present a list of practices that support and help build students' internal resources and environmental protective factors:

- Caring relationships with teachers and mentors
- Clear and consistent structures, such as classroom routines and a culture of respect
- Exposure to narratives of others who have overcome adversity
- Mirroring students' strengths back to them
- Opportunities to help and serve others[30]

ENGAGE: Recount snapshots in your own story that you could share with a group of students that include difficult circumstances in which you persevered and developed resiliency. Now reflect on one of the disciplines that you teach and jot down names of authors, leaders, and theorists who overcame long odds and demonstrated resiliency. Set a goal to share at least one per week with your students.

---

[28] Frey, Fisher, and Smith, *All Learning Is Social and Emotional*, 35.
[29] Souers, *Fostering Resilient Learners*, 154.
[30] Frey, Fisher, and Smith, *All Learning Is Social and Emotional*, 38.

Empathy

My daughter and I joined with a ministry one summer to spend a week in another city assisting families with home renovation projects such as painting and roofing that they otherwise would not be able to afford. I was asked to work with a group of middle schoolers who were assigned to paint the entire exterior of a lady's home. As we went about our work, I noticed windows on one side of her home were boarded up, and I asked if she would like to have the plywood removed or painted over? I'll never forget her response and it changed me forever. She replied, "No, leave the wood over the window, please. That's the side of the house that is hidden from the street. That's the window that thieves enter through when they pick my house to break into." In addition to that learning experience, I was blessed to hear her testimony of being a cancer survivor. As we finished up at the end of the week, our new friend wept with tears of appreciation for the magnificent change in her home. But the real transformation took place in my heart and the lives of our crew of young painters.

Once again referring to the apostle Paul's letter to the Philippians, his words are instructive to us: "Do nothing out of rivalry or conceit, but in humility consider others as more important than yourselves. Everyone should look out not only for his own interests, but also for the interests of others" (2:3–4 HCSB). Notice the balance that is stated here: put others first while advocating for your own needs. Students need to be taught how to do this. D'Erizans, Jung, and Bibbo point out that "students with disabilities need to feel like they can master the 'role of a student' in order to experience a sense of belonging. . . . Even minimal signs of social connection can have positive effects on student motivation and achievement."[31]

Author of *Unselfie: Why Empathetic Kids Succeed in Our All-About-Me World*, Borba presents nine competencies that she argues can be taught in K–12 schools:

1. *Emotional Literacy*: Step one is to learn to read emotions. "Empathy thrives in environments that prioritize face-to-face connections."[32] Teachers can help by arranging their rooms in ways that encourage communication and designing lessons that include engagement and collaboration. In addition, teachers need to be with students and model caring relationships.

---

[31] Roberto d'Erizans, Lee Ann Jung, and Tamatha Bibbo, "Don't Forget about Me!" *Educational Leadership* 77, no. 2 (October 2019): 63–64.

[32] Michele Borba, "Nine Competencies for Teaching Empathy," *Educational Leadership* 76, no. 2 (2018): 24, https://www.ascd.org/el/articles/nine-competencies-for-teaching-empathy.

2. *Moral Identity*: "A child's inner value system can inspire empathy, shape character, and motivate compassion."[33] The messaging pervasive in our society focuses on independence and personal achievement. Educators can highlight developmentally appropriate discussions, essays, and classroom wide principles to coach children on identifying "what do we stand for."

3. *Perspective Taking*: Learning to view things from a variety of vantage points, not just empathizing with people who are "like us."[34]

4. *Moral Imagination*: Literature and the arts provide abundant opportunities for students to encounter other cultures and time periods through fictional characters. Novels, short stories, poetry, films, paintings, and drama are all ways to sharpen students' imagination.

5. *Self-Regulation*: The goal here is for students to keep their emotions in check and while identifying others' feelings, empathize, and think about assisting to make the situation better. One researcher argues that "managing emotions is a better predictor of academic achievement than IQ."[35]

6. *Practicing Kindness*: Borba maintains, "Each kind act nudges kids to notice others ('I see how you feel'), care ('I'm concerned about you'), empathize ('I feel with you'), and help and comfort the hurting ('Let me ease your pain')."[36]

7. *Collaboration*: Classroom and extracurricular activities develop skills in teamwork, listening, and resolving conflicts. Each of these is significant in preparation for adulthood in a diverse world.

8. *Moral Courage*: Standing up for others requires strength of character and a willingness to take risks. "Strategies like debate, engaging class discussions, Socratic dialogue, and civic discourse help students find their voice and practice speaking out."[37]

9. *Growing Changemakers*: Challenging students to help others can stimulate empathy and help them see themselves as changemakers. There are endless opportunities to serve others throughout your neighborhood and school community.[38]

---

[33] Borba, 24.

[34] Borba, 25.

[35] Borba, 25, quoting J. Lehrer, "Don't! The Secret of Self-Control," *New Yorker*, May 18, 2009, https://www.newyorker.com/magazine/2009/05/18/dont-2.

[36] Borba, 26.

[37] Borba, 27.

[38] Borba, 22–28.

ENGAGE: Having reviewed Borba's nine competencies related to empathy, evaluate each of these in light of a biblical view of relationship building.

Author Thomas Hoerr passionately lends his voice to the SEL discussion when he unequivocally states, "Who you are is more important than what you know."[39] This conviction has led him to develop the "Formative Five Success Skills": empathy, self-control, integrity, embracing diversity, and grit.[40] Hoerr believes empathy (like the other four skills) can be taught, and he presents these six steps for assisting students in the development of empathy:

1. Listening
2. Understanding
3. Internalizing
4. Projecting
5. Planning
6. Intervening[41]

Hoerr points out that internalizing is perhaps the most difficult skill to help students develop. He describes *internalizing* as the ability to place yourself in someone else's shoes and experience that person's feelings. He assists educators in carrying out the process by recommending that students practice recognizing and understanding the perspectives of others, participate in learning through service, consciously learn about stereotypes and discrimination, and examine historical and literary figures that endured as victims of false accusations.[42]

Mindfulness

Another term that occurs frequently in the SEL literature is the word *mindfulness*. Have you encountered expressions such as "Count to ten before reacting" or "Just breathe"? Or related terms such as *meditation* or *stress reduction*? Thomas Armstrong is a popular author on the topic, and he points out that some aspects of this introspection have been around for 1,000 years in Buddhist traditions. Here's his definition:

---

[39] Hoerr, *The Formative Five*, 5.
[40] Hoerr, 9.
[41] Hoerr, 42.
[42] Hoerr, 43–44.

Simply stated, mindfulness is the practice of attending to each present moment in time with an attitude of acceptance, openness, and curiosity. By engaging in this practice on a regular basis, students and their teachers and administrators can learn to train their minds, regulate their emotions, control their behaviors, and cultivate healthier relationships with the people and events around them.[43]

There are several educational programs related to these concepts that are dedicated to training children and young adults to develop self-control and to lower stress caused by conflicts and trauma. Many studies (over 3,000) based on these concepts have produced results that are encouraging. Students who have self-regulation issues and executive function problems are showing positive gains. Academic achievement and overall health are two other promising outcomes, especially for students who have experienced trauma.[44]

However, the authors of this text challenge you to consider the biblical discipline of **prayerfulness** and encourage you to base your meditation on your faith in God. Consider these verses written approximately 2,000 years before Christ (over 4,000 years ago):

> How happy is the one who does not walk in the advice of the wicked or stand in the pathway with sinners or sit in the company of mockers! Instead, his delight is in the LORD's instruction, and he meditates on it day and night. (Ps 1:1–2)

Throughout the book of Psalms, the Hebrew word *'ashrei* reminds us that we are blessed, happy, joyful, and satisfied as we trust God and meditate throughout the day on his Word. *Meditates* in verse 2 refers to studying a passage, memorizing it, praying about it, and challenging yourself to obey it with God's help. And when possible in the teaching context the Lord places you, model prayerfulness for your students and coach them to meditate on God's Word throughout their day. The apostle Paul would echo this challenge 2,000 years later in his exhortation to the Philippians:

> Finally brothers and sisters, whatever is true, whatever is honorable, whatever is just, whatever is pure, whatever is lovely, whatever is commendable—if there is any moral excellence and if there is any praise—dwell on these things. . . . and the God of peace will be with you. (4:8–9)

---

[43] Thomas Armstrong, "School Safety Starts from Within," *Educational Leadership* 77, no. 2 (2019): 48.

[44] Armstrong, 49.

As you and your fellow students or colleagues interact with the following exercise, try to convert the goals of mindfulness to the larger biblical concepts of transformation through *prayerfulness*. Consider every dimension of who we are in Christ—mind, body, and spirit. As educators, we discuss knowledge, skills, and dispositions. Or simply, head, heart, and hands. Focus on him, "the author and finisher of our faith" (Heb 12:2 KJV).

ENGAGE: Earlier in the chapter, I asked you to review the CASEL competencies and then compare them to your Philosophy of Christian Education. I posed the question, "What's missing?" Have you been reading this chapter through a biblical lens? If so, perhaps you thought, *God's Word has a great deal to say about SEL*. Before moving on with this chapter, jot down some passages, including parables that Jesus told, that speak to the themes presented here. Here are a few examples to get you started:

- Trust in the LORD with all your heart, and do not rely on your own understanding; in all your ways know him, and he will make your paths straight. (Prov 3:5–6)
- Let no corrupting talk come out of your mouths, but only such as is good for building up, as fits the occasion, that it may give grace to those who hear. (Eph 4:29 ESV)
- Bearing with one another and, if one has a complaint against another, forgiving each other; as the Lord has forgiven you, so you also must forgive. (Col 3:13 ESV)

Conclusion

One of my favorite verses speaks to self-efficacy, growth mindset, and grit. We read in Eph 2:10, "We are his workmanship, created in Christ Jesus for good works, which God prepared ahead of time for us to do."

Imagine sharing with a generation of students that they are God's workmanship! The original word here for *workmanship* is *poiema*, which can also be translated "craftsmanship, work of art, or masterpiece." This Greek word gives us our English word *poetry*. Each child is intricately made by God. That's *what* they are. Second, we see *whose* they are . . . created in Christ Jesus. They don't belong to themselves, but they belong to Jesus. Third, we see *why* they are. Each creation of God has the expressed purpose to bring him glory and fulfill the tasks for which each is divinely created. As a teacher, I often have the sense that the Holy Spirit is telling me, "If you can't teach them anything, would you at least not mess them up and throw them off the path I have for them?" Each one who crosses the threshold of your room is a precious treasure from God. Each needs to see from you that you believe in them, respect them, and cheer for them.

CHAPTER 12

Meeting the Needs of Diverse Learners

Ann Rivera

I n this book, we have addressed human development and human learning indicating both commonalities and differences in how we learn as humans. This chapter addresses, specifically, diversity in learners in the classroom and how we can maximize the learning of all students.

Growing Classroom Diversity

The makeup of the K–12 school student population in the United States has changed dramatically over the last fifty years. So, too, have international schools. Students today are more diverse across many categories—including linguistics, culture, special needs, geography, and socioeconomics—partially driven by significant shifts in population and society. The growing diversity within today's classrooms underscores the necessity for a more deliberate, supported shift to a learner-centered education system. What does this mean at the classroom level? Consider that "an educator in the 1970s or 1980s with a classroom of 24 students might have had five or six students (20 to 34 percent) requiring specialized interventions." In a classroom of 24 students today in the USA, between 10 and 12 students (40 to 50 percent), have a disability or learning difference, are English language learners, are gifted or talented, are experiencing challenges at home or in their communities that result in trauma, or some combination of the above.[1]

Whether you are a new or experienced teacher, meeting the demands of such growing classroom diversity may seem overwhelming. It is no longer a question of *if* we should include diverse learners in one classroom setting, but *how*. Classroom diversity can have many different meanings depending on context. As a descriptive term, it refers to the wide range of differences in students' attributes and needs. In the context of schooling, relevant differences may consist of students' interests, experiences, aptitudes, abilities, learning styles, exceptionalities, gender, socioeconomic status, and immigrant and/or minority background such as cultural, ethnic, national, religious and language backgrounds.[2] At first glance, thinking about meeting the needs of diverse students seems like an impossible task; however, regardless of your content area or grade level, there are changes you can make to the classroom or approach to teaching that create a more inclusive and welcoming environment for all students.

Everyone's In: What Is an Inclusive Learning Environment?

Regular educators are responsible for all students in inclusive classroom settings. Today, inclusion is not just about children with disabilities. It is about creating an environment in which every student, including those who do not have disabilities, can be active participants in the learning community. While diverse learners may spend some part of the school day in separate classrooms or in small groups with specialists, most *special educators* provide support for inclusion education within the regular education classroom. This includes special education teachers and support personnel, as well as ESL (English as a Second Language) specialists who work together with regular educators to meet the needs of English learners.

In inclusive classrooms, students not only have access to the general education curriculum but also receive the supports they need to participate and be successful. The term used since the 1980s is *inclusion,* and it is important for teachers to have both the knowledge and ability to teach diverse learners. The most effective teachers not only know their grade-level content and subject matter, but they also know their students'

---

[1] "The Growing Diversity in Today's Classroom," Digital Promise Global, accessed January 25, 2022, https://digitalpromise.org/wp-content/uploads/2016/09/lps-growing_diversity_FINAL-1.pdf.

[2] Neda Forghani-Arani, Lucie Cerna, and Meredith Bannon, "The Lives of Teachers in Diverse Classrooms," *OECD Education Working Papers*, no. 198 (2019), OECD Publishing, Paris, https://doi.org/10.1787/8c26fee5-en.

backgrounds and the specific ways in which human development and learning are achieved. An inclusive learning environment is different from *mainstreaming* (the label used prior to inclusion), in that the goal is to differentiate instruction to meet the needs of every learner, whether they are children with special needs, gifted children who need enrichment activities, or English language learners. Inclusive learning environments provide a more effective learning environment for *all* students.

ENGAGE: Our own experiences influence our perceptions about diversity; however, finding out how they do so takes effort and reflection. Take a moment to consider the *lens* you see through when you walk into your classroom. How similar are your own experiences to those of your students? Reflect on the following questions:

- How might these similarities to my own experience affect my perceptions?
- What perceptions do I have of my students' race/ethnicity, cultural diversity, linguistic differences, disabilities, or socioeconomic status? How might these perceptions influence my instruction and the development and learning of my students?
- What or who is it I *want* to model in my classroom?

Developing a Model for Inclusion

There is no one, single model of an inclusive classroom or school. What inclusive schools have in common, however, is they are welcoming and supportive places for all students and their families. When all children, regardless of their differences, are educated together, everyone benefits—this is the *heart* of inclusive education. What does this mean for the Christian educator? A biblical view of inclusive education should challenge the Christian educator to have the mind of Christ in how we respond to, and prepare for, classroom diversity. My experience as a Christian working as an administrator and educator in both public (government) and private school settings confirms what Arthur Holmes (1985) championed: "To bring our every thought into captivity to Christ, to think Christianly, to see all of life in relationship to the Creator and Lord of all, this is not an optional appendage of secondary importance, but is at the very heart of what it means to be a Christian."[3] It is not optional to model Christ. The apostle Paul wrote, "Therefore I urge you to imitate me" (1 Cor 4:16).

---

[3] Arthur F. Holmes, "Toward a Christian View of Things," *The Making of a Christian Mind: A Christian World View and the Academic Enterprise*, ed. Arthur F. Holmes (Downers Grove, IL: InterVarsity, 1985), 11.

In this chapter, we look more closely at the role of the inclusive classroom teacher, the assets and challenges in classrooms with diverse student populations (primarily students with special needs and English learners), and what it means to teach responsively to student diversity in the inclusive classroom setting. This chapter explores the following questions:

- What is an inclusive classroom?
- Who am I teaching, and why does it matter (focus on students with special needs and English learners)?
- What is the mindset, skill set, and tool set teachers need to reach diverse learners, and how do these impact practice?

The Role of the Christian Educator in Inclusive Classrooms

Most of us can remember our favorite teacher. For some, it might be their 7th grade teacher who told funny jokes and knew just how to make algebra not seem so hard. Maybe it was a coach, or the middle school English teacher who held up the all-school spelling bee when he learned you had not been called from your class in time to participate and he knew how hard you had been preparing. (Yes, that was me. I did not win, but I never forgot what it meant to me.) Maybe it was the Christian professor who became your mentor, who saw something in you, and encouraged you to pursue a teaching career. This teacher changed you—made you see yourself in a different way, the unique way God made you. They went beyond what they taught; they helped to promote change in big or small ways.

In this section we look at the *role* of the Christian educator in the inclusive classroom who brings to the diverse community of learners a particular way of seeing student differences through a biblical view, discovering the *"why,"* which determines everything you will do and be.

ENGAGE: Who was your favorite teacher, and what impact did he or she have on you? Why do you think that teacher related to you as he or she did?

What Is Your "Why"?

What makes you get up every day and do what you do as an educator?

During a two-week, intensive urban seminar course I taught at a Christian university in the suburbs of Philadelphia, I discovered Simon Sinek, author of *Start with*

Why: How Great Leaders Inspire Everyone to Take Action, and his "know your why" theory. Each spring I took a group of pre-service teachers into the city to teach alongside Philadelphia teachers to learn the applications of educational theory and to live as visiting members of urban neighborhoods, communities, and schools. It was an impactful experience. Each evening we regrouped, debriefed, and discussed issues surrounding diversity, race, culture and language, poverty and education, and disability and ableism. We talked about what it looks like, sounds like, and feels like to teach in an urban setting.

During a discussion on what sets great teachers apart from good teachers, we viewed one of Sinek's *TedTalks*, "How Great Leaders Inspire Action."[4] Sinek maintains that what sets great organizations and leaders (teachers) apart is that they begin by focusing on the *why*. He says we should envision three concentric circles: The *why* is central to the what and how of learning and keeps in focus meaning, purpose, and passion. Our *why* determines why we get up every day and do it all over again. This is the reason this book begins with a philosophical perspective on education that answers the *why* for Christians who are educators.

ENGAGE: Share, or write briefly, your *why*. What makes you get up every day and do what you do as an educator?

My Own "Why"

In my earliest days of teaching, most of the focus was on myself rather than on the students and their learning: Am I delivering the content correctly? Am I communicating it effectively? Will the students see my insecurities? Will I be able to manage the classroom and the technology? But it was not long before something transformational happened. First it was subtle, but then it became a way of being. In *The Courage to Teach: Exploring the Inner Landscape of a Teacher's Life*, Parker Palmer says it this way: "Good teachers possess a capacity for connectedness. They are able to weave a complex web of connections among themselves, their subjects, and their students so that students can learn to weave a world for themselves."[5] I would add that Christian teachers exist

---

4 Simon Sinek, "How Great Leaders Inspire Action," TED video, YouTube, 18:34, May 4, 2010, https://youtu.be/qp0HIF3SfI4.

5 Parker J. Palmer, *The Courage to Teach: Exploring the Inner Landscape of a Teacher's Life*, 3rd ed. (London: Jossey-Bass, 2017), 11.

to help students develop connections with God and weave a view of life and learning from his perspective.

Integrating connectedness into my teaching practice changed the way I saw my role. This new mindset took me from seeing myself as a deliverer of content and information to being a facilitator in creating opportunities for students' active engagement in their own learning as they processed and internalized new information and skills. It required a high level of collaboration, problem-solving, and networking with other teachers, specialists, and families. It required not only knowing what to teach, but *how* to teach using research-proven teaching and learning practices that worked with a broad range of students with varied backgrounds, abilities, and perspectives. As I began to authentically connect with students, I started to develop the "heart of a teacher" and to have an impact on students beyond content and methods.

In her book *How to Reach and Teach All Students in the Inclusive Classroom*, Sandra Rief asks, "How do children learn that it is all right to be different—to learn, think, approach problems—in different ways? How do children come to accept others and recognize that we all have strengths in some areas, weaknesses in others?"[6] Children learn that we all have differences that are to be respected and appreciated; this learning should begin as soon as they enter school and continue, all the way up through the grades. Rief concludes by saying that this may indeed be one of the most important lessons we ever teach children. So, how do our students learn that the way God made us is unique and that our differences make us special? We see how he addresses human differences and worth in his Word. For example: "I will praise you because I have been remarkably and wondrously made. Your works are wondrous, and I know this very well" (Ps 139:14).

In his book *The Courage to Teach*, Parker Palmer says, "Whoever our students may be, whatever the subject we teach, ultimately we teach who we are." He reminds us that we typically only ask *what* and *how* we teach. Like Sinek suggests, we might dig deeper and ask *why* we teach. Palmer, however, holds that we almost never ask *who* is the self that teaches. Good teaching, he says, "comes from the identity and integrity of the teacher."[7]

There has never been a teacher of greater integrity than Jesus. Teachers can learn from his example. He engaged the disciples and expected them to interact with and

---

[6] Sandra F. Rief and Julie A. Heimburge, *How to Reach and Teach All Children in the Inclusive Classroom: Practical Strategies, Lessons, and Activities* (San Francisco: Jossey-Bass, 2006), 11.

[7] Palmer, *The Courage to Teach*, 10.

respond to what he was teaching. Formal sermons were rare; conversation was plentiful; questions were posed; problems needed to be solved; and personal stories bore eternal truths. Jesus's students were unusually diverse. They were lawyers, fishermen, women, scholars, doubters, and more. Reflecting on the intersection of our faith and our teaching—the "heart and mind"—great teachers possess both. Synthesizing both is the beginning of transformational teaching.

Special Education

Who am I teaching, and why does it matter? To answer that question, we must look more closely at two separate areas of diversity that can thrive in inclusive classrooms: students with special needs and English language learners. Elaine Mulligan reports in the Iris Resource Center that although great gains have been made, more than one million students (in the USA) still do not have access to the general education curriculum and instruction. Many who do, however, do not receive the *supports* they need to actively *participate* in that instruction. This is the case even though research evidence demonstrates that most students with special learning needs (including both students with disabilities and English language learners) can succeed in the general education classroom, given the necessary services and supports.[8]

Special education means *specially designed instruction* that meets the unusual needs of an exceptional student who might require special materials, teaching techniques, or equipment/facilities.[9] Special education is a service, not a place. Services are portable, so special education is delivered to students in the placement that works best for them, including the inclusive classroom. Consider how one Christian school decided to include a student with severe physical disabilities who, with appropriate supports, impacted a whole school community.

Including Isaac: The Isaac Postma Story

High school graduation is always a special time, but especially for one group of seniors from South Christian School in Michigan in the spring of 2019, and one student in

---

[8] See Elaine Mulligan, "What Is Inclusion and Why Is It Important?" accessed May 2012, https://iris.peabody.vanderbilt.edu/module/inc/cresource/q1/p02/.

[9] "Sec. 300.39 Special Education," Individuals with Disabilities Education Act, May 2, 2017, https://sites.ed.gov/idea/regs/b/a/300.39.

particular, Isaac Postma. Isaac is by all accounts a "bright, funny, young man who lives with spinal muscular atrophy type one, a muscular degenerative disease,"[10] which affects the part of the nervous system that controls voluntary muscle movement, preventing him from sitting upright for long periods of time. What sets Isaac apart from others with this same condition is that for twelve years he has been an accepted and valued member of this group, developing solid friendships through shared experiences as classmates in an inclusive classroom setting. "They have developed these friendships over video games, beach visits, football games, medical emergencies, ice skating excursions, performing together in *The Music Man*, Lunch Buddies, youth group and much, much more."[11]

Significant accommodations and supports were required for Isaac's condition, but the school community was determined to make it work. SMA has not kept Isaac from his love of sports, especially football. *MichiganLive* reporter Patrick Nothaft explains the role Isaac plays as an inspiration to the team, lying flat in his wheelchair in his #81 jersey. Caleb Voetberg, a junior lineman for the Sailors, became best friends with Isaac in kindergarten, and twelve years later, he draws inspiration from seeing his buddy in uniform every Friday. "It means quite a lot to have him on the team because he's been with me since kindergarten," Voetberg said. "To see him out here on the field is a huge part of my everyday life. Even with his disability his mindset is still go-go-go, and seeing his determination pushes me as an athlete."[12]

Including Exceptional Children: A Christian Perspective

More and more, Christian schools are investigating how they might include students with exceptionalities, focusing less on the child's disabilities and instead focusing on what it would take to be able to serve that child in the school. In Isaac's case, his school partnered with the All Belong Center for Inclusive Education, whose mission is to "equip congregations and schools to glorify God through purposeful, innovative inclusion of persons with varied abilities."[13]

---

[10] Katie Barkley, "Belonging among Friends: A Graduation Reflection," All Belong, May 6, 2019, https://allbelong.org/belonging-among-friends/.

[11] Barkley, "Belonging among Friends."

[12] Patrick Nothaft, "Teen with Genetic Disease Provides Inspiration as Part of Football Team," MLive, September 26, 2017, https://www.mlive.com/sports/grand-rapids/2017/09/teen_with_genetic_disease_prov.html.

[13] "All Belong," May 7, 2014, https://allbelong.org/.

ENGAGE: View the video "Including Isaac."[14] Through your teacher lens, what are your biggest *takeaways* from Isaac's story?

Special Education and Inclusion: Optional or Required?

Providing instruction for all students in their least restrictive environment (LRE) is a requirement of the Individuals with Disabilities Education Act (IDEA). Passed in 1975, this federal US law was written to ensure that all students with disabilities receive an education that meets their needs while allowing them opportunities to interact and engage with non-disabled peers as much as possible. For most students, the LRE is the regular education classroom, which includes students with or without exceptionalities, students with special needs, gifted students, and English language learners. Though gifted students are not covered under IDEA, federal law in the USA and other countries have recognized that gifted and talented students are "children with exceptionalities" and in need of specially designed instruction. Determining programs and services for gifted students in the USA varies from district to district. You may wish to find out the requirements in the country of your service.[15]

General education teachers should be prepared to address their students' wide range of ability levels and instructional needs. Unfortunately, that is not always the case. Dr. Ginger Blalock reports in the IRIS Center: "Unfortunately, misperceptions about students with exceptionalities continue to exist." She shares a story about two special needs students in a general education classroom. One has a learning disability and the other, autism. Blalock explains,

> Their teacher is surprised at how well they contribute to class discussions although one had trouble with reading and the teacher assumed that she might not understand content. However, she learned very well, auditorily. The teacher's stereotypical expectations for the child with autism were, that he might be nonverbal and have excessive disruptive behaviors, such as rocking his body and flapping his hands. Instead, the only behaviors of concern are his social

---

[14] "Including Isaac," Kala Project, YouTube video, 12:40, December 11, 2014, https://www.youtube.com/watch?v=lcPvZtt7MgE.

[15] "Gifted Education in the U.S.," National Association for Gifted Children, accessed April 26, 2022, https://www.nagc.org/resources-publications/resources/gifted-education-us.

skills, which are somewhat awkward. Robert's academic skills are at or above grade level.[16]

Teachers of diverse learners need to study our students, as no two students are alike, just as no two teachers are alike. Avoid the practice of stereotypical expectations!

ENGAGE: Think about areas in which you seem to excel and areas in which you need support. List those and think about how knowing your own strengths and weaknesses, natural abilities, and needs will help you discern the needs of your students who, like you, have both strengths and weaknesses. Determine to be yourself, be authentic, and desire to impact the lives of all of your students and their families for Christ.

Who Are Special-Needs Students?

According to the most recent data from 2019–2020, the number of eligible students "ages 3–21 who received special education services under the IDEA was 7.3 million, or 14 percent of all public school students. Among students receiving special education services, 33 percent had specific learning disabilities."[17] Eligible students are those identified by a team of professionals as having a disability that adversely affects academic performance and as needing special education and related services. There are fourteen categories of disabilities listed in IDEA:

Autism	Specific Learning Disability (SLD)[18]
Deaf-blindness	*Specific learning disabilities commonly
Deafness	affect skills in the areas of: reading (dyslexia),
Emotional disturbance (ED)	writing (dysgraphia), listening, speaking,
Hearing impairment	reasoning, and math (dyscalculia)
Intellectual disability	Speech or language impairment
Multiple disabilities (MDS)	Traumatic brain injury (TBI)
Orthopedic impairment	Visual impairment, including blindness
Other health impairment (OHI)	

---

[16] Ginger Blalock, "What Should Teachers Understand in Order to Address Student Diversity in Their Classrooms?" IRIS Center, accessed August 2021, https://iris.peabody .vanderbilt.edu/module/div/cresource/q2/p05/.

[17] "COE—Students with Disabilities," NCES, accessed January 22, 2022, https://nces.ed .gov/programs/coe/indicator/cgg.

[18] "IDEA," LDOnline, accessed January 22, 2022, http://www.ldonline.org/features /idea2004.

ENGAGE: Reflect on the list of disabilities in the chart above and determine which ones you might be able to accommodate in your classroom. List them along with possible accommodations you might be able to carry out. Answer the questions below:

- Why is access to the general education curriculum—that is, the state, national, or government (in most countries) curriculum for the general population—important for all students?
- What strategies or supports might be implemented under the general curriculum that will both meet the special needs in your classroom and be successful with all students?

Specific Special Education Laws and Policies

The following pertain to the USA; however, they might be helpful in highlighting diverse needs for any country of the world, some of which have their own laws related to serving all students.

The Basics of the Individuals with Disabilities Education Act (IDEA)

To qualify under IDEA, a child must have a disability and need special education because of the disability. In the USA, IDEA provides money for states to use to meet the needs of students with disabilities. A child does not have to be failing in school to receive special education and related services. In return, public schools must follow the complex requirements and guidelines of the law. Private schools strive to follow these guidelines and do the best they can with the funds available through tuition and sometimes government assistance. The requirements are:

- Free Appropriate Public Education (FAPE): No matter how severe the disability, every child is entitled to full access to *public* education.
- Evaluations: Every child suspected of having a disability must receive an evaluation (ChildFind).
- Least Restrictive Environment (LRE): A disabled student should be separated from general education classes only if absolutely necessary. In other words, students with disabilities are to be educated to the greatest extent possible in the general education classroom, with designated supports and services included.
- Individualized Education Program (IEP): Every disabled student receives an educational program that is tailored to his or her specific needs, outlining the

services and support the school will provide for the child to benefit from the educational program. It must be written by a team, implemented, and reviewed. IEPs are used by some private schools.

- Parent Involvement: Parents and students (if appropriate) are equal partners in the disabled students' educational process.

IDEA and Private Schools

Many parents have opted for a private school experience for their child for a variety of reasons, including a religious education. Private schools are not covered under IDEA, so the laws requiring FAPE do not apply to students who have been placed in private schools by parents. While private school students do not have the same right to FAPE (especially the "free" education) as government schools, private schools, including Christian and other religious schools, should contact their local education agency (LEA) or state education agency (SEA) to learn more about potential provisions and/or benefits that are available to children with disabilities enrolled in their schools.[19] Inclusive practices worldwide may be researched through the internet. Refer to the European Agency as an example.[20]

Section 504

While public schools must implement IDEA, private schools must adhere to a different US law, Section 504 of the Rehabilitation Act, depending on the amount, if any, of federal funding they receive. Both public and private schools are bound by Section 504. Wrightslaw explains, "Section 504 is a civil rights law that prohibits discrimination against individuals with disabilities. Section 504 ensures that the child with a disability has equal access to an education. The child may receive accommodations and modifications. Children with disabilities, who are ineligible for special education, may qualify for services and accommodations under Section 504 of the Rehabilitation Act.[21]

---

[19] "Educational Rights: Public vs. Private Schools," CHADD, November 1, 2018, https://chadd.org/adhd-weekly/educational-rights-public-vs-private-schools/.

[20] See "European Agency for Special Needs and Inclusive Education," 2021, https://www.european-agency.org/.

[21] "Section 504 and ADA: Protecting Children with Disabilities from Discrimination," Wrightslaw.com, January 22, 2022, https://www.wrightslaw.com/info/sec504.index.htm.

Private Schools and Section 504

Section 504 does not require private schools to substantially modify their programs to provide access to students with disabilities.[22] Private schools might be responsible for providing reasonable modifications, accommodations, and access to educational opportunities (such as a ramp for a child in a wheelchair, services related to students with attention deficit disorder, temporary accommodations to support student learning, or temporary or long-term health conditions, e.g., asthma, diabetes, epilepsy, heart conditions, other illnesses, etc.). When a family wishes to enroll several children in a Christian school and only one of their children has a disability, it is reassuring to know that the school will be able to serve that child with the necessary accommodations.

For Christian schools, Section 504 permits latitude in determining which students could benefit from support, as well as tremendous opportunities to determine how best to provide that help within the school's distinct culture, especially when more than one child from a family attends and just one has a specific disability. It is reassuring to Christian families to know that their school of choice for all of their children can serve a child that has a specific need through accommodations.

Implications for Teachers of Special-Needs Students

Teaching in an inclusive classroom may be your first experience working with special-needs learners. With the number of students with special needs continuing to grow, teachers must become familiar with types of disabilities and the laws and policies in their country of service that governs them. They need to look for creative, collaborative options for meeting these needs. With planning, preparation, and specialized instruction, students with exceptionalities can be served and flourish, and their families can be encouraged and supported. Next, we will look at another group of learners you'll find in inclusive classrooms, English learners (ELs), and consider how ELs are identified and assessed, EL population trends and recent demographic changes, and the laws and policies that impact their instruction. In the final section of this chapter, we'll look at the approaches and best practices for teaching diverse learners in the inclusive classroom setting.

---

[22] "Educational Rights: Public vs. Private Schools."

Teaching English Learners in Inclusive Classrooms

A second group of learners will be found in inclusive classrooms, English learners (ELs).

ENGAGE: **Who are English learners (ELs)?** Read the conversation below and ask yourself what is going on in the mind of the student and teacher, and why:

Teacher?

George, please call me "Mrs. Roberts."

Yes, Teacher.

George, please don't call me "teacher."

Yes, T . . . I mean, Mrs. Roberts.

You see, George, it's a sign of respect to call me by my last name.

Yes . . . Mrs. Roberts.

Besides, when you say it, it sounds like "T-shirt." I don't want to turn into a T-shirt!

Mrs. Roberts?

Yes, George.

Please, call me Jorge.[23]

English learners (ELs) are the fastest-growing segment of the student population in US classrooms. They are an immensely diverse group, bringing a rich cultural diversity to our schools and communities. This is true as well for international schools around the world. ELs have varied levels of English language proficiency, socioeconomic status, prior school experiences, content knowledge, and immigration status. This increasing diversity requires that every teacher has sufficient knowledge and skills to be able to meet the unique needs of those who are learning English in inclusive classrooms. The term *English language learners* (ELL), or *English learners* (EL), refers to students whose first language is not English but who are learning English. In many states, the preferred term is *EL* or *EB* (emergent bilingual), which is becoming more widely accepted. EL or EB are intended as a positive description of these students, emphasizing that they are learning in two languages, and that *both* the home language and new language are of value.[24]

---

[23] Jane Medina and Fabricio Vanden Broeck, "T-Shirt," in *My Name Is Jorge on Both Sides of the River: Poems* (Honesdale, PA: WordSong, 2014), 24–25.

[24] "English Language Learners," page 2, accessed January 22, 2022, https://prod-ncte-cdn .azureedge.net/nctefiles/resources/policyresearch/ellresearchbrief.pdf.

English Learner Statistics

According to the most recent data from the National Center for Education Statistics (NCES), there were nearly 5 million English language learners in US public schools in fall 2018, representing about 10.2 percent of public school students.[25] By 2025, it is estimated that 25 percent of public school students may be ELs.[26] English language learners in the United States speak more than 400 languages. The majority, some 80 percent, report Spanish as their home language, with another 2 percent each speaking Arabic, Chinese, or Vietnamese, and 1 percent each speaking Somali, Hmong, Russian, Haitian Creole, Tagalog, or Korean.[27] Eighty-five percent of pre-K–5th grade EL students and 62 percent of 6th–12th grade EL students are born in the United States and English is not their first language.[28] This language diversity might not be as extreme in many countries and in many international schools.

Because the number of ELs is growing with a global economy and migration, it is critical to consider how best to prepare all teachers to work with English learners they are likely to have in their class. Learning a language is a complex process; however, ELs are expected to acquire English proficiency while learning grade-level content. It is crucial that teachers not only understand the basics of learning a second language but how to plan instruction to meet their language needs in the regular classroom. Many teacher education programs now require a course in effective EL instructional strategies for all pre-service teachers, realizing that the responsibility for educating ELs does not lie solely with teachers specifically trained for ESL or bilingual education certification. All teachers may have ELs in their classrooms today.

Teaching English Learners from a Christian Perspective

Dr. Michael Lessard-Clouston, Professor of Applied Linguistics and TESOL at Biola University, spells out a certain "theology of language learning" and holds that "clear

---

[25] "Condition of Education—English Language Learners in Public Schools," National Center for Educational Statistics, 2021, https://nces.ed.gov/programs/coe/indicator/cgf.

[26] National Education Association, "English Language Learners," NEA, July 2020, https://www.nea.org/resource-library/english-language-learners.

[27] "NCTE Position Paper on the Role of English Teachers in Educating English Language Learners (ELLs)," NCTE, March 6, 2020, https://ncte.org/statement/teaching-english-ells/.

[28] Jie Zong and Jeanne Batalova, "The Limited English Proficient Population in the United States in 2013," Migrationpolicy.org, July 8, 2015, https://www.migrationpolicy.org/article/limited-english-proficient-population-united-states-2013.

connections exist between Christian faith and theology and various aspects of language learning and teaching, because language is significant to people's understanding of God, ourselves, and our world."[29] Lessard-Clouston goes on to discuss the importance of community, both linguistically and culturally, saying that "communities typically reflect differences, and one can be an insider/outsider due to language, culture, race, nationality, etc. Paul said, 'If then I do not grasp the meaning of what someone is saying, I am a foreigner to the speaker, and he is a foreigner to me' (1 Cor 14:11)."[30]

Christian educators who have ELs in their classrooms have an opportunity to show immigrants and culturally diverse families that you understand their assets and challenges and live out the principle in God's Word about how his people are to treat *strangers and sojourners* (foreigners): "You are no longer foreigners and strangers" (Eph 2:19).

ENGAGE: We all want to be an *insider*, not an *outsider*! Reflect on your personal experience learning a new language or living in a culture that was/is new to you.

- What were some challenges you had, and how did you overcome them (or imagine what you might experience if you haven't been in this situation)?
- What motivated you to learn? What hindered you?
- How will this reflection impact your perspective as you think of ELs?

Rights of English Language Learners

The education of English learners (ELs) is impacted by policies at the federal, state, and local levels in many countries. The US Department of Education spells out guidelines requiring public schools to take affirmative steps to ensure that ELs can meaningfully participate in educational programs and services and will communicate information to parents in a language they can understand. Among the requirements are: identify and assess all potential EL students, provide English learners with language programs led by qualified teachers, integrate English learners as much as possible into regular classrooms, and provide meaningful access to all curricular and extracurricular programs.[31] Federal law does not dictate the curriculum schools must use or the program model

---

[29] Michael Lessard-Clouston, "Seven Biblical Themes for Language Learning," MissioNexus, April 1, 2012, https://missionexus.org/seven-biblical-themes-for-language-learning/.

[30] Lessard-Clouston, "Seven Biblical Themes for Language Learning."

[31] "Ensuring Equal Educational Opportunities for English Learner Students," U.S. Department of Justice, July 1, 2015, https://www.justice.gov/archives/opa/blog/ensuring-equal -educational-opportunities-english-learner-students.

to teach English learners, except that programs and materials must be educationally sound in theory and effective in practice.

Although private schools are not required to offer English as a Second Language (ESL) or other services for EL students, many do. Private schools in the United States, including Christian schools, should contact their local or state education agency to learn more about potential provisions and/or benefits under Title III available to English learners and their families who are enrolled in private schools.[32]

How Are ELs Assessed?

Under the guidelines of the Every Student Succeeds Act (ESSA), most states' ELs in public schools are assessed annually by ESL specialists on English listening, speaking, reading, and writing skills through WIDA (World Class Instructional Design and Assessment). This instrument is used by 40 states and 400 international schools throughout the world to ensure schools are helping their ELs achieve English language proficiency. Students' ACCESS scores reflect their proficiency from Level 1 to Level 6. Teachers will use these scores to ensure that students are getting the proper instruction and supports they need to be successful language and grade-level content learners at their level of English proficiency. WIDA provides teachers of ELs with free instructional resources to support the planning of differentiated lessons based on assessment data for various levels of language development. Their website offers free materials.

Based on WIDA's "Can Do" philosophy that focuses on what learners *can do*, not what they can't do, teachers use "Can Do Descriptors" for all grade ranges and content areas to help them understand what students at different levels of English proficiency should be able to do in a regular content area classroom. For example, in reading, a *Level 1 Entering* 9th through 12th grade can match visual representations to words/phrases. In contrast, a *Level 4 Expanding* 9th through 12th grade can compare/contrast authors' points of view, characters, information, or events. The descriptors can help teachers look at an activity they plan and then differentiate for various EL students so that they are still interacting with the academic content but modified to lessen the language demands. The focus always remains on making grade-level content understandable.[33]

---

[32] U.S. Department of Education, Title III Part A Programs—Strengthening Institutions, last modified June 22, 2022, https://www2.ed.gov/programs/iduestitle3a/index.html.

[33] See "Proven Tools and Support to Help Educators and Multilingual Learners Succeed," WIDA, 2021, https://wida.wisc.edu/ as well as "Can Do Descriptors Key Uses Edition Grades 9–12," https://wida.wisc.edu/sites/default/files/resource/CanDo-KeyUses-Gr-9-12.pdf.

ENGAGE: Strength-based instruction (what the student *can do*) provides an important foundation for success and offers opportunities to build upon those strengths to address areas where the student is struggling. Look at this list of ELs' strengths and challenges. How might these impact your instruction?

- Strong literacy skills in their native language
- Academic skills and content area knowledge developed in their native language
- Strong family support and commitment to children's future
- Strong interest in education
- High levels of personal responsibility, resilience, resourcefulness, and commitment to success

Some of their challenges may include:

- Little or no formal schooling
- High levels of mobility in moving between schools (especially in the case of students from migrant farmworker families)
- Lack of access to effective, consistent language instruction, as in the case of students who have experienced bilingual education during one year and then English immersion in another
- Limited practice developing and using academic language
- Personal responsibilities that occupy hours during or outside of school, such as caring for siblings, working one or more jobs, and translating for families[34]

What Are the Benefits of Inclusion for Language Learning?

The most important "funds of knowledge" children bring with them to school are their cultures and their languages. Teachers need to learn all they can about the languages and cultures of their students to create optimal learning environments that promote success for ELs who are expected to learn both language and content simultaneously. Most language experts agree that it takes 5–7 years to acquire academic English, the language needed to succeed academically and professionally.[35] Students may acquire social or conversational language much more rapidly, but there is frequently a gap between social and academic English. There is individual variation in language learning, but it

---

[34] Lydia Breiseth, "What You Need to Know about ELLs: Fast Facts," Colorín Colorado, 2015, https://www.colorincolorado.org/article/what-you-need-know-about-ells-fast-facts.

[35] Breiseth, "What You Need to Know about ELLs."

takes several years for English learners to reach a high enough level of language pro-ficiency to perform on par with their native English-speaking peers. English learners cannot wait until they are fluent in English to learn grade-level content. Instead, they must continue to develop their math and reading skills as well as their knowledge of social studies and science, even while learning English. This can happen through a variety of program models, including the inclusive classroom setting.

L1 (First Language) versus L2 (Second Language) Learning and Its Implications in the Inclusive Classroom

Research in this area (called *second language acquisition*) suggests that there are three key elements to learning a new language.

1. The first is comprehensible input, which is a fancy way of saying being exposed to (hearing or reading) something in the new language and learning to under-stand it.
2. Comprehensible output is the second element, and unsurprisingly it means learning to produce (speak or write) something in the new language.
3. The third element is review or feedback, which basically means identifying errors and making changes in response.[36]

According to Stephen D. Krashen, linguist and researcher on second language acquisition, "Language acquisition is a subconscious process. We are not aware it is happening."[37] Children *acquire* their L1 (first language) naturally, even without much instruction at home and learn when and how to use it to reach their desired goals, such as asking for permission, answering a question, making a request, and so on. All their learning is contextualized in the here and now, with opportunities to connect speech to real-life objects or events (realia), and to use nonverbal techniques to make meaning, such as gestures, facial expressions, and emotions, etc. Children learning their first lan-guage proceed through a series of stages and often make errors as they try to model their speech to the language around them. They are attempting to communicate real needs.

---

[36] "Learning Languages," The Learning Center, University of North Carolina at Chapel Hill, accessed October 19, 2020, https://learningcenter.unc.edu/tips-and-tools/learning-a-second-language/#_ftnref.

[37] Douglas Magrath, "MultiBrief: L1 and L2 Acquisition: Hints for Teachers," MultiBriefs, August 31, 2018, https://exclusive.multibriefs.com/content/l1-and-l2-acquisition-hints-for-teachers/education.

The story is very different in L2 (second language) acquisition, which occurs mainly in the classroom. Krashen goes on to say, "Language learning is what we did in school. It is a conscious process; when we are learning, we know we are learning."[38] Students *learn* a second language with different aims and under different conditions. The aim of the L2 is to develop proficiency in the language of school, or *academic language.* Not only are skills of spoken language learned, but proficiency in reading and writing are expected. New information must be reprocessed in the brain as L2 learners transfer the language patterns they already know to those of the new language. According to Krashen (1988), people can acquire a second language only if the amount of input they are exposed to is sufficient and understandable, and if their *affective filters* are low. Affective filters include factors such as anxiety, motivation, attitude, and so on.[39]

Daily interaction with social and academic language can lead to quicker, greater gains in English language development if the basic elements of learning a new language are implemented in an inclusive classroom environment that is more like the L1.

ENGAGE: If Krashen is right in his assumptions about language learning and emotional filters, knowledgeable and prepared teachers can create effective spaces for ELs to develop language proficiency and learn content.

- Thinking about your own classroom (or future classroom), what strategies or approaches might you use to make the L2 (classroom environment) more like the L1(home/family)?
- List these possible practices.

Effective Practices for the Inclusive Classroom

What is the *mindset, skill set, and tool set* teachers need to reach diverse learners in diverse classrooms, and how does it impact their practice? In this section, we consider effective research-based practices that support the needs of diverse learners in the inclusive classroom setting, providing an opportunity for Christian educators to create an authentic community of belonging.

---

[38] Magrath, "MultiBrief."

[39] See Shahin Rahavard, Maryam Razaghi, and Firooz Sadighi, "L1 Versus L2 Learning: A Controversial Issue," *International Journal on Studies in English Language and Literature* 3, no. 7 (July 2015): 59–62, https://www.arcjournals.org/pdfs/ijsell/v3-i7/9.pdf.

A Mindset for Inclusion

The New Jersey Coalition for Inclusive Education reports, "The kinds of research-based educational practices which support students with disabilities in classrooms such as universal design for learning, differentiated instruction, and collaboration, are part of what experts consider best practice for all children in our increasingly multi-ability classrooms. The focus is on bringing together resources and expertise to meet the needs of all children."[40] The report gave as an example: practices to support students with disabilities often support English language learners whose learning is being impacted by stress at home. This teacher mindset also considers students who are way ahead of the rest of the class and need opportunities for expanding their learning beyond the general curriculum.[41]

Implementing inclusive teaching strategies in your classroom may begin with small, but intentional, changes to create the best learning environment for your students. A simple place to start may be a commitment to spending just a few minutes a day reading and learning about the diversity in your classroom. This one practice can make a significant change in teachers' understanding of their students. Below are several important evidence-based practices to consider when designing your inclusive classroom and curriculum.

Universal Design for Learning (UDL) and Differentiated Instruction (DI)

Universal Design for Learning (UDL) and Differentiated Instruction (DI) share the same overarching mindset that all students benefit from flexible learning environments that are accessible to all, making learning possible for every student. UDL and DI are defined by *Inclusive Education Planning* as follows: "Universal Design for Learning (UDL) is a proactive approach to designing learning experiences to be accessible for all students, while differentiation is a reactive evaluation of the needs of individual students where adjustments are retrofitted into the learning environment."[42] The terms

---

[40] "About Inclusion," NJCIE, accessed March 14, 2022, https://www.njcie.org/about-inclusive-ed.

[41] "About Inclusion."

[42] Tyra Milligan, "Universal Design for Learning (UDL) and Differentiation," Inclusive Education Planning, June 3, 2019, https://inclusiveeducationplanning.com.au/uncategorized/universal-design-for-learning-udl-and-differentiation.

are not synonymous but do function together. UDL addresses initial planning while differentiation refers to the additional planning as teachers begin to know student differences. Both are designed to accommodate the student, rather than expecting the student to accommodate to the environment.[43]

Universal Design for Learning (UDL)

How do we use UDL and differentiation in the classroom to reach the learning goals for all students? UDL offers an adaptable framework to connect every individual student to the learning experience. UDL has its roots in the concept of universal design that many of us have benefited from in our own lives. For example, the provision of access ramps. These can be used by people with wheelchairs or mobility needs but also easily used by parents with strollers, delivery people with wheeled packages, children with scooters, and safety for those uncomfortable with stairs. If these were replaced with steps, there would be limited access to everyone but those who can navigate the steps. In this example, flexibility is already *built into the system*. Everyone, regardless of their situation or physical ability, can get to the entrance of a street because the barriers have been removed.

In the classroom, UDL is an effective approach because from the very start of lesson planning, it helps you anticipate and plan for *all* learners. It includes not only the curriculum, but the learning environment, including physical spaces and the social/emotional climate. This helps ensure that the greatest range of students can access and engage in the learning process.

Developed by the Center for Applied Technology (CAST), the goal of UDL is to use a variety of teaching methods to remove barriers to learning. Three guiding principles are a tool used in the implementation of UDL in the classroom. These principles are: (1) multiple representations of information and course content, (2) alternative means of expression or demonstration of learning, and (3) varied options for engagement.[44]

By using these guiding principles when designing lesson plans, teachers can reduce or remove barriers that may interfere with student learning or with the ability to

---

[43] Milligan, "Universal Design for Learning (UDL) and Differentiation."

[44] "Center for Applied Special Technology (CAST)," Students at the Center, January 21, 2020, https://studentsatthecenterhub.org/resource/center-for-applied-special-technology-cast/.

demonstrate learning. *Multiple representations* involve activating prior knowledge by pre-teaching concepts, using advanced organizers or infographics, providing text in a digital format that can be read aloud using recording or photo/document reading apps, supplying captions on video or text for audio materials, using lots of visuals or verbal descriptions of pictures, and using videos or animation to convey concepts.

Alternative means of expression include options to record oral speech, to draw, or to present ideas through drama or role-play, to use video as a response to an assignment instead of writing, or to create a comic strip using a tech tool like *Storyboard That* to complete a writing task or produce an audio podcast.

Engagement and motivation include content, level of challenge, and supports that are varied and meaningful, such as the use of visuals, culturally significant activities, and peer tutoring,

While UDL is first and foremost about implementing a flexible pedagogy to accommodate the learning needs of students, technology can help by making the kind of personalized learning envisioned under UDL a reality.

ENGAGE: Read "30+ Tools for Diverse Learners" to find out about several free and low-cost UDL-aligned apps and websites that you can use to make learning environments more flexible and personalized.[45]

Differentiated Instruction (DI)

UDL helps to bring differentiated instruction to life in very real ways. One of the most important principles of inclusive education is that no two learners are alike. Christian educators start from this biblical premise as well. Andrea Beam and Deanna Keith explain:

> In the most significant commandment that He gave to Christians, Jesus said to "go and make disciples of all nations, baptizing them in the name of the Father and of the Son and of the Holy Spirit, and teaching them to obey everything I have commanded you" (Matt 28:19–20). This verse clearly commands us go to *all* people everywhere and teach them through whatever methods are necessary. Christian educators must recognize that to reach all—regardless of age,

---

[45] Luis Perez and Kendra Grant, "30+ Tools for Diverse Learners," ISTE, February 9, 2021, https://www.iste.org/explore/Toolbox/30%20-tools-for-diverse-learners.

race, disability, socioeconomic status, or other differences—we must differentiate in our mind-set first and our lessons second.[46]

As educators respond to the learners in diverse classrooms, they work to provide
instruction that is accessible and challenging to all students. Dr. Carol Ann Tomlinson,
known for her work with differentiated instruction, explains,

> At its most basic level, differentiating instruction means "shaking up" what
> goes on in the classroom so that students have multiple options for taking in
> information, making sense of ideas, and expressing what they learn. In other
> words, a differentiated classroom provides different avenues to acquiring con-
> tent, to processing or making sense of ideas, and to developing products so that
> each student can learn effectively.[47]

Tomlinson suggests that teachers adjust class activities according to student strengths.
Some ways teachers can differentiate are by incorporating independent study and
choice, agendas, tiered activities, centers, flexible grouping, project-based learning, and
alternate assessment.[48] Tomlinson's suggestions fit with cognitive interactive learning
and the teaching model that is informed by that theory and its multiple methods of
instruction. See chapters 5 and 6. Here are some suggested alternative methods:

1. Using reading materials at varying readability levels or that reflect a variety of
   cultures
2. Presenting ideas through both auditory and visual means
3. Meeting with small groups to reteach an idea or skill for learners who struggle
   or to extend the thinking or skills of advanced learners
4. Using tiered activities through which all learners work with the same important skills or concepts but progress with different levels of support, challenge,
   or complexity
5. Providing centers or stations to differentiate lessons by interest, topic, or ability
6. Giving students options of how to demonstrate required learning

---

[46] Andrea Beam and Deanna L Keith, "Differentiation and Faith: Improve the Learning
Process by Finding Every Student's God-Given Talents," *Christian School Education* 15, no. 1
(2011): 8. Available at: http://works.bepress.com/andrea_beam/6/.

[47] Carol A. Tomlinson, "Chapter 1: What Differentiated Instruction Is—and Isn't," in *How
to Differentiate Instruction in Academically Diverse Classrooms* (Alexandria, VA: ASCD, 2017).

[48] Carol Ann Tomlinson, "What Is Differentiated Instruction?" Reading Rockets, accessed
May 27, 2022, https://www.readingrockets.org/article/what-differentiated-instruction.

7. Allowing students to work alone or in small groups on their assignments or projects

Response to Intervention (RTI)

In any general education classroom, there will be students struggling for different reasons, both academically and behaviorally. Differentiated Instruction (DI) and Response to Intervention (RTI) can work hand in hand to support student learning using a multilevel problem-solving approach to identify students with learning and behavior needs, providing a framework for teachers and school personnel to work together as a team to address problems quickly and efficiently.

The RTI process begins with the teacher assessing the skills of each student early in the year and ongoing. The data clarifies which students are struggling and in need of intervention in specific areas. These interventions can be addressed in the classroom through differentiated instruction (Tier 1) and the use of high-quality instruction using research-based materials in the regular classroom. For example, creating small groups tailored for different skill levels, learning styles or interests, or through other instructional strategies such as technology-based or project-based learning. Tier 1 supports are often enough to address a specific academic or behavioral need. When they are not, the team makes recommendations for continued intervention, accommodations, and services at Tier 2 to decrease academic and behavioral challenges and improve student success.[49] The Iris Center reports that most students respond to Tier 1 or Tier 2 instruction; however, a small percentage (i.e., 5 percent) will not, and may require Tier 3 intervention (i.e., more intensive individualized supports such as specialists, counseling, or special education services). At Tier 3, the focus is on the needs of individual students who are experiencing significant problems in academic, social, and/or behavioral domains. This level is more intensive and individualized than it is at other levels and may involve individual or small group instruction and support from specialists, in addition to the classroom teacher.[50]

---

[49] See Matthew Burns and Negar Kordestani, "Response-to-Intervention Research: Is the Sum of the Parts as Great as the Whole?" Recognizing Interventions Supported by Research, RTI Action Network, accessed June 11, 2021 http://www.rtinetwork.org/learn/research /response-to-intervention-research-is-the-sum-of-the-parts-as-great-as-the-whole.

[50] "RTI (Part 5): A Closer Look at Tier 3," IRIS Center, 2008, https://iris.peabody .vanderbilt.edu/module/rti05/.

Essential "Soft Skills" for Inclusive Teachers

Throughout the many best practices for inclusive teaching discussed in this chapter runs a very important "invisible thread" that educators need to reach and teach diverse learners. These are the *soft skills*, the everyday interpersonal skills that cannot be measured with a certificate, an exam, or professional development credits. *Hard skills* such as content knowledge, technical skills, and language skills are often gained through education or specific training. *Soft skills* such as leadership, communication, teamwork, creativity and problem-solving, cultural competence, flexibility, and integrity enable one to express ideas, plan, organize, and get along with others. Soft skills can be far more important than purely academic and technical skills and should be cultivated.

A must skill set for Christian educators, in addition to the obvious hard skills of teacher preparation and professionalism, are the soft skills that lead to the development of healthy relationships with colleagues, students, and families. In his article "Taking a Hard Line on Soft Skills: Discipling for Healthy Relationships," R. E. Cline reminds us that "Jesus commanded his followers to learn and practice relationship in and out of the church that are pleasing to God. Those sorts of relationships don't simply occur naturally; they must be encouraged, developed, and practiced. Therefore, they must become a part of the regular rhythms of the church as we make disciples."[51] Developing *soft skills* must become part of the rhythms of our daily life as teachers as we model Christ, not only in *what* we do, but *how* we do it.

This chapter is designed to help you deepen your understanding of the most effective practices for creating inclusive classroom settings and develop a *mindset, tool set, and skill set* for inclusive education. We began this chapter by considering the biblical view of inclusive education and what it means *to think Christianly* in how we respond to and prepare for classroom diversity. By knowing our "why," who are students are, and their diverse needs, we can create communities of belonging and a community of learners that benefit all.

Extended Research and Reflection: For those using the InTASC Standards, review the first three standards and determine how this chapter addresses each of the three.

Standard #1: Learner Development. The teacher understands how learners grow and develop, recognizing that patterns of learning and development vary

---

[51] R. E. Cline, "Taking a Hard Line on Soft Skills: Discipling for Healthy Relationships," IMB, October 4, 2016, https://www.imb.org/2016/10/02/taking-a-hard-line-on-soft-skills -discipling-for-healthy-relationships/.

individually within and across the cognitive, linguistic, social, emotional, and physical areas, and designs and implements developmentally appropriate and challenging learning experiences.

Standard #2: Learning Differences. The teacher uses understanding of individual differences and diverse cultures and communities to ensure inclusive learning environments that enable each learner to meet high standards.

Standard #3: Learning Environments. The teacher works with others to create environments that support individual and collaborative learning, and that encourage positive social interaction, active engagement in learning, and self-motivation.[52]

---

[52] "Interstate Assessment and Support Consortium," Council of Chief State School Officers 2013 (Washington, DC).

SECTION 4

Understanding
the Structure of the
Disciplines We Teach

Structure of the Subject

Marti MacCullough

Understanding Structure

Understanding structure is much more than possessing content knowledge. Many twenty-first-century educators are convinced that both inside and outside factors are important in student learning and, therefore, adhere to interactive learning. Outside factors include the subject matter of the school curriculum. While many teachers have a rich content background in the subjects they teach, they may not have been exposed to studies that address the underlying structure of these subjects. This is the topic for the next section of this book.

Educational psychology and learning theory contribute to our understanding of the nature of the student and learning. This was addressed in chapters 2–4. Many teachers have had a course in educational psychology or have studied human development and learning in some way before entering the teaching profession. Most have also taken a sequence of courses in general studies that include the subjects they will ultimately teach. Some have studied one subject in depth in preparation for teaching that one subject at the higher levels of schooling. However, there is something more about the subject matter of the school curriculum that must be understood if one is to promote effective learning in a *specific subject*. In this section experts in the content areas address the nature (structure) of the various subject areas—the "what" the students learn and why this is important!

The Subjects We Teach

Each domain of study—whether mathematics, natural science, social science, history, the visual and performing arts, physical education, biblical studies, or the language arts—has its own underlying structure that makes it a distinct subject. What other reason would there be to separate the various "disciplines" of study? Each academic discipline offers its own field of knowledge and way of knowing and expressing information, emotions, and skills in that specific domain. School subjects are related, at least in part, to several formal academic disciplines all of which have in common a respect for knowledge and intellectual inquiry. However, they are very different in how the knowledge and intellectual inquiry in their discipline should be understood and learned.

Structure: Essential for Teachers

In Pennsylvania, the state in which I serve, teacher education programs are required to include the study of the nature of the content they teach. This is a requirement beyond the factual knowledge gleaned from coursework. In the Pennsylvania Code 354.25 #3, teacher education programs are required to be intentional in using structure.

> (3) The preparing institution shall ensure that candidates complete a well-planned sequence of professional educator courses and field experiences to develop an understanding of the **structure**, skills, core concepts, facts, methods of inquiry and application of technology related to **each** academic discipline the candidates plan to teach.[1] (emphasis added)

The Updated InTASC Model of Teaching Standards offers the following about content knowledge preparation.

> Standard #4: Content Knowledge. The teacher understands the central concepts, tools of inquiry, and **structures of the discipline**(s) he or she teaches and

---

[1] "Preparation of Professional Educators," Chapter 354, p. 7, August 2008, http://www.pacodeandbulletin.gov/secure/pacode/data/022/chapter354/022_0354.pdf.

creates learning experiences that make the discipline accessible and meaningful for learners to assure mastery of the content.[2]

Standard #5: Application of Content. The teacher understands how to connect concepts and use differing perspectives to engage learners in critical thinking, creativity, and collaborative problem solving related to authentic local and global issues.[3]

Under the rubrics section of the document for suggested assessment of teachers is the following:

1. The teacher understands major concepts, assumptions, debates, processes of inquiry, and ways of knowing that are central to the discipline(s) s/he teaches. 4(j)
2. The teacher understands common misconceptions in learning the discipline and how to guide learners to accurate conceptual understanding. 4(k)
3. The teacher knows and uses the academic language of the discipline and knows how to make it accessible to learners.
4. The teacher knows how to integrate culturally relevant content to build on learners' background knowledge. 4(m)
5. The teacher has a deep knowledge of student content standards and learning progressions in the discipline(s) s/he teaches. 4(n)[4]

Assessment is based on knowledge, understanding, and performance of the teachers. I would add: The teacher knows how to develop biblically integrative thinking about his or her subject (for Christian school venues). The mentioned standards are often used by international schools as well as USA schools; however, standards from other countries may also include structure as well. Check with your national or regional areas for more on structure or nature of the disciplines.

---

[2] "InTASC-Interstate Assessment and Support Consortium," Council of Chief State School Officers 2013 (Washington, DC), 8.

[3] "InTASC," 9.

[4] See InTASC Standards (24–29). Standards may be downloaded from the site below: https://ccsso.org/sites/default/files/2017–12/2013_INTASC_Learning_Progressions_for _Teachers.pdf.

What Is the "Structure of the Subject"?

Psychologist Jerome S. Bruner, one of the first to address structure of the subject, explains it this way in his classic book *The Process of Education*: "Grasping the structure of a subject is understanding it in a way that permits many other things to be related to it meaningfully. To learn structure, in short, is to learn how things are related."[5]

Providing structure for a specific subject is the process of instructing in several areas:

- *Logical organization* of a content area (a specific subject of study)
- *Key concepts* and generalizations (definitions of terms and use of vocabulary specific to the subject and big enduring ideas around which related facts are organized)
- *Method of inquiry* (how a subject should be learned by the student because of its nature; for example, science is different from history as a way of obtaining information and as a way of knowing)
- *Standard* for testing and judging truth or stated claims in the specific field of study (e.g., judging truth is different in science, history, and mathematics)

Bruner suggests four benefits of teaching the fundamental structure of the subject. (1) Understanding the fundamentals of a subject makes it more comprehensible. (2) It enhances human memory. "*Unless detail is placed into a structured pattern, it is rapidly forgotten.*" (3) Teaching fundamental principles of a subject aids in the transfer of learning, a major goal of schooling. (4) It narrows the gap between advanced and elementary knowledge.[6]

You may have heard the testimony of a student who has been "turned on" to a subject area by a teacher who was passionate about the subject. That passionate teacher may have been fully aware of the underlying structure of the subject and was able, therefore, to relate it to other subjects and to real life.

Structure's Value for Developing Biblical Worldview Thinking

How does knowing well the subjects we teach enhance learning? The value of knowing "structure" is that it simplifies and organizes the material so that it can be related to

---

[5] Jerome S. Bruner, *The Process of Education* (New York: Alfred A. Knopf, 1960), 7.

[6] Bruner, 23–26.

other information including biblical truth, specifically, biblical answers to life's biggest questions that should be addressed in a Christian school curriculum. Bruner's description of structure as "understanding (the subject) in such a way that permits many other things to be related to it meaningfully," is helpful in determining how structure can enhance biblical worldview thinking specific to each *discipline*. It promotes the student's ability to think biblically about and within a particular set of subject matter. Each expert contributing to this section will include worldview questions specific to his or her area of study.

Biblical worldview thinking is a form of critical thinking. A common belief about critical thinking is that the best thinkers are those who know something about the something they are critiquing. Good thinking demands understood and organized knowledge. Critical thinking is more than a process. It includes the understanding and use of knowledge. Therefore, one who understands the big ideas and the general organization of a subject area should be able to connect related facts better than one who does not and be able to critique new information as well.

The By-Product of Teaching the Structure of a Subject: Clear and Intelligent Thinking

Knowing the structure of a subject enhances clear thinking in a specific discipline and enables discernment of differences among different ways of knowing. Educators who know the structure of their subject and develop lessons that promote student thinking and understanding have the *potential* to go well beyond what their leaders/administrators expect of them as classroom teachers. A school leader may have taught a subject or two, but perhaps not the subject you teach. As a teacher, you should know *your* subject/s well; this includes the underlying structure.

Teaching Using "Structure"

ENGAGE: The ideal way to learn and to teach a subject area is related to its own structure. For example, would you plan to *teach* science exactly the way you would teach mathematics? Why or why not? Which two of these three subjects—mathematics, science, and the language arts—are more alike in how they are *taught and learned*? Why do you think this is so? Share your thoughts with another person if you are reading this book together.

Most teachers will declare that math and science are more alike in how they are *taught;* however, this reflects a very common misunderstanding. We know that science uses mathematics to quantify findings and to build models, and science and math are frequently addressed together, for example in STEM (Science, Technology, Engineering, and Mathematics) programs. This is natural. Science needs mathematics and mathematics meets that need.

However, science as a subject area is the most *concrete* subject of any you will teach. This is the reason teachers use hands-on materials, labs, and computer models almost daily in science from preschool all the way through the PhD level. Mathematics, on the other hand, is the most *abstract* of any subject you will teach. The subject matter of each (math and science) requires different ways of knowing (inquiry). So, why do we use hands-on materials in math lessons? We do this to make an abstract subject more concrete and real-to-life, especially in the early years of mathematics. However, we do not keep our students at the hands-on level after they have grasped the mathematical concept. That practice would hinder their learning and use of mathematics rather than enhance it. Teachers who organize mathematics around procedures rather than around big ideas often fail to pass on to their students the concepts needed to build interrelated understandings in mathematics that are basic to later studies. It may surprise you that mathematics and language arts are more alike than mathematics and science in *how* they are learned and how they should be taught. In both mathematics and language, symbols and sentences are used to represent meaning. More on the structure of each of these subjects later in this section.

The structure of the major subjects of the school curriculum are described in this section by experts in the field. Teachers should be able to describe thoroughly their own area and also know the basics of all other areas of the curriculum in order to effectively promote the connections and distinctions in subject matter. School subjects include the Bible in a Christian school. It is suggested that every educator read all the sections on structure rather than just the subject area/s in which they teach.

For those who have specialized in one subject area, the structure of their subject may be understood well and yet they may not understand the structure of other areas of study so that they can contrast and compare ways of knowing and understand how to integrate their subject with others. For those who have not specialized, the structure of the subjects they teach may be less understood.

It is the goal of this section in the book to help both elementary and secondary level teachers understand and appreciate the importance of structure in the overall subjects of the school. Obviously, early childhood and elementary teachers need to know the *basics* of the structure for most subject areas. This makes their task more difficult than a specialist but rewarding, prepares their students for higher level learning, and provides opportunities for subject-to-subject integrative thinking. Secondary teachers must know their subjects in depth to effectively promote learning and should also understand the basics of the structure of other subjects so that they can develop integrative thinking. For the Christian teacher, this includes biblical worldview thinking in his or her subject area.

Structure Differences

By way of introduction, let us think briefly about *differences* in structure.

Science as a way of knowing is the process of using the senses and extended senses (telescopes, microscopes, etc.) to observe and discover principles and laws inherent in nature. New information is tested again and again by others using the methods of science and language of mathematics. Science information is open to change as new information is obtained from extended senses such as better microscopes, telescopes, models, and additional inductive research. Christians should not view science as an enemy of the Bible (as some do) but rather acknowledge the limits *and* potentials of science in helping us understand the existence of God and the wonders of his creation.

The nature of **mathematics** is different from science. Science is very concrete, hands-on, and uses the senses and extended senses, observation, experimentation, and model building. Mathematics, on the other hand, is very abstract and includes the God-given ability to reason, to see patterns and interrelationships in quantity and space. It is often considered the language of science. Why our minds are so attuned to what we experience in the natural world is wonderful evidence of the creation of humans in the image of God who is reasonable and made both what we observe and our minds.

History is a record of actual past events that impact the present and the future. While the actual event is objective (it happened a certain way and was caused by certain events), it is recorded by humans who bring to the events their own assumptions. While historical events are recorded by fallible, biased, and limited humans and must be examined from all available sources seeking evidence for the most accurate (as it happened and why) interpretations, we can know history! Historians do their investigations using certain tests for accuracy: earliest sources, multiple eyewitness accounts, trustworthiness of the eyewitnesses, corroborating evidence from other writers of the period, and truthfulness of the writer in accounting for both positive and negative details.[7] Readers bring their own present understandings, assumptions, biases, and definitions to the history they read. Historians today should be careful to check as many records of an event as possible or as they have available, to interpret as much as possible what was actually the case when an event occurred. Otherwise, we may revise history to fit the narrative of our day as we wish. Historical records contribute to what humans are as history-producers. Christian historians should carefully judge the past human wrongs of a fallen world and acknowledge the negatives as well as the positives or the good that humans, created in the image of God, have done and can do. The actual events are part of God's story moving toward a consummation he has determined.

Literature is the compilation of the thoughts and feelings of humans expressed in language and is subject to the personal beliefs, struggles, loves, and biases each of us experience. Various genres of literature should be studied through the lens of the nature of that genre, whether poetry, prose, fiction, nonfiction, drama, etc. The language arts include all of the oral and written skills to communicate (speaking, writing, performing). These are expressive arts. Also included are the skills to receive communication—the impressive arts such as listening, viewing, and reading. Communication is one of the wonderful aspects of creatures, created in the image of God, who communicates with humankind.

If you teach **technology, music, physical education, or art,** perhaps you can write a brief sentence or two describing what those subjects are all about and how they should be learned before your read the chapter for your discipline by one of the "experts" in the field.

When teachers understand their own subjects well and the basic structure or nature of their subject, they are better equipped to compare, contrast, and relate their subject to other subjects in the curriculum and thus promote integrated rather than disintegrated learning in general. In addition, they are able to permeate their teaching with God's view of a subject area and biblical worldview thinking related to specific areas such as science, mathematics, history, and literature. Experts in the various areas will capture the structure in the pages ahead.

---

[7] Norman L. Geisler and Frank Turek, *I Don't Have Enough Faith to Be an Atheist* (Wheaton, IL: Crossway Books, 2004), 231.

CHAPTER 13

Mathematics: Structure of the Subject

Debbie MacCullough

Introduction

For nine years, I taught a required introductory math course called "Introduction to Mathematics" at a private university in the United States. In almost every first day of class (which included several sections each semester), I would have at least one student inform me that they did not like mathematics and were not looking forward to taking the course. I would ask these students what they thought a mathematics class in college would be like since they obviously had formed an opinion before entering the classroom. The responses were very similar every year: "It is going to be a lot of lectures with examples that I'm supposed to actually understand and then I go back to my room to try to figure out what the professor is actually saying—most likely with little success." My response usually was to ask them to wait a few weeks before formulating their opinion about *this* course.

Why did I do this? Because mathematics does not have to be taught through lecture and example only. In fact, the structure of mathematics lends itself to many different methods of learning and requires multiple methodologies for true learning to occur. More must be experienced than simply memorizing. In the university introductory course, we examined mathematics in a variety of ways with the goal that students learn to think about mathematics as a discipline of study from a biblical perspective. It was satisfying to have those students who had originally balked at the course leave saying things such as "It wasn't nearly as bad as I thought." Even occasionally, "I think I like mathematics now."

In the initial introduction to the section on the structure of the subject, you read that mathematics is very abstract and includes the God-given ability to reason, to see patterns and interrelationships in quantity and space. It is often considered the language of science. In this chapter, we expand the concept of the structure of mathematics, including the logical organization and key concepts that should be learned throughout the study of mathematics. In addition, we will examine methods or pedagogical approaches that assist in the learning of mathematics because they fit with the nature of mathematics itself. We will look at the standard used in mathematics for testing and judging truth. Finally, we will examine key worldview questions that can be answered (at least partially) through the study of mathematics. The goal of this section of the chapter is that the teacher who reads and understands will be better prepared to teach well and as a result have students come to class anticipating and excited to learn more, even if mathematics is not their strength.

The Structure of Mathematics

Mathematics is a language. This language is used to express the abstract notions of quantity, space, structure, and change, and the relationships among these four abstract notions. For example, how do we express changes in quantity? How do we structure spaces?

Quantity refers to "how much" of something. We use a number to describe this as well as a unit of that number. In early mathematics we teach children to count and to use one-to-one correspondence when using the counting numbers. This allows the child to find the quantity of something.

Space refers to quantity in more than one dimension. For example, the quantity of area is a two–dimensional space. Spaces can be much more abstract as mathematics progresses to higher levels.

Structure refers to sets that have certain operations and features. Most simply, we often refer to natural numbers and the simple operations of addition, subtraction, multiplication, and division. However, sets can be much more complex than this. Mathematics is the study of these structures and the relations in them.

Change refers to the study of the relationships in a structure. For example, in the structure of algebra, we often study the "variables" or changes. In calculus, we study the rate of change as a basic unit of study.

Together these basic concepts and the relationships among the concepts form the study of mathematics.

We start our learning of this language as we start the learning of most languages, with basic words and definitions and simple grammar. In mathematics, this includes learning our most basic set of quantity—the counting numbers, what these numbers represent, and simple arithmetic (our "grammar"). As we continue, we add sets of numbers (natural numbers, integers, rational numbers, and eventually algebraic expressions of numbers) while continuing to learn how the arithmetic (or operations) function with these sets. We examine space and how it relates to quantity.

For decades, mathematics teachers have wrestled with a false dichotomy related to seeing mathematics as either concept or as skill. This is a false dichotomy at any level. We must see that mathematics is *both* concept AND skill. In order to use the language of mathematics properly, we need both the concept being addressed and the skill to use it. We will continue to discuss this structure as we examine pedagogical approaches. While this is a simplistic look at mathematics, it allows us to briefly examine the logical organization and key concepts of school mathematics (the mathematics studied by children around the world before getting to university) to better understand how mathematics should be taught well.

Logical Organization

In the United States, the National Council of Teachers of Mathematics (NCTM) has published several documents and books related to the logical organization of mathematics to help teachers better teach. In all these publications, there is a logical organization that is "spiraled"—that is, taught at a simple level and then built upon in the ensuing years of study. There are five areas of mathematics included in the study of school mathematics. These are: Number and Operation, Algebra, Geometry, Measurement, and Data Analysis and Probability.

ENGAGE: Return to the structure of the subject and the four abstract notions of the language of mathematics: quantity, space, structure, and change and the relationships among these. How do each of these five areas of study indicated by NCTM in the above paragraph fit into the abstract notions? For example, algebra is the study of structure and change of quantity. It represents a space; therefore, all four abstract notions are examined within the study of algebra.

In addition to these five content areas, the NCTM also includes something that they call "process standards" in their publications. These are five process skills necessary in the study of mathematics: Problem Solving, Reasoning and Proof, Communications, Connections, Representations.

ENGAGE: Look at the five Process Standards. How are these a reflection of mathematics as a language?

When teaching mathematics, whether to a class of five-year-old students or a class of eighteen-year-old students, these five concepts and five processes are all needed to fully understand mathematics. This will require the use of much more than simple lecture in order to teach mathematics well. But to examine these pedagogical approaches, we must first understand the standard for testing and judging truth in mathematics.

Standard for Testing and Judging Truth

Because mathematics is a language of quantity, space, structure, and change, we must judge truth in a manner that encompasses this language. Most people would suggest that mathematics is a "neutral" subject—that there is no worldview involved in mathematics—therefore there really is nothing to judge. Math simply is correct or is not correct. However, as a follower of Christ, we know that there is nothing that God has not created. If God has created the quantity, space, structure, and change, and even the language to communicate these, then there are worldview issues related to mathematics. You cannot read past even the first chapter of Genesis without seeing God's own communication using mathematical language. "In the beginning . . ." he divided space, used cardinal numbers (i.e., day one, day two), and ordinal numbers (i.e., first, second). When reading the rest of Scripture, we can see that God uses mathematics in his communication and created us to use mathematics as well.

Mathematics involves two basic types of reasoning. Either *inductive reasoning*— reasoning in which we see example after example that "works" and we make a judgment that it must always work—we often call these postulates or theories. Or we will use *deductive reasoning*—reasoning that starts with an assumption that certain things always work—and we deduce, using logical inquiry methods, that something else is true. One reason we study Euclidean geometry in school is to hone both methods of reasoning. In either case of reasoning, at some point, we must make an assumption. This is where our worldview will most impact our study of mathematics. I read in a high school algebra book something to the effect that we are "stuck with" the properties of algebra because they are what they are. This is a worldview statement. So, we ask, why are they as they are?

ENGAGE: What worldview is shown in the above algebra book statement? What might be a biblical reason for why the properties of algebra are "what they are"?

To know that something is true in mathematics, we must first have convincing reasons for why something is inductively true. (For example, take a rigid structure like a triangle. Inductively we know it will not change shape if translated. The inductive proof is to move a drawing of a triangle all over the room and see if it has changed shape. It does not. This is how Euclid began his study of geometry.) The use of inductive reasoning is why problem-solving, connections, and representations are important processes for students to know and practice. Second, we must be able to take things we have already accepted as "true" in mathematics and use deduction to show that it is true. This is why reasoning and communication and representation are also important processes.

So, how do we develop the content and the processes to help students learn mathematics well?

Methods of Inquiry

The study of a language is started by first learning some basic vocabulary and memorizing (to start) some basic phrases. It is impossible to learn a language without some memorization. However, this memorization is done within a meaningful context. The same is true in mathematics. Early learners must memorize the numbers in order (1, 2, 3, . . .). However, if they do not understand one-to-one correspondence, these "digits" are nonsensical. We must have them learn to count. We need both the proper order and the one-to-one correspondence to learn to count. The same is true in many aspects of mathematics. There are things that simply must be memorized—but they must always be matched to a conceptual understanding of the "thing" being memorized. This is where methods of inquiry become critical in the study of mathematics.

The typical mathematics class, around the world up to several years ago, perhaps at a time when you were learning mathematics, was something we call the "Rule of

Three." This is a pedagogical approach where (1) the teacher tells the students how to do an arithmetic or algebraic move, (2) the teacher puts an example (or more) on the board and has a student do the arithmetic or algebraic move with the other students watching, helping, etc., and finally, (3) the students are assigned more examples to do on their own. Does this sound familiar to you?

There are times when this approach is expedient; however, we must ask ourselves if expediency or learning is our goal. When learning is the goal, this three-step process is not the best pedagogical approach. In this text, we suggest that you use a model of teaching that fits best with how humans learn. In this model, the teacher activates prior knowledge before addressing new learning, then provides new information, and finishes by allowing students to process what they have learned. Many mathematics texts now use a "5E Model" (Engage, Explore, Explain, Elaborate, Evaluate). Some books collapse "Explain/Elaborate" into one step. The 5E approach fits with the model addressed in chapter 6 of this book. No matter what lesson plan template you use, mathematics can be taught in such a way that true learning of both the content and skill take place.[1]

Suppose you desire your students to learn some basic things about area of polygons. In this unit you want your students to understand the concept that area is a measure of "how much" covers a two-dimensional space. You also want them to have the skill to find the area of differing two-dimensional spaces. As always, before choosing a pedagogical approach, we must know what we desire the students to learn—our objectives. Before we look at one pedagogical approach to this unit, stop and think through the key questions related to the pedagogical model we are suggesting in the book.

1. What do students already know that can be activated in their minds as they begin this lesson?
2. What new information will the students need to either discover or be told?
3. What do we want students to process to understand both concept and develop skill?
4. How might I assess what my students know and understand for both concept and skill?

As you read through these four key questions, you may have struggled a bit. There are several reasons for this struggle. One, there can be a lack of content knowledge

---

[1] The BSCS 5E Instructional Model: Origins and Effectiveness," BSCS Science Learning, accessed June 21, 2022, https://bscs.org/reports/the-bscs-5e-instructional-model-origins-and-effectiveness/.

regarding an area of study such as mathematics and its underlying structure; another might be a lack of knowledge in pedagogical approaches for mathematics (the goal of this section as it addresses structure of the subject). Together, in mathematics education, these two aspects of knowledge are known as "pedagogical content knowledge," or the integration of general knowledge about teaching and the content being taught. Both content and pedagogy are key requirements for mathematics teachers who desire to be successful. Understanding mathematics well enough to discern how best to teach mathematics is something many mathematics teachers have not experienced.[2]

Let us return to the unit on area. I might start the unit with an activity to activate student's prior knowledge and give them a beginning look at the concept of area.

Activation Activity: Put students in pairs and give each pair one cardboard (or plastic) rectangle. (Rectangles should all be the same size for all the pairs of students so comparison can be made.) Next, instruct the students to figure out how many of these rectangles it would take to cover their desk or a table. Once the pair of students decides on a number, they are to record it for all the pairs of students to see. From experience, I know that younger students will get very different numbers. This is because of how they orient the rectangle in counting (see Fig.1).

Pair 1 Orients: (meaning the way they place the rectangles in the figure)

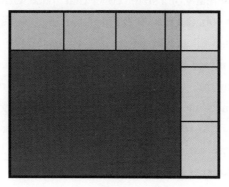

Fig. 1

This means that Pair 1 place 4 rectangles across with the long side of the rectangle parallel to the horizontal edge of the table. Next, they turn the rectangle and count 3

---

[2] See Liping Ma, *Knowing and Teaching Elementary Mathematics: Teachers' Understanding of Fundamental Mathematics in China and the United States* (New York: Routledge, 2010) for further reading.

rectangles down. They then multiply 4 x 3 and get 12 rectangles (because they know the *skill* that you multiply to find area.)

Pair 2 Orients differently:

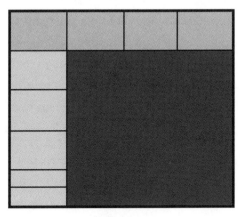

Fig. 2

Notice here that this pair does not turn the rectangle when they count the number of rectangles down a side but instead tiles down one side and counts 4½ rectangles down. They multiply 4 x 4½ and get 18 rectangles. This pair shows they understand the concept that area is how many of a shape cover that space without overlap.

This activity allows you, the teacher, to discuss which pair's method is covering the table without overlap, as well as why we do not use rectangles to describe area but use squares instead. It also allows us to probe using questions such as, "Why did we multiply?" and "Did we count the corner rectangle twice when we multiplied?" It helps the student to begin to learn, conceptually, what area is and the language we use to communicate area. Notice how this relates to the structure of mathematics: Communication and reasoning and representation are all a part of this activity. This continues throughout this lesson as the students also problem solve.

Concept Development: The lesson can then move forward to how we find area using squares. For this part of the lesson, we can use the answers we have developed to the questions from the activation activity to develop how we find the area of a rectangle using a 1 cm square. Students can use cardboard, plastic, or even "virtual" squares on a smartboard to find how many it takes to cover the space. When they do this, they will find the same answer as the other pairs because they are using the same unit. Eventually, the class will develop the algorithm that states that we multiply the number of a unit across by the number down to count all the squares covering a space. This saves us from having to fill the space and uses an abstract way to communicate how many 1 cm squares it takes to cover in all.

Many mathematics textbooks and teachers would remain in the abstract at this point. However, we recognize that in all language learning it is difficult to transfer from one situation to the next without some concrete or sensory experience. Mathematics is no different. It is unwise to expect students to be able to operate in the abstract exclusively. Most mathematics curricula will address the triangle next because it is the most basic shape. When teaching area, I often move to finding the area of an L-shaped figure. As an example, I found the following idea in the grade 4 lesson on finding the area of shapes by Akihiko Takahashi.[3]

Using L-shaped figures is a logical move because the students may have learned how to find the area of a rectangle. They can use this knowledge to figure out the area of an L-shape. Because mathematics is a language that communicates meaning, it is wise to set up a structure for the students that communicates meaning. For example, you want to carpet a very small room used in your house for storage. It is shaped like an L. You must measure it to communicate to the carpet store the size to cut. Let's see how that works.

Ask the students to find as many ways as they can to find the area of the figure (see Fig. 3).

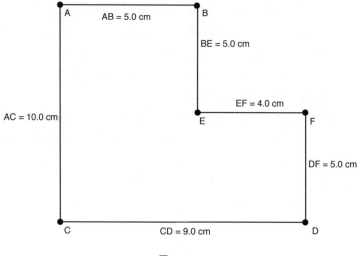

Fig. 3

[3] Akihiko Takahashi, "TTP in Action," The Lesson Study Group at Mills College, July 30, 2021, https://lessonresearch.net/teaching-problem-solving/ttp-in-action/. To access the videos, scroll to grade 4 "Finding the area of shapes."

Students must present their ways of finding the area with both drawing and a mathematical sentence. They must be able to do this by folding or by cutting and moving a piece. They cannot use a dividing line with free drawing without using established points. It will not be accurate. There are about thirteen (13) different ways this task can be done! Students are often shocked.

ENGAGE: Take a few minutes to see if you can find thirteen ways to find the area for figure 1 (remember, you *only* know how to find the area of a rectangle). Let me help you get started. You could divide line AC by extending line EF and making a new point G on that line. You now have *two* rectangles: ABGE and GFDC. Students can use the prior lesson to see that ABGE is a 5 x 5 square and GFDC is a 9 x 5 rectangle. The mathematical sentence for the area would be: (5 x 5) + (9 x 5). So 25+ 45 = 70 square cm.

Another way would be to "cut" across this newly made line GF and move rectangle ABGE so that it fits with GFDC. Now, you have a rectangle that is (9 + 5) cm long by 5 cm wide. The mathematical sentence for the area would be (9 + 5) x 5. This is 14 x 5 = 70 square cm. Notice, you should get the same result for each new way.

If you wish to see more ways, the videos with this lesson series are accessible here: https://lessonresearch.net/teaching-problem-solving/ttp-in-action/. You can find these in the grade 4 lesson on finding the area of shapes.

Next, have the students report their discovered ways to the whole class. This is practice in the process of communication and representation (an aspect of the structure of math) and a method of inquiry using a standard for measurement (truth judging). Students show, on paper, what they have done and the mathematical sentence that represents their work. The students then place the thirteen or so ways of finding the area into categories. They usually end up making three categories. Category one is usually using "known" figures (such as making the two rectangles). Category two is often one the students will call "add and take away." This is where they complete the L-shaped figure to make it into a full rectangle that is 9 x 10. They then subtract the added rectangle (4 x 5 in the upper right-hand corner). See figure 4:

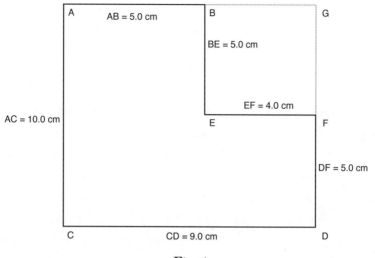

Fig. 4

Notice that the full rectangle ACDG in figure 2 is a 9 cm x 10 cm rectangle. We have added rectangle BEFG. Students then take away from the full rectangle the added rectangle (5 cm x 4 cm). The mathematical sentence is $(9 \times 10) - (4 \times 5) = 70$ square cm.

Category three is often called "cut and paste" by the students. This is where they cut the figure in some spot and move the piece they cut away to a new spot to make a rectangle. This is like the second example in the "Engage" portion (see fig. 5).

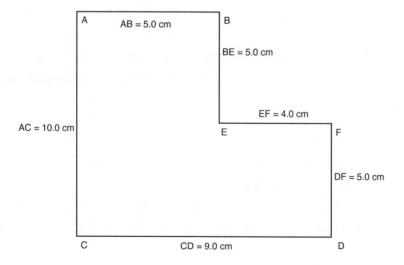

Fig. 5

In figure 5 rectangle ABHE is cut from the top of the L-shape and moved to match the lower rectangle HCDF. This makes a larger rectangle of CHEH. This is 5 cm tall and (9 + 5) or 14 cm long. This mathematical sentence would be: (9 + 5) x 5 = 70 square cm.

Notice that these instructional strategies are not "telling" the students how to find the area of an L-shaped figure. Rather, the students are figuring it out with guidance from the teacher. This is a version of the "directed inquiry" approach in which the teacher guides the students using questions or activities to direct their learning in a particular way.[4] The teacher's role during these activities is to watch the pairs of students and ask questions that will help them figure new ways. One question I have often had to ask as my students are doing this activity is "What if you had scissors? Could you find more ways to do this?" I save this suggestion for after the students have struggled some. It is interesting to see how it triggers new ways of thinking when they are stuck.

Student Processing Activities: You may also notice that when the students report and when they categorize the methods, they are processing the new information. This part of the unit is best finished by having the students write how they would find the area of a new L-shaped figure. This continues to relate to the structure of mathematics as a language of that communicates information.

Assessment Activity: We go back to the carpet for a small room to help the students relate the work they have been doing to communicating a quantity. Give the students a new L-shaped figure with different dimensions. Find the area for the carpet and give it to the teacher as an exit slip. The teacher is the carpet salesperson.

I present this example lesson to recommend creativity when thinking through ways to teach mathematics. Often, when teaching mathematics, a teacher feels the need to follow the textbook or curriculum exactly as given. But this does not consider how individual students learn, nor what a more logical order may be for students. Sometimes, a teacher must follow the curriculum as given, but a teacher could be creative, logical, and more productive in how to teach that material. What follows are some examples of pedagogical approaches for teaching mathematics.

Without a doubt, students must sometimes become "automatic" with certain facts and certain operations. That does not mean that only one method should be employed

---

[4] For more information on the "directed inquiry approach, see "Directed Inquiry versus Guided Inquiry," Discovery Science Education, accessed June 21, 2022, https://static.discoveryeducation.com/techbook/pdf/DirectedInquiryvsGuidedInquiry.pdf.

to help the students build automaticity. For example, when learning addition, subtraction, multiplication, and division facts, teachers often employ the timed worksheet. Other approaches might include songs, flashcards done in pairs (one student holds the card and "checks" as the other states the fact), and even poems. Another approach using the worksheet is to have students beat the prior score, not by becoming "faster," but by becoming more accurate.

Another way to work on the memorizing and "skill" parts of mathematics might be to do reviews of these skills in more creative ways. Playing a game or having the students create their own worksheets is one way. Another I have used is something I call "musical chairs" (see Fig. 6 for a pictorial explanation). This method takes two days but is highly effective. First, the students are given a worksheet with the same number of problems as there are students in the class, for example, 16. Each student is given ONE problem on the worksheet to solve. This allows the teacher to differentiate for different learning needs. The students must solve the problem they receive "step-by-step" in words on a separate worksheet. Note that this continues to relate to the structure of mathematics by requiring students to not only problem solve but also communicate the means of solving.

The teacher may then check to make sure each student has the correct solution to his or her problem. The next day, half of the students (for example, 8 of the 16) are seated at a desk or table, and the other half (8) are the "movers." Sitting in pairs, the students are given a set amount of time to share with the other student *how* to solve their problem. Each shares his or her solution in that time, so that both have answers. If the student who is learning how to solve the problem does not understand, the student sharing must give a better explanation.

After the preset time ends, the "movers" move one seat to the left with the end student moving to the beginning. This pattern continues until all movers have met with each of the other students. (I had small classes, so in a class of 16, 8 students have now been with 8 other students.) I then halve each half of the class (e.g., 4) and we have "sitters" and "sitters who now move" and "movers who sit" and "movers who move." This allows the students to now meet with new students. We continue until everyone has met with each other person in the room. With larger classes you can make smaller groups and smaller worksheets and have the smaller groups work independently from each other. The joy of this method is that in a class of "n" students (such as n = 16 students), each student must explain his or her work "n-1" times (or 15 times!). In addition, they hear an explanation for each of the other problems. This hones the students' skills in communication of mathematics (structure of subject).

"Musical Chairs" Method

Sitter 1 = S1
Mover 1 = M1

	Sitter	Mover		Round 1	Round 2	Round 3	Round 4	Round 5	Round 6	Round 7	Round 8

Left boxes: Sitter 1–8, Mover 1–8.

Round 1	Round 2	Round 3	Round 4	Round 5	Round 6	Round 7	Round 8
S1 M1	S1 M2	S1 M3	S1 M4	S1 M5	S1 M6	S1 M7	S1 M8
S2 M1	S2 M2	S2 M3	S2 M4	S2 M5	S2 M6	S2 M7	S2 M8
S3 M1	S3 M2	S3 M3	S3 M4	S3 M5	S3 M6	S3 M7	S3 M8
S4 M1	S4 M2	S4 M3	S4 M4	S4 M5	S4 M6	S4 M7	S4 M8
S5 M1	S5 M2	S5 M3	S5 M4	S5 M5	S5 M6	S5 M7	S5 M8
S6 M1	S6 M2	S6 M3	S6 M4	S6 M5	S6 M6	S6 M7	S6 M8
S7 M1	S7 M2	S7 M3	S7 M4	S7 M5	S7 M6	S7 M7	S7 M8
S8 M1	S8 M2	S8 M3	S8 M4	S8 M5	S8 M6	S8 M7	S8 M8

Fig. 6

After first 8 rounds

Boxes: Sitting Sitter 1–4, Move Sitter 1–4, Sitting Mover 1–4, Move Mover 1–4.

Sitting Sitter = SS   Move Sitter = MS
Sitting Mover = SM   Move Mover = MM

Round 9	Round 10	Round 11	Round 12
SS1 SM1	SS1 SM2	SS1 SM3	SS1 SM4
SS2 SM1	SS2 SM2	SS2 SM3	SS2 SM4
SS3 SM1	SS3 SM2	SS3 SM3	SS3 SM4
SS4 SM1	SS4 SM2	SS4 SM3	SS3 SM4
MS1 MM1	MS1 MM2	MS1 MM3	MS1 MM4
MS2 MM1	MS2 MM2	MS2 MM3	MS2 MM4
MS3 MM1	MS3 MM2	MS3 MM3	MS3 MM4
MS4 MM1	MS4 MM2	MS4 MM3	MS4 MM4

Rounds 13 and 14 split each of these four groups into two. Round 15 is the remaining students who have not met.

Of course, not all mathematics is skill driven, so we need other methods for learning mathematical concepts. By using the model in which students build from what they know to the new mathematics with guidance, much like the directed inquiry model, much mathematics can be learned. It is always helpful to use concrete objects ("manipulatives") when possible, to help students better understand the abstract language. For example, when learning volume, having cubes that students can use to fill up a three-dimensional space can be very helpful. When learning algebraic formulae, having algebra tiles to relate the algebra to already understood arithmetic can also be helpful.

No matter what method you choose to use, a key thing to consider is how you will have students use their words to describe what they are doing (*Structure: Language and Communication*). Remember, they are learning a language and must use their primary language to interpret what they are thinking and doing. Having students present their work should always include justifying why something is correct *(Structure: Truth-Judging)*. Other students should have the freedom to ask questions and compare their approach. There may be one right answer in mathematics, but often there are many ways to that correct answer. Some ways *always* work, others do not. It is your job, as the teacher, to help students understand which will always work and why.

For example, when teaching division of fractions, I have often used a non-standard algorithm approach to help my students understand how division of fractions really is "division" (not simply "inverting and multiplying"). The algorithm the students discover is one in which you create a common denominator and then divide the numerators to get the correct answer. This method will always work; however, it is tedious and will be difficult to use with some fractions and all of algebra. The unit plans I use help the students relate this algorithm to the standard algorithm with the explanation of why we use the "shortcut." My students are very relieved to have a shorter algorithm, and should they forget which fraction to invert (which does not happen often), they can re-create the shorter algorithm because they conceptually understand division of fractions.

Key Biblical Worldview Questions/Answers

In the final section of this chapter, we address the key biblical worldview questions that can be raised during the study of mathematics. The list is certainly not comprehensive, but it is presented to help mathematics teachers build a more biblical understanding of mathematics with their students.

Who or what is God?

God is a God of order and consistency. Although this may seem to be overused by Christian mathematics teachers, it is critical in building a biblical worldview. Mathematicians must, for mathematics to work, trust in order and consistency. However, without God, there is no logical reason to trust.

God is a communicator. We have examined how mathematics is a language. God uses quantity, space, and change in communication. When we learn to use mathematics appropriately, we are learning to be communicators of God's creative order as God desires.

Who or what is a human?

Humans are image-bearers and reflect some of God's characteristics. We think and reason because God does, and we can think about God's order, consistency, and communication. Although imperfect, we have these traits. We seek order, consistency, and desire to communicate. This worldview question and answer allows mathematics teachers to discuss why we see things, such as the golden ratio, in so many areas of life. It also allows the mathematics teacher to encourage students to be orderly and consistent and good communicators.

What is the nature of external reality?

We can describe the world around us using mathematical models. Reality reflects the nature of God. Both answers allow us to look at *why* humans can model reality mathematically and why some models fail; that is, because of human failure.

Why is it possible to know anything at all?

God has created humans with the ability to inductively and deductively reason truths that he has designed into the universe. Again, this question-and-answer fits well with many mathematical lessons.

Please notice that these questions are the "larger" or "broader," more philosophical worldview questions, but mathematics teachers may go deeper into sub-questions that are more specific to our particular content. For example, we may ask, "Why do I measure using a standard unit?" Although this is not a "worldview" specific question, my worldview will influence the answer. As followers of Christ, we know this allows us to communicate better. Another example is the question, "How do people use data to influence others?" This question can be answered from a biblical worldview.

ENGAGE: Take some time to look at a mathematics curriculum and list some worldview questions or sub-questions that may be related to the content of that curriculum.

CHAPTER 14

The Structure of Science

Paula Gossard

Romans 1:20 tells us that God is made manifest as we study his world. It is a privilege to teach about the natural world revealed to us by the work of scientists, bringing students face-to-face with God's "invisible qualities" (Rom 1:20 NIV). But many Christians perceive conflict between certain scientific findings and their reading of the Bible. How do we teach science accurately and faithfully in light of this tension? How do we make the study of the natural world engaging—not threatening—to our Christian students? And how can we teach science as a creative, iterative process and not merely as a collection of settled facts?

Science is a systematic way of investigating the natural world and coming to logical conclusions based on observable evidence. This process, and the resulting findings, are "science." In this chapter, we will liken science to a house that is built on a foundation, encompassed by walls and floors, divided into rooms where families live, and covered by a peaked roof that points upward. We will first examine the presuppositions of science—foundational assumptions on which science is based. Then we will describe the nature of science, the walls and floors that create the space in which scientists work. Next, we will learn how to engage students in the process of scientific inquiry occurring within this space. Finally, just as our home's roof covers the structure and makes the house livable, the house of science is overseen by God, the Creator. As Col 1:17 (NIV) tells us, "He is before all things, and in him all things hold together." Just as a diligent homeowner examines and maintains all parts the house so, too, a diligent science teacher must know and teach all parts of science.

Laying the Foundation: The Presuppositions of Science

"The earth is the LORD's, and the fulness thereof; the world and they that dwell therein." (Ps 24:1 KJV)

In my experience, Christian students are often reluctant to fully engage in the study of science. From their pastors, parents, conference speakers, and others, they have heard explicit condemnations of evolutionary theory or an ancient earth or, worse, that science is an atheistic, purely naturalistic enterprise determined to undermine biblical truths. Teaching students about the presuppositions of science at the beginning of the school year and, more specifically, evaluating the validity of these presuppositions from a biblical perspective, encourages Christian students in their study of modern science and its findings. For this reason, we will tackle some presuppositions of science first, before examining science teaching explicitly.

Presuppositions are "beliefs that one presumes to be true without supporting independent evidence from other sources or systems."[1] For example, one of my presuppositions in writing this chapter is that you will give the same meanings to English words as I do. Science is based on many presuppositions. An online search provides lists of scientific presuppositions ranging from just a few to more than ten.[2] We will consider three presuppositions of science here, along with the biblical basis for accepting them as true. Somewhat ironically, this approach presupposes that the reader accepts the Bible as a source of absolute truth.

Our first presupposition is that *there is orderliness, regularity, and predictability in the natural world.* Without patterns in nature, scientific inquiry would be impossible. We also presume that natural laws operate the same way in the vast reaches of the universe as they do here on earth and that this will be as true 500 years from now as it is today. Why is this so? This consistency is spoken of in terms of the covenant God made with his created order, similar to his covenant with David (Jer 33:19–26).

---

[1] "Presuppositions," Answers in Genesis, accessed May 18, 2021, https://answersingenesis.org/presuppositions/.

[2] See William Lane Craig and J. P. Moreland, *Philosophical Foundations for a Christian Worldview* (Downers Grove, IL: InterVarsity, 2003), 348.

Jeremiah 33:25 tells us that God established the natural laws governing the earth; thus, nature typically operates consistently, and scientific laws apply universally. We say "typically" because God sometimes acts outside of the boundaries of natural law: we call these actions miracles!

We can accurately perceive and understand the natural world is our second presupposition. As we have seen, "the universe is rational, reflecting both the intellect and the faithfulness of its Creator. It has pattern, symmetry, and predictability to it. Effect follows cause in a dependable manner. For these reasons, it is not futile to try to study the universe."[3] Our perceptions are not without flaws, and our understanding is not perfect, but as God's image-bearers (Gen 1:27), we have been given the ability and opportunity to study the natural world. God would not ask us to faithfully steward a world we could not understand.

The final presupposition we consider is that *natural causes exist for natural effects*. A redwood tree recently fell and killed two tourists hiking a popular trail near my home in Oregon. We did not attribute this sad event to spiteful gods occupying wind and trees, but to a natural combination of storm-driven winds, water-laden soil, and the shallow root system of redwood trees. "There are no nature spirits, no capricious gods, no fate. There is only one God (Deut 6:4) who created and rules the world (Gen 1) in a faithful, consistent manner (Ps 119:89–90)."[4] This is not to say that God cannot work outside these natural causes (again, as in miracles) but that nature generally operates by predictable cause-and-effect.[5]

Teaching Suggestions

These presuppositions are abstract, so they are often hard for students to grasp and apply. The teacher's job is to engage the students with concrete, familiar illustrations of the presuppositions, and then to ask students to supply their own examples. For elementary and middle-level students, this scaffolding is especially important.

---

[3] Kitty Ferguson, *Fire in the Equations* (West Conshohocken, PA: Templeton Foundation, 2004), 8.

[4] Deborah B. Haarsma and Loren D. Haarsma, *Origins: Christian Perspectives on Creation, Evolution, and Intelligent Design* (Grand Rapids: Faith Alive Christian Resources, 2011), 43.

[5] Note that science deals only with natural causes for natural effects. Science does not claim "there is no God" because God exists in the metaphysical realm. Likewise, scientists who look only for natural causes will not say, "God caused this earthquake."

- To illustrate the second presupposition, take grade K–5 students outdoors and ask each one to find a living thing: a weed, an ant, a tree. Have students silently observe the organism and sketch (or describe) what is seen so that other students can identify the organism when drawings (or observations) are shared. Read and discuss *The Girl Who Thought in Pictures*[6] (about Dr. Temple Grandin) with students while highlighting that we *can* understand the natural world.

- For middle-level or high school students, choose several of the presuppositions of science and develop learning tasks to examine them early in the school year. A cooperative-group jigsaw activity or a fish-bowl discussion involves your students in higher-level thinking about the presuppositions of science and their basis in biblical truth.[7] Depending on your students' levels of biblical literacy, you can ask them to think of biblical principles (e.g., "God is sovereign over all of creation") or to find specific verses or passages (Job 40:6–41:34) supporting an assigned presupposition ("There is consistency in the natural world").

- I asked my undergraduate college students to write a two-to-three-page paper guided by this prompt: "Explain how the presuppositions of science [presented in class] can be seen as consistent with a biblical worldview. Address each presupposition individually; support your thinking with Scripture or biblical principles." This was a difficult task for students with poor biblical literacy but produced a deep search of the Scriptures for those who embraced the challenge.

In her book on how scientific findings impact religious beliefs, Kitty Ferguson writes, "It is intriguing to find that religion shares much of science's basic view of reality. How is it that two approaches, science and religion, both claiming to be avenues of truth but in many ways reputed to clash with one another, should be in agreement on so basic a level?"[8] For non-Christians, the overlap between scientific assumptions and "religious" thinking is noteworthy and often puzzling. For Christians, it is no surprise that the presuppositions of scientific inquiry are also biblical truths: God endowed the creation with the characteristics that make it knowable by modern scientists. Christians

---

[6] Julia Finley Mosca, *The Girl Who Thought in Pictures* (Seattle: Innovation, 2017).

[7] See The Teacher's Toolkit, "Jigsaw," https://www.theteachertoolkit.com/index.php/tool/jigsaw; and Tolerance.org, "FISH BOWL STRATEGY," https://www.csuchico.edu/cbms/assets/documents/fish-bowl-strategy.pdf.

[8] Ferguson, *The Fire in the Equations*, 9.

believe that God reveals himself in the created world and in the Bible: it would be odd if there was *not* overlap between science and Christian faith.

Review the presuppositions of science throughout the school year. Remind students that these assumptions, fundamental to the practice of science, are biblical truths. This encourages students to enjoy rather than fear learning science.

Walls and Floors Create Space: The Nature of Science

"Science is built up of facts, as a house is built of stones; but an accumulation of facts is no more a science than a heap of stones is a house."[9]

When I ask students what science is, their answers usually focus on science as a collection of facts. But science is also a process, a methodical way of investigating the natural world and coming to logical conclusions based on observable evidence. This process is characterized by guidelines, values, and assumptions collectively known as the nature of science (NOS). Research shows that explicitly teaching the nature of science enhances students' understanding of science content and increases students' interest in science.[10] In this section, we will examine five tenets of the nature of science and the important distinctions between scientific theories and laws.[11]

Tenet 1: *Scientific knowledge is tentative, but also reliable and durable.* In this case, tentative doesn't mean uncertain. It means changeable. Scientific knowledge changes in light of new evidence or new ways of thinking about current evidence. Scientific laws and theories can and do change to more accurately describe or explain the natural world. Thus, scientific knowledge does not find "absolute truth." This is not a weakness of science but is a characteristic of how we arrive at scientific knowledge. People who understand the nature of science never say "science proves" but rather "scientific evidence strongly supports" a particular claim.

---

[9] Henri Poincaré, *Science and Hypothesis* (London: Walter Scott, 1905), 141.

[10] "Reasons for Teaching the Nature of Science," Science Learning Hub, October 7, 2011, https://www.sciencelearn.org.nz/resources/411–reasons-for-teaching-the-nature-of-science. This is a helpful resource if you need to be convinced about the value of teaching the nature of science. Other NOS web pages by this New Zealand organization are also worth your time.

[11] "Tenets of the Nature of Science," Science Learning Hub, New Zealand Government Curious Minds, October 7, 2011, https://www.sciencelearn.org.nz/resources/413–tenets-of-the -nature-of-science.

Tenet 2: *Science is empirical, based on observation of the natural world.* Scientists depend on empirical evidence—observational data—to develop scientific knowledge. This data takes many forms, from naked eye observations (of rocks and minerals, for example) to sophisticated chemical analyses (as of meteorites using mass spectrometers). Scientists draw conclusions based on data alone, not based on feelings, hunches, or metaphysical beliefs. "Any scientific explanation must be consistent with empirical evidence, and new evidence brings the revision of scientific knowledge [see NOS Tenet 1]."[12]

Tenet 3: *Science is inferential, imaginative, and creative.* Scientists interpret data. In other words, they make inferences. Inferring requires imagining possible explanations (called hypotheses) for what is observed. Developing methods to test these hypotheses requires creativity. Albert Einstein remarked, "After a certain high level of technical skill is achieved, science and art tend to coalesce in [a]esthetics, plasticity, and form. The greatest scientists are artists as well."[13] You will notice that the traditional "scientific method" is not included in this chapter on teaching science. While it is important for students to understand controlled experiments (the hallmarks of experimental science), there is no single set of steps that scientists follow as they work. All scientists are problem solvers: they approach problems in various contexts (historical, theoretical, practical, experimental) and develop imaginative, creative ways to find solutions.

Tenet 4: *Science is subjective and theory laden.* Is scientific inquiry a purely objective search for knowledge about the natural world? No! Scientists do try to be objective. But science is a human endeavor and humans are influenced by their prior knowledge, theoretical beliefs, training, culture, opinions, and biases. Observations and inferences are both colored by human subjectivity. The scientific community recognizes this and attempts to offset it using peer review. In the peer review process, colleagues examine other scientists' work to identify possible biases. Generally, this review is done when research is published in journals or presented at conferences. Thus, scientific findings are made public and are available for anyone to examine with the goal that scientific conclusions are as objective as possible.

Tenet 5: *Science is socially and culturally embedded.* Science operates within a specific culture at a certain time in history. Politics, religion, economic systems, traditions, and other features of culture all influence the practice of science. The questions that

---

[12] "Tenets of the Nature of Science," Science Learning Hub.

[13] Alice Calaprice, *The Ultimate Quotable Einstein* (Princeton, NJ: Princeton University, 2011), 379.

concern scientists change as culture changes. So, too, do acceptable methods of investigation. Here is one example. From the early to mid-1900s, scientists worked at finding a vaccine for polio. Jonas Salk developed a vaccine using killed-virus cells. He tested this vaccine on resident children in institutions for the physically and intellectually disabled, presumably without their expressed consent.[14] More recently, scientists raced to produce a COVID vaccine. Rather than using killed-virus cells, researchers used messenger RNA (mRNA) to deliver new genetic information to the cells of vaccinated people, telling those cells to create protection against the virus. Scientific discoveries of the past half-century radically changed the way vaccines are developed. And today, widespread testing of COVID vaccines was performed only with the informed consent of study participants,[15] a requirement brought about by societal and governmental outrage at scientific research conducted on unsuspecting people without their consent.[16]

An important clarification: People often use the term *theory* to mean an opinion or a guess. Thus, scientific theories are also often thought of as mere guesswork, whereas scientific laws are viewed like the laws of society: standards that must be obeyed. Neither of these conceptions is correct.

Scientific laws are descriptions of the natural world based on empirical data that are often—though not always—represented by mathematical equations. Laws describe natural phenomena: they reveal patterns, relationships, and generalizations. An example of a scientific law is Newton's Second Law of Motion: $F = ma$. Laws never become theories. Let me repeat, *scientific laws never, ever become scientific theories.*

Scientific theories are natural explanations (also called models) of groups of related events or observations. Most theories can be expressed in one sentence, although their power to explain is far-reaching. Scientific theories often explain scientific laws. For example, Gregor Mendel expressed laws governing his principles of inheritance, but he had no idea about the real explanation: genes, and subsequent genetic theory.

---

[14] See "Jonas Salk, MD," History of Vaccines, accessed June 27, 2022, https://historyof vaccines.org/history/jonas-salk-md/overview.

[15] See Timothy Cardozo and Ronald Veazey, "Informed Consent Disclosure to Vaccine Trial Subjects of Risk of COVID-19 Vaccines Worsening Clinical Disease," *International Journal of Clinical Practice* 75, no. 3 (March 2021): e13795, https://doi.org/10.1111/ijcp.13795.

[16] The Tuskegee Study of Untreated Syphilis is a disturbing illustration of this tenet. It is a good opportunity for older students to study how the history of racial injustice in the US impacted the practice of science in the 1930s. It also provides excellent fodder for discussing how Christians should interact with society.

Remember: *laws describe; theories explain*. A law is not "better" or "more reliable" than a theory. Both are well-supported by empirical data. Both are widely accepted by the scientific community. And one never, *ever* turns into the other!

Teaching Suggestions

Teaching the nature of science is not a "once-and-done" proposition. It takes intentional effort on the part of the teacher to continually direct his or her students' attention to the nature of science.

One way to teach students about the nature of science is to have them work with actual scientists. There are at least two ways to accomplish this:

1. *Citizen science* involves students in collecting data for active research projects. The United States government maintains a citizen science web page that can be searched by topic,[17] as does National Geographic.[18] I searched "kelp forests" when teaching a recent marine biology class. As a result, my students analyzed satellite images on their computers to identify the locations of kelp forests worldwide for a study on the effects of climate change on kelp forest distribution.[19]

2. Look for opportunities to *partner with scientists*. An internet search of "student-scientist partnership" yields fruitful results. My marine biology students also partnered with scientists studying the impact of climate change on the Southern Ocean. By "adopting" a data-collecting float, the class was able to dialogue with scientists about the ongoing project. This "powerful opportunity for elementary- and secondary-aged students to engage directly with world-class scientists and learn about their research by naming and tracking SOCCOM floats" engaged my class for the entire year. We identified characteristics of the Southern Ocean using data from our float (named "Mesosaurus"). The creative engineering of the floats highlighted the third NOS tenet as well.[20]

---

[17] https://www.citizenscience.gov/#.

[18] https://www.nationalgeographic.org/idea/citizen-science-projects/.

[19] https://www.zooniverse.org/projects/zooniverse/floating-forests.

[20] https://soccom.princeton.edu/content/adopt-float-program. SOCCOM stands for Southern Ocean Carbon and Climate Observations and Modeling.

Many classroom activities requiring no science content knowledge springboard students into thoughtful discussions of the nature of science. These can be used with students of all ages, from kindergarten through college. Two of my favorites are Mystery Boxes and the Great Fossil Find.[21] These hands-on activities involve students in an investigation followed by a teacher-led discussion of what they did to solve the "puzzles" and how, in this way, they acted as scientists. These activities and subsequent discussions reveal the nature of science without "lecturing" the students: the teacher guides students to the NOS tenets through class discussion.

Life in the House of Science: Inquiry-Based Pedagogy

"Tell me and I forget, teach me and I may remember, involve me and I learn."[22]

Since you're reading this chapter, you are probably interested in science teaching strategies other than lecturing or having the students read pages in their textbooks followed by answering questions for homework. Inquiry-based learning is one way to engage students in *doing* science instead of being told *about* science. This section describes inquiry-based learning and provides a framework for developing an inquiry-based science lesson.

What is inquiry-based learning? Inquiry-based learning is a learner-centered pedagogy that emphasizes hands-on activities, investigation, and posing of questions. Science learning becomes a process of students constructing and acquiring knowledge in a way that mimics scientific inquiry.

How does inquiry-based learning differ from traditional learning? This table highlights some of the key differences between traditional teacher-centered instruction and student-centered inquiry-based learning.[23]

---

[21] See https://evolution.berkeley.edu/evolibrary/teach/ensi/ensi_great_fossil_find.html and https://evolution.berkeley.edu/evolibrary/teach/ensi/ensi_great_fossil_find.html.

[22] Often incorrectly attributed to Benjamin Franklin, this quote originates with Chinese Confucian philosopher Xun Kuang, who lived from 312–230 BC. See https://www.goodreads .com/quotes/7565817-tell-me-and-i-forget-teach-me-and-i-may for more about the origin and subsequent translation of this quote.

[23] This table was compiled using the information at Concept to Classroom, https://www .thirteen.org/edonline/concept2class/inquiry/index.html. This website contains an excellent workshop about inquiry-based learning. It includes videos of inquiry-based learning in real classrooms and gives examples of inquiry-based "facilitation plans."

Traditional Learning	Inquiry-based Learning
Focused on content mastery	Focused on developing problem-solving and information-processing skills
Teacher dispenses "what is known" about a subject	Teacher facilitates learning and emphasizes "how we come to know"
Students receive information and memorize facts	Students construct a representation of knowledge through active involvement in hand-on investigations, research, and posing questions
Assessment often focuses on the "right" answers	Assessment focuses on determining the progress of skills development in addition to content understanding
Focused on preparation for the next grade or the next high-stakes test	Focused on helping students develop lifelong learning skills and inquiring attitudes
Use of resources is often limited to what is in the classroom or school building	Students are encouraged to find and use outside resources
On-target questions that would cause deviations from the lesson plan are met with "We will get to that later."	On-target questions are met with "How do you suggest we investigate that question?"

How do we implement inquiry-based learning? The 5E instructional model is one way to "[provide] a carefully planned sequence of instruction that places students at the center of learning. It encourages all students to explore, construct understanding of scientific concepts, and relate those understandings to phenomena or engineering problems."[24] This model fits nicely with cognitive interactive learning addressed in this book. We will examine the five Es (Engage, Explore, Explain, Elaborate, Evaluate) to see how they promote inquiry-based learning for students of any age. A lesson plan for elementary students on "Simple Circuits" illustrates each phase. After completing this lesson, the students will be able to (1) define a "circuit" and name its parts, (2) construct a working simple circuit, and (3) explain how a flashlight operates. The 5Es fit the cognitive interactive model developed in this book.

- **Engage:** In the first phase of the 5E learning cycle, the goal is to engage students using an activity or by asking a question. The goals are to reveal students'

---

[24] "5E Model of Instruction," San Diego County Office of Education, accessed June 21, 2022, https://ngss.sdcoe.net/Evidence-Based-Practices/5E-Model-of-Instruction. This website provided the information used to summarize each of the 5Es. Helpful lists of "student behaviors" and "teacher behaviors" are also found here.

prior knowledge, to uncover misconceptions, and to excite them about further learning. We want students' minds focused on a phenomenon, object, problem, situation, or event, and for them to ask questions such as "Why did this happen?" "What do I already know about this?" "What can I find out about this?" and "How can this problem be solved?"

Example: Read the section of *Dear Mr. Henshaw* by Beverly Cleary where Leigh Botts wants to build a burglar alarm on his lunch box. Ask students how they think Leigh might be able to build a burglar alarm. Record student answers on a white board.

- **Explore:** It is very important for students to participate in common, concrete experiences, which will later be used to develop concepts and introduce terms and explanations in the next phase. Thus, during this phase, students engage in hands-on investigations. They should observe patterns, identify variables, ask testable questions, record observations, and consider cause-and-effect relationships. The teacher's role is to facilitate student investigation by providing time, materials, and probing questions.

Example: Students are given wires, a light bulb, and a battery and are asked to make the bulb light up. They draw their ideas first and discuss their ideas with group members before using the materials. Upon construction, students record whether the bulb lights. The teacher asks questions like "Why did you decide to do it that way?" "Why do you think that works (or doesn't work)?" and "Can you design a different setup that still makes the bulb light up?"

- **Explain:** First, the teacher asks the students to share their investigations and their explanations. Using what students share as a springboard, the teacher provides scientific terms, definitions, and explanations. This phase is teacher-directed but emphasizes the students' shared experiences. Activities and resources used in this phase include lecture/note-taking, textbooks, videos, and online articles. After the teacher's explanation, the students articulate their newly constructed understanding of the concept. The teacher corrects any misconceptions.

Example: Have students share diagrams of successful and unsuccessful setups on the board and explain why they think the bulb did or did not light up. Ask students if they see similarities between the setups that worked. Introduce the term *circuit* and explain that a working circuit must include an unbroken *pathway* (the wire) so energy can travel from the *energy source* (the battery) to the *appliance* (the light bulb) and back to the battery again (forming a closed circuit and lighting the bulb). Examine the diagrams of working circuits. Ask students to identify each of the parts and to trace the flow of energy through the circuits. Examine the diagrams of non-working circuits and ask students what was missing or out of order in each one. Correct any misconceptions that arise during this discussion.

- **Elaborate:** The goal in this phase is for students to apply, extend, or elaborate on the concepts, processes, or skills they are learning. Students do additional investigations, design new applications of the concept, or apply what they have learned to other disciplines. Misconceptions are revealed in this phase too. It is important for the teacher to be sure students are using vocabulary and definitions correctly.

  Example: Distribute a flashlight to each group. Ask them to figure out and describe how it works using the new terms and concepts. Each group investigates the flashlight, asking questions, tinkering with variables, recording observations, and developing an explanation which is then shared with the class. The teacher guides the class to a correct explanation of how the flashlight works.

- **Evaluate**: Students need feedback on the quality of their explanations and the accuracy of their understanding. This feedback occurs in two ways: formative feedback is given throughout the learning cycle as the teacher interacts with students individually, in small groups, and as a class. Summative feedback is also necessary so that everyone knows if the learning objectives are met. This phase is, in essence, assessment of student learning.

  Example: Students are given a worksheet with diagrams of circuits. They are asked to label the parts of each circuit, to tell whether the light bulb lights up or not, and to explain their answers. Each student also constructs one of the circuits to verify his/her conclusion, which they then share with a classmate who constructed a different circuit.

Teachers have understandable concerns about implementing inquiry-based learning. Primary among these is that the outcomes of inquiry-based learning are different from what is often assessed by school districts or states. Science, historically, has been assessed as an accumulation of facts, not as the development of scientific skills and dispositions. Parents fall prey to this idea too, and may complain when their children are not memorizing lists of terms or completing an entire textbook. Part of the work of incorporating inquiry-based learning is making sure that all educational stakeholders are aware of its importance. Where possible, assessments at the school, district, and state levels should be adjusted to reflect the emphasis of inquiry-based learning on life-long science process skills along with students' comprehension of scientific terms and concepts. Furthermore, with good inquiry teaching and learning, concepts and skills are learned and retained for future use in building science content and skills.

The Roof Covering the House: Science and Christian Faith

"Great are the works of the LORD; they are pondered by all who delight in them." (Ps 111:2 NIV)

If you are a Christian teaching science, every lesson reveals God the Creator, whether explicitly in a Christian school or implicitly in a public school. This is one of the joys of being a science teacher! But for the sake of your students, you must also resolve how you will teach scientific topics that seem to conflict with what the Bible says. Examining your own thoughts about how science and faith interact is a helpful place to start.

First, it is important to clarify your view of the relationship between science and biblical Christianity (or theology, if you wish), for whether you have recognized it or not, this is one presuppositional pillar in the foundation from which you teach. Four views of this relationship, proposed by Ian Barbour in 1966, are still in use today.

1. The first view of the interaction between science and theology is that they are in *conflict* or *opposition*. That is, science and Christian faith are in combat over the same territory: one must be right and the other must be wrong.
2. The second view is *independence*: Science investigates the natural world and theology deals with values, meaning, purpose and the supernatural. They both have important things to say, but study entirely different domains using entirely different techniques.[25]
3. The third way science and theology might interact is *dialogue*. In this view, an understanding of the sciences influences our view of theology, and an understanding of theology (and the Bible) informs our approach to the sciences.

---

[25] The term "non-overlapping magisteria" is associated with this view: Stephen Jay Gould, "Nonoverlapping Magisteria," *Natural History* 106 (March 1997): 16–22.

4. Finally, the fourth view is *integration*. This is the view that insights from science and theology can form an integrated whole, an "inclusive metaphysics" in Barbour's words.[26]

In the first two views, science and Christian faith are mutually exclusive, which seems an uncomfortable position for a Christian teacher of science to hold. At best, one would have to teach from a position of constant tension or compartmentalization. In my opinion, the last two views are views that are most compatible with belief in *one* God who created the matter and energy of the natural world along with the physical laws that govern it. For more information on investigating an atheistic scientific view of the origin of the universe see the book *I Don't Have Enough Faith to Be an Atheist*.[27]

Next, because most areas of perceived conflict between science and faith revolve around origins (of the universe, planet Earth, living things, and humans), a second presuppositional pillar in a Christian science teacher's foundation is how he or she interprets Genesis 1–11 and other creation passages in the Bible. Although Christians agree that God created all matter and energy, they do not all agree about *how* he did it nor what Scripture tells us about these origins.

In the book *Origins* (which I strongly urge every science teacher to read), Christian interpretations of creation passages are divided into two categories: *concordist and non-concordist*. In the concordist view, God made the earth using the sequence of events described in Genesis 1. Within this category are the Young Earth, Gap, Day-Age, and Appearance of Age interpretations. In the non-concordist view, God created the earth using a different timing and order of events than that described in Genesis 1. In this category are the less familiar Proclamation Day, Creation Poem, Kingdom-Covenant, Ancient Near Eastern Cosmology, and Temple interpretations. All of these interpretations are explained, contrasted, and critiqued in *Origins*.[28]

What has this to do with teaching science? Everything! How one interprets the creation passages in Genesis and elsewhere impacts how you teach the science related to origins questions. Likewise, the degree of confidence you have in the scientific findings

---

[26] These views were first presented by Ian Barbour in *Issues in Science and Religion* (1966) but are taken here from a highly recommended article by the Rev. Dr. Michael Fuller, an Anglican priest with a background in organic chemistry: "Science and Theology: An Introduction," Thinking Faith, October 29, 2010, https://www.thinkingfaith.org/articles/20101029_1.htm.

[27] Norman L. Geisler and Frank Turek, *I Don't Have Enough Faith to Be an Atheist* (Wheaton, IL: Crossway Books, 2004).

[28] Haarsma and Haarsma, *Origins*.

related to origins impacts how you are likely to interpret Scripture. Recognize that your biblical worldview conclusions unavoidably influence how and what you teach. Make every effort to teach evidence-based theories of science accurately and with professional integrity. Science teachers need to teach current scientific evidence that enhances a biblical view of creation and the design of the universe without resorting to attacking Christians who take a position different from their own. Engage students in age-appropriate discussion. When teaching scientific topics with which one has biblical concerns, it is prudent to be aware of your tone of voice and facial expressions. Nonverbal communication can undermine a lesson's worth of excellent instruction.

At the same time, point out where observational support for scientific theories is weak or currently under development. Be sure the critiques are scientifically valid and not fabricated, fanciful, or inaccurate. Engage students in an age-appropriate discussion about the various ways in which Christians harmonize or question the findings of science with their biblical worldviews. If Christians are to interact humbly with others in "the household of faith" it is important for students to learn that not all Christians hold identical beliefs related to scientific and theological questions (Gal 6:10 KJV). All should be respected.

Teaching Suggestions

- With the approval of your school administrators, high school students (and perhaps middle school students) could discuss the information contained in this section, specifically the four views of the relationship between science and theology and the various Christian interpretations of creation passages in the Bible. Although students and their families generally prefer a specific interpretation, realizing that committed Christians hold different views opens students to considering scientific support for origins questions that they previously may not have encountered. The goal here is not to raise doubt in students' minds but to help them appreciate that the natural world *and* the Bible are *interpreted* sources of knowledge. In a Christian school, creating an interdisciplinary unit on this topic with the Bible and history teachers might be profitable.
- Again, for older students and with the support of your administration, develop a learning activity that pairs NOS Tenet 4 with an analysis of Christian websites presenting science and faith perspectives.[29] Students will readily grasp

---

[29] The most well-known Young Earth creationist group is https://answersingenesis.org/ and a Young Earth scientist's perspective is found at https://isgenesishistory.com/todd-wood/;

that both the Bible and observations of the natural world are interpreted by Christians who arrive at many different conclusions. This nicely illustrates that science and theology are both subjective human endeavors that represent Christians' best efforts to know God through nature and through his Word. The key issue for Christian teachers to address is that God exists and that he created everything; how and when he did is a question with various answers among Christians, and these answers should not divide us.

- Teaching suggestions for elementary school teachers are not given primarily because I do not think wrestling with these topics is necessary or appropriate for younger students. Raising such questions would only confuse them. They are not yet developmentally ready to analyze or digest this information. Each teacher must gauge the readiness of his or her students and the educational community at large before engaging in either of the activities suggested here.

Intentional Biblical Worldview Integration

Finally, having dealt in some measure with the most difficult part of teaching science as a Christian, we now turn to the most rewarding aspect. As science teachers, we draw our students' attention to God's revelation of himself in the natural world with every lesson we teach.[30] In public schools, we trust the truth of Rom 1:20 referenced earlier, that God's invisible attributes will manifest themselves in the hearts and minds of those we teach. In Christian schools, science teachers joyfully and explicitly point students to God, the Creator, during their lessons. For example, many teachers use the phrase "the creation" in place of "natural world" as they teach science class, highlighting God's creative work. Praying before a lesson or pausing in the midst of a lesson to thank God for his providence and wisdom in creation require little effort on our part. But these are not sufficient if our students are to engage in deeper biblical integrative thinking.

Science education specialist Susan Koppendrayer reminds us that "teaching science allows educators the amazing opportunity to become advocates, evangelists, and

---

Old Earth creationism is well represented by https://reasons.org/; evolutionary creation by https://biologos.org/; and intelligent design by https://intelligentdesign.org/study/ and the Center for Science and Culture at https://www.discovery.org/id/. The spectrum of Christian positions on these issues is also well represented in book form.

[30] Psalm 19:1.

tellers of the story found in God's creation."[31] Part of telling this story is asking your students to intentionally connect science and God's Word, his character, and his work in creation. We did this when we analyzed the biblical underpinnings of the presuppositions of science. Koppendrayer suggests five questions for teachers to consider when teaching science from a biblical worldview. These questions provide excellent starting points from which to begin biblical worldview integrative discussions with students, no matter what their ages.

1. What is creation saying about God?
2. What damage is done by separating creation and Creator?
3. What does God want us to know about his creation?
4. What does God want us to do with his creation?
5. What is the proper role of science education in God's creation?[32]

Teaching Suggestion

Develop a set of biblical integration questions to use with students in the classroom using Koppendrayer's questions as starting points. Replace the word *creation* with concepts related to the specific *topic* you are teaching. Not every question will be useful for every lesson, but with prayer and reflection, you will come up with at least one or two thoughtful biblical integrative prompts. Here are some sample questions for the lesson plan on simple circuits found earlier this chapter:

•   From Question 1: What do we learn about God by studying electrical circuits?
•   From Question 2: What damage is done by separating God from the study of electricity?
•   From Question 4: How can we be good stewards of God's creation when it comes to generating and using electricity?
•   From Question 5: What should we learn about God and ourselves as we think about complete and incomplete circuits? Similarly, give students an open-ended writing prompt along these lines: "My relationship with God is like an electrical circuit because . . ."

---

[31] Susan Koppendrayer, "5 Questions to Ask When Teaching Science from a Biblical Perspective," Christian Schools International, August 14, 2019, https://www.csionline.org /articles/5–questions-to-ask-when-teaching-science-from-a-biblical-perspective.

[32] Koppendrayer, "5 Questions."

From its presuppositional foundations to the roof that covers the structure, we see that science is a house built on the truths of God's Word and the character of God that is revealed in nature. Christian students should not fear science but should embrace it as a human attempt to examine God's creativity and wisdom displayed in the natural world. May the Lord grant us strength for the task and joy in the journey as we help students see science in this way.

CHAPTER 15

Structure of the Subject: English and Language Arts

Charlotte Gleason

Introduction

So much of teaching requires us to first "sell" our disciplines. You know the student; she raises her hand and asks, "When am I ever going to use this?" After we stop bristling, we launch into the merits of our discipline, whether it be transitive property or sentence variety. In our weaker moments, we respond with the threat of an upcoming test or a grade on a report card. The student's question, however, should be one we continually revisit: Why does what I'm teaching matter?

In the ELA (English Language Arts) classroom, our defense seems obvious. The four components of language arts—reading, writing, speaking, and listening—impact daily communication. Individuals need these skills to navigate a world buzzing with technology in its many forms. Those who lack in any of these areas struggle to navigate today's world, missing opportunities to join conversations and make connections. Research consistently connects poor literacy to financial and social hardship. One study even tied poor literacy to "a range of adverse health outcomes."[1] Even though students

---

[1] Darren A. DeWalt et al., "Literacy and Health Outcomes," *Journal of General Internal Medicine* 19, no. 12 (2004): 1238.

acknowledge the worth of skills like reading and writing, they often fail to make the connections in the classroom. They question how a Shakespearean sonnet or a metaphor will contribute to a strong educational foundation. Unfortunately, teachers often perpetuate these ideas by their failure to connect the dots in this discipline.

In this chapter, I begin by discussing the categories assigned to ELA, but I will also diagnose the problem with a compartmentalized approach. The components of ELA are parts of a whole, working together as one. When they are treated as one, students make lasting connections and increase their retention of the material. My focus is on perhaps the most mistreated ELA component—grammar. The model lesson will showcase how grammar's natural place needs to be among literature and writing, its natural habitat. I use Amy Tan's "Fish Cheeks" as my textbook, showcasing methods that allow students to see how her intentional use of language impacts her overall theme. The end goal is for students to master mechanics in order to develop their own writing voices. In doing so, they will be better heard by their audiences. I address how this integrated approach to teaching ELA reflects God's own design for human communication.

Structure

In a majority of primary and secondary ELA curriculums, students experience aspects of this discipline apart from one another. For example, teachers begin the class with a grammar exercise. Once they have completed this task, they close the workbook or change the slide, indicating to students a conclusion instead of a continuum. Even vocabulary development is taught outside of the very literature that students study during class. In many high school college preparatory classes, teachers provide separate vocabulary workbooks to ready students for standardized tests. Students memorize definitions for objective quizzes, but they fail to retain the meaning or recognize these words in a different context. Meanwhile, the literature they study remains a separate entity. These works, however, contain words, and they contain the stuff of grammar: commas, clauses, phrases, fragments, and the list continues. ELA teachers ask students to discuss the meaning of these works, but they do so without asking them to address many of the ingredients they need to aid their comprehension.

In my approach to teaching ELA, I focus on what I call the big four: *content, style, organization,* and *mechanics.* I often have students ask me which of these categories I weigh the most. Their question, unfortunately, derives from a message they have heard in other disciplines. Teachers tell students they "grade for content." I respond to this question by stressing each of the big four has equal weight. How can I understand the content if the mechanics cloud the meaning? Will I engage with the content if the work uses vague language? What if I fail to see the logical development of the essay? If one part is weak, it impacts the whole.

Even an integrated approach to teaching ELA, however, requires us to teach bits and pieces in isolation. In the upcoming model lesson, I will explain how the mini-lesson acts as a necessary springboard for ELA instruction. It allows ELA teachers to zoom into a part and then zoom out to show their students where the part fits in the entire picture. Whether students are reading, writing, speaking, or listening, the big four must be addressed. The end goal, then, is for students to recognize how techniques and terminology for each of these categories can be applied to a poem, an essay, or any of the content in an ELA class.

Logical Organization

The big four—content, style, organization, and mechanics—is a simplified view of the Common Core standards in the United States as well as the NCTE/IRA standards (National Council of Teachers of English/International Reading Association). In the United States, Common Core categorizes the standards as anchors, specifically reading, writing, speaking/listening, and language. The scope of ELA is far-reaching and connected to all other disciplines. Reading and writing takes place across the curriculum. When ELA teachers strengthen the reading, writing, and speaking skills of students, all other disciplines benefit.

A review of the NCTE/IRA's twelve standards for the English Language Arts reflects the breadth of this subject.[2] The standards include comprehension and production of all kinds of texts, including fiction, nonfiction, and digital media. How ELA teachers achieve these standards varies, but the most effective curriculums integrate each aspect and allow students to make real world connections.

Standards for Testing and Judging Truth

The final NCTE/IRA standard summarizes what they believe should be the goal for any ELA teacher: "Students use spoken, written, and visual language to accomplish

---

[2] "NCTE / IRA Standards for the English Language Arts," National Council of English Teachers, November 2012, https://ncte.org/resources/standards/ncte-ira-standards-for-the-english-language-arts/.

their own purposes."[3] They want students to recognize the power of language and to know how to wield that power. As Christian ELA teachers, however, we want written and verbal communication to accomplish God's purposes. In fact, God chose writing to convey his own words. John 1:1 even equates Jesus Christ with "the Word." Jesus Christ became the living Word, allowing his creation to hear and understand his great narrative of redemption. God knows our minds are finite: his words provide us with enduring reminders of God's commandments and promises.

Because humankind is made in God's image, individuals bear witness to his truths whether they intend to or not. We often see truth in the works of those who do not know God. In a fallen world, we also see evidence of lies and blasphemy. God's Word provides us with an absolute standard to evaluate all other words. We can also celebrate the Bible as a great work of literature, but we must remember it is set apart from all other books. In the Bible, God used different genres, varied authors, and powerful literary techniques to communicate with the world and guide his children until his return.

The challenge for many students in ELA is the subjective nature of the discipline. God's Word provides the standard of truth for us, but as mentioned above, God uses a variety of ways to do so in the Bible. Everyone has a favorite Bible verse, and their reasons are as varied as the people who choose them. We do not have the time to discuss aesthetic standards for beauty, but I encourage my students to recognize that God has created objectivity and subjectivity. In the ELA classroom, we see examples of both. A complete sentence needs a subject and a predicate: this does not change. Someone's interpretation of a poem, however, does change. ELA teachers provide their students with objective tools to analyze, interpret, and write about subjective matter. The result, then, does not often end with a single answer and certainly not a single voice.

Methods of Inquiry

Approaches to teaching ELA vary based on the teacher's pedagogical background and the expectations of his or her school. It is difficult to characterize a typical ELA classroom; however, ELA teachers tend to emphasize that with which they are the most comfortable. As a result, two stereotypes of English teachers circulate in pop culture:

---

[3] "NCTE / IRA Standards for the English Language Arts."

the "grammar Nazi" and the English teacher as depicted by Robin Williams in *Dead Poet's Society*. One narrows her focus on grammar, and the other narrows his focus on literature. The two must meet to create the most effective ELA classroom.

Before teachers deliver the content to their students, they need to first consider the question posed in the introduction: Why does what I am teaching matter? Whatever the objectives for the lesson, we need to first consider their place in the larger world. Some educators list the essential questions at the beginning of their lesson and share them with their students. Jay McTighe and Grant Wiggins emphasize that the goal of these questions "should strive to develop and deepen students' understanding of important ideas and processes so that they can transfer their learning within and out-side school."[4] The end goal allows students to make subject-to-life connections with the content they learn. In their work, McTighe and Wiggins suggest several example ELA essential questions. When answered, these responses reach beyond the scope of the ELA classroom.

- What do good readers do, especially when they don't comprehend a text?
- How does what I am reading influence how I should read it?
- Why am I writing? For whom?
- How do effective writers hook and hold their readers?
- What is the relationship between fiction and truth?
- How are stories from other places and times about me?[5]

Another way to address the "what matters" in a lesson is to write the big idea—the why it matters in written form. This idea forces teachers to think broadly. Instead of creating questions, the teacher writes the ideological goal of the lesson before the practical outworking of the lesson plan unfolds. She answers why the content matters. In many instances, several lessons or an entire unit will fit under this one idea. Writing such a statement challenges us to consider how the content and the presentation of the content points students to a larger meaning.

---

[4] Jay McTighe and Grant Wiggins, "Chapter 1. What Makes a Question Essential?" *Essential Questions: Opening Doors to Student Understanding* (Alexandria, VA: ASCD, 2013), https://www.seedpaknwboces.org/pd-resources/what-makes-question-essential.

[5] McTighe and Wiggins, "Chapter 1. What Makes a Question Essential?"

Example Lesson Overview

As addressed earlier, the goal in the lesson is to show how to integrate each aspect of ELA. A work of nonfiction appropriate for middle level students or higher is used. The work, Amy Tan's "Fish Cheeks," describes Tan's personal experience when she was fourteen, navigating life as a Chinese American. When her parents invite their pastor's family for a Christmas dinner, Tan relives the humiliation she felt as the Chinese customs and food selection surprise the visitors. Toward the close of the story, Tan recalls the words of her mother: "But inside you must always be Chinese. You must be proud you are different. Your only shame is to have shame."[6]

In this lesson, the students will not only read and comprehend her story; they will notice how Tan's language, specifically her use of strong verbs, enhances the theme of the story. My hope is that you will see how instruction about grammar naturally enters the discussion about this work. Teachers need not segregate the content in Tan's work from her mechanics, organization, and style. For example, when students observe Tan's mechanics, they see how it enhances her style. The content, then, becomes more accessible and appealing to the readers.

As a Christian English educator, I want my big idea to reflect biblical truth. How is God's voice heard in the Bible? How does he use different writers to communicate his narrative of redemption? How does the ability to communicate reflect our status as image-bearers?

Big Idea

Writers depend on many tools and methods to communicate their messages, but they do so for a common goal: communication. They want to be heard. For those who feel marginalized or different, this desire is especially great. Writing provides an opportunity to share their voice with one reader at a time. To keep their readers engaged, writers learn how to manage every aspect of language—from the punctuation they use to the genre they choose. Effective writers wield the power of writing to express their thoughts and to be heard. As image-bearers, we can do the same. Humans think, talk,

---

[6] Amy Tan, "Fish Cheeks," *The Brief Bedford Reader* (2000):95, New Canaan Public Schools, accessed June 17, 2022, https://www.ncps-k12.org/cms/lib8/CT01903077/Centricity /Domain/638/LA/Short%20Story%20-%20Fish%20Cheeks.pdf.

write, speak, and communicate because God does; he has equipped us with the capacity to develop this human ability.

Objectives

The student will be able to identify the strong verbs Amy Tan uses in "Fish Cheeks" to "show" instead of "tell" in her writing and be able to express in writing the theme of identity in Tan's story.

Activation/Engagement Activity

To begin the lesson, I will consider a relevant subject to life connection that can be made with the students. This part of the lesson represents how I will "hook" my readers so they will want to continue, and their minds will be engaged with what lies ahead. In much the same way, I want students to connect to the content—even if they are unaware they are doing so. One word we will revisit throughout this lesson is *identity*. This is a theme of the essay.

The "name tag method" challenges students to consider how we identify others and ourselves. Students will need to decide what questions they need to ask to determine who they are. The process begins with teacher planning. Before class, write a variety of famous names on name tags or sticky notes. Choose names the students will be able to identify: musicians, actors, athletes, and historical figures. As students enter the room, provide them with the name tag by placing (sticking) it on their back; tell them not to look at the names (no peeking!). When they are seated, instruct the students that their task is to discover who they are. Give students three minutes to circulate, asking their classmates to give them hints about their identity. Do not give them the questions ahead of time. They will naturally ask questions; this is what we do. They will consider what types of questions we ask and why we always default to "What do you do?"

The initial goal is for students to correctly guess their names. After the three-minute guessing time, ask the students to share the types of hints they were given in answer to their questions. List their responses on the board, allowing them to see the language and categories they used to identify people. Some examples may include physical appearance, gender, vocation, and association.

This activity leads your students into a natural conversation about identity or the answer to the question, "Who am I?" Ask the students to create a simple word web with "Identity" at the center.

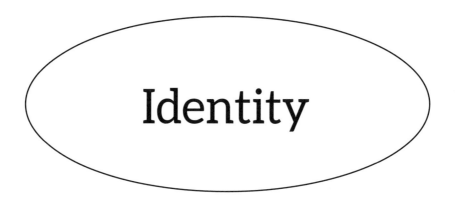

Students should list words and/or phrases they associate with "identity" in one minute. Word webs also offer ELA teachers an opportunity to integrate mechanics as students consider the content. I encourage my students to use concrete nouns (things you can experience with your senses) instead of abstract nouns or adjectives when they are brainstorming. As much as possible, I use grammatical terms throughout my lessons. These terms do not need to be reserved for a five-minute exercise or a worksheet review. This is part of understanding the structure of the language arts as a unified whole.

Several key questions will prompt the students as they begin to brainstorm: What are the characteristics of the concept of identity? How do these characteristics answer the question, Who am I? After the time ends, ask students to share with a partner. As you circulate, you will want to collect a few of their ideas to share with the entire class when you regroup. For example, students might list words such as *daughter*, *musician*, or *basketball player*; others may give a phrase such as "Who I am" or "I am a child of God."

In a Christian school setting, I would include in this activity, or later in the lesson after discussing human identity, several questions about our identity as human beings, first, and as belonging to Jesus Christ for those of us who Christians. What was God's design for humankind in the creation account (Gen 1:27)? What does it mean to be an image-bearer? In the New Testament, Paul reminds us that we are "his workmanship" (Eph 2:10). What does this mean? What happens when people do not see themselves as a work of God? We are also reminded in the Bible not to be ashamed of who we are. At some point in the lesson, the teacher can assign a brief research assignment to find Scripture references that answer the question, Who am I? (a question that King David asks in Psalm 8 and then answers). Lead into Amy Tan's story stating that we will see how humans long to discover their identity and often resist the identities they have been given. These longings reflect our need for the truth in determining who we are as humans and as individuals that only our Creator can help us understand. Later in the lesson, students learn how our life experiences and cultural backgrounds shape us but that they need not define us if we are God's children.

Concept Development

Now that the students have considered what they already know about identity and their own identity in Christ, introduce them to Amy Tan and her story "Fish Cheeks." Share Amy Tan's cultural background and experiences by providing part of her biography.[7] I like to ask my students this question after I introduce any author: How do you think this author's experiences may have impacted his or her writing? The answers to this question allow students to better contextualize the works of these individuals.

At this point in the lesson, students have connected to the idea of identity and recognized Amy Tan's unique perspective as a Chinese American. Before they read the story, however, prepare them to better appreciate her writing. The inclusion of a grammar mini-lesson does just this. Amy Tan's short story becomes their textbook, allowing students to recognize how the big four—content, style, organization, and mechanics—are a part of a whole. The selection of grammar to teach from a story is based on observations I have made about students prior to the lesson. First, I must be aware of the writing needs of my students. Many secondary students rely on the use of being verbs in their writing. This habit leads to the overuse of passive voice and a lack of specific language. Students succeed at telling in their writing (that is, giving information), but they fail to show in their writing (that is, painting a picture of what they are saying to bring the reader into the experience). I want them to use vivid verbs in their writing, but to do so, they must understand not only what they are but their function in a sentence.

I also need to make careful observations about the work of literature. What work will model this technique and provide students with a model-worthy example? How is an author's content more powerful because of his or her intentional organization, mechanics, and style? When using real literature as a grammar textbook, it is helpful to use contemporary works. We can learn how to build a plot from William Shakespeare or how to structure a sonnet from John Donne, but their eighteenth-century English often clouds students' grammatical understanding. By no means should we avoid

---

[7] Since Amy Tan is a contemporary author, we have the advantage of reading a biography she wrote about herself. You can find her biography here: http://www.amytan.net/about.html.

reading these works, but for grammar integration, contemporary literature often works more effectively.

By design, the grammar mini-lesson is meant to be short (5–10 minutes).[8] For this lesson, I begin with a short activity to remind students what they already know about verbs. I provide students with a series of sentences, and they must do what the sentences say.

> You are sad.
>
> You weep with abandon.
>
> You are happy.
>
> You grin and giggle.
>
> You are sleepy.
>
> You slouch in your chair, close your eyes, and snore.

After this activity, ask the students which sentences were easier to perform. They will point to the sentences with active verbs as their simple predicates. Think aloud with your students, allowing them to interject as you do so. Encourage them to use grammatical terms such as *subject* and *predicate*. You want them to see that all the sentences are grammatically correct. In fact, they are similar in length. The difference, then, is not the number of words I use; it is the type of words I use. At this point, explain how the sentences with "are" use *being verbs*. We will call them the *telling sentences*. The other sentences are the *showing sentences*. The verbs give the readers a clear idea of what the subject is doing. Strong writers frequently use *vivid verbs* as the simple predicates.

The first five minutes of your lesson are spent on direct instruction. For the remainder of the mini-lesson, students will complete a simple activity. Throughout the remainder of the lesson, students will continue interacting with the idea of showing verbs. Students will write several before-and-after sentences to showcase their learning. Provide them with the telling sentences, and have the students transform them into

---

[8] Constance Weaver offers twelve guidelines for teaching a grammar mini-lesson. Weaver, along with Lucy Caulkins and Nancie Atwell, are invaluable resources for how to integrate grammar into the context of reading and writing. This article provides a summary of some of their ideas: https://www.usi.edu/media/2962428/teaching-grammar-and-mini-lessons.pdf.

showing sentences. If you have several advanced writers, encourage them to use a vivid verb in a complex sentence or write multiple showing sentences about the same idea. Notice how the example sentences could be related to the topic we have been discussing: identity.

Esther was feeling insecure about her outfit.

Juan is scared to answer the question.

Jane is a police officer.

I was dreading the new school year.

After three minutes, ask your students to choose their best showing sentence. Each student reads his or her sentence, and the class determines which telling sentence it addresses. Encourage them to consider the relationship between mechanics, style, and content. When writers understand how a sentence functions, they have the power to manipulate their style. In doing so, their content becomes not only clear but memorable.

The activation activity, initial concept development, and mini-lesson will take about thirty minutes of a class period. After students read their sentences, you transition to Amy Tan's "Fish Cheeks." As they listen to the story being read, give them these listening prompts:

- How does Amy Tan use language that "shows" in her story?
- How does Tan feel about her identity as a Chinese American in this story?

I encourage you to read the story aloud to your students. As much as possible, model how to read well, using expression and clear enunciation. Students will need to have a copy of the story before them as you read. Encourage them to underline words, images, and phrases they notice. After you complete reading the story, give students two minutes to write their responses to the listening prompts. Follow this time of writing with a "soft call." Students know I will call on anyone, but they know they can ask me to come back if they feel unprepared.

Student Processing Activities

After a brief time of responding to the listening prompt, students work in small groups to complete a processing sheet. This time of collaboration offers students time to verbally process the story before they process the work through writing. As you will see, I have created a handout to guide the students through their discussion, asking them to first underline the simple predicates in a paragraph from Tan's work. Students see grammar in action, and in seeing this, it becomes more relevant. This is helpful in developing understanding of the structure of the language arts. Toward the end of the assignment, the students begin to unpack the theme of "Fish Cheeks."

In a traditional forty-five-minute class, the students will not complete the three elements in one class period. Determining where to stop is an individual class matter, but allowing students to fit into their thinking and understanding what has been addressed for this initial period is vital. Because one of the objectives is related to the theme of identity, perhaps this should be discovered in the first part of the lesson, and because strong verbs are vital to meeting the objective, the brief grammar lesson and review should be included in day one. Even in a longer class period, this review allows the teacher to formatively assess the class's understanding of vivid verbs and their value. As students interact with the language of the story one word at a time, they begin to see how Tan's showing language allows her to better communicate her point. As students progress through the steps, the teacher should be proactive about circulating and listening for student insights. I often ask students to share insights when we regroup as a whole class. Being aware of specific, excellent thinking guides in the calling on students to participate orally and builds confidence. Included here is a series of steps to follow for this lesson.

The Language of Identity

In Amy Tan's "Fish Cheeks," she writes about her own experience with a culture clash. She spends most of the evening embarrassed about her Chinese culture, wishing to be more American. In your groups, complete the steps below and end with a discussion on the theme of Tan's work by identifying evidence for the theme.

Step 1: *Verb Search*. Read this passage aloud from "Fish Cheeks." Underline the simple predicates in each sentence; several have been completed for you.

> Dinner <u>threw</u> me deeper into despair. My relatives <u>licked</u> the ends of their chopsticks and <u>reached</u> across the table, dipping them into the dozen or so plates of food. Robert and his family waited patiently for platters to be passed to them. My relatives murmured with pleasure when my mother brought out the whole steamed fish. Robert grimaced. Then my father poked his chopsticks

just below the fish-eye and plucked out the soft meat. "Amy, your favorite," he said, offering me the tender fish cheek. I wanted to disappear.[9]

Discuss: How does Tan use verbs in this paragraph to give readers a picture of what she saw? How did Tan feel about the behavior of her family members? How do you know?

Step 2: *Story Skim*. Highlight three additional examples of Tan expressing her embarrassment of her family. You may not use the paragraph in Step 1.

Discuss: What images does Tan use to show the contrast between Chinese and American culture?

Step 3: *Point of View Guide*. In Tan's story, she recalls the words and actions of her mother after their guests were gone:

> "You want to be the same as American girls on the outside." She handed me an early gift. It was a miniskirt in beige tweed. "But inside you must always be Chinese. You must be proud you are different. Your only shame is to have shame." And even though I didn't agree with her then, I knew that she understood how much I had suffered during the evening's dinner.[10]

Discuss: Imagine that you are Amy Tan's mother. Share with your group members how you felt about Amy's behavior during the Christmas dinner. Explain why you chose the gift you did for your daughter.

Respond & Write: You may wish to discuss these questions before you respond in writing in your notebook.

1. Amy Tan ends her story with this observation: "For Christmas Eve that year, she had chosen all my favorite foods." What does this observation convey about her mother? What does it convey about Amy Tan's own likes and dislikes?
2. How did Amy Tan's language allow her readers to experience the dinner with her? What image was especially vivid to you and why?
3. Paraphrase these words of Amy Tan's mother: "But inside you must always be Chinese. You must be proud you are different. Your only shame is to have shame."

---

[9] Tan, "Fish Cheeks."
[10] Tan, "Fish Cheeks."

After the students complete each step in the handout, ask them to share their responses. If the teacher has done the work of preparing students to contribute, he or she will find that student responses will embolden others to share as well.

Assessment

Students need to show their individual understanding of the content. The final assessment that may be initiated on day two of the lesson challenges students to connect their learning to their own worlds. How can they communicate their ideas about identity in an engaging manner? The final assessment requires students to consider the big four (content, mechanics, style, and organization) and model how these work together in their own writing.

Writing assignments are not the only summative assessments in an ELA classroom, but they should certainly be frequent. For younger students, episodic or narrative writing assignments are developmentally appropriate. Middle school students should be moved beyond these types of writing to strengthen their critical and creative thinking skills. The writing assignment for this lesson can be adapted for a diverse group of students. I would give them the following writing prompt with specific requirements. Notice how the requirements reflect each category of the big four serving the structure of the language arts. The final two requirements—strong verbs and sentence/word variety—reiterate the symbiotic nature of style and mechanics. If we do not understand how language works (mechanics), how are we to best showcase our voice (style)?

Respond and Write: Amy Tan's "Fish Cheeks"

In Amy Tan's "Fish Cheeks," she shares how she struggled with her identity as a Chinese American. As Christians, we acknowledge that our cultural background and life experiences are God-given, but they do not define us. God's Word tells us who we are as humans and especially who we are in Christ as a Christ-follower. As humans we should see all people of every color, race, gender, and socioeconomic group of equal value, created in the image of God. Diversity and unity are God's idea. This is a good opportunity to develop the concept of acceptance of others as they are.

In two developed paragraphs, explain what Tan's mother meant when she told Amy, "Your only shame is to have shame." After you address this statement, explain what it means for you to be unashamed of who you are as a human being and as one "in

Christ." Express how you can appreciate the unique experiences and culture God has given to you in the human family and in God's diverse family of Christians.

Like Amy Tan, use showing language, not telling language. Be sure to include the following in your paragraphs:

- Topic sentences
- 6–8 sentences per paragraph
- Specific references to Tan's story
- Specific examples of your background/experiences
- Strong verbs
- Sentence and word variety
- Biblical references for human dignity and who we are as humans who are Christians

☑ *Create a word bank of strong verbs you might use in your paragraphs.*

Key Biblical Worldview Questions and Answers

The first biblical worldview question I address is one we began to address earlier: *Who or what is God?* The Bible reveals God as a communicator, and as ELA teachers, we need to recognize the unique position of God's Word compared to other works of literature.[11] The Bible is our source of truth. We seek to find these truths in our reading, writing, speaking, and listening. God's creation, including human authors, cannot help but point to God's "eternal power and divine nature" (Rom 1:20 ESV). We are made in his image and are communicators by nature.

As we understand God as a communicator, we then ask, *How do we know what is true?* ELA studies humanity through stories. This study naturally leads to questions

---

[11] See "Standards for Testing and Judging Truth," pages 337–38 in this book.

about what is true and what is the nature of reality. Fictional stories are not real, but they allow us to better understand true things. C. S. Lewis's Chronicles of Narnia, for example, shows us how evil can be redeemed for good. The poetry of Gwendolyn Brooks allows us to recognize the need for justice in a fallen world.

We addressed earlier how the language arts do not shy away from the subjective. When individuals are confronted with ambiguity, they look for absolutes for comparison. In a sense, the subjective nature of ELA drives individuals to seek truth and consider why others might disagree. Practically, many academic writing assignments require students to create an arguable thesis statement and use evidence and reason to convince their audience of the same. ELA teachers instruct their students to support their opinions with conviction; they develop truth seekers. Students learn how to defend their opinions and convince their audience their educated opinions are true. Especially in biblical worldview thinking, the point of truth should always focus on what God has revealed about an issue rather than just a personal opinion.

The final question I address connects to our model lesson. *What is a human being?* Whether we read fiction or nonfiction, these works have authors. Writing, then, is human thought on paper. The more we engage with literature, the more we learn about those who God created in his image. In an ELA classroom, we enter the minds of villains and heroes. We see the full extent of human depravity, but we also see the potential. We see glimpses of the way the world and humankind are meant to be.

ELA does not only challenge us to consider the full scope of humankind—the pretty and the ugly. It also challenges us to consider our own identity. In Amy Tan's "Fish Cheeks," we interact with a girl who resented her identity. In doing so, we consider our own identities. As we see characters failing to discover who they are or attempting to define themselves, we see how humans yearn to be known. This desire again points us to God's intent for those who bear his image to flourish as God intended, knowing who they are and who they can be in Christ.

While the outlined lesson above does not give a complete picture of how the lesson will be delivered in a class of students, I trust that it helps to trigger the thinking of the reader about the four big elements of the language arts and how they can be integrated into one lesson rather than treated as individual elements, for indeed they all work together in communication!

CHAPTER 16

World Languages

James Nyagetiria, Nairobi, Kenya

Introduction and Personal Background

According to the *Oxford English Dictionary*, *language* is "the system of communication in speech and writing used by people of a particular country or area."[1] Learning a new language exercises the brain as one uses new grammar and vocabulary. At the beginning of every academic year, I remind my students of our school mission statement: "Rosslyn Academy inspires and equips each student to develop their God-given gifts for Christ-like service in the world community."[2] That service is enhanced by learning a second or third language.

Why do I remind students of our mission statement? I want them to value what they will be learning and motivate them to study well so they can use language for God's glory to change the world in various spheres of human life. Currently, I have a student whose parents are missionaries in Burkina Faso. They are doing translation of Bible verses into French and from French to English. This is a perfect example of

---

[1] *Oxford Advanced Learner's Dictionary*, s.v. "language," accessed March 14, 2022, https://www.oxfordlearnersdictionaries.com/us/definition/english/language.

[2] "Mission and Values," Rosslyn Academy, accessed January 28, 2022, https://rosslyn academy.org/mission-and-values/.

using God-given talents to serve in the world community. Some of my former students are now teachers of French in different parts of public Kenyan schools as well. This is a great joy.

Our international academy is an authentic Christian school where students excel in various subject areas, in part, because of our Christian values. I have been teaching French as a Foreign/World Language for nineteen years and have had the opportunity to teach in different systems of education: Kenyan (five years), British (six years), and now in American, starting my seventh year. In addition to teaching, I have also had the privilege of heading the World Languages and Examinations Departments in several institutions of learning.

Before I introduce French as a language, I usually ask the students these questions: Why would you like to learn French? What are some of the French words you know already? Who are the famous French footballers and musicians that you know, if any? It is a good idea to share some of the things you know about France. After all, the course will address the language of France and other French-speaking countries in the world. In upper-level classes, I ask students why they are interested in continuing to higher levels such as French 3 and AP French. The answers help the teacher to understand the motivational level of the student and a little about how he or she might use the language in the future. My colleagues who teach other world languages such as Spanish and Korean do the same for their students.

We often get interesting responses such as "I would like to work with the United Nations," "French will help me communicate with French speakers in Europe," "I would like to play for a football club like Paris Saint Germain," "My parents are missionaries who work in French West Africa so I would like to continue their missionary work," and "My brother told me that your classes are lively and memorable!" (I like this last one especially!) Students take World Languages based on their interest. Teachers should value and use the diverse interests of the class.

Learning a New Language

Languages are not always easy to learn—vocabulary, parts of speech in grammar, various dialects, and new sounds must be heard, listened to carefully, and formed, often with a mouth that is foreign to that new language. Learning a world language is an astonishingly good gift from our good and gracious God. It is encouraging to see students get excited as they use new vocabulary and can actually begin to converse. Good language teaching, as with all teaching, must be done by teachers with passion for

God's glory and with the apostle Paul's encouragement in mind: "Whatever you do, do it from the heart, as something done for the Lord and not for people" (Col 3:23).

Structure of a Language

Britannica defines language as "a system of conventional spoken, manual [signed], or written symbols by means of which human beings, as members of a social group and participants in its culture, express themselves. The functions of language include communication, the expression of identity, play, imaginative expression, and emotional release."[3]

There are five major components of the structure of a language: *phonemes, morphemes, lexemes, syntax, and context*. Along with grammar, semantics, and pragmatics, these components work together to create meaningful communication among individuals.[4]

Phonemes are units of sound that can distinguish one word from another in a language like French, for example, p and b in French words *pain* (bread) and *bon* (good). Every language has some common phonemes and some phonemes unique to the language. It is essential to have good comprehension of the phonemes for both listening and speaking in the language.

Morphemes are the smallest meaningful parts of a word in a language that can have a meaning, for example, "unable": *un* and *able* are morphemes. Morphemes are used within language as building blocks of words and vocabulary. When learning a language, it is helpful for listening, reading and speaking the language.

Lexemes are a language's basic units of meaning. In English, for example, we have the words *dancing, danced*, and *dancer*. The lexeme is dance. That is the word at its basic unit of meaning with no prefixes or suffixes. The others mentioned above are examples of "variable lexemes." Languages also have "invariable lexemes." These are words in which there are no variations. In English, a good example is the word *the* (only one word corresponds to this word and there are no variables). **Idioms** also fall into a category and are called "multiple lexemes." These are words that combine to form a specific

---

[3] "Languages," Britannica, accessed January 28, 2022, https://www.britannica.com/browse/Languages#:~:text=Language%2C%20a%20system%20of%20conventional.

[4] "Introduction to Language," Boundless Psychology, Lumenlearning.com, 2019, https://courses.lumenlearning.com/boundless-psychology/chapter/introduction-to-language/.

meaning. An example in English is "at the crack of dawn," meaning very early in the morning at sunrise. We study lexemes for all forms of comprehension of a language.

Syntax is how morphemes are arranged to form phrases and sentences. Syntax includes things like word order, agreement, and gender. Syntax is a subset of grammar and often covers the complexities within a language beyond the grammar.

Context is the setting and circumstances where language is used. For instance, the saying that "the early bird catches the worm" can be used in different settings to convey a message. One context may relate to a person arriving at a market and finding the best fruit because he or she arrived early. Another context may be that a business was the first to market a particular product and is doing very well. The context changes while the meaning of the idiom remains the same.

Grammar is the whole structure of various parts in a language. This includes all parts of speech like nouns, verbs, and adjectives. It includes the rules of the structure of language. Most language learners are familiar with the idea of grammar, but each world language studied has its own rules of grammar.

Semantics is the study of the meaning of various parts of a language. Semantics in language study goes beyond a simple definition of a word but examines when a specific definition of a word is appropriate. Semantics includes understanding labels and categories as well as specific definitions. Higher levels of semantics include being able to understand ambiguous words with multiple meanings or figurative language. A strong development of semantics is necessary to express oneself clearly as well as to be able to understand other speakers.

Pragmatics deals with how language is used and in which contexts it is used. It is the social aspect of learning a language such as knowing when a phrase is appropriate and in which context. Pragmatics includes a lot of cultural aspects of what we say and how we say it. Because language learning is about communication, pragmatics is a key to pulling together the other structures within language learning.

Teaching a world language is a process that requires a teacher to plan well to teach different aspects of a language: listening comprehension, reading comprehension, essay writing, and oral use of the language. The structure of a language is presented here to assist the reader in understanding the overall structure of language learning. In the section on methods of inquiry, we will examine how to put these together in a way that will help the student learn holistically the language being studied.

Logical Organization

In what order should a student learn language skills? In the chapter on mathematics, there is an interconnectedness of the discipline of mathematics, however students must learn certain things first. This is true as well for languages. What is a logical way to approach the learning of a language?

In the Kenyan System of Education, the Ministry of Education provides a syllabus that is used across the country. It is a guide that outlines what should be covered at different levels of language learning with clear learning objectives. The ministry also approves which textbooks and materials should be used to accomplish its mission of imparting knowledge to learners. The Ministry of Education officials who are in charge of World Languages plan organized and impromptu visits to schools to see how learning is taking place. This is true in many parts of the world.

Teachers are taught how to prepare schemes of work and lesson plans with clear objectives and learner-centered methodology. The guidelines are designed to ensure that learners are exposed to listening, reading, essay writing, and oral activities. At times it is difficult for some schools with limited resources to effectively use the plan. I am privileged to be in an International Christian American School where resources are available and standards are encouraged.

In the United States, National Standards for Foreign Language Learning are published by the American Council on the Teaching of Foreign Languages (ACTFL).[5] The standards task force identified five goals for language learning regardless of the reason for study: Communication, Cultures, Connections, Comparisons, and Communities—the five Cs of world language education.[6] These areas of language study are adopted by many states and are the focus of language teaching in the United States and some international schools as well.

Whether teaching French 1 or an AP class, I always ensure that I have included all the components of language learning but tend to give more time for oral language used in group discussions. At our school, we have peer observations where we invite colleagues to come and observe our lessons. This is a good practice and allows for the sharing of best practices. Our teachers also attend professional development workshops where we talk about best practices in language learning.

---

[5] https://www.actfl.org/resources/world-readiness-standards-learning-languages/standards-summary.

[6] Denise Minor, "Standards of Foreign Language Teaching the Five C's," *On Being a Language Teacher*, March 2014, 115–23, https://doi.org/10.12987/yale/9780300186895.003.0006.

Standard for Testing and Judging Truth

The reason why people learn a language is to enable communication in that language. Learning a new language is not easy and demands a lot of patience to learn and use correctly various grammar aspects such as adjectives, nouns, and adverbs. Different languages have different grammar rules. For instance, in French, all objects are either masculine or feminine and an adjective must agree with the noun; there must be subject-verb agreement as well. A lot of grace and assistance must be extended to learners as they begin to figure out unique aspects of a new language.

In the biblical account of the Tower of Babel, there is an interesting, albeit negative, account. The people refused to scatter, to be fruitful, and inhabit the earth. They were content to stay there in their comfort zone. The people at Babel all spoke the same language, and their communication enabled them to do some incredible building albeit with the wrong attitude and actions that were not pleasing to the Lord. Genesis 11:6 records: "The Lord said, 'If they have begun to do this as one people all having the same language, then nothing they plan to do will be impossible for them.'" While this is a negative example because they were demonstrating pride and disobedience to God, the story does indicate a truth that could be positive as well. When people can converse in the same language, they can accomplish much. As well, when language is a barrier, accomplishment of aims and desires is difficult. Missionaries have understood this for centuries.

When the Lord sent the apostle Paul to Cornelius (Acts 10), he was sending a Jew to a Gentile with the message of the gospel and made it clear to Paul, and those Hebrew believers with him, that God was saving the Gentiles as well as the Jews who believed in Jesus. The large household of Cornelius heard Paul's message in their own language much like many did on the Day of Pentecost. While this was a miracle of God, it shows the importance of language not only to people but to God.

Humans communicate because God communicates. We are created in his image, and one of those "image-bearing" characteristics is the ability to communicate in languages. God chose to communicate through the prophets of old through language, through his Son, Jesus, and through the Bible in written form. Language is important!

To determine if something is true in language, grammar rules have to be well used with proper conjugation of verbs. Whatever is read or heard must be understood in relation to the context. It is a thinking process, and it involves the context of the speaker and the writer. Various genres of language use must be understood. This makes analysis of literature in a new language complex. And, of course, not everything we hear or read is truth. In every language, communication must be held to the standards of evidence in each genre. In a new language as well as a first language, students must learn how to select and use valid and quality literature to be consumed by it.

Methods of Inquiry

Linguistics is the study of the structure of language. The subject is language itself, spoken and written. Because language is a means of communication and meaning—getting and making—it serves as an instrument to enhance the methods of inquiry in other disciplines. Like mathematics that uses sentences, letters, symbols, and numbers to communicate patterns of relationship and functions as a language of science, language serves as a means of communicating, for example, laws and theories (descriptions and explanations) in science. Language also serves to communicate human thought and experiences, history, culture, and more. Language and thinking are intertwined.

Language studies overlap with the fields of applied linguistics, modern world languages and literature, education, anthropology, cultural studies, sociology, history, political science, psychology, and cultural studies. Law, technology, and media are also involved in language studies. Therefore, the specific methods of inquiry in these other disciplines of study are integrated with language when language is used to communicate their content.

Teaching a Language

In a formal setting such as a school, learners are introduced to the alphabet and some basics such as greetings and departure salutations. As one prepares for a lesson, the lesson objectives must be clear and measurable. Before introducing a topic or sub-topic, the teacher should prepare questions to ask, including what the students may already know about the topic, plan for time for students to do research on the topic, and prepare student processing activities that will promote class discussions. See chapters 5 and 6 for lesson-planning ideas. Especially important is the concept in teaching of engaging the students right at the beginning of class though a motivational activity that focuses the mind toward the lesson of the day and comments about what will be learned using prior knowledge and the usefulness of the topic. For instance, when teaching about the French Culture (touristic attractions in France), I will ask students to list all the tourist attractions in France they know about and why they are important to the French people and perhaps to the rest of the world. They will be assigned a certain amount of time to research this in groups of four using their laptops and the internet. They will share their findings. I may add some they did not find.

When I address the Eiffel Tower, students are asked to answer the following questions: Who designed it? How long did it take the builders to construct it? Why was it constructed? What were some of the challenges they encountered in their work? (This question is important and may provide an opportunity to discuss the rebuilding of the walls of Jerusalem under the leadership of Nehemiah, noting the many challenges and obstacles and the strength of the people to continue to work in spite of these.) What makes the Eiffel Tower one of the most attractive tourist destinations in Paris? What economic importance does it have? To make it more interesting, I will give students a link for songs they can learn about the tower and show them how beautiful it looks at night. This introduction allows the teacher to introduce grammar by asking them to identify verbs and adjectives they have used to describe the tower as they talked about it and to introduce the aspect of gender—the tower is of female gender.

There are many ways of making a language class lively: students can predict a given topic using social and contextual clauses to guess at the topic, use repetition and practice when conjugating verbs in various tenses, use acronyms, take part in skits to enhance their grammar skills with adjectives and adverbs, and sing songs and watch movies in the World Language under study. I also insist that students take notes to have an external record of the key concepts and skills of the lesson. This enables them to better internalize what they are learning. Using a variety of teaching and learning styles will enable diverse learners to benefit from the learning process. Some students are better visual learners while others learn through listening and participating in practice. It is the responsibility of the teacher to attempt to meet the learning needs and preferences of all students. Variety in methodology assists in this endeavor.

Assessment

Formative assessment often involves group tasks such as coming up with a skit on eating in a restaurant that requires some use of menus and orally ordering a dinner or buying a ticket for a destination at the train station or airport. Each student should contribute to the skit in order to practice vocabulary and sentence structure. The teacher can circulate and listen as students respond. Since mistakes are a part of learning, I will then let them know that it is okay to make mistakes; however, I will teach them the correct vocabulary of structure. Written assessments with clear objectives are also important in language learning. Often these are used in summative assessment after the students have had an opportunity to master a lesson or unit.

Key Biblical Worldview Questions and Answers

In the final section of this chapter, we address the key biblical worldview questions that can be raised during the study of world languages. This list is not exhaustive but will help World Languages teachers to build a more biblical framework for understanding world languages and allow for more integrative thinking.

Who or what is God?

God is all-knowing. He is a communicator by nature. He reveals much about himself through the means of language. He spoke and used prophets to speak and write his laws; kings and musicians to write poetry of praise and human emotions; scribes to record history of his plan through Abraham to bring redemption to humanity in Christ. He spoke through his Son, Jesus, and he used many New Testament authors to communicate history, the life of Christ, the birth of biblical Christianity, letters to the churches on important issues of the faith, and he revealed information about the future through John in the book of Revelation.

During creation, God used verbal commands such as recorded in Genesis 1:3: "Let there be light" and 1:26: "Then God said, 'Let us make man in our image, according to our likeness. They will rule the fish of the sea, the birds of the sky, the livestock, the whole earth, and the creatures that crawl on the earth.'" The key issue is that God spoke. Moses, a human being created in his image, also spoke and recorded God's words for others to read in these first chapters of Genesis.

What is a human being and how do we learn? What is the nature of external reality?

The science of linguistics has revealed that language seems to be a natural part of the development of the humans we interact with in our environment. Almost all humans learn their "native" language quite naturally, and the earlier the better in learning a second language. However, humans can learn more than one language, and this is a gift that can be used by God. Humans are communicators by nature and have the capacity to be social and cultural creatures facilitated by language.

Why is it possible to know anything at all?

The Bible presupposes that humans can learn. *Humans, created in the image of God, have been given the ability to know God himself and his created order—that is reality.* God has created man to be able to communicate in different languages for his glory.

Conclusion

Much like the English language arts, we can see that teaching a new language is an integrated task. As we teach vocabulary and context, we also teach the more detailed aspects of that language. All of this is done within differing contexts, including the cultural context and the worldview context.

ENGAGE: How does this chapter help to address InTASC Standard #4?

Content Knowledge: The teacher understands the central concepts, tools of inquiry, and structures of the discipline(s) he or she teaches and creates learning experiences that make these aspects of the discipline accessible and meaningful for learners to assure mastery of the content. The teacher knows how to integrate culturally relevant content to build on learners' background knowledge. The teacher has a deep knowledge of student content standards and learning progressions in the discipline(s) he or she teaches.

CHAPTER 17

Social Sciences: History and Geography

Travis Bradshaw, Daniele Bradshaw, and Lucia Lary-Shipley

Introduction

History and geography are two of the social studies disciplines that work together to teach students how to "make informed and reasoned decisions for the public good as citizens of a culturally diverse, democratic society in an interdependent world."[1] Christian educators of these subjects work to engage students in experiencing Creator and Sustainer God, while also leading students to discover their individual significance. We will look at history and geography through a biblical lens in this chapter.

History, the aggregate of past events, is more than the rote recitation of a sequence of dates. Similarly, geography, the study of the uneven distribution of things in time and space, is more than the memorization of maps and place names. Both are exciting fields of study with much to be discovered, described, and documented for subsequent generations. Both are essential for understanding the past, present, and future, based on consumption patterns, population shifts, and increased interconnectedness.[2] Further,

---

[1] See Alexandra E. Cirone and Thomas B. Pepinsky, "Historical Persistence," SSRN, June 23, 2021, https://papers.ssrn.com/sol3/papers.cfm?abstract_id=3873011.

[2] See Cirone and Pepinsky, "Historical Persistence."

teaching history and geography effectively will equip students with needed reasoning skills, new modes of inquiry, and improved learning processes.

This chapter provides an overview for understanding the study of history and geography, followed by research, best practices, and reflective practice. Also included are ways to interact with the text by (1) considering prior experiences or schema, (2) engaging in active learning exercises, (3) explaining new concepts through elaboration, and (4) projecting the application of new concepts to your classroom. The authors of this chapter will present the integration of biblical truth with practical instructional applications through history and geography lessons. These lessons should enable students to realize humanity's movement within the natural world and recognize God's movement within their own lives.

The Study of History: More Than Dates

History is often viewed as fixed and finished, thereby calibrating the focus toward the present and future. Temporal contemplations may be limited to thoughts of how today affects tomorrow, or how today will be judged when it takes its place in the past. For contemporary historians, however, they see their field as fluid because each new generation of historians will likely perceive past events with a fresh perspective.[3] Some regard history as a set of *resolved* issues that led to the present; however, some see history as a set of issues that led to *conditions* of the present. For example, some may consider the building of a highway as a completed project. However, historians may discuss business, hospital, and university development, along with population growth near interstates. Historians may also examine these roadways in terms of subthemes that have emerged, such as ongoing environmental impacts, the conditions that affect nearby residents' well-being, or individual contributions. Therefore, it is through the study of history that our current human condition is revealed.

History from a Biblical Worldview Perspective

The Bible provides us with a great deal of history. A number of God-inspired authors transcribed historical accounts of past events so that future generations may study and

---

[3] See Robert Chadwell Williams, *The Historian's Toolbox: A Student's Guide to the Theory and Craft of History*, 2nd ed. (Armonk, NY: M. E. Sharpe, 2007), 43.

learn from this body of work, which includes the creation, the flood, the exodus of the Israelites from Egypt, the giving of the Ten Commandments, the records of the kings of Israel, and the spreading of people groups around the known world. The New Testament presents the earthly ministry of Jesus, including the pivotal moments of the crucifixion and resurrection. The Acts of the early church and other narratives comprise a historical record of actual events.

Secular historians support records of Israeli kings and historical figures from the Bible, but may question other portions of Scripture, such as creation or a worldwide flood.[4] Where biblical and secular viewpoints diverge, Christian historians maintain the biblical veracity of past events.

Apart from divinely inspired Scripture, we evaluate the authenticity of historical records. Lucia Lary-Shipley cautions, "Each discipline is only as good as the texts from which it teaches. If the texts are flawed, so too is the knowledge learned."[5] Historical geographer Ruth Craggs describes historical evidence as (1) fragmented, (2) partial, and (3) socially constructed. Regarding fragmented evidence, information is not always recorded, especially circumstances considered mundane or unflattering to the author. With partial evidence, written records represent the views, priorities, biases, and knowledge levels of individual authors. For socially constructed evidence, records are based on the cultural, political, economic, social, and religious contexts of authors. Hence, historical evidence is limited and judged for what it can and cannot tell us.[6] Further, we should acknowledge our own understandings, assumptions, and biases that we bring to the study of history.

---

[4] Lawrence Mykytiuk, "Archaeology Confirms 50 Real People in the Bible," *Biblical Archaeology Review* 40, no. 2 (March/April 2014): 42–45, 48–50, https://www.baslibrary.org /biblical-archaeology-review/40/2/4; see also Lawrence Mykytiuk, "Archaeology Confirms 3 More Bible People," *Biblical Archaeology Review* 43, no. 3 (May/June 2017): 48–52, https://www .baslibrary.org/biblical-archaeology-review/43/3/6.

[5] Lucia Lary-Shipley, "Pre-Columbian Societies and Early Encounters Response Paper," SSCI E-100B: Graduate Research Methods and Scholarly Writing in the Social Sciences: Government and History (class paper, Harvard University, Cambridge, MA, September 25, 2017), 4.

[6] See Ruth Craggs, "Historical and Archival Research" in Key Methods in Geography, ed. Nicholas Clifford et al. (Los Angeles: Sage, 2016), 111–12.

Purpose of Historical Study

Historians should study the human condition with the purpose of improving the collective quality of humanity. This can be accomplished through analyzing the successes and failures of human affairs within a given time and space. In turn, this knowledge then guides future generations. Frank L. K. Ohemeng states, "This idea of knowledge accumulation through conjuncture of distinct causal streams is not only applicable in the study of revolution; it can also be used as a framework to understand issues pertaining to public policy, management, development, and governance in general."[7]

Just as students of history are better prepared from knowledge garnered from the past, so too are Christians. By studying history and conducting personal reflection, Christians can move forward with enhanced knowledge, using the God-given powers of observation and discernment. Both can be honed by studying the Bible and seeking the Holy Spirit's guidance. The Bible is unique among historical documents, as a compendium of past events and the living Word of God. Because all the Holy Writings are consecrated, divine, and made alive by him, God's Word is both a sustenance and a guide for us. By learning biblical truths, individuals are strengthened and accompanied on their journeys through life. The Bible can be life changing as it teaches us how to be right with God.[8] As such, biblical examples can be integrated into the classroom for study and reflection. Teaching students that all truth is God's truth and then building upon that premise "brings alive in one's heart and mind the grand concept of a Christ who is the image of the invisible God by whom all things were created, who is before all things, and by whom all things hold together."[9]

Research and Best Practices

Thucydides (460–400 BC) of Athens, Greece is considered the father of the historical research method. He was the first to apply strict standards toward evidentiary support and cause-and-effect analyses.[10] Researchers have expanded the techniques first

---

[7] Frank L. K. Ohemeng, "Comparative Historical Analysis, A Methodological Perspective" in *Global Encyclopedia of Public Administration, Public Policy, and Governance*, ed. Ali Farazmand (Cham, CH: Springer, 2020), 4, https://doi.org/10.1007/978-3-319-31816-5_1205-1.

[8] 2 Tim 3:16 NLT.

[9] Frank Ely Gaebelein, *The Pattern of God's Truth: Problems of Integration in Christian Education* (Chicago: Moody, 1968), 23.

[10] See Charles Norris Cochrane, *Thucydides and the Science of History* (New York: Oxford, 1929).

employed by Thucydides. In his 2021 book, *The Princeton Guide to Historical Research*, Zachary M. Schrag compares learning historical research skills to an athlete learning a sport. There may be a plausible order to conducting research; however, "in practice, you should expect to deploy these skills as needed, jumping back and forth, repeating some tasks and skipping others," depending on what you are researching.[11] Robert Chadwell Williams defines historical research as a process of discovery and constructionism based on available evidence.[12]

Gall and others describe historical research as the "process of systematically searching for data to answer questions about a phenomenon from the past to gain a better understanding of the foundation of present institutions, practices, trends, beliefs, and issues in education."[13] Williams states the historical research method attempts to explain (1) idea origins, (2) event causes, (3) event consequences, (4) cultural context of an event, (5) accountability for an act, (6) social history of an event, and (7) broad trends in society during an event.[14] Central to the process of choosing which data to utilize is the consideration of (1) data appropriate to the question to be answered, (2) original data collection methods, (3) data meanings at the time of original data collection, and (4) what meanings from the data are relevant in the modern world.[15] By this careful gathering of evidence, one can construct a historical analysis.[16]

ENGAGE:

1. Review with your students what the historical research method attempts to explain.
2. Have your students choose a biblical event, like the flood or Jesus's crucifixion, and research it using some of the historical research methods identified above. (If you are a pre-service teacher without a class, consider discussing these ideas with a classmate, professor, or mentor.)

---

[11] Zachary M. Schrag, *The Princeton Guide to Historical Research* (Princeton, NJ: Princeton University, 2021), 3.

[12] See Williams, *The Historian's Toolbox*, 11.

[13] Meredith D. Gall, Joyce P. Gall, and Walter R. Borg, *Educational Research: An Introduction*, 8th ed. (Boston: Pearson, 2007), 529.

[14] See Williams, *The Historian's Toolbox*, 52.

[15] See Gaye Tuchman, "Historical Methods" in *The SAGE Encyclopedia of Social Science Research Methods*, ed. Michael Lewis-Beck, Alan Bryman, and Tim Futing Liao (Thousand Oaks, CA: Sage, 2004), 463, accessible from http://dx.doi.org/10.4135/9781412950589.

[16] See Williams, *The Historian's Toolbox*, 104.

Modern Historic Resources

For the recording of past events, historians rely on primary and secondary data sources such as demographic records (birth, death, marriage, military, tax), newspaper articles, journals, books, letters, diaries, and architectural drawings.[17] Additional sources include documents, maps, artifacts, images, cliometrics, and genetic evidence.[18] Government agencies, schools, universities, companies, learned societies, charities, sports teams, private collections, community-based collections, documentaries, and even reality television are potential resources for historic information.[19] The twenty-first century has seen an explosion of digital archives available from governments, universities, libraries, and museums that allow students to explore via the internet.

The US Library of Congress, the US National Archives and Records Administration, and the UK National Archives are examples of agencies with extensive historical print and digitized resources. Individual company records like those of Ford, IBM, and the Bank of England can also provide historical information.[20] Individual church records noting baby dedication/christening, baptism, marriage, and death records assist in estimating population size, life expectancy, and other metrics within communities.

ENGAGE:

1. In preparation for leading a class, conduct internet searches with the US Library of Congress and your nearest major university about history topics of local significance.
2. Identify at least three web resources to supplement these findings from other resources.
3. With a peer, discuss and describe how your future students might utilize these resources when writing about a local historical topic.

History Themes

Themes, elements, and standards form the basis of study, instruction, and assessment. There are varying educational standards, such as national, regional, state standards,

---

[17] See Tuchman, "Historical Methods," 463.
[18] See Williams, *The Historian's Toolbox*, 56–74.
[19] See Craggs, "Historical and Archival Research," 115–17.
[20] See Craggs, 116.

Common Core Standards, etc. In the USA, the College, Career, and Civic Life Framework (C3), which has information on history, geography, religious studies, and other topics, provides information for social studies.[21] The National Council for the Social Studies (NCSS) provides ten themes that represent a way of organizing knowledge about the human experience.[22] The themes are broad and aim to cover the gamut of human activity.

ENGAGE:

1. Review a curriculum guide for content in a history course.
2. Categorize the required teaching topics by the ten social studies themes.
3. Reflect on how a theme-based approach may help you facilitate learning with students.

Reflective Practice

Now that you have read this broad overview of history, take a few minutes to consider the definitions, descriptions, and key concepts that you have encountered. Ask yourself: What do I think God's Word would tell me about the pursuit of history? In what ways could I incorporate that into my teaching? What have others observed, researched, or reported about the study of history? Finally, in thinking about your prior interactions with history, how might this chapter contribute to, or even improve upon, your past experiences?

The Study of Geography: More than Maps

According to National Geographic, "Geography is the study of places and the relationships between people and their environments."[23] Broadly, geographers study resource distribution, geographic characteristics, and social structures that affect people.

---

[21] See "College, Career, and Civic Life (C3) Framework for Social Studies State Standards," National Council for the Social Studies, accessed July 6, 2021, https://socialstudies.org/standards/C3.

[22] See "National Curriculum Standards for Social Studies: Introduction," par. 8, National Council for the Social Studies, accessed June 22, 2022, https://www.socialstudies.org/standards/national-curriculum-standards-social-studies-introduction.

[23] "What Is Geography," par. 1, National Geographic Society, accessed June 20, 2021, https://www.nationalgeographic.org/education/what-is-geography/.

Specifically, these include natural and human resources as well as physical, cultural, political, and economic differences. *Forbes* recently reported that 74 percent of non-geographers intentionally integrate geography in their curricula.[24] Geographical awareness is critical because it helps us make informed decisions for us, our community, our country, and our planet. "Geography helps connect us with our daily lives by providing relevant information for making consumer decisions; helping us understand and improve our interactions with the rest of the world; allowing decision-makers to use geospatial technologies to understand and address contemporary issues; permitting us to choose the best site for schools, businesses, or homes (location, location, location); and assisting us in finding resources and using them in a sustainable manner."[25]

Geography from a Biblical Worldview

From a geographical perspective, the Bible calls for us to take care of the earth and its inhabitants. The Lord God took man and placed him in the garden of Eden to work it and to watch over it (Gen 2:15). The earth and everything in it, the world and its inhabitants, belong to the Lord (Ps 24:1). We are better equipped to care for God's physical and human creations through the study of geography.

Churches and some Christian academies and international schools increasingly rely on database software to keep track of their members and to maximize transportation-related (geography) time and capital expenditures. Demographics, addresses, program code(s), ministry code(s), volunteer code(s), and attendance patterns are routinely tracked. These systems coordinate volunteers for services and special events, which enables the institution to better serve families and community.

Regional or statewide religious organizations can also employ geographers to identify optimal locations for new churches and potential new schools, so that more people can be reached for Christ. For instance, ideal locations include those on high-trafficked roads near population centers with ample parking and ADA (Americans with

---

[24] Vicki Phillips, "Survey 62% of Teachers Say Learning about Geography Is 'Extremely Important,'" par. 5, *Forbes*, December 12, 2020, https://www.forbes.com/sites /vickiphillips/2020/12/01/survey-62-of-teachers-say-learning-about-geography-is-extremely -important/?sh=f43f1d825f08.

[25] Maps for All, "Geographic Literacy," par. 3, Maps for All, accessed June 20, 2021, https:// www.mapsforall.org/geographic-literacy.

Disabilities Act) compliant facilities.[26] To assist in this, geographers examine the location of existing churches or schools and then seek growing population centers within the service area where there is a need. Geographers select optimal locations based on location-specific religious polling, education polling, rental costs, land and construction costs, funding levels, and cultural and linguistic characteristics, among other factors.[27]

ENGAGE:

1. Review the video library of the US Census Bureau for videos that explain how geographic data is collected and utilized within the US or your country of service.

2. Have students list and discuss utility (water, electrical, sewer, phone, cable, internet, cell phone) and government service providers (bus, subway, highway, bike trails, parks) that display maps.

3. Contact a local or state religious office to inquire about their geographic tools for church revitalization, new church plants, or new schools.

Purpose of Geographical Study

The purpose of studying geography should be to make a positive impact upon one's community, country, and planet through the specialized examination of the relationship between people and their environment. Those who study geography look for distributions and patterns in various phenomena. The powers of observation and detection that geographers utilize help them represent the complexity of the real world, in both physical and human geography.

Physical Geography

Physical geography deals with God's created world and the human manipulation of it. This includes the study of continents, oceans, rivers, mountains, forests, rocks, soils,

---

[26] See Travis Heath Bradshaw and James Henry Hobson, "Using Community Knowledge for Place-based Ministry: Interdisciplinary Engagement from Geography and Urban Ministry," *Faith and the Academy* 4, no. 2 (2020): 45–47, https://issuu.com/libertyuniversity/docs/110057_spring_2020_ace_journal_issuu.

[27] See Travis Heath Bradshaw, "Evangelistic Churches: Geography, Demographic, and Marketing Variables that Facilitate Their Growth," (PhD diss., University of Florida, 2000).

minerals, climate, weather, biodiversity, and the like.[28] In a physical geography context, Christians believe that God created the heavens and the earth (Gen 1:1); God keeps the physical processes of the universe in motion (Gen 8:22); and God steps in to manipulate the physical world, whenever he sees fit. Further examples include: the flood as detailed in Genesis 6–9 and calming the stormy sea as outlined in Mark 4.

Physical geography involves exploring God's creation. Physical geographers primarily rely on observations and quantitative assessment of observed phenomena, as noted in the Bible. Numbers 13 records that Moses sent out twelve people to survey the region of Canaan prior to the Israelites inhabiting the land. The Parable of the Great Banquet from Luke 14 records the foolishness of buying land without first seeing it and buying oxen without first seeing them work.

ENGAGE:

1. Look at satellite images of your community.
2. Label familiar features of the community, such as rivers, mountains, lakes, schools, churches, and businesses.
3. Encourage students to research, compare, and contrast natural and human manipulated environments within your local community.

Human Geography

Human geography addresses everything related to humans and their manipulation of the world around them. This includes the study of culture, religion, transportation, urban systems, rural systems, politics, languages, music, clothing, food, dwellings, buildings, and manufactured goods.[29] Human geographers also look at demographic shifts, employment by industry, imports and exports, educational attainment, life expectancies, and similar phenomena for country and regional comparisons.

Human geographers use both qualitative and quantitative methods of assessment. Qualitative observations come through the lens of researchers, who may hold multiple viewpoints. For example, a historical geographer may review time period sources from both inside and outside the community of study. A contemporary geographer may

---

[28] See Stephen Reynolds et al., *Exploring Physical Geography*, 3rd ed. (New York: McGraw Hill, 2021).

[29] See Mark Bjelland, Daniel Montello, and Arthur Getis, *Human Geography*, 13th ed. (New York: McGraw Hill, 2020).

interview community neighbors, community leaders, community members, and others to look for corroborating evidence.

Quantitative/statistical tests are often performed on datasets in both social and physical sciences. Quantitative assessments in the social sciences are typically labeled as significant, when they are right 95 percent of the time, referred to as the 95 percent confidence level. Physical sciences sometimes seek confidence levels at 99 or 99.9 percent.[30] To better illustrate this distinction, for example, an economic geographer (a social scientist) may predict how many people will dine at a local restaurant this week. Variances are acceptable if they are within 5 percent of their initial estimate. Whereas, a physical geographer who documents a boundary line map between counties or states must be exact.

Finally, geography is also considered a data science discipline. For much of recorded history, geographers have explored the world and documented their findings. Today, GIS (geographic information system) is increasingly linking demographic, environmental, consumption, services, and other datasets for specific locations. Smartphones access databases to locate positions and represent the location of landforms, roads, restaurants, gas stations with pricing, hotels with pricing, parks, bus stations, key landmarks, and other searchable items. People, vehicles, pets, computers, and cell phones can all be tracked and monitored based on technologies created by geographers. Recent advances include robotic vacuum cleaners and lawn mowers programmed to utilize detailed maps of their surroundings. Artificial intelligence (AI) is a growing field within geography, with applications in traffic management, urban development, crowd sourcing, risk assessment, and healthcare.[31] "GeoAI is still evolving and has the potential to be one of the future trends in GIS that makes the biggest impact on daily life. In addition to land use and infrastructure analysis, GeoAI can also be applied to health systems, agriculture, and many more industries."[32]

---

[30] Ana-Maria Šimundić, "Lessons in Biostatistics," *Biochemia Medica* 18, no. 2 (2008): 154–61, https://www.biochemia-medica.com/assets/images/upload/xml_tif/Simundic_AM_-Confidence_interval.pdf.

[31] Maged N. Kamel Boulos, Guochao Peng, and Trang VoPham, "An Overview of GeoAI Applications in Health and Healthcare," *International Journal of Health Geographics* 18, no. 7 (2019), https://doi.org/10.1186/s12942-019-0171-2.

[32] USC Dornsife Spatial Sciences Institute, "3 GIS Technology Advancements in the Last 5 Years," *USC Blog*, par. 14, July 12, 2021, https://gis.usc.edu/blog/3-gis-technology-advancements-in-the-last-5-years/.

ENGAGE:

1. View a video discussing how GIS is used in the modern world.
2. View a video on GPS animal tracking.
3. Have students research and discuss their family's daily uses of GPS.

Research and Best Practices

Geographers observe and collect information through three primary methods: (1) fieldwork, (2) remote sensing, and (3) data mining. First, fieldwork consists of in-person observation and data collection. "Fieldwork allows geographers to make direct observation in places where local data are missing or unreliable."[33] It is used for detailed observation of an area, looking inside of human-created structures or naturally occurring formations (such as caves, sinkholes, or valleys where remote sensing images cannot provide sufficient detail). It is also used to interact with people, animals, and nature. Further, it may be utilized to analyze interesting phenomena identified from satellite or aerial photos.

Fieldwork extends beyond research to pedagogy. Field trips are incorporated into many geography courses. "They are designed to teach students about the environment in which they live and to encourage them to be inquisitive about the processes that shape landscapes and cultures."[34] This is important for promoting environmental and cultural awareness. If you are a teacher of social studies, consider taking your class on field trips.[35] Encourage students to journal about vacations, hiking, camping, and other excursions.

Second, remote sensing uses cameras to take pictures from satellites or aircraft. These images are utilized to make observations of physical, biological, and cultural features of the earth's surface. Remote sensing has applications in farming, transportation, urban planning, disaster assessment, weather forecasting, and a number of fields. Remote sensing expanded rapidly with satellite proliferation in the 1960s.[36]

---

[33] National Research Council, *Rediscovering Geography: New Relevance for Science and Society* (Washington, DC: National Academies, 1997), 51.

[34] National Research Council, 52.

[35] See Hayley Peacock and David Holmes, *Progress in Geography Fieldwork: Key Stage 3* (London: Hodder Education, 2020) for sample fieldwork inquiries.

[36] "NASA Remote Sensing Accomplishments," NASA Earth Observatory, accessed August 26, 2021, https://earthobservatory.nasa.gov/features/RemoteSensing/remote_09.php.

Third, data mining uses algorithms, statistics, and database systems to look for patterns.[37] It involves processing, visualizing/graphing, and updating information into usable forms. "Data mining is the process of finding anomalies, patterns, and correlations within large data sets to predict outcomes or to create new information."[38] Geography as a data science discipline spread rapidly with the introduction of supercomputers but has erupted in the twenty-first century along with smartphone and other GPS technologies.

Modern Geographic Resources

Geographers rely on a variety of tools to collect and display information.[39] Examples of these tools are surveying equipment, compasses, satellites, airplanes, weather and temperature monitors, pollution sensing equipment, database analysis, interviewing (face-to-face, online, phone), on-the-ground field observations, and cameras. Geographers display data with 2D and 3D maps, atlases, globes, aerial photos, satellite photos, camera photos, electronic mapping files, models, and a wide variety of graphic images.

Familiar geography data displayers are Google Maps, Google Earth, and the US Census Bureau. Companies and governments collect geographic data. This data is then utilized by governments, Geographic Information Systems (GIS) software producers, researchers, and private companies.

Geography Themes

National Geographic provides six essential elements expanded to eighteen standards to categorize geographic information.[40] The elements and themes span the gamut of

---

[37] See Gloria Phillips-Wren, Anna Esposito, and Lakhmi C. Jain, "Introduction to Big Data and Data Science: Methods and Applications," *Advances in Data Science: Methodologies and Applications, Intelligent Systems Reference Library* 189 (Cham, Switzerland: Springer, 2021), https://doi.org/10.1007/978-3-030-51870-7_1.

[38] "Data Mining: What It Is and Why It Matters," par. 1, SAS, accessed June 20, 2021, https://www.sas.com/en_us/insights/analytics/data-mining.html.

[39] See Joseph J. Hobbs, "Objectives and Tools of World Regional Geography" in *World Regional Geography*, 7th ed. (Boston: Cengage, 2022), chapter 1.

[40] See "National Geography Standards," National Geographic Society, accessed August 26, 2021, https://www.nationalgeographic.org/standards/national-geography-standards/.

human and physical geography and link geographic research to other fields of study. They are periodically updated as global interconnectedness and information increase.

ENGAGE:

1. Look at the six geographic elements and hypothesize how they were expanded into eighteen practical standards.
2. Research and reflect on how your teaching can be enhanced by organizing your classes by geographic elements or themes.

Reflective Practice

Take a moment to consider the geographic portion of this chapter. Contemplate the definitions, descriptions, and key concepts that you came across. Ask yourself, What do I think God's Word would tell me about the study of geography? How could I integrate that into my teaching of this subject? What have geographers observed, researched, or reported about studying geography? Finally, in thinking about my prior knowledge of geography, how might this chapter contribute to, or even improve upon, my past experiences?

Assessment

The social studies disciplines of history and geography have some overlap. Both contribute to the interdisciplinary understanding for enhanced knowledge and skills on a topic.[41] For example, educators who teach about transportation changes throughout history will usually include components of technology, engineering, planning, business, and other subjects.

Teaching history and geography effectively will equip students with needed reasoning skills, new modes of inquiry, and improved learning processes. However, educators should carefully differentiate between the instructional process and the assessment process. Educators can use engaging applications of history and geography to personalize instruction and assessments. Differentiation involves adjusting the instruction in order to meet student needs. According to David Sousa and Carol Ann Tomlinson, differentiation should account for "(1) an invitational learning environment, (2) quality curriculum, (3) persistent formative assessment, (4) responsive instruction, and (5)

---

[41] See George Maxim, *Dynamic Social Studies*, 11th ed. (New York: Pearson, 2018), 8.

leading students and managing flexible classroom routines."[42] Historical and geographical instruction and assessments can be customized to varying student interests, grade levels, and abilities. For example, assessments can include discussions, essays, projects, quizzes, tests, portfolios, etc. With any aspect of assessment, expectations and grading criteria must be clear, especially for creative historical and geographical assignments.

Incorporating Biblical Perspectives in the Classroom

Christian historians and geographers understand that God created and sustains the universe. As Christian educators, we know our biblical worldview guides our lines of inquiry; however, do we realize that the quality of our Christian influence in the classroom is directly related to our own Christian walk?[43] Because this is so, the best way to integrate biblical principles for the benefit of others is to first ensure they are deeply engrained in us. So, stop and ask yourself: Is there an area of my life that needs attention? How can I solve this need? Staying in God's Word is a good first step.

We need to remember that the Bible does not specify just one teaching method. Instead, it upholds a whole host of strategies surrounding one central theme. Students are more likely to respond to the message of God if it is presented in a personal way.[44] Our challenge is for students to understand these subjects in light of their biblical emphasis while fulfilling our biblical mandate to learn from the past, explore God's creation, and evangelize the world.

When teaching history, we must remember that the Bible contains the record of creation and early civilization. It documents historical events from creation to Jesus's life and ministry, to the disciples' dissemination of Christianity. The Bible lists many place names and denotes their historical significance. It provides us with examples of how to grow and develop as individuals, church bodies, school communities, and people groups. Concerning Job's struggles as applicable to our lives, the Bible states, "For inquire, please, of bygone ages, and consider what the fathers have searched out. For we are but of yesterday and know nothing, for our days on earth are a shadow. Will they not teach you and tell you and utter words out of their understanding?" (Job 8:8–10 ESV).

---

[42] David Sousa and Carol Ann Tomlinson, *Differentiation and the Brain: How Neuroscience Supports the Learner-Friendly Classroom*, 2nd ed. (Bloomington, IN: Solution Tree, 2018), 11–12.

[43] See Gaebelein, *The Pattern of God's Truth*, 35.

[44] See Harro Van Brummelen, *Walking with God in the Classroom: Christian Approaches to Teaching and Learning*, 2nd ed. (Colorado Springs: Purposeful Design, 2009), 10.

When teaching geography, we can look to the Bible for its highlights of the differences among earth's physical and human features. It gives examples of people who populated specific geographic regions of the earth. For instance, Numbers 33 lists over forty places that the Israelites visited before they entered the Promised Land, and Numbers 34 goes into detail describing the geographic borders of Israelite territory. Further, the Pauline Epistles give detail about the geographic territories where Paul ministered. Finally, the Bible commands us to be witnesses in Jerusalem, in all Judea and Samaria, and to the ends of the earth (Acts 1:8). This answers the question of, What makes us human? It is those who can make decisions, move to new locations, and develop communities. We are social creatures by nature, and God commands us to inhabit the earth. When humans chose to disobey God by staying in one place and building the Tower of Babel, God interrupted their ability to communicate through the assignment of new languages, which caused them to scatter. God created the earth to be inhabited.

According to Harro Van Brummelen, relaying these historical and geographical truths to students is conceivable by keeping the following points in mind. As mentioned, we first must examine ourselves. Second, we need to make God's message feel personal for each student. Third, we should teach the educational content aspects of the Bible. Fourth, we must allow biblical values and ethics to set the climate of our classroom. Fifth and finally, we guard ourselves against giving false testimony and portray historical events fairly. The worldview issue here is that humans, created in the image of God, are history-makers and communicators by nature, thus we record our history for succeeding generations just as God inspired authors to do through his written Word.[45]

Methods for Further Engagement

Teaching is often performance based, and it effectuates varying levels of cognitive activity. Gaea Leinhardt identifies three approaches that educators may find helpful in varying contexts. These are (1) didactic leader, (2) discovery, and (3) facilitator. In the didactic leader model, the educator is central and is the transmitter of knowledge. For the discovery model, the educator constructs a situation where the student has the tools necessary for discovery and is able to build new knowledge from existing intuitions through the selection of personal interest topics. With the facilitator model, the

---

[45] See Brummelen, *Walking with God in the Classroom*, 31–32.

student constructs knowledge under guided social conditions where the educator is an arranger or collaborative facilitator. The educator poses questions and directs student attention on specific portions of the enterprise.[46] Examples that correspond to each of these three approaches follow and, unless otherwise noted, are for both history and geography instruction.

Didactic Model

Utilize Existing Resources

Educators should utilize existing resources to aid in their teaching. There are numerous text outline, picture, audio, and video resources on standard K–12 history and geography lessons. Internet searches yield ideas for specific lesson topics, such as with The Ohio State University (history), Geography for Geographers, and National Geographic (geography). Some professional organizations provide supplemental resources such as websites, lesson plans, journals, etc. for student learning. For example, in history and social studies, the National Council for Social Studies,[47] National Council for History Education,[48] and the American Historical Association[49] provide resources. In geography, the National Council for Geographic Education[50] and National Geographic Society[51] provide professional support. For example, the Association of American Geographers has a Bible Specialty Group.[52]

---

[46] See Gaea Leinhardt, "On Teaching," in *Advances in Instructional Psychology*, vol. 4, ed. Robert Glaser (London: Routledge, 2019), 13–16.

[47] See "Publications and Resources," National Council for the Social Studies, accessed January 20, 2022, https://www.socialstudies.org/publications-resources.

[48] See "Resources," National Council for History Education, accessed January 20, 2022, https://ncheteach.org/educator-resources.

[49] See "Teaching and Learning," American Historical Association, accessed January 20, 2022, https://www.historians.org/teaching-and-learning.

[50] See "Teacher Resources," National Council for Geographic Education, accessed January 20, 2022, https://ncge.org/main_page/teacher-resources/.

[51] See "Education Resources," National Geographic Society, accessed January 21, 2022, https://www.nationalgeographic.org/society/education-resources/?nav_click.

[52] See "Bible Specialty Group," Association of American Geographers, accessed January 21, 2022, https://community.aag.org/communities/community-home?CommunityKey=639c98d9 –cce1–46eb–90d2–f4cd5eae98ad.

Utilize Video

Videos can be valuable resources for student education. There are many YouTube channels related to history and geography. The History Channel, National Geographic Channel, Smithsonian Channel, and American Heroes Channel may assist with instruction. Films can be shown in class, assigned as homework, or assigned for extra credit.

Maximize Textbook Resources

Textbook resources provide support for residential and online teaching.[53] Examples include: (1) making textbook-based PowerPoint presentations or lesson outlines available to students and parents; (2) having students take adaptive practice quizzes; (3) having students review interactive maps and cartographic tools, videos, and other media; (4) highlighting links to additional readings, resources, and datasets; and (5) utilizing specific web-based metrics to analyze student activities.

Utilize Podcasts

Podcasts highlight historical and geographic topics. Most topics discussed in secondary schools have a variety of internet searchable podcasts. Many publishers offer online links to podcasts pertaining to specific textbook content. Assign specific podcasts for your students and encourage them to explore additional resources.

Discovery Model

Utilize Creative Assignments

Allowing students to choose presentation/writing topics piques interest in conveying knowledge. A variety of student-chosen assignments can be integrated into history and geography classes. Students can be creative with their visual art, graphic organizers, timelines, presentations, and writing assignments.

---

[53] See David Arendale and David Ghere, "Teaching College History Using Universal Instructional Design," in *Pedagogy and Student Services for Institutional Transformation: Implementing Universal Design in Higher Education*, ed. Jeanne L. Higbee and Emily Goff (Minneapolis: University of Minnesota, 2008), 118, https://hdl.handle.net/11299/200460.

Utilize Games and Simulations

Simulations can assist students. Examples of simulations include preparing a meal or building a model house with available foods, tools, and materials from various regions and time periods.[54] Online simulations, such as ones from the National Museum of American History (history) and the University Corporation for Atmospheric Research (physical geography), also provide interactive images and perspectives for students.

Utilize Role Play

Role playing appeals to some students. Examples include having history students role-play historical figures and having geography students represent various countries in Model UN–style debates.[55]

Utilize Place-Based Education Resources

Place-based education allows local history and geography to come alive. Place-based education institutions focus on local history, local industry, and prominent citizens. For example, historical societies often provide recorded oral history interviews with local citizens, avenues for genealogy research, and information on regional industries. Guest speakers can provide valuable perspectives to enhance instruction. Place-based learning can be done at any place around the world.

Utilize Drone Footage (Geography)

Drone footage shot at individual schools, on school-sponsored field trips, and within the local community can promote geography as a part of a larger STEM program. The NASA Globe project is an example of a school-sponsored program that utilizes drones.[56]

---

[54] See Arendale and Ghere, 123–24.

[55] See "Model UN," United Nations Foundation, accessed June 20, 2021, https://unausa.org/model-un/.

[56] See "The Globe Program," accessed June 20, 2021, https://www.globe.gov/.

Compare Images

Comparing satellite images and aerial photos over various time periods allows historians and geographers to review physical and human changes on earth's landscape. Examples include levels of development along coast lines or interstates, before-and-after disaster (tornado, hurricane, or tsunami) photos, downtown aerial photos from newspaper archives, and lake or reservoir water levels during floods or droughts.

Utilize Application-Based Activities

Use application-based activities to show real-world examples. Examples include: (1) assessing hurricane or tsunami risks in coastal areas; (2) discussing the positive and negative impacts of bottled water usage; (3) utilizing census data and business name applications to review demographic shifts in urban neighborhoods; (4) connecting water pollution and industrialization; (5) analyzing surface temperatures in the concrete jungle versus green space, such as Central Park in the middle of New York; and (6) mapping local roads, storm drains, or utilities.[57]

Utilize Concept Mapping (Geography)

Concept mapping helps students to think spatially. Have students describe and/or draw their home, their school, and their local area from memory. As an extension activity, compare the school maps of students.

Facilitator Model

Share Examples

Personal examples can enhance overall course learning. History courses can be enhanced through student discussions on museum visits, historical place visits, historical interactions, interviews, and personal study. Geography courses can be enhanced by individual students describing their diverse living locations, global vacations, work travels, military postings, or missionary activities. Educators need to guide student discussions toward relevant historical or geographic themes for the required lesson content. It is important

---

[57] See Phillips, "Survey 62% of Teachers Say Learning about Geography Is 'Extremely Important.'"

to make subjects exciting and relevant, while also conveying how content is applicable for study in the modern world.

Evaluate Writing and Media Samples

Have students evaluate a variety of texts, such as primary sources, secondary sources, biographies, autobiographies, map versions, and videos for perceived strengths, biases, and limitations. Encourage students to research varying perspectives from different sources. This helps them to think critically about assessing information in an informed manner.

Activity Samples

In chapters 2–6, the underlying work of several developmentalists, Piaget and Vygotsky; one philosopher, Dewey; and learning theorist Jerome Bruner are used to develop the current cognitive interactive theory most prominent today. Educators can support student understanding through discussions and collaborations. In structured inquiry, the educator poses a question and an outline of the procedure.[58] Inquiry-based learning, also addressed in the chapter on the structure of science, involves the educator leading students in questions and discussions. It is designed to develop critical thinking skills. To enhance the discussion, educators guide students through general resources on the inquiry topic. Inquiry and active learning are essential for historical and geographical understanding. Below are examples of inquiry-based activities for history and geography.

Historical and Geographical Food Study

In a favorite foods study, students learn about the history of selected foods and how they have been discovered, consumed, modified, produced, and transported around the world. The study highlights trade routes, transportation technologies, physical geography environments, and cultural practices.

Start with an activity designed to activate prior knowledge. This allows students to highlight personal choices and describe associations. For example, a student may

---

[58] "Inquiry-based Learning," Lumen Learning, accessed June 20, 2021, https://courses.lumenlearning.com/educationx92x1/chapter/inquiry-based-learning/.

describe a preference for Italian food for Sunday lunches. Explain that a food location designation typically refers to foods associated with a particular country. Extend the lesson to historical research on the discovery origin of the food. Provide the needed articles and maps to reinforce and supplement the information.

Select an appropriate video on the trade route or geographical origin of the selected food item. For example, this may involve information on the Silk Road trade route, the Columbian Exchange trade route, or the Sub-Saharan trade route. Select an appropriate video on time-space convergence (the concept of the time needed for people or goods to move from one location to the other). Select one or more videos on the food supply chain and transportation considerations.

Students then take an inventory of their pantry, refrigerator, and freezer, noting the country-of-origin label for the foods. Students describe how their food inventory items were transported to their local grocery store or to their home. This will generate discussion of global transportation and packing technologies, including those that require refrigeration, humidification, and freezing technologies. For instance, the educator or a student might describe a favorite meal of buffalo meatloaf, delivered to a home in dry ice. As another example, the educator or student may describe a favorite dessert of ice cream traveling by freezer railcar to a freezer semi-trailer to a grocery store. The idea is to encourage discussion related to food transportation.

Have students choose a favorite food for a writing assignment and/or presentation. Suggested assignment requirements include food country or region of discovery, region(s) of current production, transport mode(s), special transportation requirements to support food freshness, average length of time from harvest to table, context of typical food consumption, environmental impact of food production and transport, and references. Consider having your students relate their project to the ten social studies themes.[59]

Geographical Activities

Begin by activating prior knowledge, while allowing students to highlight personal choices. Encourage students to think spatially about their favorite place to visit and to consider the wide variability in the physical and human-created environment. For example, a student can describe how he or she loves to visit the mountains to enjoy skiing and snow tubing or perhaps visit a large city to patronize theaters or ethnic

---

[59] See "National Curriculum Standards for Social Studies: Introduction," par. 8.

restaurants. Download Google Earth or Google Maps for students and zoom in to country, state/region, city/county, local government administration offices, and school sites. Spend time on the satellite, road map, and street level image layers to introduce the geographic concept of scale. When teaching about a particular geographic area, highlight that area and encourage students to make a list of at least three interesting things about it.

In a destination-themed travel activity, allow students to talk about how they travel to their favorite destination and what they do along the way. Students may describe travel by hiking, biking, car, plane, train, ferry, or cruise ship. They may describe listening to music, watching movies, or observing landscapes while on their journey. This will invite discussions of the movement of people and information, climate differences, landscape features, and personal preferences.

Have students choose a favorite place to research for a writing and/or presentation. Allow students to write about their church, a restaurant, or favorite local place, if needed, as the purpose is to think geographically. Assign a writing/presentation section related to each of the six essential geographic elements.

InTASC Ideas

The following are sample geography lesson ideas based on InTASC Standard 8. Standard 8 states, "The teacher understands and uses a variety of instructional strategies to encourage students to develop deep understanding of content areas and their connections, and to build skills to apply knowledge in meaningful ways."[60]

The educator can prepare and present a lesson on local cultural landscapes, with an emphasis on cultural diversity. The topic falls under the broad geography element "human systems" and is labeled as geography standard 10, "The characteristics, distribution, and complexity of Earth's cultural mosaics."[61] Suggested topics to be covered include buildings, houses, cemeteries, signs, billboards, restaurants, houses of worship, ethnic enclaves, and immigration patterns. Present examples and customized videos on

---

[60] Council of Chief State School Officers (April 2013), Interstate Teacher Assessment and Support Consortium, InTASC *Model Core Teaching Standards and Learning Progressions for Teachers 1.0: A Resource for Ongoing Teacher Development* (Washington, DC: Author). Standards can be downloaded at https://ccsso.org/sites/default/files/2017-12/2013_INTASC_Learning _Progressions_for_Teachers.pdf.

[61] See "National Geography Standards," National Council for Geographic Education, accessed August 26, 2021, https://ncge.org/teacher-resources/national-geography-standards/.

local cultural landscapes and cultural mosaics. Local libraries, universities, historical centers, and news outlets may supplement lesson content.

Assess students on the presented lessons, using traditional assessment methods such as multiple-choice, true-false, short-answer, and other items. Allow students the choice of their second assessment. Suggestions include: (1) a narrated video showing and verbally describing culturally diverse locations in the student's local area, (2) a narrated presentation with pictures and bullet point descriptions of culturally diverse locations in the student's local area, (3) a picture collage with bullet points showing culturally diverse locations in the student's local area, or (4) a table with place name, location, and description of diversity for culturally diverse locations in the student's local area.

Another example involves the use of lesson plans and historical resources from the National Archives and Records Administration.[62] Educators can select primary resources for various topics and include options of corresponding document analysis activities and geographical activities. By encouraging students to practice as historians and geographers, educators facilitate knowledge and understanding.

Interacting with the Material

To reap the benefits of knowledge learned, continue thinking about how this material could be applied to your current or eventual classroom. Consider the student ages and apply the concepts appropriately. Begin by contemplating schema, which is simply the assimilation and accommodation of knowledge.[63] This can be accomplished by reflecting on their past experiences. How do they compare or contrast with the concepts presented in this chapter? How do you think the "Engage" activities in this chapter will work for you in an actual educational practice? Do you feel confident explaining these concepts in your own words? How may these history and geography concepts take shape in your future classroom?

---

[62] See "Educator Resources," National Archives, accessed January 21, 2022, https://www.archives.gov/education.

[63] See Paul DiMaggio, "Culture and Cognition," *Annual Review of Sociology* 23 (August 1997): 263–87, https://www.annualreviews.org/doi/abs/10.1146/annurev.soc.23.1.263.

Conclusion

This chapter provided a broad overview for understanding history and geography; the corresponding definitions, descriptions, and key concepts of each; the current research and best practices of both; and opportunities for you to engage in your learning. Additionally, we gave you examples founded on proven education pedagogy so that you can confidently teach your future students history and geography, meet those all-important discipline standards, and still maintain a biblical worldview in your classroom. All of this was accomplished by recognizing the importance of the social studies mission of helping students become informed citizens, and then enriching this mission with a Christian perspective. We endeavored not only to encourage an informed citizenship, but a Kingdom citizenship, as well.

Dr. Martin Luther King Jr. taught that education should empower a person to screen and weigh evidence and to distinguish between truth and error and between reality and fantasy. Education's function, then, involves arduous, critical thinking.[64] By effectively teaching history and geography, Christian educators can augment students' reasoning, decision-making, observation, and discernment skill sets.

---

[64] See Martin Luther King Jr., "The Purpose of Education," in *The Papers of Martin Luther King, Jr.*, vol. 1, *Called to Serve, January 1929–June 1951*, ed. Clayborne Carsone, Ralph Luker, and Penny A. Russell (Berkeley: University of California, 1992), 10, https://kinginstitute.stanford.edu/king-papers/documents/purpose-education.

CHAPTER 18

Structure of Technology

Betsy Sentamu

Introduction

In his posthumous collections of anecdotes, essays, and stories titled *The Salmon of Doubt*, Douglas Adams, author of the cosmically comic novel *Hitchhiker's Guide to the Galaxy*, says:

I've come up with a set of rules that describe our reactions to technologies:

1. Anything that is in the world when you're born is normal and ordinary and is just a natural part of the way the world works.
2. Anything that's invented between when you're fifteen and thirty-five is new and exciting and revolutionary and you can probably get a career in it.
3. Anything invented after you're thirty-five is against the natural order of things.[1]

Considering the subject of this chapter and the quote from Adams above, so much of the technology we teach in our classrooms will be native to our students, whereas we, at one point in our own lives, had to learn it. Turning on and off a device, saving and sending an image file, and opening an application are things I can photographically remember learning for the first time as I sat in my parents' office using a computer

---

[1] Douglas Adams, *The Salmon of Doubt: Hitchhiking the Galaxy One Last Time* (New York: Ballantine Books, 2005), 94–95.

tower and monitor my father had brought home. All four siblings gathered around with wonderment in our eyes and impatience in our fingertips as we waited for our turn to press the protruding letters on the keyboard. Now, a tower sits in the corner of the dining room, long forgotten and collecting dust. Today, my son swipes a tiny screen while he sits on the bean bag doing his history homework. I never taught him how to swipe or click or drag; those things were never really "new" to him. From birth, he adapted to technology just like learning to walk. It was never foreign or special or even exciting to him like it was to me. He is more comfortable with most technology than I ever will be. It is arguably the one subject matter in life that, generally speaking, our children and students can teach us more about than we can teach them, that is, about the functions of technology.

So, what then? What is necessary to teach in a technology class to students who can process NFT circles around us faster than we can Google what that means? While we must remember that some of our students may not have had access to as much technology as others and therefore will need our help in this area, wisdom and discernment and efficiency in the use of technology is our focus. These are aspects of our subject that are not native and cannot be omitted because in so doing our students will be shaped in their use of technology by practices and values shaped by the culture at-large in a non-Christian world.

Structure

Learning that promotes the structure of a subject was defined in the introduction of this section as "Grasping the structure of a subject is understanding it in a way that permits many other things to be related to it meaningfully."[2] Technology by its very nature is a subject area that, when understood well, supports and permits all other subjects to be related in a systematic way and makes learning and communication today more meaningful.

We begin by defining what we mean when we say technology. *Technology* is a term that can be interpreted in different ways. The original term comes from two Greek words, *techne* and *logos* (transliterated into "skill or craft" and "words").[3] It is understood today as far more and refers to a systematic treatment and application of knowledge

---

[2] Jerome S. Bruner, *The Process of Education* (New York: Alfred A. Knopf, 1960), 7.

[3] "Technology," Technology and Christian "Values," accessed July 11, 2022, https://web.engr.oregonstate.edu/~funkk/Technology/technology.html.

in the creation of mechanics, tools, and systems to aid the human experience. Almost every definition for "technology" involves the practical use of tools and systems to solve human problems and affect better productivity. In the twentieth century, the development of computer technology was a prolific and essential form of applied knowledge to aid in the efficiency and speed of the productive workforce. This is the focus of our content in teaching Educational Technology. Technology is the use of the tools and mechanics and also the systems put in place and available. Now, well into the twenty-first century, computer technology takes on new forms as the tools get smaller, more accessible, and more easily manipulated by younger and younger users.

Technology includes not only the devices on which our students do their homework, but the systems that have been created for our efficiency. As an example of a system that is more efficient, take chapters and numbered verses we now have that were not a part of the original manuscripts of the Bible. That was a system, in broad terms—a technology—that was applied to the collection of text and translations to help the readers share and interpret passages more efficiently. Technology is about efficiency. But as we look at technology from a biblical perspective, we acknowledge that life is not just about efficiency; it is about relationships and effectiveness that honors God. Because of this, our Ed Tech curriculum in a Christian school must go beyond what might be found in government schools. Students must develop the wise use of technology (that which God has providentially allowed humans to create) and begin to experience a biblical understanding of taking a tool and shaping it into a resource for missional purposes. The tool is always secondary to its usage and purpose. For example, relationships always supersede efficiency. So, we consider what we gain with technology but also consider what we lose. With this consideration in mind, we form our scope and sequence and applications of computer technology to the skill level and development of our students today.

The question we strive to answer in a technology course is this: In what ways can we be efficient, creative, and God-honoring with the relationships and resources at hand? What is the best way to love God and love others while using technology? Remembering that technology is the application of knowledge to mechanics and systems and our call as Christians is to honor God in everything we do.

Logical Organization

There is a natural organization of key performance indicators, beginning with learning the technology to use and then leveraging technology to best serve human endeavors and transform the human learning experience. Throughout the school years, students are given more and more access to systems that will challenge their level of responsibility and maturity in the use of such systems. The delicate balance is to release access to technology at a rate that matches the brain development and judicial capabilities of each age group. The organization and rate of access is similar to the approach we would take in teaching a child to cook. There are tools, basic rules to follow, and real and present risks, but we begin there and move beyond that to actually cook a meal; beyond that, "the world is your oyster."[4] Let us begin with the tools.

Hardware and Basic Operations

Early education is focused on the hardware and devices, the tools. Learning objectives at the early elementary level are that students demonstrate a sound understanding of basic operations and concepts of technology systems. Navigating an operating system to change preferences, using a mouse and keyboard, locating files, and other basics are the focus. Students begin to transfer the knowledge they have learned in reading, writing, mathematics, and even art to a digital space. What this looks like will vary greatly depending on the age of your students, when you introduce technology, to what extent you desire to go at that level, and the resources you have at your disposal. Much depends on student access. If you have, primarily, a desktop computer to use during a technology lab period, the early focus is utilizing and navigating a piece of machinery to do tasks similar to what the students would be otherwise doing orally or on paper. This may be tracing a letter with their finger on a tablet or typing a thought on a Word document and using the skills that are required to demonstrate these tasks, such as typing. The goal at this stage is to utilize the technology in efficient ways.

Production Tools

Once students can demonstrate an understanding of how to operate the technology machine, the learning objectives are to utilize the systems, information, and software available to them. Practices utilize key production software such as Microsoft Word, Excel, and PowerPoint, as well as standard computer tools such as a calculator, dialogue

---

[4] This is a saying often given to youth, meaning that everything is open to you if you just take the opportunities as they come. One of them might yield something as precious as a pearl in an oyster.

boxes, image editors, and video players. In the early introduction to technology tools, motivation is a major focus. Students are keenly aware of and often unimpressed by the tools at hand; however, the reasons and goals for which to use the technology are foreign to many and must be prominent. In an introduction to an activity that utilizes basic functionality, it is wise to take a moment to reflect on the responsibility and role technology plays in their lives. For example, you may design an assignment for students to share about their favorite family experience using Microsoft Word or PowerPoint. In this case, students are getting to know one another, sharing about themselves, and building relationships while practicing typing, learning different software tools, reinforcing skills, and demonstrating appropriate uses for the technology.

Communication Tools

As we move up the pyramid of Bloom's taxonomy of learning goals,[5] once we have established proficiency in the basic native and productivity tools, it is time to introduce more communication, collaborative, and creative tools to develop their analytical usage of technology. Students are introduced to cloud-based software, resources, and services, which allow them not only to explore and connect pieces of information, but to share and collaborate while learning. Learning activities become more collaborative in nature while allowing students the joy of discovering and learning online. Developing activities should be in concert with teachers of other subject areas in which the same students are required to do research or find information that will contribute to the week's learning goals. Provide several specific links and safety guidelines for searching and navigating the internet and then allow their curiosity to lead them on a learning journey.

An introduction and practice for emailing and other communication tools is included at this stage. Students learn what is appropriate usage of different technology and systems and what is not appropriate. Different types of communication take place within emails versus another messaging system. As students begin using communication and collaborative tools, it is important to establish the link between human relationships and technology. While technology makes life and communication more efficient, relationships can be damaged by not understanding how to use technology. Focus on developing relationships that mirror character that is informed by a biblical

---

[5] Patricia Armstrong, "Bloom's Taxonomy," Vanderbilt University Center for Teaching, 2010, accessed June 15, 2022, https://cft.vanderbilt.edu/guides-sub-pages/blooms-taxonomy/.

view of human beings that foster acceptance, love, and encouragement of one another. Students' habits and practices of responsible usage of technology that honor people and honor God begins sooner rather than later.

Ethical Use

The topic of appropriate use of the thoughts and writings of others is important as research assignments are utilized in tech class. The need to address copyright laws and plagiarism will become evident and must be addressed as projects and research papers are submitted for assessment. While it is wonderful to see students develop an interest and love of learning, when they are given freedom to discover information sources that add to their learning, their integrity will be tested as content is readily available and the temptation to copy is always present. Providing practice in summarizing in their own words what they are analyzing and examining will be increasingly important as students grow in their use of technology and become responsible digital citizens.

Research Tools

By the time students advance to middle school and high school, they will be using technology tools for researching, curating, and processing data into presentations. Unlike the sleek design and use of most new hardware being developed, researching on the internet is not so "sleek" or intuitive. Maneuvering through the massive amount of information available on the internet to find accurate and relevant information can be difficult and might even be considered an art form. Teaching learners how to judge credibility, identify bias, and seek truth in data research is arguably the most important skill students should acquire under the guidance of a trusted and caring adult. Activities that challenge students to dig into primary resources for data and weed through secondary and tertiary commentaries will develop awareness and discernment in understanding the fallibility of internet data. Critical thinking skills are part of a solid technology education.

Creative Use

God is creative, and he created us in his image—to create (Gen 1:26–28). The first mandate given to humanity was to create, to bear fruit. He gave us a work to do in having dominion over part of his created order. A systems approach was used as God classified the animal kingdom; for example, he listed in Genesis 1, creatures of the sea, birds, livestock, and creatures that move along the ground. Then he asked Adam to name the animals; this, too, is creating a system of communication. The creative use of technology is a highlight of working with students and can be considered the development of the use of tools allowed by God and discovered and created by humankind to be used in the cultural mandate he gave us. The creativity with which students harness and manipulate technology is a wonderful reflection of their Creator.

Students, especially in high school, are highly motivated and interested in innovative technology and may end up making a career in this area. This is an excellent period in their lives to encourage them to use new tools, to create responsibly, and to evaluate the ways in which their creative use of technology affects their own lives and relationships with others. Christian educators are called to help students weigh the gains and losses in using technology personally or socially, but should also be challenged to use technological resources in the mission of sharing Christ with the world. The creative use of technology will constantly challenge the moral compass of students and adults alike but will also provide some of the most inspiring and God-glorifying moments when we help our students develop God-honoring stewardship of current-day resources.

Digital Citizenship

Digital citizenship is the way in which a person conducts himself or herself in the use of computers and the internet and digital devices to engage in society. In Christian education, this includes a student's witness to the world via technology as much as by his or her words and actions toward neighbors and classmates daily. It is essential to reinforce the connection between real life and individual digital representations. A dangerous phenomenon occurs when one is sitting behind a screen. There is often a physical disconnect, and at times a cognitive dissonance between the real and the digital experience, which can lead to things written that can have lasting, negative consequences in human relationships. Address these issues early in Ed Tech classes.

The topic of digital citizenship includes the well-being of students as they engage in social media, the balance of digital and in-person human experiences, privacy and security, the individual digital footprint, media literacy in research and proper usage of data, collaboration, communication, and online bullying. Exercises at all levels with appropriate grade-level examples will demonstrate the human connection to digital expressions and help to reinforce an understanding that we are humans communicating with humans *and* are representing Christ in everything we do whether physical or digital. We are to love the Lord with all our heart, mind, and soul and to love others as ourselves. Matthew 22:36–40 tells us that on these "two" commandments hang all the laws and the prophets. (The two are love God first and love others.) This is a summary of God's expectations for us in all of life and that includes our digital life.

Standard for Testing or Judging Truth

Technology is an instrument for information exchanges, and as such is subject to the standards for judging truth in the discipline under study. For example, if being used in science, truth-judging is done through inductive and experimental research using the senses and extended senses. Knowledge gain is always open to further investigation as more and better extended senses are invented to investigate, for example, the enormous spatial Universe or tiny molecules.

Truth-judging in mathematics uses reason and deduction as well as serving as a language to describe what is discovered in science. In today's world, too often people have succumbed to the postmodern thinking that there is no objective truth outside the mind of the human being by which we can measure other "truths." While God's Word does not include all truth that exists, it is true in all it affirms, and it is considered an outside standard for knowing objective truth. The loss of objective truth-seeking in science, in mathematics, in history, in biblical information through a variety of genres, has become a problem with the use of technology as well as for culture in general. This is one reason why a Christian school exists. We (teachers and students) have a standard for truth-judging that stands outside the human mind and can be sought (as truth seekers). It is the Word of God, and God himself is the source of all truth wherever it is found.

Biblical answers to life's biggest questions are found in his Word and are used to appreciate, connect, and use knowledge found in all subjects of the curriculum. As well, biblical answers to the big questions of life are also used to see distinctions or to contrast or correct non-biblical views. It takes the process of critical thinking to discern that which agrees with Scripture and that which does not, and this is the foundation of digital and media literacy. Indeed, worldview thinking is essentially the process of critical thinking in which the Word of God is the standard for truth-judging in the final analysis.

Other Standards

The International Society for Technology in Education (ISTE) has published seven standards for students that have been adopted by all fifty states in the USA. These standards include: Empowered Learner, Digital Citizen, Knowledge Constructor, Innovative Design, Computational Thinker, Creative Communicator, and Global Collaborator. You can find more information and learning objectives for each standard at the ISTE website.[6]

While the standards do address identity and reputation as well as the permanence of digital actions, they give no guidance for the character of that identity. Awareness of one's identity as a person is a good thing; however, Christians apply biblical standards for character and conduct to digital interactions and creative use of technology. This is part of a discipleship process to which we are called as Christian educators. Key questions to remember: Are students honoring God in their use and interactions in the digital space as they would in a human space? Are students using the technology resources available to them to be more efficient as good stewards? Are students loving others? Do students place the proper value on technology?

A growing focus for Educational Technology is on Media Literacy (ML) or the approach to processing information that uses the ability to not only access but also to analyze, evaluate, and communicate media messages in various formats. All media carry biases just as any word or information-producing source does. With this in mind, the process of critical thinking becomes more necessary today in Ed Tech.

Concept Development

How do we develop the content and the processes that help students learn technology well? The approach to learning addressed in the early chapters of this book provides a template and the theory behind it for planning effective lessons for any learning event including technology. Meaningful learning activities are used within the template to carry out the purpose of each element. Meaningful activities are age-appropriate activities that mirror real-life experiences. In elementary school, it might be an assignment to find a tasty dinner recipe online, email it to you and their parents, and then prepare that part of the dinner for their family. In middle school, I have assigned students the task

---

[6] "ISTE Standards: Students," ISTE, 2021, accessed June 22, 2022, https://www.iste.org /standards/iste-standards-for-students.

of creating a video that teaches the class one new skill that they have developed well. In high school, students can choose any form of technology to share their testimony or favorite Scripture to be played on the school monitor (if you have one). The goal is to design activities that are generous enough to allow free use of age-appropriate technology while providing enough guidance to accomplish the learning objective and meet the key learning indicators. In Christian education, we have the privilege of discipling students while they learn content. Ed Tech is a wonderful subject to allow that discipleship to take center stage while still covering the learning objectives.

Assessment

Formative assessment is a part of every lesson; review chapters 6 and 7, which address effective assessment practices. Summative assessments are more formal and are always the target of the big ideas in the curriculum. Each state or nation has its own list of key indicators, which have been informed by a set of standards such as the ITSE standards. In a technology course, assessments are focused on the demonstration of technology knowledge, and on the understanding and application of technology rather than the content development of the project itself, especially if the assignment aligns with the requirements in another course. For example, for tech assignments, a teacher must be careful not to apply judgment based on subjective taste or preference or creative style, but rather on the ability to utilize the appropriate tools to accomplish the task. If the project is for another teacher, the other teacher can create a rubric for making judgments. Tech rubrics will be used by the tech teacher. Christian teachers in any class are called to give correction and guidance when a digital expression is not reflecting a Christlike interaction or representation. Evaluating through testing is appropriate, especially in the elementary school grades as students are practicing the functionality and basic operational skills of the hardware and software. As students get older, project-based assessments will help to determine if students can demonstrate the learning objectives in technology.

Rules for Using Technology in the Classroom

Most schools today have a list of rules for technology usage in the regular classroom. Some teachers require that handheld technology—phones and iPads—be turned off and placed in a holding place during class. Some suggest obtaining and using a bag that is usually used for storing shoes but works well with smartphones and the like. Rules for in-class personal computer use are the preference of the teacher and depend on how the computers are to be used in the day's lesson. Think through your rules carefully.

A special set of rules is required for Ed Tech classes. Here is an example of one list adapted from a list posted by Jessica Sanders.[7]

1. Visit approved internet sites only.
2. Never provide your personal information online.
3. Tell your teacher if you see something uncomfortable or inappropriate.
4. Never download nor print anything without the teacher's permission.
5. Leave your workspace neat and clean.
6. Place devices on chargers when not in use.
7. Be careful when using the mouse and touch the keyboard gently.
8. Do not eat or drink near devices.

For lab usage, the teacher is tasked with the responsibility of sanitizing the keyboards and equipment between usages to prevent the spread of germs.

ENGAGE: You may think of other important rules to add. Take time to write out a complete list of rules that you believe will effectively allow for care of all of the equipment and for the ease of learning. Give a justification for each rule. Try to state your rules in the positive form rather than a negative form so as "never" or "don't."

Key Biblical / Worldview Connections

The integration of a biblical worldview is and should be deep since our faith informs every interaction we have, whether digital or human. Biblical integrative thinking is an integration of the mind in which the student and teacher *together* explore God's view on a topic. One question often asked concerns the use of technology at all, especially with young children. Should young children have access to computers or tablets? Should they be allowed to access the internet? What safety measures and barriers are in place to filter and protect my child from false or harmful information? These are important questions in which some of the answers are related to the "why" of technology. In the broadest sense, if technology is applied knowledge to create efficient human experiences, and God uses technology as we see throughout Scripture, then we who

---

[7] Jessica Sanders, "10 Classroom Rules for Using Technology," *Whooo's Reading Blog*, August 3, 2015, http://blog.whooosreading.org/10classroom-rules-for-using-technology/.

are created in his image with a purpose on this planet to reflect his image must address these questions as best we can by using principles of living and loving from Scripture.

In thinking through how God used systems to make his created order efficient, we might refer to Genesis 1. God created a system of day and night. He created and divided water and land and the universe in total. These are systems and order that we count on for our survival (Ps 8:3–6). Without these "systems" there would be chaos. God also chose to tell his story in the form of text, using the system of written language as we know to be Scripture we have today. Throughout Scripture we see cities built, towers raised, temples assembled, and sculptures crafted by his order and to his specifications (Exod 31:1–6). Jesus used carpenter tools and Paul wrote letters, each a form of technology for its day.

John wrote, "Though I have much to write to you, I do not want to use paper and ink. Instead, I hope to come to you and talk face to face so that our joy may be complete" (2 John 1:12). John, while using a medium, a technology, to write, considers it inferior to a face-to-face experience. However, he did write in the absence of being present. We are glad he did. A fellow writer, Paul, also used writing and a technology, and he encouraged us as follows:

So whether you eat or drink or whatever you do, do it all for the glory of God. Do not cause anyone to stumble, whether Jews, Greeks or the church of God— even as I try to please everyone in every way. For I am not seeking my own good but the good of many, so that they may be saved. (1 Cor 10:31–33 NIV)

Are we using and teaching students to use technology for our own broken, selfish sinful desires and pleasures, or are we using technology to help promote human flourishing and divine glory? Our distinction as Christian educators must be to warn of the dangers inherent in some uses of technology and yet use God's gifts and resources that he allowed humans to invent and develop, to glorify him. "Our Lord and God, you are worthy to receive glory and honor and power, because you have created all things, and by your will they exist and were created" (Rev 4:11).

CHAPTER 19

The Arts (Visual and Performing)

Debbie Lynn Wolf

What comes to mind when you think of the arts? Take a moment and consider this realm of learning. The arts have followed the foundational subjects, often referred to as the three "Rs," Reading, 'Riting, and 'Rithmetic, as the forgotten fourth "R" in historical scholastic contexts. Often overlooked from an academic perspective, the arts provide a unique aspect of education. Francis Schaeffer describes this general pattern of disregard for the arts:

> As evangelical Christians we have tended to relegate art to the very fringe of life. The rest of human life we feel is more important. . . . We have misunderstood the concept of the Lordship of Christ over the whole of man and the whole of the universe and have not taken to us the riches that the Bible gives us for ourselves, for our lives and for our culture.[1]

The arts are distinct disciplines often corralled together because of their aesthetic qualities and complex, and sometimes, overlapping subject matter and skills. They are unique academic subjects because they have the potential to entertain as well as educate, developing skills for a lifetime of enjoyment, while providing experiences more

---

[1] Francis A. Schaeffer, *Art & the Bible* (Downers Grove, IL: InterVarsity, 1979), 7.

than just actual information, and the intensity of those experiences may be life changing and unforgettable.

The arts offer opportunities to experience various perspectives, different ways of "knowing," and can challenge and inspire students to contemplate worldview questions. The emotional and intellectual stimulation they provide creates unique opportunities for students to respond personally and individually as they grapple with worldview issues. An aesthetic encounter may provide deeper and more profound meaning by surpassing words or thoughts. Through the arts, we can fathom richer experiences of all aspects of life.

The arts can be a compelling tool in the redemptive process—God can use the arts to change lives. For example, in 1 Sam 16:23, David plays his harp and ministers to Saul on multiple levels: "Saul would then be relieved, feel better, and the evil spirit would leave him." Leonard Seidel in *God's New Song* points out that the Hebrew meaning of this passage indicates that when David ministered to Saul through playing his harp, he played *skillfully*, and provided relief physically (*Saul would then be relieved*), mentally (*feel better*), and spiritually (*the evil spirit would leave him*).[2] God can use the power of an artistic experience to minister on multiple levels. In this example, we also see social benefits of the arts in that David ministered to Saul through his skillful playing. Because the arts communicate, the social functions of art transcend the personal intrinsic value to influence an ever-expanding social circle.

Perhaps you can relate to the power of the arts in your own education. If you enjoyed a rich education in the arts, you will most likely recall vivid, positive aesthetic experiences. Perhaps your memories of the arts are even stronger than your memories of other classes. Because of this, and because of the power that an artistic experience affords, I would like to propose that the arts are pivotal and perhaps paramount in promoting Christian worldview thinking in our students. Ryken, in *The Liberated Imagination*, suggests this view:

> I wonder if young people who abandon their Christian faith after high school
> or college might not have been better able to withstand the appeals of a secu
> lar world view if they had explored the world views in art and literature more

---

[2] Leonard J. Seidel, *God's New Song: A Biblical Perspective of Music* (Springfield, VA: Grace Unlimited, 1980), 4–9.

seriously when they had the chance to weigh them with a measure of intellectual detachment.[3]

The arts can help students reflect on learning and application of worldview in all subjects because they can serve as catalysts for teachers to provide memorable worldview integration. An understanding of the structure of the arts may enable these disciplines to be more accessible to those who desire to harness their power in creating opportunities for worldview thinking in any classroom.

The Arts: A Multifaceted Discipline

An overview of the arts must include an understanding of their aesthetic properties along with the multifaceted structure of each art form, as each art discipline has its own elements. Each also has a collection of work that must be understood in an historical/ cultural/social/artistic context, and each requires knowledge and skills to be creative and to participate meaningfully and successfully, whether actively (as performer, presenter, or producer) or reactively (as observer, critic, or commentator). In this way, the arts are both product and process: as product in the elements of each discipline and collection of work, including works performed, presented, or produced by the students; and as process in the participatory experiences as cognitive, psychomotor, and affective learning develop. Both product and process contribute to promoting aesthetic experiences in arts education.

In *Art and Soul: Signposts for Christians in the Arts*, Brand and Chaplin express the importance of the aesthetic component:

> There is something in us that instinctively responds to aesthetic excellence, something that can never quite be defined in rules of composition or theories of perception. But, learning the rules and theories does help. It helps us understand **how** the work weaves its aesthetic magic. . . . It is this aesthetic dimension that turns something into art, as opposed to a purely functional form of communication. . . . Any interpretation of art which does not take the aesthetic surface into account, seriously misses the point.[4]

---

[3] Leland Ryken, *The Liberated Imagination: Thinking Christianly about the Arts* (Wheaton, IL: Harold Shaw, 1989), 147.

[4] Hilary Brand and Adrienne Chaplin, *Art and Soul: Signposts for Christians in the Arts*, 2nd ed. (Carlisle, UK: Piquant Editions, 2007), 142.

Teachers should always strive to foster the wonder of the arts for their students by planning for aesthetic experiences along with cognitive, psychomotor, and affective development. Like other subjects, the arts are both concepts and skills, but in addition, the arts are more than just concepts and skills, more than product and process—the aesthetic component is essential. The arts unite the head, hand, and heart by forcing integration of thought, skill, and feeling in the instruction and application of learning. Teachers should caution against emphasizing skill development, technique, or cognitive processes to the extent that students miss the overall aesthetic affect. The cerebral and technical aspects should not detract from the thrill of the artistic experience. Accordingly, this coverage of the structure of the subject of the arts will begin with aesthetics.

Aesthetics

Aesthetics is a unifying factor of the arts: in addition to overlapping characteristics and shared components, each of the arts offers aesthetic experiences. While these experiences may be difficult to define, the following six characteristics provide a general description: an aesthetic experience . . .

1. possesses no practical or utilitarian purpose, but is valued for insight, satisfaction, and enjoyment as an end in itself
2. stimulates feelings and inspires an emotional reaction
3. requires careful thought and intellectual deliberation
4. engages a focus of attention or thoughtful contemplation
5. must be experienced first-hand
6. results in a richer, more meaningful awareness and realization of life.[5]

Aesthetic experiences occur in varying degrees depending on the quality of the stimulus and the sensitivity of the spectator. A rich education in the arts would likely improve students' ability to perceive and appreciate artistic endeavors throughout life.

When thinking of arts education, what specific courses come to mind? Do you think of the visual arts? Music? Historically, these two subjects have been the most

---

[5] Harold Abeles, Charles Hoffer, and Robert Klotman, *Foundations of Music Education*, 2nd ed. (New York: Schirmer Books, 1994), 75.

prevalent, but arts education has become much broader. Educational forums now recognize the arts as dance, music, theater, visual arts, and media arts.[6]

Many countries have a set of standards providing structure for curriculum in the arts. In the United States, the National Standards for Arts Education addresses all five art disciplines with one set of standards that applies to each individual discipline.[7] These standards reveal commonalities among the Arts but also provide a basis for understanding the structure of each discipline. While schools may not offer separate or distinct courses in each discipline, students should gain some experience in all of these art forms throughout elementary and secondary grades. For example, music classes may include experiences in dance and theater; physical education classes may include experiences in dance; and literature classes may include experiences in theater.

The National Standards for Arts Education promotes arts education for all students, upholding that "a future worth having depends on being able to construct a vital relationship with the arts."[8] This relationship is cultivated through discipline and study, such as with all other academic subjects, and is an educational right for all students, not limited to the "talented" few.[9] The National Standards for Arts Education states that **every student** should be able to achieve the following:

- Communicate at a basic level in the five arts disciplines—dance, media arts, music, theater, and the visual arts.
- Communicate proficiently in at least one art form.
- Develop and present basic analyses of works of art.
- Demonstrate an informed acquaintance with exemplary works of art from a variety of cultures and historical periods.
- Relate various types of knowledge and skills within and across the arts disciplines.[10]

---

[6] "National Core Arts Standards: Dance, Media Art, Music, Theatre, Visual Arts," National Coalition for Core Arts Standards, 2015, www.nationalartsstandards.org.

[7] "National Core Arts Standards."

[8] "National Standards for Arts Education," Americans for the Arts, 2015, https://www.americansforthearts.org/by-program/reports-and-data/legislation-policy/naappd/national-standards-for-arts-education-what-every-young-american-should-know-and-be-able-to-do-in-the.

[9] "National Standards for Arts Education."

[10] "National Standards for Arts Education."

The National Standards of the Arts consists of eleven core anchor standards developed around four processes (creating; performing/presenting/producing; responding; connecting), resulting in a cohesive design for addressing cognitive, psychomotor, and affective domains of learning, while revealing the multidimensional focus of developing appreciation, understanding, and skill required in all arts education:

1. **Creating**: conceiving and developing new artistic ideas and work
   Anchor Standard #1. Generate and conceptualize artistic ideas and work.
   Anchor Standard #2. Organize and develop artistic ideas and work.
   Anchor Standard #3. Refine and complete artistic work.

2. **Performing/Presenting/Producing**
   Anchor Standard #4. Select, analyze and interpret artistic work for presentation.
   Anchor Standard #5. Develop and refine artistic techniques and work for presentation.
   Anchor Standard #6. Convey meaning through the presentation of artistic work.

3. **Responding**: understanding and evaluating how the arts convey meaning
   Anchor Standard #7. Perceive and analyze artistic work.
   Anchor Standard #8. Interpret intent and meaning in artistic work.
   Anchor Standard #9. Apply criteria to evaluate artistic work.

4. **Connecting**: relating artistic ideas and work with personal meaning and external context
   Anchor Standard #10. Synthesize and relate knowledge and personal experiences to make art.
   Anchor Standard #11. Relate artistic ideas and works with societal, cultural and historical context to deepen understanding.[11]

The National Standards for Arts Education addresses these four artistic processes (creating; performing/presenting/producing; responding; connecting) separately and sequentially, yet these four processes are also often encouraged and experienced concurrently. For example, when improvising in dance, music, or theater, students may simultaneously engage in the four processes: students are creating as they perform,

---

[11] "National Core Arts Standards, Dance, Media Art, Music, Theatre, Visual Arts." Note: The three-verb combination *performing/presenting/producing* allows for reference to the variation in the processes developing among the disciplines (performance skills for dance, music, and theater; presenting skills for visual arts; and production skills for media arts) but also allows for reference to the variation of the processes developing within each of the disciplines.

and at the same time, they are responding by analyzing and adjusting their performance as needed. They are connecting by relating to other performers, classmates, and
their audience or by recalling previous experiences. Teachers may plan simultaneous or
sequential development of students' creativity to imagine or personalize the production
or performance while awakening students' response to adjust or appreciate these experiences. Additionally, teachers may help students connect with thoughts, feelings, and
attitudes inspired by the experience, perceived by the creator/artist/composer/author-
playwright/producer, realized by others, and related to other ideas and art forms before
or following an introduction to an artwork. These four interrelated and interdependent
processes (creating, performing/presenting/producing, responding, and connecting) are
vital to arts education.

Each art discipline has its own distinguishing elements. Aaron Copland, the
American composer, offers this advice in understanding the elements of art:

> You can't develop a better appreciation of the art merely by reading a book about
> it. If you want to understand music better, you can do nothing more important
> than listen to it. Nothing can possibly take the place of listening to music.[12]

His example addresses the art of music, but his advice applies to learning about all art
forms: experience in the art is necessary to understand the elements of the art. In the
next section, I have followed his advice in my description of the elements of each of the
arts by providing links that supply visual and auditory examples to offer appropriate
context for learning about each.

Dance

Dance education includes the study of dancing, dance making, and appreciation of
dances and dancers from around the world and throughout history. According to the
National Dance Education Organization (NDEO):

> The art of dance uses movement to communicate meaning about the human
> experience. It is far more than exercise or entertainment. It is a powerful medium
> to express one's values, thoughts, and aspirations about the lives we live and the
> world in which we live. Education in the art of dance develops the knowledge
> and skills required to create, perform, and understand movement as a means

---

[12] Aaron Copland, *What to Listen for in Music*, rev. ed. (New York: McGraw-Hill,1957), 15.

of artistic communication. A comprehensive education includes improvisation, technique, choreography, performance, observation and analysis. Exposure to dance history and cultures, kinesiology and anatomy, and movement theories further enriches the dance educational experience.[13]

The common elements, or core characteristics, of all forms of dance are the body, action, space, time, and energy. Identifying and understanding these elements provide context in observation, analyzation, discussion, performance, and creation of dance. Rudolf Laban analyzed and categorized all movement into four elements: flow, space, time, weight; his work initially influenced dance, but now applies to all art disciplines. For more information on the elements of dance, refer to https://www.elementsofdance.org/.[14]

Music

In the United States, music education includes courses for all grade levels in general music and both large and small ensemble experiences in choral, band, orchestra, and other vocal and instrumental groups. Lessons for instrumental students may begin in elementary school and may continue through high school. Secondary schools (grades 5–12) may offer specialized music courses in theory, composition, history, guitar, keyboard, and music technology. Additionally, music programs may provide more challenging and specialized training in various ensembles and extracurricular opportunities for all grade levels. Music encompasses a massive body of knowledge in music theory, music history and world music traditions, music technology, and musical works of all genres. Music skills include listening, moving/dancing, singing, playing instruments, improvising, creating, and reading musical notation, but also include the ability to analyze, integrate, evaluate, and relate music to society, culture, history, and other disciplines.

---

[13] "About Dance Education," The National Dance Education Organization, 2021, https://www.ndeo.org/About/Dance-Education/Dance-Studios.

[14] "Elements of Dance," last updated September 2018, https://www.elementsofdance.org/. Project Coordinator and Online Architect: Diane Aldis; Research Assistance: Genevieve Muench; BASTE graphics: Amy Fasteneau. A project of the Perpich Center for Arts Education in partnership with University of MN Dance Program including support from University Research Opportunity Program (UROP).

The elements of music are rhythm, melody, harmony/tonality, timbre, form, texture, and expressive devices (dynamics, articulation, tempi).[15]

Theater

Theater is a complex, collaborative art form showing thoughts, emotions, perspectives, or experiences by blending words, voice, gesture, sound, and visual effects to express meaning in live or recorded, improvised, or scripted performance. This "showing" actually becomes the most distinguishing component of theater because this transforms other art forms into theatrical performance. For example, dance becomes theater when dancers portray a story; music becomes theater when singers act out the lyrics; visual art becomes theater when an artist constructs before an audience. The elements of theater include the following: performers, audience, director, theater space, design aspects (scenery, costume, lighting, sound), and text (focus, purpose, point of view, dramatic structure, dramatic characters).[16]

The six elements of theater that Aristotle identified in *Poetics* are also prominent in describing this art form: plot, character, thought, diction, song (rhythm/music), and spectacle.[17]

Visual Arts

The vast domain of Visual Arts, as defined by The National Art Education Association, extends beyond the traditional fine arts of drawing, painting, printmaking, photography, and sculpture. Visual arts also includes environmental, architectural, and industrial

---

[15] For more in-depth understanding of the elements of music, refer to "Elements of Music," Jooya Teaching Resources, 2021, https://juliajooya.com/2020/10/11/what-are-the-8-elements-of-music/; and Kaitlyn M. Bove, "Elements of Music," Dr. Bove's Virtual Courses, 2021, https://kaitlinbove.com/elements-of-music/.

[16] For a greater description of these elements, refer to Michael Roche, "Elements of Theater," Roche Website, William Penn Charter School, December 7, 2009, https://sites.google.com/a/penncharter.com/roche-website/7th-grade-drama/aspects-of-theater.

[17] Aristotle, *Aristotle's Poetics* (New York: Hill and Wang, 1961). For more information on Aristotle's six elements, refer to Tylie Shider, "Decoding the 6 Aristotelean Elements of Drama," PWC, The Playwright's Center, 2021, https://pwcenter.org/playwriting-toolkit/decoding-6–aristotelean-elements-drama. For lesson plan examples for all grade levels, refer to "Theatre Educator PRO," Educational Theater Association, 2021, https://learn.schooltheatre.org/click-to-teach-lesson-plans.

arts; design, communication, product, and interactive arts; conceptual, performance, participatory, street, mural, and folk arts; and works of art in clay, fiber, glass, metal, paper, wood, and other materials, such as jewelry and ceramics.[18] The elements of the visual arts are color, line, shape, form, value, texture, and space. Artists use these elements according to the principles of design: balance, contrast, emphasis, movement, pattern, rhythm, and unity.[19]

The visual arts has historically encompassed media arts, but since the early 2000s, media arts has surfaced as a distinct artistic discipline. The National Art Standards of Australia, UK, and America now address media arts as a separate art form. The elements of media arts are space, time, light, motion, color, and sound.[20]

The arts are recognized and sanctioned as vocational and avocational pursuits in Scripture: we have God's approval for participation and appreciation of the arts. A survey of references to the arts in the Bible reveals some important considerations regarding these subjects.

Arts in the Bible

Dance

While the dance of Salome (Matt 14:3–12; Mark 6:17–29) demonstrates this art form exploited with grievous results, dance is most often referenced in positive contexts of celebration and worship. Consider the following examples. Miriam led the women of Israel in dance commemorating God's overthrow of Pharaoh's army in the Red Sea (Exod 15:20–21). David danced before the Lord as the ark was paraded back to Jerusalem (2 Sam 6:14–17); Christ referenced dancing in the parable of the prodigal son at the celebration hosted by the father, rejoicing in the prodigal's return (Luke 15:25–32). Psalmists include dancing as part of the musical offering of praise and devotion (Ps 149:3). Many Old Testament writers contrast dancing with mourning as the

---

[18] "National Visual Arts Standards," The National Art Education Association, accessed June 22, 2022, https://www.arteducators.org/learn-tools/national-visual-arts-standards.

[19] For more information on the elements and principles of design in Visual Arts, refer to "The Elements of Art," The J. Paul Getty Museum, accessed July 28, 2021, https://www.getty.edu/education/teachers/building_lessons/formal_analysis.html.

[20] For more information on Media Arts, refer to "What Is Media Arts," Saint Paul Public Schools, 2021, https://www.spps.org/Page/23303; and William Anderson, "Elements and Principles of Media Art," SchoolWorkHelper, 2019, https://schoolworkhelper.net/elements-and-principles-of-media-art/.

definitive expression of joy (Ps 30:11; Eccl 3:4; Lam 5:15). Scripture frequently presents dancing in references with playing tambourines; accordingly, such dancing may have been self-accompanied, but nevertheless, dancing is commonly associated with instrumental accompaniment (Exod 15:20; Judg 11:34; Ps 149:3; Jer 31:4). Criticism and disrespect of this worship style resulted in judgment (2 Sam 6:14–20).

Music

Music is the most predominant art form mentioned in Scripture; Seidel lists 602 direct references to music in the Bible.[21] Although most references involve praise and worship, references to music in other aspects of daily life include self-expression, celebration, military purposes, and songs to accompany work. God has revealed much about this art form, but I will only include a few notable examples helpful for teachers here:

- Music can minister on mental, emotional, physical, and spiritual levels (1 Sam 16:23).
- God expects everyone to make music; music is not limited to the talented (Ps 100).
- Both singing and playing instruments are tools in worship (Ps 150).
- Study and skill development were necessary and required by the priest musicians (2 Chron 34:12–13).
- Musicians labored day and night; practice is necessary and required (1 Chron 9:33).
- Singing should be a spiritual expression with understanding (1 Cor 14:15).
- Music is to be used to teach and to admonish spiritual truth (Col 3:16).
- A variety of musical resources, psalms, hymns, and spiritual songs should be used (Eph 5:19).
- Music is used for self-expression and associated with joy (Jas 5:13).

Theater

Paul the apostle presents two theatrical references in his epistles of 1 Corinthians and Titus. Ryken reports 1 Cor 15:33, "Bad company corrupts good morals," is a quote from the play *Thais*, by the Greek dramatist, Menander.[22] In Titus 1:12, Paul quotes

---

[21] Seidel, *God's New Song*, 107.
[22] Ryken, *The Liberated Imagination*, 47.

from the Cretan philosopher-poet Epimenides and states that he agrees with him in verse 13. With these references, Paul demonstrates his familiarity with Greek literature and uses these theatrical references to emphasize his argument. Paul turns to secular art to emphasize spiritual truth.

Visual Arts

Many allusions to the visual arts appear throughout Scripture. Reference to various media in the visual arts include the following examples: architecture (Jer 22:14); embroidery (Exod 35:35); engravings (Exod 35:35); fabrics (2 Chron 2:13–14); paint (Jer 22:14); pottery (Jer 18:3); precious stones (2 Chron 3:5–7); sculpture (2 Chron 3:5–7); weavings (Exod 35:35); and works of gold, silver, and bronze (2 Chron 2:13–14).

References to artisans in Scripture include the following: architect (Jer 22:14); carpenter (2 Chron 3:5–7); designer (2 Chron 2:13–14); engraver (Exod 35:35); embroiderer (Exod 35:35); gardener (Jer 29:5); painter (Jer 22:14); silver purifier and refiner (Mal 3:2–3); smelter (Mal 3:2–3); spinners (Exod 35:25); stonemasons (2 Sam 5:11); tailors (Exod 28:3); tentmakers (Acts 18:3–4); and weavers (Exod 35:35).

The preponderance of these references points to the importance of this discipline and God's concern and attention to it. In two scenarios, constructing the tabernacle in Exodus 31 and building the temple in 1 Kings 6, we have a detailed record of how God directed and enabled artists to produce incredible work for his glory, demonstrating that God desires and ordains artistic endeavors, and equips the artists. Note the four specific terms (*wisdom, understanding, knowledge, craftsmanship*) used in describing God's empowerment of the master craftsman of the tabernacle in Exod 31:9, "I have filled him with God's Spirit, with wisdom, understanding, in ability in every craft." God called the artist to service and provided wisdom, understanding, knowledge, and skill to complete the artistic demands. Artistic skill is a talent given by God, but it still requires hard work to develop and produce works of art for his glory.

In Acts 17:22–31, we find an example of Paul using the visual arts to provoke contemplation on worldviews. Paul observed the art displayed in the Temple of the Athenians, specifically, the altar inscribed "To an Unknown God." He uses this observation to introduce the Athenians to his own God. By referring to their art, he is able to compare their worldview with his own. We can follow Paul's example by using art as a stepping-stone in approaching worldview questions. Art allows for such cross-cultural comparisons and opportunities for discussion and contemplation of worldview questions.

We follow the example of Christ when we ask questions to help students contemplate worldview integration. Asking questions seems to be a vital teaching strategy of Christ's earthly ministry. During his ministry, Christ asked many more questions than he answered. According to Copenhaver, Christ asked an astounding 307 questions, but he only answered three of the 187 questions asked of him recorded in the Gospels.[23] Although he knows all things and has all the answers, he raised questions. Perhaps it is not as important for teachers to require or supply answers as it is to ask questions for students to deliberate and to seek answers from God's Word. The arts are a tool for asking worldview questions. Students have the chance to personally experience these questions, rather than merely think about, discuss, or receive instruction and information about them. The arts open opportunities to explore, ponder, and process worldview thinking and acting.

The arts can be especially helpful to all teachers in providing a forum to ask questions they are seeking to answer by offering students aesthetic experiences, or at least, promoting conditions for such possibilities. Teachers can provide opportunities for students to participate in artistic endeavors or present a work of art for their students to perceive, analyze, and interpret, and thereby engage them in contemplation of worldview questions. Teachers can ask students to respond to worldview questions by expressing themselves through one of the art forms.

Teachers can also provide opportunities for worldview integration by planning for student response to specific works of art. Teachers can guide students into worldview thinking by analyzing and interpreting a work of art in several ways. For example, teachers could reveal background information on the artwork by describing the social and historical context and any iconographical characteristics, such as symbolism, metaphor, allegory, and biographical information on the artist to direct student attention to consideration of the values, assumptions, and other factors influencing the artist and society at this time. An alternative approach could be an examination of the stylistic evolution of the work and public reaction to the new artistic developments. A third approach could be to examine the work of art from an aesthetic perspective, considering what the artist is trying to communicate and if the artwork demonstrates integrity in form and function in relaying this message. For more detail in analyzing and

---

[23] Martin B. Copenhaver, *Jesus Is the Question: The 307 Questions Jesus Asked and the 3 He Answered* (Nashville: Abingdon, 2014), 67.

interpreting works of art to reveal worldview integrative ideas, I recommend consulting Brand and Chaplin's *Art and Soul: Signposts for Christians in the Arts.*[24]

Worldview Questions and the Arts

In this final section, we will examine how the study of the arts can address each of the worldview questions posed by Sire in *The Universe Next Door.*[25]

1. What Is Prime Reality?

Of special significance is the relationship of the arts with depicting reality. According to Ryken, "There can be no doubt that the arts are one of the chief means by which the human race grapples with and interprets reality."[26] The arts help us to realize what we have experienced, what we believe; they help us to consider what is important and what is true. Experiences in the arts can bring insight to what we have been feeling, considering, or believing all along, or alternatively, provide new perspectives to consider.

Recently, a Jewish music teacher recalled for me his first experience of singing the "Hallelujah Chorus" from Handel's *Messiah* in his high school choir. He said he knew he was singing something he did not believe, but because it was so beautiful and so inspiring, he wanted to believe it. The arts provide aesthetic experiences that make the heart tender. Teachers should be careful to choose works of art wisely and make the most of the emotional effect art may elicit by directing attention to spiritual matters.

2. What Is the Nature of External Reality—the World around Us?

Ryken describes the importance of art in enlightening our perspective of reality: "Experiencing a work of art is a bifocal experience. A work of art is a lens or window or lattice through which we see ourselves and our world."[27] The arts reveal ourselves and our world by intensifying focus, providing new perceptions of the familiar, and introducing unusual ways of thinking, imagining, and feeling. Once we encounter this new

---

[24] Brand and Chaplin, *Art and Soul*, 142.

[25] James W. Sire, *The Universe Next Door*, 6th ed. (Downers Grove, IL: InterVarsity, 2020), 8–9. For a deeper look into the role of the arts in interpreting worldviews, I recommend using Ryken's *The Liberated Imagination: Thinking Christianly about the Arts*, 125–62.

[26] Ryken, 31.

[27] Ryken, 33.

slant on reality through the arts, we can return empowered and invigorated to face reality with greater understanding and appreciation. According to Ryken, "Artists turn our pain into art so we can bear it. They turn our joys into art so we can prolong them."[28] The arts may help to reveal thoughts and emotions previously concealed, unexplored, or unspoken, and then the arts can serve to share and intensify emotions. Such aesthetic moments can point to the Creator of all art, the Deliverer of all our sin and sorrow, the Source of all our joy.

3. What Is a Human Being?

God created humankind in his image, and through the arts, humans demonstrate that they, like the Creator, are creative. The arts reveal universal human qualities, emotions, and experiences. According to Ryken:

> Because He created reality, and mandated man's rule over the world, God ordained man's concern with human experience and culture, and because His creation was "good" (beautiful and functional), God also ordained man's attention to beauty and artistic expression. Because God created man in His image, He perpetuates His creativity in man's creativity, endorsing the creative process, imaginative thinking, and the celebration of originality.[29]

Brand and Chaplin caution against evaluating art solely based on whether or not it conveys a Christian message. "Our appreciation of a work of art should not depend on whether it happens to share our worldview. Rather, art is about a shared experience of what it means to be human."[30] Ryken agrees:

> The arts, then, tell us the truth about foundational human experience. . . . The arts are the most accurate index to human preoccupations, values, fears, and longings that we possess. If we wish to know what it means to be a human in this world, we can go to the stories, poems, songs, and paintings of the human race. . . . The arts possess such truth regardless of the philosophic or religious perspective of an artist.[31]

---

[28] Ryken, 32.
[29] Ryken, 14.
[30] Brand and Chaplin, *Art and Soul*, 146.
[31] Ryken, *The Liberated Imagination*, 132–33.

In sharing the humanity expressed in an art form, we can direct students' thoughts to the commonalities and differences in worldviews as Paul did in confronting the Athenians about their quest to honor the unknown god. He noted the universal human need to find God expressed in their art and used this shared experience to reveal God to them.

4. What Happens to a Person at Death?

Artists, including dancers, musicians, and playwrights, as well as visual and media artists, have attempted to address this question through the ages. Works of art reveal countless interpretations of death, the afterlife, and eternity in myriad forms throughout history. An examination comparing the depiction of death in any work of art with what Scripture reveals will promote worldview thinking in powerful and personal ways.

Scripture portrays aspects of death through the arts: for example, in 2 Cor 5:1, "For we know that if the earthly tent we live in is destroyed, we have a building from God, an eternal house in heaven, not made with hands," death is depicted in architectural terms. In 1 Cor 2:9, we read that God's preparations are beyond imagination for those who love him, and Christ assures his own that in heaven there are many mansions, in John 14:2.

Throughout eternity, the arts will be a means of praising and glorifying God. Scripture reveals that the arts are evident after death and for all eternity: the perspectives of death and eternity from dance, music, theater, and visual arts as referenced throughout God's Word provide a multifaceted understanding of death and eternal life. Consider the following examples:

- Music will be experienced as a divine and eternal activity because God himself sings. "The LORD thy God in the midst of thee is mighty; he will save, he will rejoice over thee with joy; he will rest in his love, he will joy over thee with singing" (Zeph 3:17 KJV).
- Revelation 14:3 describes the redeemed singing their new song before the throne.
- Prophetic psalms, such as Psalm 149, describe his people offering praise through music and dance to the Lord when he establishes his kingdom.
- Both music and visual arts are addressed in 1 Cor 15:51–57. The last trumpet will sound, and we will be clothed with the imperishable when Christ returns.
- The spectacle of Rev 19:1–5 seems to convey many of the elements of theater.
- The description of New Jerusalem in Rev 21:10–27 portrays the ultimate beauty of glorified visual arts.

5. Why Is It Possible to Know Anything at All?

Because God made us in his image, we can learn from him and about him and his creation. The arts allow us to demonstrate our knowledge, our imagination, and our creativity. As God reveals himself through his creation, we reveal our minds, our hearts, and ourselves through the arts. As mentioned previously in this chapter, God has empowered artists with wisdom, understanding, knowledge and their artistic skill.

6. How Do We Know What Is Right and Wrong?

"The arts are perhaps the chief means by which a society focuses attention on its own values."[32] Analyzing the values expressed by works of art in social, cultural, and historical contexts will give greater meaning to this question. Examining works of art addressing morality through thematic reference to aspects of creation, the fall, sin, redemption, and glorification provides a foundation for contemplating questions regarding values. For example, teachers could approach this question by having students examine visual artwork, listen to music, watch excerpts of ballet, films, or media art tackling themes of good versus evil and relate the interpretation to the standards God establishes in Scripture.

7. What Is the Meaning of Human History?

The arts provide a review of human thought, philosophy, and achievement through the ages. Through the arts, we can contemplate the meaning of history. According to Ryken, art "organizes the experiences of the entire race. Works of art are the collective memories of what human experience is like, arranged into the patterns of the imagination."[33] The arts have kept record of human perspectives throughout the ages, providing a means to relate the past to the present, revealing history. Teachers can have students examine works of art, analyze what the artwork discloses about a particular time and place in history, and then relate this to God's plan and faithfulness through his Word. Art easily enhances the understanding of history.

---

[32] Ryken, 36.
[33] Ryken, 35.

8. What Personal, Life-Orienting Core Commitments Are Consistent with This Worldview?

Every facet of the artistic experience (creating, performing/presenting/producing, responding, connecting) should result in glorifying God. The purpose and meaning of glorifying God with all our being should illuminate all our endeavors, artistic and otherwise. Through the arts, one is able to realize this, communicate this, and meditate on this. As Brand and Chaplin explain, "Art can create a longing for God or an awareness of God, but it cannot give us a life lived under God. That involves more than a pleasurable aesthetic experience."[34] Francis Schaeffer extends this application to the Christian life:

> No work of art is more important than the Christian's own life, and every Christian is called upon to be an artist in this sense. He may have no gift of writing, no gift of composing or singing, but each man has the gift of creativity in terms of the way he lives his life. In this sense, the Christian's life is to be an art work. The Christian's life is to be a thing of truth and also a thing of beauty in the midst of a lost and despairing world.[35]

The arts help us to express our beliefs and continually help us to dedicate ourselves to fulfilling these commitments. Teachers can have students create, perform/present/produce, relate or connect to the arts to examine and personalize worldview questions.

I began this chapter asking the reader to consider the arts. I again ask you to consider the arts as a channel for challenging your students with worldview questions and for offering them new perspectives to contemplate. This fourth "R," the arts, may never receive the same recognition and attention as other subject areas, but the arts may be the most powerful in students' lives for opening their minds to worldview thinking. The arts permeate Scripture in offering multidimensional perspectives in understanding God's truth and examples of opportunities for glorifying God. The arts provide possibilities for examining all the worldview questions, while ministering to the hearts of students in diverse ways that transcend words. All teachers should consider the arts to further integrate the Word of God within each specific discipline and to effectively promote a personal biblical worldview for all students.

---

[34] Brand and Chaplin, *Art and Soul*, 89.

[35] Schaeffer, *Art and the Bible*, 63.

CHAPTER 20

Health and Physical Education

Dick Beach

Introduction

As an undergraduate student, I took a course called History and Philosophy of Physical Education as part of my program of study. However, my appreciation for that course many years later is much greater than it was at the time. It is now a similar feeling to completing a 500-piece puzzle and then remembering what that same puzzle looked like with all those pieces scattered randomly across the table. Looking back, one can easily trace the origins and threads of themes still prominent in health and physical education. But there is a perception of underlying discontinuity summed up in the writing of Fred Leonard (1866–1922), a professor and historian who wrote in an editor's preface to his book, *A Guide to the History of Physical Education*: "The shore of physical education is strewn with the wrecks of systems and movements, many of them good in themselves, but left to drift when the personal support and enthusiasm of the founder was removed from the helm."[1] He went on to say that only in some great national crisis were efforts made that were great enough to survive the test of time and change.

---

[1] Fred Eugene Leonard, *A Guide to the History of Physical Education*, Internet Archive, 1923, accessed May 1, 2021, https://archive.org/details/guidetohistoryof00leon/page/n13/mode/2up.

Leonard's comment referenced almost 2,000 years of history related to health and physical activity. My view of the subject after a forty-year career in the field is a microcosm of his. There was so much change in such a relativity short period of time, including movements and ways of doing things introduced then discarded, seemingly overnight. There have been crises sufficient in magnitude and scope to contribute to the change.

Structure of This Discipline of Physical Education and Health

As a subject to be studied, physical activity has been part of the educational process as far back as the fourth or fifth century BC. There are several reasons for that. First, prominent historical figures such as Confucius and Hippocrates observed that people who were physically active were less likely to acquire disease and so encouraged activity in educational settings. Indeed, Hippocrates is said to have stated, "Walking is a man's best medicine."[2] Others, such as the Athenians, were able to establish a link between physical activity and function of the mind, an outcome consistently found by researchers to this day.[3] Philosophers, and later the apostle Paul, found a link between activity and moral and spiritual development. Even later Martin Luther is recorded as having spoken of physical activity as being more beneficial than the medical practices of his day.[4]

This linkage of body, mind, and spirit was also implemented in settings not exclusively educational such as the Young Men's Christian Association. There has been a long-standing connection between physical activity and characteristics of good health such as lack of disease, a sound mind, and good character. For much of America's history, health and physical education have existed together in schools in an informal curriculum that was primarily activity-based and at times as simple and unstructured as recess and occasional talks by a school nurse.

---

[2] David C. Batman, "Hippocrates: 'Walking Is Man's Best Medicine!'" *Occupational Medicine* 62, no. 5 (July 2012):320–22. https://pubmed.ncbi.nlm.nih.gov/22764266/.

[3] See Brock Armstrong, "How Exercise Affects Your Brain," *Scientific American*, December 26, 2018, https://www.scientificamerican.com/article/how-exercise-affects-your-brain.

[4] See Martin Luther, "The Table Talk of Martin Luther: On Sickness and the Causes Thereof," trans. William Hazlitt, accessed May 1, 2021, https://ccel.org/ccel/luther/tabletalk/tabletalk.v.xxxii.html.

Change and the Emerging Focus on the Importance of the Subject

It is useful to understand how cultural crises foster change. There were three events that occurred within a relatively short period during the 1950s that precipitated change in health and physical education. The first crisis came to light in the 1950s and centered on youth fitness. In the 1940s Dr. Hans Kraus, a New York physician, developed a battery of muscular fitness tests along with a colleague, Sonja Weber. This test became known as the Kraus-Weber tests and was widely recognized and utilized as a good means of determining physical fitness. In the early 1950s Bonnie Prudden, a well-known fitness expert, did wide-scale administration of the test to school-age children in the United States and several countries in Europe. Prudden found that over half of American school-age children failed the test compared with failure rates of under 10 percent for a similar sample in European countries.[5] Kraus and Prudden published the results of these tests, which became public record and the source of considerable media attention.[6] Prudden was later invited to present her findings to President Dwight Eisenhower who was dismayed by the revelations.

The second crisis involved the president himself. In September of 1955, while playing golf in Colorado, Eisenhower developed chest pains and was hospitalized and found to have had a massive heart attack. A Massachusetts cardiologist, Dr. Paul Dudley White, was recruited to consult on Eisenhower's case and gained a good deal of notoriety in the process. He was already an outspoken advocate for activity and lifestyle as a means of preventing heart disease, and his association with the president gave him an effective pulpit from which to advocate for his positions.[7] The third crisis originated on October 4, 1957, when the Russians jumped out to an early lead into space launching a satellite called Sputnik.[8] This was during the Cold War when tensions were already high. The Russian success served to focus our nation on determining the

---

[5] See "About Bonnie Prudden," Bonnie Prudden Educational Institute, accessed May, 1, 2021, https://bonnieprudden.org/about-bonnie-prudden/.

[6] See Hans Kraus and Bonnie Prudden, "Comparison of Fitness of Danish and American School Children," *Research Quarterly, American Association for Health, Education and Recreation* (1961).

[7] See Henry Blackburn, "Paul Dudley White, MD," University of Minnesota, accessed May 1, 2021, http://www.epi.umn.edu/cvdepi/bio-sketch/white-paul-dudley/.

[8] See Alvin Powell, "How Sputnik Changed U. S. Education," *Harvard Gazette*, October 11, 2007, https://news.harvard.edu/gazette/story/2007/10/how-sputnik-changed-u-s-education/.

reasons we were behind. Attention quickly centered on the need to improve science and engineering curricula specifically. However, all of education came under scrutiny. The three crises combined to create an environment for reform that impacted all aspects of education including health and physical education programs.

Reforms

Some responses were almost immediate, others took longer. President Eisenhower established the President's Council on Sports, Fitness, and Nutrition within a year of receiving the Kraus-Weber results.[9] The organization has a goal of promoting programs and initiatives that motivate people to lead active, healthy lives. While there have been some implemented initiatives that have been beneficial, such as the Presidential Youth Fitness Programs, others have had limited success in stemming the tide of health issues associated with a lack of physical activity.

Paul Dudley White's message of activity as a means of preventing cardiovascular disease specifically, and other diseases more generally, however, fell on receptive ears. It hearkened back to the emphases held by Confucius and Hippocrates millennia earlier. The publicity associated with the results of the Kraus-Weber tests initiated a change in the way physical education was perceived by the public and brought about calls for change in the emphasis of content and the way it was delivered; instead of an overemphasis on sports and games, there was more concern for outcomes contributing to good health.

The health and physical education profession responded with calls for improved curricula, more class time, better credentialing of practitioners, and a general emphasis on making health and physical education more a part of the educational mainstream. Professional organizations such as the American Alliance for Health, Physical Education and Dance (now the Society for Health and Physical Educators or SHAPE) advocated for more class time and improved credentials for practitioners. Prominent educator Muska Mosston introduced his Spectrum of Teaching Styles to the physical education profession.[10] He was also among the first to advocate for a change in terminology away

---

[9] See "About the President's Council on Sports, Fitness and Nutrition," US Department of Health and Human Services, accessed April 25, 2021, https://health.gov/our-work/pcsfn/about-pcsfn.

[10] See "About Muska Mosston," Spectrum of Teaching Styles, accessed May 11, 2021, https://spectrumofteachingstyles.org/.

from *physical education* to *kinesiology* at the university level. Dr. Kenneth Cooper developed his aerobics system,[11] published numerous books on the benefits of activity, and established the Cooper Institute.[12] The Institute has remained a leading advocate for the benefits of activity in school and community settings.

While other countries have experienced similar changes in physical education and health programs, this review of the history of physical education in the United States as it relates to health is important in establishing the "structure" of the subject. Structure reviews the logical reasons for the subject, the general outline of topic content, the way of judging truth related to the content, and the relationship of the subject to other subjects and learning in general.

One Result Leading in Change of Curriculum

What may not have initially been intended as the result of historical research and conclusions was a split of health and physical education into two separate fields. Much of the impetus for this was generated by changes in credentialing for teachers of health. The National Commission for Health Education Credentialing[13] led the way in that process. The result, in the United States, was that credentialed specialists were teaching health education, and traditional physical educators were teaching just physical education. Today, some states require both areas in one certification so that both are given equal emphasis in an integrated way. However, there exists not only significant differences between the two fields but they have, effectively, become separate disciplines in spite of how they might be credentialed by governments or national organizations. So, as we look at structure, we examine them as two separate but related entities: health education and physical education.

---

[11] See "Kenneth H. Cooper, MD, MPH Full Bio," Cooper Aerobics , accessed May 2012, https://cooperaerobics.com/About/Our-Leaders/Kenneth-H-Cooper,-MD,-MPH-Full-Bio .aspx.

[12] See "Mission Statement and Core Values," Cooper Institute, accessed June 22, 2022, https://www.cooperinstitute.org/mission/.

[13] See "Health Education Credentialing," National Commission for Health Education Credentialing, accessed April 2021, https://www.nchec.org/health-education-credentialing.

Logical Organization of Health Education

USA National Health Education Standards are quite specific in describing the components of health education.[14] We reference these standards but assume that other countries have similar standards for review by practitioners. Health education is a social science. Researchers study societies or communities with a particular emphasis on the relationships among members of society with the primary goals to prevent disease, disability, and premature death by encouraging voluntary behavior change. They seek to improve health knowledge, attitudes, skills, and behavior through the development of strategies based on an individual, group, institution, community, and larger system. The purpose of health education is to positively influence the health behavior of individuals and communities as well as the living and working conditions that influence their health. Health education is delivered in educational settings through a sequential, structured curricula to students in kindergarten through twelfth grades. When implemented successfully, health education contributes to overall community health by providing individuals with the knowledge by which to make behavioral changes underlying healthy living. Healthy living is a God-given goal for humans whom he created in his image!

Logical Organization of Physical Education

The United States Centers for Disease Control (CDC) describes the organization of modern physical education as consisting of a sequential K–12 curriculum that is based on the national standards for physical education,[15] providing instruction that is both cognitive and physical in nature and designed to develop motor skills, knowledge, and behaviors for physical activity and physical fitness.

Sequence is one of two major components of a curriculum, *scope* being the other. Sequence starts with the establishment of fundamental movement patterns and then moves on to more advanced movements as readiness dictates. Sequential progression is always important but especially so when a more advanced movement is based on one more basic. Motor skills underlie the completion of any intentional movement. The specific components of motor skills will be addressed under Key Concepts below.

---

[14] See "National Health Education Standards," Centers for Disease Control and Prevention, accessed April 2021, https://www.cdc.gov/healthyschools/sher/standards/index.htm.

[15] See "Physical Education," Centers for Disease Control and Prevention, accessed April 2021, https://www.cdc.gov/healthyschools/physicalactivity/physical-education.htm.

The intentional introduction of a cognitive instructional component helps ensure that the "how" of a movement, which may be mostly physical, is accompanied by the "why." This is particularly true when learning new skills for which technique is important. Performance may suffer temporarily when learning proper technique; students want to know why.

Key Concepts in Health Education

The US National Health Education Standards were developed in 1995 by a joint committee representing the American Public Health Association, the American School Health Association, and the American Association for Health Education (AAHE). There are eight separate standards defining what students should know and be able to do at four different grade levels. The key concepts in health education are geared toward achievement of these standards. Other countries have their own standards that are not only worthy but essential for those in country to follow. In this chapter, I offer input with which I am familiar.

The most basic concept is developing a student's ability to understand that good health derives from activities that promote the ability to function at the best possible level, while at the same time avoiding infectious disease. A second concept is understanding how other elements in our environment such as family, friends, culture, media, technology, and other factors (e.g., value system) influence behaviors that affect our health. A third concept centers on developing proficiency in being able to access correct information and quality products and services that affect our health. In other words, to become wise health consumers. A fourth concept involves a student being able to develop the ability to use interpersonal communication skills to enhance health and avoid activities that constitute a health risk. A fifth concept targets a student developing and demonstrating the ability to make good choices to enhance health. A sixth concept centers on students learning and demonstrating the ability to use goal-setting skills to enhance health. A seventh concept builds on goal setting by turning those goals into consistent practice of health-enhancing behavior and health risk avoidance. The final concept deals with students developing and demonstrating the ability to advocate for personal, family, and community health.[16]

From a Christian perspective, each of these basic concepts must be viewed through the overall goal to live a life on this planet as healthy as possible for the glory of God,

---

[16] See "National Health Education Standards."

serving him with our whole being; this includes our bodies. This objective puts into practice the admonition of the apostle Paul in his letter to the Corinthian church where he references bodily self-discipline as a way by which to enhance ministry efficacy (1 Cor 9:17).

The standards referenced above lay out expectations for knowing and doing at four different grades levels. Below you will find performance indicators or learning outcomes for the first standard listed as an example of how the expectations would vary by grade.[17] These indicators may be used by one not familiar with a set of national standards to begin to promote student health.

Pre-K–Grade 2

- Identify healthy behaviors that impact personal health.
- Recognize there are multiple dimensions of health.
- Describe ways to prevent communicable diseases.
- List ways to prevent common childhood injuries.
- Describe why it is important to seek health care.

Grades 3–5

- Describe the relationship between healthy behaviors and personal health.
- Identify examples of emotional, intellectual, physical, and social health.
- Describe ways in which safe and healthy school and community environments can promote personal health.
- Describe ways to prevent common childhood injuries and health problems.
- Describe when it is important to seek health care.

Grades 6–8

- Analyze the relationship between healthy behaviors and personal health.
- Describe the interrelationships of emotional, intellectual, physical, and social health in adolescence.
- Analyze how the environment affects personal health.

---

[17] See "Standard 1: Performance Indicators," Centers for Disease Control, accessed May 15, 2021, https://www.cdc.gov/healthyschools/sher/standards/1.htm.

- Describe how family history can affect personal health.
- Describe ways to reduce or prevent injuries and other adolescent health problems.
- Explain how appropriate health care can promote personal health.
- Describe the benefits of and barriers to practicing healthy behaviors.
- Examine the likelihood of injury or illness if engaging in unhealthy behaviors.
- Examine the potential seriousness of injury or illness if engaging in unhealthy behaviors.

Grades 9–12

- Predict how healthy behaviors can affect health status.
- Describe the interrelationships of emotional, intellectual, physical, and social health.
- Analyze how environment and personal health are interrelated.
- Analyze how genetics and family history can impact personal health.
- Propose ways to reduce or prevent injuries and health problems.
- Analyze the relationship between access to health care and health status.
- Compare and contrast the benefits of and barriers to practicing a variety of healthy behaviors.
- Analyze personal susceptibility to injury, illness, or death if engaging in unhealthy behaviors.
- Analyze the potential severity of injury or illness if engaging in unhealthy behaviors.

The action verbs defining each learning outcome or performance indicator are like those proposed by Bloom[18] in his taxonomy, addressed in chapter 6. These action verbs describe the cognitive processes by which learners encounter and work with knowledge they discover. You see higher order activities such as propose and predict used as performance indicators for grades 9–12 while performance indicators at lower grade levels use action words from lower-level learning outcome categories.

---

[18] See "What Is Bloom's Taxonomy?" Bloom's Taxonomy, accessed May 15, 2021, https://www.bloomstaxonomy.net/.

Key Concepts in Physical Education

The Society of Health and Physical Educators (SHAPE) has coined the phrase "physical literacy" and describes a physically literate person as one who is able to pursue a lifetime of healthful physical activity. Physical literacy has been achieved when the student has learned the skills necessary to participate in a variety of physical activities, knows the implications and the benefits of involvement in various types of physical activities, participates regularly in physical activity, and is physically fit and values physical activity and its contributions to a healthful lifestyle.[19]

The first concept centers on the student demonstrating competency in a variety of motor skills and movement patterns beginning with the development of fundamental movement patterns, a foundation on which all other movements are based. The second concept is cognitive in nature and involves developing the ability to effectively apply principles, strategies, and tactics to movement and skill performance. The third concept involves developing the knowledge and skills to achieve and maintain levels of physical activity and fitness by which to enhance fitness. The fourth concept derives from developed attitudes and encourages demonstration of personal and social behavior that is responsible and respects others as well. The fifth concept centers on teaching students to recognize the various values that derive from physical activity, including social interaction enhancement, challenge of self and others, the use of activity as a means of self-expression, and enhanced health.[20] An individual student's progress in mastering these concepts can be evaluated using the standards that follow for the three grade level groupings referenced.[21]

Elementary School Outcomes (K–Grade 5)

By the end of elementary school, students will be able to demonstrate competence in basic motor skills and a combination of skills. They will also be able to possess

---

[19] See "Physical Literacy," SHAPE America (Society of Health and Physical Educators), www.shapeamerica.org, accessed January 17, 2022, https://www.shapeamerica.org/events/physicalliteracy.aspx.

[20] See "The Essential Components of Physical Education," 2015. SHAPE America—Society of Health and Physical Educators, accessed April 2021, https://www.shapeamerica.org//upload/TheEssentialComponentsOfPhysicalEducation.pdf.

[21] See *Grade-Level Outcomes for K-12 Physical Education*, SHAPE America—Society of Health and Physical Educators, accessed January 17, 2022, https://www.shapeamerica.org/standards/pe/upload/Grade-Level-Outcomes-for-K-12–Physical-Education.pdf.

basic movement concepts in small practice tasks, gymnastics, and dance, and will be able to identify several basic fitness concepts. Students in these formative years should be able to accept their abilities and others' abilities in physical activities and be able to understand the benefits of a physically active lifestyle.

Middle School Outcomes (Grades 6–8)

By the end of middle school, students should be able to apply several strategies in modified game play and demonstrate fundamental movement skills in several different settings and environments. Students in this age group should also be able to participate in self-guided physical activities, collaborate and work together with other classmates, and accept individual differences. They should also be actively engaged in physical activity for both self-expression and enjoyment.

High School Outcomes (Grades 9–12)

By the end of high school, students will be fully prepared to demonstrate their readiness for careers or college through their ability to plan and implement any number of personal fitness programs. They will also be able to demonstrate their competency in at least two lifetime activities while modeling responsible behavior associated with physical activity. These young adults should also be actively participating in physical activities that challenge them, encourage social interaction, and result in self-expression and personal enjoyment.

Methods of Inquiry for Health Education

While health education is considered a social science, it draws on other sciences including biological, psychological, medical, and environmental science as sources of knowledge.[22] *Health is defined as a state of physical, mental, and social well-being in which disease and infirmity are absent.*[23] Inquiry into other sciences provides understanding of how each might contribute to health. While it is understood that the nature of science is an investigation into the natural world using the senses and reason, it is also understood that science knowledge gained is always open to further investigation and change.

---

[22] See "National Health Education Standards."

[23] See Constitution of the World Health Organization—Basic Documents, Forty-fifth edition, Supplement, October 2006.

Physical education and health teachers must keep up with the changes that might significantly improve the understanding of the students.

Biological sciences study living organisms including their reproduction and growth. The human body has structure in the form of cells, tissues, organs, and systems.[24] The normal operation of these various levels of structure results in function outcomes. We call the structure of anything anatomy.[25] Physiology is normal function and can refer specifically to any of the four levels of structure or the body in total.[26] Anatomy and basic exercise physiology contribute to the body of knowledge underlying health education. Both anatomy and physiology are based on chemical processes including cell structure and function and molecular interactions. Important areas of inquiry within biological science would be nutrition, or what we put in our bodies, and activity, including the types and amounts. Both nutrition and activity are significant influences not only on structure but function. Physical well-being is enhanced by normal structure and function of the body in concert with normal psychological function.[27]

Psychological sciences deal with mental processes including, but not limited to, how we learn, what determines our personality, and what shapes our attitudes. Behaviors, or the things we do, are influenced greatly by all three of these factors. As no two people are exactly alike, it is to be expected that there would be a range over which learning capabilities, personalities, and attitudes could vary but still be normal. Departures from that range are generally called disorders and take many different forms. Severe disorders in the learning area are called learning disabilities and can be caused by genetic factors or neurobiological factors.[28] In the personality area, severe disorders fall into three general categories called clusters.[29] Cluster A disorders are characterized by odd or eccentric patterns of thinking, such as extreme social

---

[24] See Webster-Dictionary.org, s.v. "biological science," accessed January 18, 2022, https://www.webster-dictionary.org/definition/biological%20science.

[25] See Webster-Dictionary.org, s.v. "anatomy," accessed January 18, 2022, https://www.webster-dictionary.org/definition/anatomy.

[26] See Webster-Dictionary.org WordNet Dictionary, s.v. "physiology," accessed January 18, 2022, https://www.webster-dictionary.org/definition/physiology.

[27] See "Health-Related Quality of Life: Well-Being Concepts," Centers for Disease Control and Prevention, accessed January 18, 2022, https://www.cdc.gov/hrqol/wellbeing.htm.

[28] See "Types of Learning Disabilities," Learning Disabilities Association of America, accessed May 17, 2021, https://ldaamerica.org/types-of-learning-disabilities/.

[29] See "Personality Disorders," Psychology Today, accessed May 17, 2021, https://www.psychologytoday.com/us/basics/personality-disorders.

detachment, distrust, or unusual beliefs. Cluster B disorders feature unstable emotional states and erratic behavior, which can involve aggression toward or manipulation of others. Cluster C disorders involve anxious or fearful patterns of thinking and relating to others. Much of healthy living involves the ability to exist in meaningful relationships, and so the psychological sciences become an important area of inquiry for health education. Mental well-being is determined by normal function in all areas relating to the psychological sciences.[30]

Medicine, by definition, involves the treatment of diseases by various means.[31] Disease involves a functional breakdown, usually of a body system. Functional breakdown can occur a variety of ways. A common cause of breakdown is infection, meaning that a harmful substance has been introduced in the body and interferes with normal system function. Examples of these harmful substances include germs and poisons. Germs are small organisms and may take the form of bacteria or virus.[32] The study of the causes of infection is a branch of epidemiology.[33] Preventive medicine includes epidemiology as well as the study of any other causes of functional breakdown including factors such as nutrition or activity levels.[34]

Environmental science is described as an interdisciplinary science pursuing study of how natural and man-made processes interact with one another and ultimately affect the plants and animals living on the earth.[35] This becomes an important area of inquiry for health education in that living beings are very dependent on the regular intake of food, air, and water from the environment to sustain normal function, or good health. All three of these substances are known to be potential sources of infection. It is important to know how to protect their origin or remediate contamination in order to

---

[30] See "Personality Disorders," Psychology Today.

[31] See Merriam-Webster.com, s.v. "medicine," accessed January 18, 2022, https://www.merriam-webster.com/dictionary/medicine.

[32] See "Germs: Understand and Protect against Bacteria, Viruses and Infection," Mayo Clinic, January 18, 2022, https://www.mayoclinic.org/diseases-conditions/infectious-diseases/in-depth/germs/art-20045289.

[33] See "epidemiology," McGraw-Hill Concise Dictionary of Modern Medicine, accessed January 18, 2022, https://medical-dictionary.thefreedictionary.com/Epidemiolgy.

[34] See "Health Care: Preventive Care," U.S. Department of Health & Human Services, accessed January 18, 2022, https://www.hhs.gov/healthcare/about-the-aca/preventive-care/index.html.

[35] See "What Is Environmental Science?" Environmentalscience.org, accessed May 17, 2021, https://www.environmentalscience.org/.

avoid unhealthy consequences. All of these areas of inquiry use the methods of science, a field of study open to further investigation and changes.

Methods of Inquiry for Physical Education

Physical education draws from several fields of study. These include anatomy, physiology, exercise physiology, biomechanics, biochemistry, and motor learning. In total, these are often referred to as movement sciences or kinesiology.

Anatomy is the study of structure of organisms and their component parts. Understanding the structure of the human body underlies our ability to understand how it moves. The study of anatomy by physical educators focuses mostly on the skeletal and muscular systems and their interaction. Muscles exert pull on bones, and that is the means by which movement is initiated and controlled. Study of nervous system function is also important as it is the nervous system that provides stimulation to muscles, causing them to shorten or allowing elongation.

Physiology is the study of the function of an organism and the various systems of which it consists. **Exercise physiology** expands that study, focusing on the function of the body and body systems in an exertion state, or above normal activity levels. There are several principles that come into play when the body is exerted or exercised. Adaptation involves change that occurs because of exertion.[36] Muscle, when exerted, typically gets larger, increases the amount of force it can produce, and is able to produce force for a longer period. As adaptation occurs, body function achieves new "normal" levels, so exercise must be adjusted over time for adaptation to continue. This is the overload principle.[37] Exertion can occur at higher levels of intensity or for longer periods of time. Body systems will respond differently to exertion at higher intensity than for exertion for longer periods of time. These differences in response are typical of the specificity principle.[38]

---

[36] See "Physiological Adaptation," Biology Online, accessed January 18, 2022, https://www .biologyonline.com/dictionary/physiological-adaptation.

[37] See Mark D. Peterson et al., "Progression of Volume Load and Muscular Adaptation During Resistance Exercise," *European Journal of Applied Physiology* 111, no. 6 (2011): 1063–71, https://doi.org/10.1007/s00421-010-1735-9.

[38] See "Principle of Specificity," Oxford Reference of Sports Science & Medicine, accessed June 22, 2022, https://www.oxfordreference.com/view/10.1093/oi/authority.20110810105645

Biomechanics is the study of mechanical laws applied to human movement. Most important of these laws are those developed by Sir Isaac Newton, referred to as Newtonian Physics. Newton built on the work of predecessors such as Galileo in developing his three laws of motion: the law of inertia, the law of acceleration, and the law of reaction.[39] All human movement is affected by these laws in some way and so they constitute much of the focus of inquiry into biomechanics.

Biochemistry is the study of chemical processes in living organisms. In humans, chemical processes underlie the function of body systems such as the respiratory, digestive, muscular, and nervous systems. Chemical processes allow us to breathe, convert food into energy useable by cells, stimulate muscles to contract, and transmit nervous stimuli throughout the body.

Motor learning can be described as the study of movement learning or causation. It refers to the study of psychological and neural mechanisms that underlie skilled movement. Psychological concepts such as arousal and attention and neural mechanisms such as memory, intelligence, and pain sensation would all be related to motor learning or motor neuroscience.

Implications

Physical Activity

Despite the attention given to learning styles, the teacher and student should remember that physical education is primarily about activity, and so movement is the best modality by which to teach and learn. I have been playing golf and riding a bicycle for the better part of fifty years, and I can guarantee you that both of those activities are learned best with club in hand and feet on the pedals. That is not to say that there are no other approaches you can interject. They say a picture is worth a thousand words, but getting the kinesthetic feel of a movement is better than either.

210#:~:text=principle%20of%20specificity%20Quick%20Reference%20A%20basic%20 training,a%20person%20must%20emphasize%20that%20component%20in%20training.

[39] See Andrew Zimmerman Jones, "Introduction to Newton's Laws of Motion," ThoughtCo, February 12, 2020, https://www.thoughtco.com/introduction-to-newtons-laws -of-motion-2698881.

Make It Fun!

Good physical educators make learning fun. When learners are enjoying what they are doing, it generates an intrinsic motivation that they can depend on through the learning process.

Teachers should develop effective use of cue words to assist learners. Cue words may paint a word picture or help the learner with a movement concept. They are usually short descriptive phrases and may just be a reminder to employ an important skill component. One example I have found useful is the "baby bird" illustration somebody gave me as it relates to swinging a golf club. Gripping the golf club too tightly develops tension in the swing and causes you to lose distance and feel. Holding the club like you would hold a baby bird causes you to impart just enough force to control the club but discourages the development of too much muscle tension.

Variety

Another important learning strategy in physical education is introducing variety. Students tend to concentrate on things they already do well. Pushing them out of their comfort zone exposes them to their weaknesses. Working on weaknesses is the key to skill mastery.

More One-on-One Instruction

Physical education has typically been taught using the cohort method with a large group of students and one instructor. Team teaching came into practice to help move the instruction more toward individualized and personalized learning. Teachers need to be intentional and creative about finding ways to accomplish more individual instruction. One such way to accomplish this is to use older students to teach basic skills on a low ratio basis to younger students. The result is highly effective outcomes with less time invested by the single instructor. An additional benefit is the reinforcement of the skill for the older student.[40]

---

[40] Saga Briggs, ""How Peer Teaching Improves Student Learning and 10 Ways to Encourage It," InformED, June 7, 2013, https://www.opencolleges.edu.au/informed/features/peer-teaching/#:~:text=The%20main%20benefits%20of%20peer%20teaching%20include%2C%20but,discourse%2C%20allowing%20for%20greater%20understanding.%20More%20items...%20.

Assessment

I conclude this section with some additional comments about the fourth component SHAPE referenced as part of a quality physical education program, regular assessment. This is an area, based on my observations, that I think could be done much better.

Standards, by definition, call for a means of determining achievement of that standard. Standards without assessment to determine achievement are not really standards. Assessment is the measurement and evaluation of performance. It sounds simple and should be straightforward. Assessment tools for physical education have been developed and validated for years. There are test batteries in existence to evaluate virtually every known physical activity. All the standards that make up the key concepts addressed earlier are measurable and can be evaluated. States such as New York have had standardized assessment tools for more than fifty years. Many countries around the world have published standardized assessments as well.[41]

The big debate in physical education for many years has been over how to evaluate assessment results. Norm-referenced evaluation involves comparison of an individual's results with others in their population. That works if you have a sufficient number in the sample and if you just want to know where one's performance stands relative to his or her peers. However, it does not address one's status relative to a standard.

Many assessment specialists advocate the use of criterion-referenced tests, which are designed to measure student performance against a fixed set of predetermined criteria or performance standards.[42] When dealing with health issues such as obesity, you want to know whether an individual is healthy as measured by a typical standard, or just a little more healthy or unhealthy than his or her peers. Application of standards and use of a criterion-referenced tests are essential in measuring health.

Formative evaluation is that which occurs during and early in learning. I have found this type of evaluation gives the student an idea of his or her progress regardless of outcome, can assist in motivation, and can provide direction on specific skills on which to work. Well-designed formative evaluation can be an effective part of your

---

[41] New York State Education Dept., Albany, *The New York State Physical Fitness Screening Test for Boys and Girls Grades 4–12 (1976 Revision): A Manual for Teachers of Physical Education,*" available for download at https://eric.ed.gov/?id=ED133356.

[42] See "Criterion-Referenced Test," Great Schools Partnership, The Glossary of Education Reform, updated April 30, 2014, https://www.edglossary.org/criterion-referenced-test/.

instructional assessment process as well as indicating where changes in instructional methods might be warranted.

Finally, assessment should have, as one of its goals, the ability to discern differences in performance or goal achievement that should addressed. This is often not practiced in physical education classes but should be. One very simple way to achieve this is to use continuous rather than discrete measures when determining fitness status. Discrete measurement intervals often infer equality in outcome or status, particularly where intervals used are quite large. When goal achievement is determined using discrete measurements, reaching a higher goal can seem very difficult depending on the size of the discrete measurement interval.

Standard for Testing and Judging Truth in Health Education

Realistically, standards for testing and judging truth in curricular content for physical education and health fall into one of two categories for the Christian educator: (1) Does God's Word speak to this issue specifically or in general principle? and (2) What is the scientific research behind the information; has it been peer reviewed for quality? Science information is open to change as more research is conducted, data analyzed, and conclusions suggested. Both God's Word (special revelation) and his world (general revelation) are sources for information.

When the Bible speaks to an issue directly or in principle, the Christian teacher should use it to help students develop biblical integrative thinking. What does God say about health and activity and the social issues related, for example? When science information seems to be in clear conflict with the curriculum, the Scripture speaks with unchanging authority. However, when the curriculum reporting the science does not conflict with something clearly stated in Scripture, use it freely. It is common grace to have scientific discoveries and their applications. Part of the mandate of Scripture is to have dominion over God's creation and use it for his glory.

As a self-described social science, it appears to this writer that establishing standards for testing and judging truth in health education is potentially difficult for several reasons. A casual look at the key concepts reveals many that are problematic in several ways. First, several concepts are culturally defined, and as culture changes, they change. Behaviors relating to health that were forbidden just a few decades ago are now allowed or even encouraged. Take the use of marijuana as an example. People used to go to jail for using and distributing it. Now it is fully legal in fourteen states and legal for medical use in all but two states. The same can be said of family, peers, and the media as influences related to behaviors. In an ideal world, a family would be the most significant factor in influencing positive health behaviors. We understand the powerful influence peers have on each other, and there is as much potential for negative influence as positive. In spite of the changes in legality for a substance, the Christian must ask, What is a biblical principle that may apply? How should Christ-followers care for their bodies and why?

There are content areas within health education that espouse secular values that run contrary to a Christian's moral dictates. For example, some modern trends in sex education have been so altered by secular cultural influence that they now create a moral dilemma. These include current trends relating to sexual orientation. A Christian teacher will be called upon to address these culturally accepted behaviors from a biblical perspective with love and understanding. It is not my view but God's view on life and learning that matters most. His Word is unchanging and absolute when it speaks to specific issues and the big questions of life.

Do not be afraid to research what the Bible says about an issue specifically or in principle so that you can have open discussions and create activities to challenge students to seek God's view in his Word. In my view, that makes Christian school education and homeschooling more attractive, and indeed, perhaps more necessary today than ever before, here in the United States and around the world.

Standard for Testing and Judging Truth in Physical Education

Much of the content area in physical education is based on principles of motor learning or human physiology. When God created humans, he gave us a body he designed and tells us to present our bodies to him as part of our service to him (1 Cor 6:12–20). Healthy, functioning bodies are vital to living for his glory. While there is little said in Scripture concerning motor development, God has given us the ability to discover information about our bodies through science. Motor control and human exercise physiology are active areas of inquiry. New facts are being learned all the time. I cannot blame my high school football coach for restricting water intake and giving us salt pills during those hot weeks in August. He was using the best information available at the time. Football coaches should have moved on from that practice given more current research. Similarly, methods used to increase flexibility "back in the day" have been proven to be counterproductive and new methods dominate practice today. Practitioners have a responsibility to stay current.

Issues in Health Education and Physical Education

I conclude with some comments on issues that are prevalent relative to these two areas of education. The most glaring issue is the lack of positive outcome as it relates to health. Despite documented benefits where good practices are followed, the results in general have been abysmal. Obesity is one such area—for both children and adults. According to the Centers for Disease Control, in 2018 over 40 percent of the US population was obese.[43] That represents a 12 percent increase in the last twenty years. Obesity results in medical costs in the amount of $147 billion annually.[44]

Drug abuse is rampant. According to the Vermont Department of Health,[45] non-fatal overdoses increased more than 137 percent in one year from 2019 to 2020. Drug overdose fatalities were up in a one-year period more than 28 percent in the states of Kentucky and Colorado and the city of Chicago.

Advocacy groups such as SHAPE and the CDC have called for daily PE and a minimum total time per week.[46] They have also encouraged government funding be made available for professional development. Those calls have remained largely unanswered. Twenty-eight US states allow some sort of waiver to the daily require-ment. Less than half the states require any specific amount of time. Only ten states allocate funds for professional development for PE and health teachers. Only six states require physical education in every grade, and just six states have requirements that meet or exceed total time per week recommendations. This is true in other nations as well.[47] This should not be so in Christian schools. Time intentionally assigned for physical education is a must to the health of a population and community!

States are much more likely to meet recommended requirements for staffing and providing support for professional development. However, there is considerable

---

[43] Division of Nutrition, Physical Activity, and Obesity, National Center for Chronic Disease Prevention and Health Promotion, Overweight & Obesity, "Adult Obesity Facts," CDC website, last reviewed September 30, 2021, https://www.cdc.gov/obesity/data/adult.html.

[44] Division of Nutrition, Physical Activity, and Obesity, "Adult Obesity Facts."

[45] See Suzette Gomez, "Opioid-Related Deaths Are on the Rise in America," Addiction Center, December 4, 2020, https://www.addictioncenter.com/news/2020/12/opioid-deaths-on-the-rise.

[46] See "Loopholes Stalling Progress in Physical Education Across the US," SHAPE America, accessed May 2021, https://www.shapeamerica.org/advocacy/son/upload/shape-of-the-nation-infographic1.pdf.

[47] See Melissa Davie, "Australian and New Zealand Teenagers among Most Inactive in the World," *Guardian*, November 21, 2019, https://www.theguardian.com/australia-news/2019/nov/22/australian-and-new-zealand-teenagers-among-most-inactive-in-the-world.

inequity in terms of what is covered in the curriculum from state to state and from country to country.

There is solid research[48] indicating that quality, school-based health education programs can improve the health and well-being of children and youth as well. There is positive data pointing toward the potential of these disciplines to contribute toward resolution of major health issues if emphasized properly both in the US and around the world. Furthermore, Christians should see care for health and body as a charge, as we are the "temple of God" on this planet and should keep the "vessel" as strong and healthy as possible (Eph 5:29).

Establishing healthy behaviors for younger people is easier and more effective than changing unhealthy behaviors once they become established. Reminds me of my grandmother telling me, "An ounce of prevention is worth a pound of cure."

Key Biblical Worldview Questions Related to Physical Education and Health

Worldview questions and answers are considered a framework for understanding and give meaning to life. There are several that are vital in the two subject areas addressed in this chapter that are derived from the nature of the disciplines.

Who Is God?

God is the Creator. What did he create? The Apostles' Creed answers simply: "heaven and earth." Genesis 1 gives a much more complete response and shares who and what he created—all things including humankind, man and woman, *in his own image.* This means that I am his creation given unique capacities that mirror, to some degree, the divine nature of God.[49]

---

[48] See "Health Education in Schools—The Importance of Establishing Healthy Behaviors in Our Nation's Youth," American Cancer Society, the American Diabetes Association, and the American Heart Association on Health Education, June 2008, https://www.heart.org/-/media /files/about-us/policy-research/prevention-obesity-prevention/health-education-in-schools -ucm_467656.pdf?la=en.

[49] "What Does 'Imago Dei' Mean? The Image of God in the Bible," Christianity.com, June 25, 2019, https://www.christianity.com/wiki/bible/image-of-god-meaning-imago-dei-in-the -bible.html.

God is personal and triune; in the person of Jesus Christ, he is my Savior. His death on the cross purchased, at great price, my freedom from sin and a restored relationship with him. Lastly, based on my salvation through faith in Christ, God in the person of the Holy Spirit has taken up residence in my body. How does this relate to health and physical education? God is the sovereign Creator and authority of the universe who holds us accountable for how we treat our bodies, that which he made in his image and within which he resides.

Who Am I?

I am a created being, in the very image of God; I am his. He owns me. While salvation is a gift for which I did not work, I have a work to do here on earth as God directs. I am to think, decide, and choose to act in such a way as to please him in obedience and thankfulness for what he has done for me. Ephesians 2:8–10 gives us a complete picture: "For you are saved by grace through faith, and this is not from yourselves; it is God's gift—not from works, so that no one can boast. For we are his workmanship, created in Christ Jesus for good works, which God prepared ahead of time for us to do."

When I take this seriously, it should have significant implications for how I care for my body and encourage my students to do likewise; however, my body does not define who I am in Christ but rather serves as an instrument of his, and for his glory.

What Are the Implications Related to These Worldview Questions for a Practitioner of Health and Physical Education?

Expressed another way, what personal and professional behaviors should derive from my relationship to God? Being made by God and in his image gives us tremendous value. And indeed, viewed properly it gives tremendous value to all those with whom we come in contact. I am relational by nature as an image-bearer. Fully appreciating the value God has placed on each of his creations should have a profound impact on our relationships. It shapes how we view humanity, those students we see every day. Relationship building is a vital part of physical activity in sports, in group experiences, and in lifelong activities such as walking, biking, golfing, swimming, and the like.

I used to be somewhat discouraged by 1 Tim 4:8, particularly that first phrase: "For the training of the body has limited benefit, but godliness is beneficial in every way, since it holds promise for the present life and also for the life to come."

As I think about this verse, I noticed there are two comparisons at play in the verse that help us put physical training in perspective. First, physical activity compared to godliness. What clear-thinking Christian would not affirm that godliness is superior? The second comparison is between life on earth compared to eternity. My conclusion is, yes, my current physical body is only going to last me for the time God allows me on this earth, but I would be a fool not to maintain it so I can function at the very best for my age and circumstances all for his glory.

Furthermore, the Bible addresses our bodies as the very residence of the Holy Spirit. First Corinthians 6:19–20 asks, "Don't you know that your body is a temple of the Holy Spirit who is in you, whom you have from God? You are not your own, for you were bought at a price. So, glorify God with your body."

Encourage every student to go to every length possible to glorify God appropriately with body and mind. Schools, especially Christian schools, need great physical education and health programs as part of the regular curriculum and not as add-ons.

CHAPTER 21

Structure of the Bible

Susan J. Allen and April Murrie

Introduction

More so than any other curricular or extracurricular opportunity, the Christian teacher who becomes a Bible teacher has a unique privilege to connect his/her personal teaching philosophy and testimony of faith with a full class period of God's Word that has the potential to change lives that day and for eternity. Perhaps the reader of this text has never considered the notion that you are training someone's grandmother or grandfather! The lessons you teach can impact families for three or more generations.

How do we know this to be true? The psalmist begins in Psalm 1 with the promise to believers who embrace Scripture of a changed life:

> His delight is in the LORD's instruction,
> and he meditates on it day and night.
> He is like a tree planted besides flowing streams
> that bears its fruit in its season,
> and its leaf does not wither.
> Whatever he does prospers. (Ps 1:2–3)

This passage describes a fabulous vision for your classroom and your students as you teach them, and they engage in learning—the students delight in God's Word and meditate on it beyond the classroom and your class meeting time. The co-authors of this text along with the contributors were the recipients of someone's ministry at some time in the past. Now we are raising families and some of us have grandchildren. And we are writing to you. So we know the impact YOU can have in the lives of children and parents. Once his Word takes hold, the young believer will continue to grow and flourish.

Let's Visit a Christian School Classroom

Imagine a Bible classroom that has an atmosphere of both warm reception and electric expectation. As you walk into the room before class begins, you notice the space is beautifully inviting with lovely art pieces on the walls, classical music playing in the background, and greenery growing along the windowsills. Desks grouped together in quads send a message of student teamwork and collaboration. Projected on the board is a thoughtfully provocative question for students to consider when they first come into the classroom. As students begin to eagerly jostle their way through the door into the room, the Bible teacher stands at the entrance and personally greets each student by name to welcome them to class.

As students fill the classroom, they notice the question on the board right away, sit down, and begin to jot down ideas about the day's discussion question. They are accustomed to an invitation and expectation to interact with God's Word. When everyone is present, the teacher invites teams to discuss the question, and the students, who already know the expectations for thoughtful engagement in group discussions, begin to listen to each other.

A lively discussion ensues, and the teacher walks around the classroom and checks in with each group. After groups have finished, the teacher calls on different individuals to report the highlights of their discussion and warmly encourages each student who shares. The teacher then explains how the initial discussion topic introduces the objective for the day. The teacher invites everyone present to be still. A peaceful hush falls over the classroom, as taking time for silence is a regular part of this classroom routine before a student prays to invite Christ to be the center of learning that day. There is a clear sense that students and teachers alike expect that Christ will indeed be present as they study the Word of God together.

As the instructor continues the lesson, everyone is listening and engaged, and their participation doesn't end. Students move around the classroom to discuss ideas together, and you notice that they treat each other with respect and kindness. There are also moments for learners to pause for personal thought, reflection, written reflections, Bible searches, and connection with God. Before the end of class, groups are processing and sharing the ideas discussed that day. This gives the teacher a chance to informally assess their learning. The fifty minutes of class goes by in what feels like just a few minutes, and as students leave the room, the teacher stands by the door to have them submit the exit slip that answers a question related to the day's discussion and warmly says, "Have a great day."

Furthermore, this Bible class has implications that ripple throughout the rest of the school. Students are not only learning from the Bible, but they are also understanding and responding to God's perspective on life and being formed into Christlikeness. They start to approach learning in their other disciplines with a lens of humility and eager anticipation, because they are starting to see that all truth is grounded in relationship to Jesus. They are less anxious, quicker to listen and ponder, and eager to seek understanding and act upon what they learn. Their time in this Bible class is changing them as people and as students. Sounds ideal, doesn't it? Do you think that this scenario is possible?

ENGAGE: Review the description of this Bible class in light of previous concepts in this text. How do the instructional techniques reflect the chapter that discusses Mind, Brain, and Education Research? Also, how does the atmosphere both in the classroom and in the school community reflect the concepts related to Social-Emotional Learning?

What makes a Bible class the kind that students look forward to and talk about for years to come? The differences between substandard and excellent Bible classes can be seen in critical distinctions between teachers' approaches to pedagogy and content. Underneath these differences in pedagogy and content are definitive principles that shape every aspect of the classroom. This chapter will present three foundational principles that undergird excellent Bible teaching and will then describe how they translate to excellence in both pedagogy and content in the classroom. We invite you to join us as we consider how to structure Bible classes to be a transforming learning experience for students of all ages.

Nature and Structure of Bible and Biblical Study as a Discipline

Scripture as Narrative

First, to engage with Scripture we must understand that it is essentially a story, a meta-narrative.[1] All narratives are relational and invite active connection. From the YouTube

---

[1] For more on this idea, see Craig G. Bartholomew and Michael W. Goheen, *The Drama of Scripture: Finding Our Place in the Biblical Story* (Grand Rapids: Baker Academic, 2004).

commercial that is telling viewers a story that their meaning is found in their beauty to the movie whose story is telling them that their purpose is found in personal achievements, narratives surround us all day every day. As humans, we look to stories to find meaning, purpose, and belonging. Therefore, what we encounter when we engage with the narrative of Scripture is a story that we can enter and engage with today. We read this story with the author bringing it to life in us through the work of the Holy Spirit. As students engage with the narrative of Scripture, they find themselves invited to live in the story.

When my children were younger, they had certain favorite stories, and they would dress up and imagine themselves as part of them. They would go into these imaginary worlds for hours on end—they loved it. Though most of us can relate to doing something like this in our childhood, we often think of this imagining as something we leave behind as we grow older. We do not realize that the longing to be part of a meaningful story lives deep within the soul of each human being. The Bible tells us the truth about where we came from, who we are, and where we can find purpose.

As we embrace Scripture, the characters of the Bible are not strangers but are intimately connected to us. We first meet God our Father and learn of his great love. We meet Jesus and see how he perfectly reveals God to us, for he is God in the flesh, divine and human. We also meet the fathers and mothers of our faith and find that they are our family members because we are each grafted into the family of God. We realize that their stories are connected to who we are today. As we help our students enter the biblical story using the techniques of excellent pedagogy described in this book, it brings the story to life and invites them to enter in to find meaning, belonging, and purpose. They discover that God's story can be theirs as well.

The narrative of Scripture has five parts much like the acts of a play: Eternal God, Creation, Fall, Redemption, and Restoration.[2] The acts of the story answer the big questions of life and help to make sense out of life on planet earth and individual existence. When we teach our Bible classes against the background of the drama of Scripture, it gives context and meaning to everything we teach. For instance, if I am teaching a Bible class to the younger grades on the life of Jesus, I will spend time bringing the story of Christ into the greater context of the five acts of Scripture (Eternal God, Creation, Fall, Redemption, Restoration). My students will need to understand that Jesus is God, made flesh. As my students and I engage with the story of Christ through the Gospels, we will constantly refer to how his words and works parallel so

---

[2] See chapter 1 for additional information on this narrative framework.

many of the stories and prophecies of the Old Testament. Study of the Scriptures will be integral to discovering Jesus foretold in the Old Testament. We do not just talk about these things . . . we will engage, embody, and entrust them. The context of the larger narrative brings the learning to life.

The narrative of Scripture provides an opportunity to engage with critical questions that are in the heart of every person. As we go through the Creation narrative, for example, we discuss how this helps us to understand many critical questions such as "From where did the world (universe) come into being? What is God like? Why are we here? What is our purpose? What is wrong with our world that people hate, suffer, conduct war and oppression?" The narrative of the fall helps us to understand the biblical answer to this question. "What are the consequences when people do not obey God?" When we enter the narratives of redemption and restoration, we address, "Where can we find salvation, the 'fix' to the problem? What happens after death? Is there hope for the world?" As we go through the narrative of Scripture, we find that each one of life's greatest questions is answered.

Structure of the Bible Itself

The Bible is made up of sixty-six books in one book written by about forty different human authors. The human authors wrote independently of each other over a period of fifteen centuries, in three languages on three continents employing their own literary styles, vocabulary, and idiosyncrasies to record historical narratives, poetry, prayers and songs, prophecies, personal letters, theological treaties, and other literature genres. Surprisingly, to many who study the Bible who are not Christians, there is a singleness and coherency that is pervasive throughout as God's truth is revealed throughout the unfolding of his grand story.

There seems to be no other reason for sixty-six books in one, written over a very long period to portray a unified narrative, than to assert as the Scriptures do, that "all Scripture is inspired by God and is profitable for teaching, for rebuking, for correcting, for training in righteousness" (2 Tim 3:16).

Scripture Narrative as a Series of Progressive Covenants That Provide Meaning to the Whole Big Story of the Bible

To engage with Scripture through the perspective of loving God and others, we must not only use the framework of a narrative and worldview questions embedded in God's big story, but also the series of covenants between God and humans that are considered parts that tell the whole story with emphasis on the relationship of a personal God who relates to humankind. A covenant may be simply defined as an agreement between two parties. In Scripture, this is often an "I will" type statement made by God to humans. The Bible records that humans, too, made agreements with God in terms of "we will do"—such as the agreements of the Israelites from time to time to obey God.

Covenants unfold progressively throughout Scripture and must be connected together to understand the big narrative of God's Word. Covenants are founded on freely chosen relationship, not in duty or obligation. The covenants God makes with his people throughout Scripture reflect his unfailing love and incredible kindness (as well as his judgment)—principles that are still just as true today as they were thousands of years ago. A covenant is the context in which we are invited to relate to God, so as we notice them throughout the narrative of Scripture, we can grow in our own personal relationship with him and grow in our knowledge of him. This knowledge of him becomes the foundation for all wisdom.[3]

The progression of the covenants, beginning with creation, are the parts that together become the whole of God's unfolding story in the Bible. Humans seem to learn best by thinking from whole to parts to whole. "The covenants (plural) or covenant (singular) are considered as the key to the main storyline by covenant theologians and dispensationalists . . . dispensationalists have normally used the covenants as a way of dividing history into the various dispensations. The covenant or covenants are important to both positions."[4]

Relating to Scripture through the context of covenants should change how we interact with God and others. Instead of seeing a relationship with God as a drudgery or a duty (which is how transactional relationships often feel), we live in the unending joy of a covenant relationship. When it is an agreement of God's own making, I can be assured that I am known, I am safe, and I am loved. This relationship is not disposable—I can trust his Word because it will not change. As I interact with the Bible using this relational context, I find that instead of finding it boring, I find it full of delight. From this place of delight, loving others becomes more natural. Instead of pretending to love others, I find the love I have received from God spilling over to others.

---

[3] See the works of Esther Meek on this topic: Esther Lightcap Meek, *Longing to Know* (Ada, OK: Brazos, 2003); *Loving to Know: Introducing Covenant Epistemology* (Eugene, OR: Wipf & Stock, 2011); *A Little Manual for Knowing* (Eugene, OR: Wipf & Stock, 2014).

[4] Peter Gentry, "The Significance of Covenants in Biblical Theology," *Southern Baptist Journal of Theology* 20, no. 1 (2016): 9–33.

This context of relationship and covenant also answers deep questions of the human heart, those worldview questions addressed earlier. Every human wants to know where he or she can find worth, identity, belonging, and unfailing love. A covenantal view of Scripture, in part, answers each of these questions. Students can "taste and see" the answers to these questions as they come to know Christ. When understanding some of the structure of the Bible, a teacher can more naturally engage students with these deep questions of the heart.

Epochs of Biblical History

Another approach to understanding structure of the Bible is to view it chronologically as a series of epochs in which God is revealing himself and his redemptive story to humankind through a timeline. The major epochs are creation; fall; result of the fall culminating in the Noahic flood; Abraham's call to become a nation (the Hebrew nation) through which the Savior would enter the world and through which the light to the Gentiles would come; Christ's birth and life; the birth of the church; expansion of the church; work of the church; future of the church; and the future return of Christ to make all things new. This is a great historical plan and movement by God and should be incorporated into the big narrative of the Bible as a whole and not as separated sections.

Scripture as Christ-Centered

"The Son is the radiance of God's glory and the exact representation of his being, sustaining all things by his powerful word" (Heb 1:3 NIV).

To engage Scripture through the lens of loving God and others, we must participate with Scripture as Christ-centered. In other words, we must understand that the overarching purpose of the Bible is to reveal to us the person of Christ that we may know the Father. Why? Because Jesus "is the exact representation" of God's glory, and when we have seen Christ we have "seen the Father" (John 14:9). Viewing Scripture as Christ-centered also leads us to a foundational question of every human heart: "Who or what is truth?" We all want to know who to trust to show us the way through life. Most of our students follow Instagram, YouTube, and Google in the hopes of finding truth, but many of them have figured out the hard way that the source of truth cannot be found on the internet. Perhaps more than ever, this generation is longing to find the truth. What an amazing gift that Jesus is Truth; consider the implications of this. When we teach Scripture as Christ-centered, we are inviting our students to find Truth. Very simply, Christ is the key to understanding each part of the biblical narrative. Christ is also the key to experiencing a relationship with God. Christ enables us to receive the love of God, and it is in Christ that we can love God and others. The centrality of Christ cannot be overstated!

As a high school Bible teacher, I modeled taking Christ's teachings seriously, and this is something we often discussed together as we engaged with Scripture. When we took a week to read the Gospel of Mark in class, I also invited students to engage with Jesus as someone who is alive, citing examples of all who came to interact with him during his ministry on earth. Throughout the whole class, I modeled wonder and love for Christ, and in so doing, invited my students to do the same. My ultimate goal was to see my students come to know Christ personally. Christ truly is the same yesterday, today, and forever (Heb 13:8). He continues to draw people to himself, and our Bible classes are a place to glorify him and welcome his presence.

Effective Practices for Bible Teaching

Effective practices for teaching Bible are founded on principles and practices that are selected because they fit with how humans learn in general as well as understanding our content, the nature and structure of the Bible. The inspiring Bible classroom described in the introduction to this chapter is an outgrowth of these principles in action (see pages 442–43). At this point in reading this book, it may be assumed that the foundation has been laid for understanding human learning and its application to learning in general.[5] One thing for sure in using cognitive interactive learning, the student must be mentally, actively involved with the lesson at hand. Good Bible teaching is never straight lecture and "where did we leave off yesterday in our outline?"

In this chapter we consider teaching Bible specifically, and while using the overall philosophical and psychological foundations in chapters 1 and 2, we will add the following. There are three interconnected biblical principles for learning the Bible. Bible education is transformational. Bible education is relational. Bible education's goal is knowledge that produces action.

> For this reason also, since the day we heard this, we haven't stopped praying for you. We are asking that you may be filled with the knowledge of his will

---

[5] Refer to chapters 2–6, pages 47–157.

in all wisdom and spiritual understanding so that you may walk worthy of the Lord, fully pleasing to him: bearing fruit in every good work and growing in the knowledge of God. (Col 1:9–10)

Bible Education Is Transformational

First, we consider the belief that Bible education is formational and transformational, not just informational. It does *inform* our worldview, but it is designed to form a view of life and learning that transforms and renews our minds to think God's thoughts and to respond to him, bringing about life-giving change. Learning, as most teachers know, is defined as a *change* in behavior and actions. It is this kind of change that is paramount in Bible teaching.

The goal of Bible education is to see students conform to God's view of life and grow into people who love God, obey his teachings, love others, and are people of Christlike character. Jesus invited people into a changed way of living, and Bible teachers (indeed all Christian teachers) are called to do the same. This transformational view of education may run counter to much of today's educational landscape when it becomes memorized information for standardized tests. Humans can know all the right facts and be unchanged. What we love is what motivates us to act.

This stagnate view of education as simply information to be memorized to be regurgitated on tests, is historically quite new. Prior to the Enlightenment, education was about forming a person of virtue, whose desires were well formed. Two historical examples are helpful here: In ancient Greece, education was through apprenticeship to a master. While various subjects were certainly taught, and master teachers knew their content well, students learned by imitating their teacher in tasks with the hope of mastering what they were learning as their teacher had. In the Hebrew tradition, the example of rabbi and disciple gets at a similar idea. The disciple imitated the rabbi with the explicit outcome being that the disciple would become like his rabbi. Likewise, Christian education is concerned with who the student is becoming, not only what he or she is learning.

Bible Education Is Relational: The Teacher as Model

In the chapter on philosophy of education informed by a biblical worldview, Dr. MacCullough addresses the roles of the teacher, one of which is to relate to the students as an example and role model whose standard is Christ. The models of Master/

Apprentice and Rabbi/Disciple also illustrate the second biblical principle: Bible education is relational. Teachers are their students' "first text."[6] Jesus knew this and invited his students to "come and see." Paul likewise invited his students to "imitate me as I also imitate Christ" (1 Cor 11:1). We join Jesus and Paul by inviting our students to take "whatever you have learned or received or heard from me or seen in me—[and] put it into practice" (Phil 4:9 NIV). Bible class, and school at large, is therefore a community of scholars in which students apprentice. Teachers invite students into the authority and tradition of their discipline of knowledge so that the students can imitate their teacher and reach the point where they can say, "I see for myself."[7] Make no mistake, the students always become like the teacher. Your students will become like you.

If we do not understand this key principle, it may lead to a deep disconnect in the classroom where the teacher believes the curriculum *is* the educational experience rather than the teacher/student relationship with each other and the content. A colleague of mine would ask his students at the end of each year, "What did I teach you this year that I didn't know I was teaching you?" Their answers were incredibly enlightening to what the "sometimes hidden curriculum" was despite what the lesson objectives were for the day. David Smith calls this the "pedagogy gap," where the actual pedagogy may not match the intended pedagogy.[8] Often one of the biggest pedagogical gaps in the Bible classroom comes when the teacher is not modeling relational connectedness to Christ and others.

Bible teaching must begin with the transformation of the teacher's heart. Teachers must take seriously their discipleship to Jesus as their ever-present teacher in all of life, including their academic discipline. Maturation into Christlikeness is an act of the Spirit in which we participate through classic spiritual disciplines such as worship, prayer, silence, solitude, and commitment to community in the church. Acts 2:42 includes in the task of the church, devotion "to the apostles' teaching"—the very Word of God. There is a vertical and horizontal aspect to teaching the Bible. Both are essential in order to be effective in Bible teaching. This leads to the third principle.

Bible Knowledge Produces Action

Bible learning involves content and biblical knowledge. It is crucial that we define knowledge biblically and accurately. In general, prior to the Enlightenment, knowledge

---

[6] We are grateful to Andrew Elizalde for this idea.

[7] Leslie Newbigin, *The Gospel in a Pluralistic Society* (Grand Rapids: Eerdmans, 1989), 46.

[8] David I. Smith, *On Christian Teaching* (Grand Rapids: Eerdmans, 2018), 1–13.

was embedded in community and tradition and passed on through relationships. After the Enlightenment, for many, knowledge was reduced to information, facts, and data.[9] While information, facts, concepts, and data are a part of knowledge, in themselves they do not necessarily translate into the high description of knowledge in the Bible. The biblical description of knowledge is much more robust. Knowledge in Scripture is often connected to wisdom or the wise use of knowledge and requires an action on the part of the knower in obedience to truth. In Col 1:9–10, cited above, the apostle Paul prayed that the people at Colossae would learn the Word of God by knowing it, understanding it, and responding to it so that they would grow and bear fruit. Biblical knowledge can therefore be described as obedience to the truth.[10] It is formative and transformative. This is crucial for Bible teachers to understand. Knowing facts, but not acting in obedience to them, makes one "hearers" and not "doers of the word" (Jas 1:22).

This principle of knowledge bears out in all of life. If I hire a plumber to come fix my pipes at my home, I not only expect that he will understand what a pipe is, how the water moves through it, where the leak might be, and what might have caused the leak, I expect him to *use* all that information to fix the pipes. Or think of the makeup of athletes and what makes them successful. They must know the rules of the game, and they must understand the skill needed to play the game. But it is not until the rules and skills become embedded in their muscle memory and cognitive map of the game that they can become masterful athletes. In the same way, information divorced from an embodied application is of little use for us in reality. Our students must grasp the notion that God absolutely intends for us to live in full conformity to reality. True knowledge changes how we interact in the world; true knowledge forms us. These things are "written for our instruction" (1 Cor 10:11).

These interconnected principles help to inform excellent pedagogy related to the content to be learned in the Bible classroom. When we infuse these principles into every part of the classroom, we build an environment that echoes the effective classroom described in the introduction. Conversely, when we mistake Bible teaching as solely disseminating facts, teach in a way that is relationally disconnected, or offer no engagement in response to truth, it leads to substandard Bible classes. How do these principles practically inform the content we teach and our pedagogy?

---

[9] For information on "knowledge" (but pre- and post-Enlightenment), see "The Enlightenment," Alpha History, September 20, 2020, https://alphahistory.com/frenchrevolution /enlightenment/.

[10] Parker J. Palmer, *To Know as We Are Known* (New York: HarperOne, 1993), 65.

ENGAGE: Select a passage of Scripture with a view toward preparing to teach it to a particular age group. Examine the passage in light of the questions below.

Approaching the Scriptures with God in mind (hermeneutical questions):

1. What does this passage tell me about God? (Who he is: character, promises, covenants, love, attributes etc.)
2. What [persons] of God is the text describing (Father, Son, Spirit)? And what is his/their role?
3. How does the text point us to the person and work of Christ?
4. What comfort do you find knowing what the text says of God?
5. What does the text say about our response or responsibility?
6. How does this text remind us that we are not God but need God?
7. What does this passage tell us about ourselves? Our sinful inclination?
8. What does this passage tell us about what God desires from us?
9. How is God able to help us accomplish what he desires for us?
10. Why does God want us to know what he is revealing from the text I/we are studying?[11]

Pedagogical Practices

Jesus is Master only because he is Maestro. "Jesus is Lord" can mean little in practice for anyone who has to hesitate before saying, "Jesus is smart." He is not just nice, he is brilliant. He is the smartest man who ever lived. He is now supervising the entire course of world history while simultaneously preparing the rest of the universe for our future role in it (John 14:2). He always has the best information on everything and certainly also on the things that matter most in human life.[12]

The biblical view of knowledge as knowing, understanding, and responding to truth, and the relation of truth to wisdom, is vital in the formation of students into the people God intend us to be. Jesus, as the Master Teacher, demonstrates how he led people to understanding and encouraged response. There are three practices that

---

[11] Ken Coley and Blair Robinson, *Equipping Fathers to Lead Family Worship* (Nashville: Randall House, 2021), 48–49.

[12] Dallas Willard, *The Divine Conspiracy: Rediscovering Our Hidden Life in God* (San Francisco: HarperCollins, 1998), 95.

Bible teachers can model based on Jesus's example: ***Engage*** *the student, allow him or her to* ***embody*** *the lesson, and* ***entrust*** *the Holy Spirit to guide the student to obey the truth and demonstrate knowledge.* In this next section we will observe how Jesus practiced this pedagogy and point out the underlying principles implied in that pedagogy.

Engage the Student

Jesus frequently engaged his students through story (parable), questions or riddles ("Which of the sons did the will of his father?"), imagery (mustard seed), tactile engagement (drawing in the dust), surprise ("Your sins are forgiven"), list ("Who do you people say I am?"), rebuke ("Unless you become like little children you will not enter the kingdom"), problems ("You give them something to eat"), songs (after singing a hymn they departed), and many more examples. Engaging our students is crucial to stirring their desire to meet Jesus. In Jesus's ministry he was regularly making space for the student to notice and wonder, to notice what they might desire and therefore love.

Like Jesus, Bible teachers must wisely consider how to engage students well, to tap their desire, and prepare them for learning the lesson of the day. In chapter 6, Dr. Debbie MacCullough explains the concept of engagement for all lessons. There is a need for the same pedagogical activation in Bible class as well. The purpose for this engagement is to get the minds of the students thinking in the direction of the lesson.

While well-chosen creative engagements can be particularly fun (and we encourage you to have fun with your lessons), do not underestimate the simple power of a thoughtful question and time for reflection to engage students. Essential questions for your discipline or your lesson can be a great starting point and continued touch point for your class. Essential questions invite students to consider big ideas and enduring understandings about your discipline. For example, an essential question for an Old Testament survey class for middle school students might be "Why is sin such a big deal?" For a high school class on the Minor Prophets, the question might be "What does God's anger show us about his character?" For a discipleship group, it might be "Is anger ever good?"

We encourage you to think creatively about even more ways you can awake wonder in your students through imagery, activity, music, food, color, smell, etc. Engaging your students well is issuing them an invitation into learning and inviting them to love by engaging their desire to meet truth.

Embody the Lesson

"Education is implication. It is not the things you say which children respect; when you say things, they very commonly laugh and do the opposite. It is the things you assume which really sink into them. It is the things you forget even to teach that they learn."[13]

Jesus always embodied learning and taught by actively involving the students in the learning. He invited his students to obey with their bodies—for example, "Follow me," "Come and see," "Go and do likewise," "Become like little children."[14] It is crucial to remember that being human means being embodied. An early heresy in the church was Gnosticism, the belief that matter was bad, and the spiritual was superior.[15] The incarnation flatly refutes that matter is bad—Jesus's very life shows us that being human, with its bodily limitations, is good. He had a human body and ate, drank, walked, talked, and so on, and so do your students. Use these sensory experiences in learning.

It is common for some educators to reduce knowledge to cognition apart from response just as we mentioned that some educators reduce knowledge to simply facts. The biblical definition of knowledge is much more robust. I imagine the whole spectrum of the color wheel in 3D and animated. Knowledge in Scripture always requires an inside response and action on the part of the knower to make sense out of it and store it for use in real-life situations. Truly learned truth will result in changes in the whole person and not just in factual information. We are what James K. A. Smith calls "liturgical creatures"[16]—we are shaped by formative practices. We should consider time for our students to rest, to run, to listen, to wonder, to act out what we are studying, to ponder and question. We need to help our students use their whole being to learn.

The body and the mind are both important in learning because meaning, or how students internalize information on their way to understanding, is often made through action. This is where cognitive interactive learning that focuses on inside and outside factors uses a variety of physical methods to stimulate and impress the mind and aid in storing and using new information. Meaning is not passively discovered by observation.

---

[13] G. K. Chesterton, *The Man Who Was Orthodox*, ed. A. L. Maycock (London: Dobson, 1963), 96.

[14] Matt 4:19; Matt 18:3; Luke 10:37; John 1:46 (NIV).

[15] Jack Zavada, "What Is Gnosticism? Definition and Beliefs Explained," Learn Religions, accessed January 31, 2022, https://www.learnreligions.com/what-is-gnosticism-700683.

[16] James K. A. Smith, *Desiring the Kingdom: Worship, Worldview, and Cultural Formation* (Ada, OK: Baker Academic, 2009), 40. The term he uses is "liturgical animals."

Read that sentence again and let it sink in. Recent brain science research confirms that meaning is found in feedback from action.[17]

Furthermore, there is deeply formative power when a community of learners participates together in activities that involve the body and actions together. "There is much research to support the notion that acts seen and acts done are coded together in the brain and are therefore tightly linked to one another."[18]

Wise teachers scrutinize their own formation, their pedagogy, and their curriculum to harness the best learning for their students. We encourage you to thoughtfully consider how you can harness both body and mind in both helping your students learn and in forming a welcoming classroom that becomes a caring and effective community of learners.

Entrust the Holy Spirit to Guide the Student

INSIGHT ISN'T INFORMATIONAL; IT IS TRANSFORMATIONAL[19]

Jesus consistently entrusted learning and meaningful action to those who followed him. He chose unworthy and flawed humans in which to entrust the gospel; he chooses ordinary teachers to pass on the treasure of learning to a new generation. He warned teachers that hearing his words and not acting on them was disastrous (Matt 7:26). We are intended to build upon what we learn.

Trusting learners to process biblical information as they experience your lessons requires humility, faith, and love. But above all, it requires our trust in God's Spirit to use his Word taught well, to do the teaching and nudge the response. We always point to God's view of issues and not to our own, whether the voice of the teacher or student. His Word is the standard for both teacher and student.

CAUTION

One of the effects of reducing biblical knowledge to simply a set of information is that it robs the student of the wonder and power of a personal relationship with a personal God who speaks through his Word. It requires very little commitment on behalf of the learner to simply know names, accounts, people, and places in the Bible without some

---

[17] Warren S. Brown and Brad D. Strawn, *The Physical Nature of Christian Life: Neuroscience, Psychology, & the Church* (New York: Cambridge University, 2012).

[18] Brown and Strawn, 56.

[19] Meek, *A Little Manual for Knowing*, 72.

context and connection to the big story and worldview questions and answers. The teacher's end goal must be to provide opportunity for students to demonstrate their obedience to the truth.

Entrusting the internalizing of truth taught to the students—as they process new information and connect it to prior knowledge—requires the teacher to let them talk and not fear they will misinterpret the Word of God. If they do, and we all make mistakes in reading God's Word because of human limits in knowing, the teacher can guide the student to Scriptures to help correct the conclusions. It is okay to say to the students, "I am not sure about that; let's do some research from Scripture together." This is a part of learning. We fit in new information and change our thinking, and sometimes we just need more information. It is the Word of God that is the standard for truth—not the teacher or the student. It is absolutely essential for students to understand this in a day and age when we focus on "my truth" and "your truth" (and both can be called truth) rather than God's voice and his Truth. This means that learners not only act upon information but they humbly understand "Thus says the Lord" and receive it as well.

How Do We Encourage Ownership of Learning?

What are some practical ways to entrust your students with learning? Consider making more time for reflection in the classroom. Silence is a tangible trust act on the teacher's part, and while not a cultural part of American education, it is used effectively in many cultures. Have the students write their questions and comments as they reflect. Ask questions. Jesus asked questions and used these to reveal hearts. How can you guide your students to truth through careful questioning and reflection rather than through a full lecture? At the upper levels of school, questions should be posed and discussed before you include a mini-lecture in your lesson.

Mini-lectures should be 8–10 minutes or less in length and should be surrounded by questions and activities such as writing and discussions. Younger students can have their minds activated by using questions that will be answered as you tell a biblical story or read a passage. Ask them to be ready to share their answers at the end.

ENGAGE: Select a passage of Scripture and think through preparing to teach using the lesson outline below. Of course, the individual steps can be moved to a different place in your outline or omitted all together. Some teachers find this outline versatile to use for most lessons.

- **Connection with the learner.** Begin with a "hook" that connects with prior learning and experience.

- **Context of time and culture of the passage.** Select important aspects of the cultural, historical, or geographical setting of the passage.
- **Context of biblical setting in the book of study.** Clarify how the passage fits with the overall themes of the book.
- **Content of the particular passage of the lesson** (the emphasis for that lesson and the section that requires the most time). What is the Lord saying to us?
- **Checking for comprehension of the learners.** Take time to assess your students' level of understanding.
- **Checking for conviction of the learners.** What are aspects of their lives about which the Lord is speaking to them?
- **Challenge for application by the learners.** How might they think, feel, or respond differently today and this week based on this study?[20]

Not All Bible Learning Is Equally Good

There are biblical examples of poor learning of God's Word. For example, there were false teachers who plagued the New Testament church because they were not Christ-followers, nor they did not know their content well. Most epistles warn of false teachers infiltrating the young churches with teachings contrary to the core teachings of Scripture. Whether by calling for legalism or license, these false teachers taught a way of life opposed to what Christ taught and modeled; yet many in the young church had a difficult time applying what they had been taught to be able to recognize these errors. Many of the false teachers were dynamic and compelling speakers, but their teaching did not lead to obedience to the truth.

Bible Teachers Must Be Students of the Word of God[21]

On the other hand, the Pharisees had the truth and memorized much, but their lives were full of pride, and they often added to the Scriptures the "traditions of men."[22] Effective Bible teachers study their students and improve their pedagogy not just to be

---

[20] Ken Coley, "Excels in Teaching God's Word," in Steve Parr, ed., *Sunday School That Really Excels* (Grand Rapids: Kregel, 2013), 182–83.

[21] See 2 Cor 10 and Gal 3–4.

[22] See Matt 15:1–6.

liked or to be interesting (although that is not bad) but to help students know, understand, and respond to the truth.

Bible Class Content and Worldview Questions

While there is no magical number of general or major worldview questions, it is wise to create a list of five to eight big questions of life, answer each one biblically, and be aware that various Bible narratives and passages include answers to these questions. This awareness will aid the Bible teacher in using a worldview approach to fortifying biblical answers to worldview questions that will be needed by students as they study in other content areas. This practice helps other teachers of mathematics, science, language arts, PE, music, history, social studies, etc.

All worldview questions are addressed in the Bible. The key is to know the biblical answers and be ready to fortify the answers through the regular Bible curriculum.[23]

Conclusion

We began this chapter with what many would view as an ideal yet somewhat unrealistic narrative of a Bible class. The goal of this chapter has been to build skills that will make this type of class more prevalent and realistic.

We invite you to take these ideas and those in the rest of this book and merge them into your own discipleship journey and the journey you take with your students. You might ask as you plan a lesson, "How would Jesus teach my class if he were the teacher tomorrow?" We pray that as you envision new ways to teach the Bible, you will be able to take these simple ideas and bring them to life in your unique context.

---

[23] See chapter 22, "Developing Biblical Worldview Thinking through Curricular Integration," 459–71.

Developing Biblical Worldview Thinking through Curricular Integration

Debbie MacCullough

Throughout this text, each author's biblical worldview is obvious and openly admitted. We believe that God is the author of truth and that our understanding of truth should impact all that we do. We do not separate God's truth from "other" truths. In addressing the educational topics in this book, the process of biblical worldview thinking is portrayed throughout. Our goal is to have Christian educators form the habit of biblical worldview thinking in all they do. Furthermore, it is our goal to help educators pass on to their students the habit of thinking Christianly through the process described in this chapter, and this is accomplished through curricular integration using as the integrating core, God's view of life and learning.[1]

---

[1] For a brief history of curricular integration in general, see chapter 2 of Martha MacCullough, *Undivided: Developing* a *Worldview Approach to Biblical Integration* (Colorado Springs: Purposeful Design, 2016).

What Is a Worldview?

A worldview is a set of beliefs that: (1) shape our interpretation of the world, (2) affect the value we place on things in this world, and (3) determine our behavior toward the world.[2] Often, our worldview has not been examined; it is simply that from which we function that has been absorbed over time from our family, our culture, our gender interactions, media, even our generational influences. However, as Christians, our worldview should be derived from the Bible. Therefore, we refer to a "biblical worldview" within this text. While we all have a worldview, elements in that view may not be biblical. The Bible is both a verifying source and a corrective to our way of viewing life and learning. The only way to continue to align our worldview to a biblical worldview is to examine God's Word where we find scriptural answers to the big questions of life.

A good starting point for developing a biblical worldview is to have a framework from which to work. Simon Smart wrote, "The grand story of the Bible—of *Creation, the Fall* of humanity, *redemption* through Jesus Christ, and the world headed towards *New Creation*—provides the framework within which people can live their life with meaning and purpose."[3] Some people refer to this as "God's Big Story." This framework of Creation, Fall, Redemption and Restoration can assist us to better develop answers to the big questions of life.

The goal of biblical curricular integration is to develop biblical worldview thinking and acting through the intentionally planned lessons in the curriculum of the school. It is not the Bible, or the subject matter per se, that needs to be integrated. God's truth is truth wherever it is found, whether we acknowledge this or not. It is the human *mind* that must be integrated because it is filled with contradictory beliefs and often unbiblical views. Curricular integration informed by a biblical worldview involves planned activities to help students develop thinking that leads to the development of a progressively more biblical view of God and his created order. This involves a change of mind at the cognitive level and a disposition of the heart on the part of teachers and students. We are in this process together! For these reasons, we do not refer to "integrating" a lesson; rather we refer to including a biblical worldview integrative activity where

---

[2] See the Summit Ministry website review of worldviews for the source for this author-created definition. "Worldviews," April 2010, https://www.allaboutworldview.org/worldviews.htm.

[3] Simon Smart, *A Spectator's Guide to World Views: Ten Ways of Understanding Life* (Sydney, AU: Blue Bottle Books, 2007), 10.

appropriate in the regular lessons of the school day. The activity is designed to help the students develop a biblically integrated mind, and it takes time!

Biblical Worldview Integrative Activity, Counterexamples

One way to understand biblical worldview integration activities is to understand what they are not. Not all the activities to be described are wrong or bad, but they are not necessarily biblical worldview integrative activities. One such activity is including a Bible verse at the top or bottom of a worksheet. This is not biblical *integration*. It is not wrong, and it may, perhaps, be used to develop an integration activity. However, standing alone, it is not integration. Another such activity is something like reading every verse from the concordance on a particular subject (such as horses) when teaching a unit on that subject. Little in this activity of reading verse after verse will help the student develop a biblical worldview regarding horses. Within a biblical integrative activity, some verse reading may very well be necessary, but it will be done with a learning target in mind and have students look for specific issues or answers to the big questions of life. Another mistaken approach to biblical integration is for a teacher to think that praying or having class devotions equals biblical integration. Although neither of these are objectionable activities, and although they may help in the discipleship of the students, they are not necessarily biblical worldview integrative activities. The spiritual formation and discipleship of the student is a key overall target within Christian schooling, and although it is intertwined with a biblical worldview, it is different from biblical worldview integration that will be explained later in this chapter.

Another mistaken approach that is often considered biblical integration is what might be considered the "casual approach." Many teachers think they will bring a Christian perspective to their teaching simply because they are Christians. They may use the "teachable" moment on a playground, or they may refer to the greatness of God in a mathematics or science lesson. Again, this is not an objectionable thing, but if this is the only means of incorporating biblical worldview thinking into their teaching, students may see this type of thinking as rather personal (for my teacher and not me) and possibly not connect with (or integrate) the content being learned.

What Is Biblical Integration?

Intentional integration is something that is planned, happens throughout the academic day, and occurs in all learning areas. Developing lessons and units in which the student is learning to think in an integrated way from a biblical worldview perspective takes planning. This chapter will examine some structures and methods that will help a teacher in the planning of these activities for units and lessons.

ENGAGE: Take some time to "free write" about the following situation and question.

Suppose you are on a committee to oversee planning the curriculum for a new school. You are to decide what content your students will learn from the earliest years until graduation. There are no governmental regulations that you must follow (such as, at grade 3 all students learn . . .); and there are no parental expectations (my child must learn . . .); rather, simply your faith in Christ and your accountability to God for what a child needs to learn to function as a human being on this planet. What would you teach in your school to prepare your students for life and why? Because this is a very broad, difficult question, we give one area as an example:

> *Our school will teach the following communication skills: reading, writing, speaking, and listening. God has created humans as communicators, and he calls each of us to use communication. Therefore, it is critical that students learn to communicate well in each of the language arts areas.*

What else would you teach and why?

The "Engage" activity is to help you begin to see that much of what we are required to teach by governments, regional and national standards, academic tradition, or parental expectation, has a solid biblical basis. God created us with the ability to learn, and he has much for us to learn about himself and his entire creation! To help students develop thinking from a biblical worldview regarding all of life, the teacher's mind must be transformed by God. Christian educators must study God's Word and must know our subject matter well. We must be followers of Christ who love and study his Word. This includes both teachers and students.

Thinking about My Subject in Light of a Biblical Worldview

The next element in the process is to begin to critically think about the subject matter from a biblical perspective. Many teachers have been taught in primary through secondary school from a prevailing cultural worldview that differs from a biblical worldview. Teaching is not neutral. Many of us learned from teachers who promoted a naturalistic/materialistic worldview, or perhaps a mystical/transcendental worldview—worldviews that focus on nature rather than the Creator, or self and personal feelings rather than God's truth. Because of this, we must work to "relearn" our content with a "renewed mind" from a biblical perspective. This can only happen when we practice critical thinking about our subject matter in light of God's view of the issues at hand.

A tool to help us in this quest is to use worldview questions to help us in framing a biblical worldview from which to think. Several authors have used the questions approach, which includes the larger questions of life such as: "Who or what is God? What kind of god is it? Who or what is a human? What is wrong with the world? What happens when we die?"[4] These questions can then be broken into "sub" questions that are even more specific. The question, "Who or what is a human?" includes the subquestions, "Who am I?" "What is my purpose in life?" "Are all humans born innately good or bad?" These questions can also be organized under the approach of God's story mentioned above.

A bonus to focusing upon biblical worldview integration is that curricular integration in general should occur among subject areas. God's world is not divided into "subject areas." The divisions of subjects (disciplines) in academic institutions is a construct that humans have made to help make sense of God's world. When we help our students think from a biblical worldview, the connectedness of knowledge learned is highlighted. Geography, science, history, communication, and even mathematics can all be a part of the study of water conservation, as you will see in the example provided in the next section of this chapter.

A second tool combines these big questions of life with the framework: Creation, Fall, Redemption, and Restoration. Within each of these four historical aspects of God's story we can add questions regarding the content to be taught. To be sure, the Christian starts with the God of creation, the author of the Story, and affirms his eternal existence.[5] The Bible declares that this all-powerful, intelligent being is the God of the Bible, the foundation of a biblical worldview.

---

[4] James Sire, *The Universe Next Door*, 5th ed. (Downers Grove, IL: InterVarsity), and Martha MacCullough, *Undivided: Developing a Worldview Approach to Biblical Integration* (Colorado Springs: Purposeful Design, 2016).

[5] There is an excellent presentation of the scientific and forensic evidence for the existence of a higher being who is incredibly intelligent and all-powerful in the book, *I Don't Have Enough Faith to Be an Atheist* by Norman L. Geisler and Frank Turek (Wheaton, IL: Crossway, 2004).

How Do We Plan for Integrative Activities?

Let's examine how we can do this using a sample science unit on water conserva-tion. The tools of the framework and the essential worldview questions can be used to examine the worldview embedded in the lesson and connect it to a biblical view or contrast (distinguish) it from a biblical view.[6] For *creation* we ask, "What was God's original intention for creation, and how does conservation fit God's original purpose?" For the *fall*, I ask, "What went wrong, how has God's purpose been distorted, and what can humans do as a part of having 'dominion over' to help the situation?" For *redemption*, "How does God want us to respond and care for his creation?" For *restora-tion*, "Where is future hope found, and what would restoration look like to all of cre-ation?" For each of these questions, a biblical view must be studied by the teacher and then lesson activities designed to have the students examine God's view on the subject. A questions approach begins with the question, "What is the nature of the created world?" (big question) and a sub-question, "How does water fit with his creation—for what purposes and uses?" Additional sub-questions might be "What has happened to both the world and humankind to distort God's original purpose for water (the fall of humankind)? How can humans work with God to restore to some extent the original purposes and uses (conservation)?"

ENGAGE:

Write down your answer to each of the questions below considering the idea/concept of water conservation. (Find biblical evidence for your answer. This can be done in pairs or groups. Use the internet to quickly find passages and verses that relate to this topic.)

- What was God's original intention for water and its use?
- What went wrong, and how has God's purpose been distorted?
- How does God want us to respond and care?
- Where is future hope found, and what would restoration look like?

In the very first verse of the Bible, we have a record of God's creation and the prominent place of water. Genesis records that God created the heavens and the earth and that it was formless and empty. Darkness was over the surface of the deep "and

---

[6] These ideas were taken from Sue Starling et al., *Connecting Learners with God's Big Story: Illuminating Curriculum in Australian Christian Schools* (n.p.: Christian Schools Australia, 2016), http://circle.adventist.org/download/2017CSA_GBS.pdf.

the Spirit of God was hovering over the surface of the waters" (1:2). God created an expanse (that he called "sky") to separate the waters above it, and waters under the expanse on day two, and then he said let the water under the sky be called "seas" and the dry ground "land." We also see from Genesis 1 that water was created for living creatures in the seas and for humans. Our understanding of general revelation (what God reveals through his creation) allows us to know that humans, indeed all living things, need water to live. In Genesis, we also learn that God intended for humans to care for and tend to the earth, and this includes water. But we also see in that same book of the Bible that God's purpose was distorted at the fall and all creation was affected. Eventually, water became destructive (for God's purposes in the flood). Humankind's sin may lead to destructive practices related to water today as well. When we consider how God wants us to respond to his creation, we know that he desires for us to care for his earth, for he mandated this when he created Adam.

We need clean water to live, and so do the animals and the plant world. Caring for water is part of our dominion over the earth. We need to conserve and use but not misuse water. In the future, God will restore this earth and we will have clean, plentiful water. There are surely more answers than given here, but this tool allows a teacher to begin to construct a biblical worldview regarding the specific content to be taught. This biblical thinking is required for teachers to accomplish the task of preparing activities for students to investigate these issues.

Planning for Students to Develop a Biblically Minded View of Water Conservation

Once you have answered these questions regarding a unit to be taught, you can begin the planning of worldview integrative activities for your unit or lesson. The first step is to choose which question/answer you wish to highlight in your unit. You may select just one or several for the unit; however, for one lesson, it is best to limit the activity to answering just one key worldview question.

One goal of quality Christian schooling is that students are exposed to a biblical worldview throughout all academic subjects and at all grade levels through the process of teaching the regular curriculum. This allows the student to build a biblical worldview regarding all of life. A good place to start is to answer a few key questions before writing the unit and lessons. These questions are:

- What are the key ideas (content concepts or skills) the students will learn in this unit/lesson?
- What are the key biblical worldview framework questions that are addressed in this unit? Answer these questions from a biblical perspective with evidence.
- Where do I see connections or perhaps contradictions (distinctions) to the biblical answers I gave to the framework questions?
- Which one or two key ideas do I wish my students to think about?
- What will be the big worldview question and answer that we will examine as we study the material?
- What activities can I have my students do to think about this worldview question? Notice that developing the activities for the students is preceded by the teacher's own study and preparation. This is a must for effective worldview teaching.

Let us return to the unit on water conservation. First, we list key ideas and concepts that would be taught. For our example we will discuss these for a grade 1 or 2 student.

Key Ideas

- Water plays a pivotal role in our daily life; we use water every day.
- Not all water is fresh water. Only a small percentage of water on the earth is fresh water.
- As population grows, water resources can be limited.
- Definition of water conservation and why we all are impacted by it.

Connections, Contradictions, Continued Study

As we examine the key ideas, we can reflect upon our framework and see connections to answers given. We know that God intended for humans to have water and to have dominion (care) over that water. We know that because of sin (the fall), we do not always care for water sources as we should. Also, we recognize that our response to the misuse of water should be to care for our resources better, as God intended for us to do. Water conservation is not just a "science-world" idea, it is a God-ordained plan.

ENGAGE: What other connections or contradictions to a biblical view do you see in your curriculum materials or resources? This is the next question to ponder. For this activity determine any connections or contradictions you might notice in a lesson on conservation with which you are familiar. Write these down for reference. _____

_____

Limiting the Idea(s) to What Will Be Used in the Unit

The next question to ask is: What worldview idea will you focus on in the unit or lesson? In some schools, a curriculum guide will determine the direction and key worldview question and answer for focus. Other schools will not have curricular guidance and the teacher will need to decide. For our example, let us focus on connections that cover three areas: creation, fall, and redemption. God gave humans the responsibility to care for our earth (including our water). Humans over the course of history have not used water as God intended because we are flawed as sinners. As Christians, we should care about God's creation, use it and not misuse it; water conservation is one way that we can do this.

Developing Worldview Integrative Activities

Lastly, we examine what kind of activities we might have our students do to develop biblical worldview thinking about the issue of water conservation. This is the key to developing quality biblical worldview integrative units and lessons. These are student processing activities and not the teacher telling or "preaching" a biblical view. To create these activities, it is helpful to recall concepts from prior chapters. Bloom's taxonomy is used to help guide the teacher in writing objectives and learning targets with higher thinking requirements. At the lowest level of the taxonomy, "remember," a student will simply put knowledge into long-term memory and be able to recall this knowledge. At higher levels, the student will have to think more deeply and critically about knowledge to evaluate, apply, or create. In essence, biblical worldview thinking is thinking that evaluates and draws conclusions. These are higher order thinking skills; however, basic knowledge is essential.

Biblical worldview thinking is essentially the process of critical thinking using God's objective truth as the standard for evaluating and judging. "Critical thinking is the intellectually disciplined *process of actively* and skillfully conceptualizing, applying, analyzing, synthesizing, and/or *evaluating information* gathered from, or generated by, observation, experience, reflection, reasoning, or communication, as a guide to belief and action."[7] Notice that it is both an active process and requires information. Notice as well, the phrase "guide to belief and action." One reason we must encourage our students to think critically is to help them to develop beliefs and actions that are informed by God's Word.

To help move students to higher levels of thinking, we must write objectives, specifically worldview objectives, in which the student is challenged to think critically and biblically about the content under study. We must use questions that raise the level of thinking. Using the water conservation unit, let us look at examples of different levels of questions that correlate with different levels of Bloom's taxonomy.[8]

- "Do you know what water conservation is?" This requires just a "yes" or "no" answer. This type of question should be avoided and instead use "How would you describe water conservation (or define it)?" *This is a remember question and does not help a teacher to know if the student remembers with understanding.* But it is important information.

- "What are three ways we can conserve water?" *This question requires the student to remember and understand the two lowest levels of Bloom's taxonomy.*

- "Why do you think we should be concerned about conserving water?" *This question moves up the taxonomy and requires the student to analyze the issues related to how much water we have, population growth, and the scarcity of some resources.*

- "How does God desire Christians to respond to the shortages of usable water?" *This requires a high level of thinking as the student must synthesize the information learned and create solutions to the problem.*

When developing worldview activities, the students will need the basic knowledge of the unit and lessons to think critically. Critical thinking is more than a process; it always includes a standard for judging—that is, information (in this case, science and Bible). In our example, they will need activities to learn how we use water as humans, explore how much water on the earth is fresh water and usable by humans, and discover how population impacts the amount of water available. This information can be

---

[7] A statement by Michael Scriven and Richard Paul, presented at the 8th Annual International Conference on Critical Thinking and Education Reform, "Defining Critical Thinking" (1987), https://www.scirp.org/(S(lz5mqp453edsnp55rrgjct55))/reference/References Papers.aspx?ReferenceID=2595525.

[8] The examples shown are adapted from Brian Oshiro's TEDxXiguan, "Encourage Critical Thinking with 3 Questions" presentation, YouTube video, 17:11, February 28, 2019, https://www.youtube.com/watch?v=0hoE8mtUS1E.

assessed with "what" type questions. For example, "What is fresh water?" To encourage greater thinking, a teacher should make connections by asking "why" type questions. For example, "Why are there, at times, shortages of water?" Finally, to get to the highest level, a teacher can have the student problem-solve with a "how" type question. For example, "Why might God want us to use and protect water available to us and **how** can this be done?" The how question leads to the creation of a project or to a problem-solving activity.

By considering the questions and activities that might be used in the unit and lesson plans before the actual planning, a teacher can then determine what, specifically, should be included in the content designed to meet the objectives.

Developing Biblical Worldview Integrative Units and Lessons That Include Worldview Objectives

Finally, the teacher develops unit and lesson objectives, including the worldview objectives. As we addressed in prior chapters, using backward design, we first write objectives, followed by possible correlating assessments. Assessment: How will you know that the students have met the worldview objective? What will they do to show this? Next in planning, think through possible prior knowledge that could be activated, and new information they may need, and design student activities to process the new information. When planning a worldview integrative unit and lesson, it is important to remember the overall learning aim for students to learn the content being taught and view it from a biblical worldview or lens. This is not a Bible lesson but rather a subject area lesson in which a biblical worldview is examined (connected to, or contrasted from, the content) to develop the habit of biblical worldview thinking.

Example of Unit Objectives

- The student will be able to explain how water is a daily critical resource for all humans.
- The student will be able to describe how much water on the earth is fresh and usable compared to all available water.
- The student will be able to correlate population growth and water scarcity.
- *The student will be able to create a personal plan for a Christian to conserve water and explain why this is important in the Christian life.* (This is the worldview integrative objective.)

ENGAGE: What assessment activities (formative and summative) might be done with these unit objectives?

Potential assessments might be to have small group discussions of how we use water every day or have the students draw pictures of how we use water. Students could be asked to circle pictures (from those provided) of bodies of water that are fresh water. Using pictures, students could decide which cities and towns might have more plentiful water and which may have less and why this is so (populations and availability correlation). The assessment of the worldview objective is to create a personal plan for water conservation. Students of the lower age level may have small group discussions or pair-share on the topic of why a Christian should conserve water and then brainstorm together ways they could do a better job at conservation, such as not running the water the entire time they are brushing their teeth, etc. Finally, children may write a plan for how they will care for God's earth by conserving water or draw a picture depicting something they will do to conserve and tell why their plan is important especially for Christians who love God and his creation.

Within the lessons of this unit, the students will first examine how often they use water and for what purpose. In a grade 1 or 2 class, this would be done by keeping a record, with the help of a parent or guardian, of the water they use. Class discussions would include reviewing these records and talking about the purpose for using that water. Students need to connect with the lesson at hand and be motivated to learn more. They will examine where water originated by reading Genesis 1 and sharing what they know about water on the earth. They will learn vocabulary related to bodies of water (lakes, rivers, oceans, etc.) and will use these in a geography lesson. The students will be involved in a small demonstration using water in cups and in a larger, clear bin. Each student will pour water from the cup carefully into the bin. This will represent all the water on earth. The teacher will use an eyedropper to remove approximately 3 percent of the water in the bin and put it in a small container. This represents the amount of fresh water on the earth that is available to use. Another activity will have the students use dry sponges to absorb water. In the curricula used to develop this unit, the students use sponges to see how water is used. The more sponges, the less water there will be. Students are asked what the sponges represent and are led to see that areas of a larger population use more water.

Most curricula stop at this point and move to the concept of conservation. To help to develop biblical worldview thinking, do not stop at this point to begin the concept of conservation. Use the content addressed above to ask students what we know about how God has designed the earth to replenish the water. From where does that water come? (The students' prior knowledge may very well include the water cycle.) Point to God's design, how the Scriptures connect the very food we eat to rain that we understand as part of the cycle. Wow! We even need water to eat and live! Ask why we might have water shortages? What part can we play in preserving good water? How can we care for the water God has provided? These are the kind of questions and or activities that help the student to develop a biblical worldview.

Conclusion

Your biblical worldview should permeate all the activities of teaching, such as classroom environment, your philosophy of teaching, and much more. Specifically, lesson planning requires the teacher's personal study and attention to biblical worldview thinking about the subject at hand. However, not every lesson will lend itself to a biblical worldview integrative activity. When a teacher uses a unit approach to planning, a logical decision can be made about where students will have the best opportunities to examine their own worldview related to a particular topic from a biblical perspective. Some units may have only one lesson in which that worldview question can best be examined. Other units may have a place in every lesson of the unit. Using the approach we suggest allows a teacher to carefully analyze the content, the biblical worldview addressed in that content, and the nature of their students, in order to develop units and lessons in which the students meet the learning targets while developing a biblically integrated mind. It takes time, but it is worth the effort in changed minds and lives.

SELECTED BIBLIOGRAPHY

Abeles, Harold, Charles Hoffer, and Robert Klotman. *Foundations of Music Education.* 2nd ed. New York: Schirmer Books, 1994.

Adams, Douglas. *The Salmon of Doubt: Hitchhiking the Galaxy One Last Time.* New York: Ballantine Books, 2005.

Adler, Mortimer J. *Ten Philosophical Mistakes.* New York: MacMillan, 1985.

Agarwal, Pooja K. "Retrieval Practice: A Power Tool for Lasting Learning." *Educational Leadership* 77, no. 8 (May 2020).

Ambrose, Susan A., Michael W. Bridges, Marsha C. Lovett, Michele DiPietro, and Marie K. Norman. *How Learning Works: 7 Research-Based Principles for Smart Teaching.* San Francisco: Jossey-Bass, 2010.

Anderson, Richard C., Ralph R. Reynolds, Diane L. Schallert, and Ernest T. Goetz. *Frameworks for Comprehending Discourse.* Urbana, IL: University of Illinois, 1976.

———. "Frameworks for Comprehending Discourse." *American Educational Research Journal* 14, no. 4 (1977): 367–82.

Arendale, David, and David Ghere. "Teaching College History Using Universal Instructional Design." In *Pedagogy and Student Services for Institutional Transformation: Implementing Universal Design in Higher Education*, edited by Jeanne L. Higbee and Emily Goff. Minneapolis: University of Minnesota, 2008. https://hdl.handle.net/11299/200460.

Aristotle. *Aristotle's Poetics.* New York: Hill and Wang, 1961.

Armstrong, Thomas. "School Safety Starts from Within." *Educational Leadership* 77, no. 2 (2019).

Arum, Richard. *Judging School Discipline: The Crisis of Moral Authority.* Boston: Harvard University, 2003.

Barkley, Elizabeth F. *Student Engagement Techniques: A Handbook for College Faculty.* San Francisco: Jossey-Bass, 2010.

Barron, Laurie, and Patti Kinney. *We Belong: 50 Strategies to Create Community and Revolutionize Classroom Management.* Alexandria, VA: ASCD, 2021.

Barrows, Samuel, Paul E. Peterson, and Martin R. West. "What Do Parents Think of Their Children's Schools?" *Education Next* 17, no. 2 (2017). https://www .educationnext.org/what-do-parents-think-of-childrens-schools-ednext-private -district-charter/.

Bartholomew, Craig G., and Michael W. Goheen. *The Drama of Scripture: Finding Our Place in the Biblical Story.* Grand Rapids: Baker Academic, 2004.

Batman, David C. "Hippocrates: 'Walking Is Man's Best Medicine!'" *Occup Med* 62, no. 5 (July 2012):320–22. https://pubmed.ncbi.nlm.nih.gov/22764266/.

Beam, Andrea, and Deanna Keith. "Differentiation and Faith: Improve the Learning Process by Finding Every Student's God-Given Talents." *Christian Education* 15, no. 1 (2011). http://works.bepress.com/andrea_beam/6/.

Benson, Jeffrey. *Improve Every Lesson Plan with SEL.* Alexandria, VA: ASCD, 2021.

Bigge, Morris, and Samuel Shermis. *Learning Theories for Teachers.* Allyn & Bacon Classics ed. Boston: Pearson, 2004.

Bjelland, Mark, Daniel Montello, and Arthur Getis. *Human Geography.* 13th ed. New York: McGraw Hill, 2020.

Borba, Michele. "Nine Competencies for Teaching Empathy." *Educational Leadership* 76, no. 2 (2018). https://www.ascd.org/el/articles/nine-competencies-for-teaching -empathy.

Boulos, Maged N. Kamel, Guochao Peng, and Trang VoPham. "An Overview of GeoAI Applications in Health and Healthcare." *International Journal of Health Geographics* 18, no. 7 (2019). https://ij-healthgeographics.biomedcentral.com /articles/10.1186/s12942-019-0171-2.

Bove, Kaitlyn M. "Elements of Music." Dr. Bove's Virtual Courses, 2021. https://kaitlin bove.com/elements-of-music/.

Boyles, Nancy. "Learning Character from Characters." *Educational Leadership* 76, no. 2 (October 2018).

Brackett, Marc. "Intelligence We Owe Students and Educators." *Educational Leadership* 76, no. 2 (October 2018).

Bradshaw, Travis Heath. "Evangelistic Churches: Geography, Demographic, and Marketing Variables that Facilitate Their Growth." PhD diss., University of Florida, 2000.

Bradshaw, Travis Heath, and James Henry Hobson. "Using Community Knowledge for Place-based Ministry: Interdisciplinary Engagement from Geography and Urban Ministry." *Faith and the Academy* 4, no. 2 (2020): 45–47. https://issuu.com/libertyuniversity/docs/110057_spring_2020_ace_journal_issuu.

Brand, Hilary, and Adrienne Chaplin, *Art and Soul: Signposts for Christians in the Arts.* 2nd ed. Carlisle, UK: Piquant Editions, 2007.

Brookhart, Susan M. *How to Give Effective Feedback to Your Students.* Alexandria, VA: ASCD, 2008.

Brown, Peter C., Henry L. Roediger, and Mark A. McDaniel. *Make It Stick: The Science of Successful Learning.* Cambridge: Belknap, 2014.

Brown, Warren S., and Brad D. Strawn. *The Physical Nature of Christian Life: Neuroscience, Psychology, & the Church.* New York: Cambridge University, 2012.

Bruce, F. F. *The Letter of Paul to the Romans: An Introduction and Commentary.* 2nd ed. Grand Rapids: Eerdmans, 1985.

Brummelen, Harro Van. *Walking with God in the Classroom: Christian Approaches to Teaching and Learning.* 2nd ed. Colorado Springs: Purposeful Design, 2009.

Bruner, Jerome S. *The Culture of Education.* Cambridge, MA: Harvard University, 1996.

———. *The Process of Education.* New York: Alfred A. Knopf, 1960.

Calaprice, Alice. *The Ultimate Quotable Einstein.* Princeton, NJ: Princeton University, 2011.

Canter, Lee. "Assertive Discipline Is More than Names on the Board and Marbles in a Jar." *Phi Delta Kappan International* 71, no 1 (September 1989).

———, and Marlene Canter. *Assertive Discipline: A Take-Charge Approach for Today's Educator.* Seal Beach, CA: Lee Canter, 1976.

Cardozo, Timothy, and Ronald Veazey. "Informed Consent Disclosure to Vaccine Trial Subjects of Risk of COVID-19 Vaccines Worsening Clinical Disease." *International Journal of Clinical Practice* 75, no. 3 (March 2021): e13795. https://doi.org/10.1111/ijcp.13795.

Carey, Benedict. "Why Flunking Exams Is Actually a Good Thing." *New York Times*, September 4, 2014. https://www.nytimes.com/2014/09/07/magazine/why-flunking-exams-is-actually-a-good-thing.html.

———. *How We Learn: The Surprising Truth About When, Where, and Why It Happens.* New York: Random House, 2015.

Carroll, Lewis. *Alice's Adventures in Wonderland.* London: MacMillan, 1865.

Centers for Disease Control. "School Health Policies and Practices Study (SHPPS)." CDC.gov. Division of Adolescent and School Health, 2016.

Chesterton, G. K. *The Man Who Was Orthodox.* Edited by A. L. Maycock. London: Dobson, 1963.

Chiu, Ming Ming, and Bonnie Wing Yin Chow. "Classroom Discipline Across Forty-One Countries: School, Economic, and Cultural Differences." *Journal of Cross-Cultural Psychology* 42, no. 3 (2011).

Christianity.com Editorial Staff. "What Does 'Imago Dei' Mean? The Image of God in the Bible." June 25, 2019. https://www.christianity.com/wiki/bible/image-of-god-meaning-imago-dei-in-the-bible.html.

Cochrane, Charles Norris. *Thucydides and the Science of History.* New York: Oxford, 1929.

Coley, Ken. "Excels in Teaching God's Word." In *Sunday School That Really Excels*, edited by Steve Parr, 182-83. Grand Rapids: Kregel, 2013.

Coley, Ken, and Blair Robinson. *Equipping Fathers to Lead Family Worship.* Nashville: Randall House, 2021.

Coley, Kenneth S. *Teaching for Change: Eight Keys for Transformational Bible Study with Teens.* Nashville: Randall House, 2017.

Copenhaver, Martin, B. *Jesus Is the Question: The 307 Questions Jesus Asked and the 3 He Answered.* Nashville: Abingdon, 2014.

Copland, Aaron. *What to Listen for in Music.* Revised edition. New York: McGraw-Hill, 1957.

Craggs, Ruth, "Historical and Archival Research." In *Key Methods in Geography*, edited by Nicholas Clifford, Meghan Cope, Thomas Gillespie, and Shaun French, 111-12. Los Angeles: Sage, 2016.

Craig, William Lane, and J. P. Moreland. *Philosophical Foundations for a Christian Worldview.* Downers Grove, IL: InterVarsity, 2003.

Csorba, Les T. *Trust: The One Thing That Makes or Breaks a Leader.* Nashville: Thomas Nelson, 2004.

Davie, Melissa. "Australian and New Zealand Teenagers among Most Inactive in the World." *Guardian*, November 21, 2019. https://www.theguardian.com/australia-news/2019/nov/22/australian-and-new-zealand-teenagers-among-most-inactive-in-the-world.

Dean, Ceri B., Elizabeth Ross Hubbell, Howard Pitler, and BJ Stone. *Classroom Instruction that Works: Research-Based Strategies for Increasing Student Achievement.* Alexandria, VA: ASCD, 2012.

D'Erizans, Roberto, Lee Ann Jung, and Tamatha Bibbo. "Don't Forget about Me!" *Educational Leadership* 77, no. 2. (October 2019).

DeWalt, Darren A., Nancy D. Berkman, Stacey Sheridan, Kathleen N. Lohr, and Michael P. Pignone. "Literacy and Health Outcomes." *Journal of General Internal Medicine* 19, no. 12 (2004).

Dewey, John. *Experience and Education*. London: MacMillan, 1938.

———. *How We Think*. Buffalo, NY: Prometheus Books, 1991.

———. *The Later Works, 1925–1953*. Edited by Jo Ann Boydston. Carbondale, IL: Southern Illinois University, 1984.

———. *The Collected Works of John Dewey, 1882–1953*. "What I Believe," *Later Works* vol. 5, *1925–1953*. Edited by Jo Ann Boydston. Carbondale, IL: Southern Illinois University, 1969–1991.

DiMaggio, Paul. "Culture and Cognition." *Annual Review of Sociology* 23 (August 1997): 263–87. https://www.annualreviews.org/doi/abs/10.1146/annurev.soc.23.1.263.

Doyle, Terry. *Helping Students Learn in a Learner-Centered Environment: A Guide to Facilitating Learning in Higher Education*. Sterling, VA: Stylus, 2008.

Dueck, Myron. *Grading Smarter, Not Harder: Assessment Strategies That Motivate Kids and Help Them Learn*. Alexandria, VA: ASCD, 2014.

Dweck, Carol. *Mindset: The New Psychology of Success: How We Can Learn to Fulfill Our Potential*. New York: Ballantine Books, 2006.

Eavey, Charles B. *History of Christian Education*. Chicago: Moody, 1964.

Felder, Richard M., and Rebecca Brent. "Active Learning: An Introduction." *ASQ Higher Education Brief* 2, no. 4 (2009): 1–5.

———. *Teaching & Learning STEM: A Practical Guide*. San Francisco: Jossey-Bass, 2016.

Ferguson, Kitty. *Fire in the Equations*. West Conshohocken, PA: Templeton Foundation, 2004.

Fisher, Douglas, and Nancy Frey. *Checking for Understanding: Formative Assessment Techniques for Your Classroom*. Alexandria, VA: ASCD, 2007.

Fisher, Douglas, Nancy Frey, and John Almarode. *Student Learning Communities: A Springboard for Academic and Social-Emotional Development*. Alexandria, VA: ASCD, 2021.

Forghani-Arani, Neda, Lucie Cerna, and Meredith Bannon. "The Lives of Teachers in Diverse Classrooms." *OECD Education Working Papers*, no. 198 (2019). https://doi.org/10.1787/8c26fee5-en.

Francis, David, Ken Braddy, and Ken Coley. *Shepherd: Creating Caring Community*. Nashville: Lifeway, 2017.

Fredericks, Anthony D. *Ace Your First Year Teaching*. Indianapolis: Blue River, 2017.

Frey, Nancy, Douglas Fisher, and Dominique Smith. *All Learning Is Social and Emotional: Helping Students Develop Essential Skills for the Classroom and Beyond*. Alexandria, VA: ASCD, 2019.

Frey, Nancy, Douglas Fisher, and Sandi Everlove. *Productive Group Work: How to Engage Students, Build Teamwork, and Promote Understanding*. Alexandria, VA: ASCD, 2009.

Froebel, Friedrich. *The Education of Man*. Translated by W. N. Hailmann. New York: D. Appleton, 1887.

Gaebelein, Frank Ely. *The Pattern of God's Truth: Problems of Integration in Christian Education*. Chicago: Moody, 1968.

Gall, Meredith D., Joyce P. Gall, and Walter R. Borg. *Educational Research: An Introduction*. 8th ed. Boston: Pearson, 2007.

Gallo, Carmine. "Your Audience Tunes Out after 10 Minutes: Here's How to Keep Their Attention." *Forbes*, February 28, 2019. https://www.forbes.com/sites /carminegallo/2019/02/28/your-audience-tunes-out-after-10–minutes-heres -how-to-keep-their-attention/?sh=3745f3f47364.

Geisler, Norman L., and Frank Turek. *I Don't Have Enough Faith to Be an Atheist*. Wheaton, IL: Crossway Books, 2004.

Gentry, Peter. "The Significance of Covenants in Biblical Theology." *Southern Baptist Journal of Theology* 20, no. 1 (2016): 9–33.

Gielen, Uwe P., and Samuel S. Jeshmaridian, "Lev S. Vygotsky: The Man and the Era." *International Journal of Group Tensions* 28, nos. 3/4 (1999). http://lchc.ucsd.edu /mca/Mail/xmcamail.2007_04.dir/att-0170/TSHC_-_LEV_S._VYGOTSKY _THE_MAN_AND_THE_ERA.pdf.

Goleman, Daniel. "Embattled Giant of Psychology Speaks His Mind." *New York Times*, August 25, 1987.

Gould, Stephen Jay. "Nonoverlapping Magisteria." *Natural History* 106 (March 1997): 16–22.

Gregory, Gayle H., and Carolyn Chapman. *Differentiated Instructional Strategies: One Size Doesn't Fit All*. Thousand Oaks, CA: Corwin, 2013.

Guskey, Thomas R. "Does Pre-Assessment Work?" *Educational Leadership* 75, no. 5 (2018).

Gutek, Gerald L. *Historical and Philosophical Foundations of Education: A Biographical Introduction*. 2nd ed. Upper Saddle, NJ: Prentice Hall, 1997.

Haarsma, Deborah B., and Loren D. Haarsma. *Origins: Christian Perspectives on Creation, Evolution, and Intelligent Design.* Grand Rapids: Faith Alive Christian Resources, 2011.

Hart, Hendrik, Johan Van der Hoeven, and Nicholas Wolterstorff. *Rationality in the Calvinian Tradition.* Eugene, OR: Wipf & Stock, 2011.

Heckman, Bruce. "Schools as Communities of Grace." In *Schools as Communities: Educational Leadership, Relationships, and the Eternal Value of Christian Schooling,* edited by James L. Drexler. Colorado Springs: Purposeful Design, 2007.

Herbart, Johann Friedrich. *The Science of Education: Its General Principles Deduced from Its Aim; And, The Aesthetic Revelation of the World.* United Kingdom: S. Sonnenschein, 1892.

Himmele, Persida, and William Himmele. *Total Participation Techniques: Making Every Student an Active Learner.* Alexandria, VA: ASCD, 2017.

Hobbs, Joseph J. "Objectives and Tools of World Regional Geography." *World Regional Geography.* 7th ed. Boston: Cengage, 2022.

Hoerr, Thomas R. *The Formative Five: Fostering Grit, Empathy, and Other Success Skills Every Student Needs.* Alexandria, VA: ASCD, 2017.

Holmes, Arthur F. "Toward a Christian View of Things." In *The Making of a Christian Mind: A Christian World View and the Academic Enterprise,* edited by Arthur F. Holmes. Downers Grove, IL: InterVarsity, 1985.

Howard, Tim. *Discussion in the College Classroom: Getting Your Students Engaged and Participating in Person and Online.* San Francisco: Jossey-Bass, 2015.

Hudgins, Thomas W. *Luke 6:40 and the Theme of Likeness Education in the New Testament.* Eugene, OR: Wipf & Stock, 2014.

Hunter, James Davison. *The Death of Character: Moral Education in an Age Without Good or Evil.* New York: Basic Books, 2000.

Hutchens, Robert Maynard. *Education for Freedom.* Baton Rouge: Louisiana State University, 1943.

Jackson, Robyn R. *Never Work Harder Than Your Students & Other Principles of Great Teaching.* Alexandria, VA: ASCD, 2009.

James, Glenn, Elda Martinez, and Sherry Herbers. "What Can Jesus Teach Us about Student Engagement?" *Journal of Catholic Education* 19, no. 1 (2015): 129. https://digitalcommons.lmu.edu/ce/vol19/iss1/7/.

James, William. *Talks to Teachers on Psychology.* New York: Henry Holt, 1899.

Jeeves, Malcolm, ed. *Rethinking Human Nature: A Multidisciplinary Approach.* Grand Rapids: Eerdmans, 2011.

Jennings, Patricia A. *Mindfulness for Teachers*. New York: W. W. Norton, 2015.

Jensen, Eric, and Liesl McConchie. *Brain-Based Learning: Teaching the Way Students Really Learn*. Thousand Oaks, CA: Corwin, 2020.

Kilpatrick, William K. *The Emperor's New Clothes: The Naked Truth about the New Psychology*. Wheaton, IL: Crossway Books, 1985.

King, Martin Luther, Jr. "The Purpose of Education." In *The Papers of Martin Luther King, Jr.* Vol. 1, *Called to Serve, January 1929–June 1951*, edited by Clayborne Carsone, Ralph Luker, and Penny A. Russell. Berkeley: University of California, 1992. https://kinginstitute.stanford.edu/king-papers/documents/purpose-education.

Klein, Stephen B. *Learning Principles and Applications*. 5th ed. Los Angeles: Sage, 2009.

Knight, George R. *Philosophy & Education*. 4th ed. Berrien Springs, MI: Andrews University, 2006.

Koppendrayer, Susan. "5 Questions to Ask When Teaching Science from a Biblical Perspective." Christian Schools International, August 14, 2019. https://www.csionline.org/articles/5-questions-to-ask-when-teaching-science-from-a-biblical-perspective.

Kraus, Hans, and Bonnie Prudden. "Comparison of Fitness of Danish and American School Children." *Research Quarterly, American Association for Health, Education and Recreation* (1961).

Lang, James M. *Small Teaching: Everyday Lessons from the Science of Learning*. San Francisco: Jossey-Bass, 2016.

Lary-Shipley, Lucia. "Pre-Columbian Societies and Early Encounters Response Paper." SSCI E-100B: Graduate Research Methods and Scholarly Writing in the Social Sciences: Government and History. Class paper. Cambridge, MA: Harvard University, September 25, 2017.

LeBar, Lois. *Education That Is Christian*. Old Tappan, NJ: Fleming H. Revell, 1958.

Leinhardt, Gaea. "On Teaching." *Advances in Instructional Psychology: Volume 4*. Edited by Robert Glaser. London: Routledge, 2019.

Lemov, Doug. *Teach Like a Champion: 49 Techniques That Put Students on the Path to College*. San Francisco: Jossey-Bass, 2010.

Leonard, Fred Eugene. *A Guide to the History of Physical Education*. Internet Archive, 1923. https://archive.org/details/guidetohistoryof00leon/page/n13/mode/2up. Accessed May 1, 2021.

Lockerbie, D. Bruce. *A Passion for Learning: A History of Christian Thought in Education*. Colorado Springs: Purposeful Design, 2007.

Luther, Martin. "The Table Talk of Martin Luther: On Sickness and the Causes Thereof." Translated by William Hazlitt. https://ccel.org/ccel/luther/tabletalk /tabletalk.v.xxxii.html.

Ma, Liping. *Knowing and Teaching Elementary Mathematics: Teachers' Understanding of Fundamental Mathematics in China and the United States.* New York: Routledge, 2010.

MacCullough, Martha. *By Design: Developing a Philosophy of Education Informed by a Christian Worldview.* 2nd ed. Colorado Springs: Purposeful Design, 2017.

———. *Flourishing in the Classroom: A Guide for Classroom Management and Student Discipline Informed by a Christ-Centered Worldview.* Wheaton, IL: Wheaton Press, 2019.

———. *Undivided: Developing a Worldview Approach to Biblical Integration.* Colorado Springs: Purposeful Design, 2016.

Magrath, Douglas. "MultiBrief: L1 and L2 Acquisition: Hints for Teachers." MultiBriefs, August 31, 2018. https://exclusive.multibriefs.com/content/l1-and-l2 -acquisition-hints-for-teachers/education.

Marzano, Robert J. *Classroom Assessment & Grading That Work.* Alexandria, VA: ASCD, 2006.

Maxim, George. *Dynamic Social Studies.* 11th ed. New York: Pearson, 2018.

Maxlow, Kate Wolfe, and Karen Sanzo. *20 Formative Assessment Strategies That Work.* New York: Routledge, 2018.

McKibben, Sarah. "Grit and the Greater Good: A Conversation with Angela Duckworth." *Educational Leadership* 76, no. 2 (October 2018).

McTighe, Jay, and Grant Wiggins. "Chapter 1: What Makes a Question Essential?" *Essential Questions: Opening Doors to Student Understanding.* Alexandria, VA: ASCD, 2013. https://www.seedpaknwboces.org/pd-resources/what-makes-question -essential.

McTighe, Jay, and Harvey F. Silver. *Teaching for Deeper Learning: Tools to Engage Students in Meaning Making.* Alexandria, VA: ASCD, 2020.

McTighe, Jay, and Judy Willis. *Upgrade Your Teaching: Understanding by Design Meets Neuroscience.* Alexandria, VA: ASCD, 2019.

Medina, Jane, and Vanden Fabricio Broeck. "T-Shirt." In *My Name Is Jorge on Both Sides of the River: Poems*, 24–25. Honesdale, PA: WordSong, 2014.

Meek, Esther Lightcap. *A Little Manual for Knowing.* Eugene, OR: Wipf & Stock, 2014.

———. *Longing to Know.* Ada, OK: Brazos Press, 2003.

———. *Loving to Know: Introducing Covenant Epistemology.* Eugene, OR: Wipf & Stock. 2011.

Miller, Donald. *A Million Miles in a Thousand Years.* Nashville: Thomas Nelson, 2009.

Minor, Denise. "Standards of Foreign Language Teaching the Five C's." *On Being a Language Teacher*, March 2014: 115–23. https://doi.org/10.12987/yale/9780300 186895.003.0006.

Moreland, James Porter. *Love Your God with All Your Mind.* Colorado Springs: NavPress, 1997.

Mosca, Julia Finley. *The Girl Who Thought in Pictures.* Seattle, WA: Innovation Press, 2017.

Mykytiuk, Lawrence. "Archaeology Confirms 50 Real People in the Bible," *Biblical Archaeology Review* 40, no. 2 (March/April 2014). https://www.baslibrary.org /biblical-archaeology-review/40/2/4.

———. "Archaeology Confirms 3 More Bible People," *Biblical Archaeology Review* 43, no. 3 (May/June 2017). https://www.baslibrary.org/biblical-archaeology-review /43/3/6.

National Research Council. *Rediscovering Geography: New Relevance for Science and Society.* Washington, DC: National Academies, 1997.

Neill, Alexander Sutherland. *Summerhill: A Radical Approach to Childrearing.* New York: Hart, 1960.

Neisser, Ulric. *Cognitive Psychology.* New York: Appleton-Century-Crofts, 1967.

Newbigin, Leslie. *The Gospel in a Pluralistic Society.* Grand Rapids: Eerdmans, 1989.

Newton, Gary. *Heart-Deep Teaching: Engaging Students for Transformed Lives.* Nashville: B&H, 2012.

Noddings, Nel. *Philosophy of Education.* Boulder, CO: Westview Press, 1995.

Oaklander, Mandy. "The Art of Resilience." *Time*, June 2015.

Ohemeng, Frank L. K. "Comparative Historical Analysis, A Methodological Perspective." *Global Encyclopedia of Public Administration, Public Policy, and Governance*, edited by Ali Farazmand. Cham, Switzerland: Springer, 2020. https:// doi.org/10.1007/978-3-319-31816-5_1205-1.

Ott, Craig. *Teaching and Learning Across Cultures: A Guide to Theory and Practice.* Grand Rapids: Baker Academic, 2021.

Palmer, Parker J. *The Courage to Teach: Exploring the Inner Landscape of a Teacher's Life.* 3rd ed. London: Jossey-Bass, 2017.

———. *To Know as We Are Known.* New York: HarperOne, 1993.

Peacock, Hayley, and David Holmes. *Progress in Geography Fieldwork: Key Stage 3*. London: Hodder Education, 2020.

Peterson, Mark D., Emidio Pistilli, G. Gregory Haff, Eric P. Hoffman, and Paul M. Gordon. "Progression of Volume Load and Muscular Adaptation During Resistance Exercise." *European Journal of Applied Physiology* 111, no. 6 (2011): 1063–71. https://doi.org/10.1007/s00421-010-1735-9.

Phillips, Vicki. "Survey 62% of Teachers Say Learning about Geography Is 'Extremely Important.'" *Forbes*, December 12, 2020. https://www.forbes.com/sites/vicki phillips/2020/12/01/survey-62-of-teachers-say-learning-about-geography-is -extremely-important/?sh=f43f1d825f08.

Phillips-Wren, Gloria, Anna Esposito, and Lakhmi C. Jain. "Introduction to Big Data and Data Science: Methods and Applications." *Advances in Data Science: Methodologies and Applications, Intelligent Systems Reference Library* 189. Cham, Switzerland: Springer, 2021. https://doi.org/10.1007/978-3-030-51870-7_1.

Plantinga, Cornelius, Jr. *Not the Way It's Supposed to Be: A Breviary of Sin*. Grand Rapids: Eerdmans, 2002.

Poincaré, Henri. *Science and Hypothesis*. London: Walter Scott, 1905.

Popham, W. James. *Transformative Assessment*. Alexandria, VA: ASCD, 2008.

Postman, Neil. *The End of Education: Redefining the Value of the School*. New York: Random House, 1995.

Powell, Alvin. "How Sputnik Changed U. S. Education." *Harvard Gazette*, October 11, 2007. https://news.harvard.edu/gazette/story/2007/10/how-sputnik-changed -u-s-education/.

Purkey, William Watson, and John Michael Novak. "An Introduction to Invitational Theory." *Journal of Invitational Theory and Practice* (September 2015).

Rahavard, Shahin, Maryam Razaghi, and Firooz Sadighi. "L1 Versus L2 Learning: A Controversial Issue." *International Journal on Studies in English Language and Literature* 3, no. 7 (July 2015): 59–62. https://www.arcjournals.org/pdfs/ijsell/v3 -i7/9.pdf.

Reed, Ronald F., and Tony W. Johnson. *Philosophical Documents in Education*. 2nd ed. New York: Longman, 2000.

Reynolds, Stephen, Robert Rohli, Julia Johnson, Peter Waylen, and Mark Francek. *Exploring Physical Geography*. 3rd ed. New York: McGraw Hill, 2021.

Rief, Sandra F., and Julie A. Heimburge. *How to Reach and Teach All Children in the Inclusive Classroom: Practical Strategies, Lessons, and Activities*. San Francisco: Jossey-Bass, 2006.

Rollins, Suzy Pepper. *Teaching in the Fast Lane: How to Create Active Learning Experiences*. Alexandria, VA: ASCD, 2014.

Rousseau, Jean-Jacques. *Emile*. Translated by Allan Bloom. New York: Basic Books, 1979.

———. *On Education*. Translated by Allan Bloom. New York: Basic Books, 1979.

———. *The Social Contract*. Book I, Chapter 1. France: 1762.

Rusk, Robert Robertson. *The Philosophical Bases of Education*. 2nd ed. London: University of London, 1956.

Ryken, Leland. *The Liberated Imagination: Thinking Christianly about the Arts*. Wheaton: IL: Harold Shaw, 1989.

Sanders, Cheryl E. *Lawrence Kohlberg's Stages of Moral Development*. Britannica. Accessed January 10, 2022. https://www.britannica.com/science/Lawrence-Kohlbergs-stages -of-moral-development.

Sanders, Jessica. "10 Classroom Rules for Using Technology." Whooo's Reading Blog, August 3, 2015. http://blog.whooosreading.org/10-classroom-rules-for-using -technology/.

Sandford, Julie, et al. "Improving Classroom Management." *Educational Leadership* 40, no 7 (April 1983). In Wong, Harry, *The Well-Managed Classroom*. Professional References for Teachers. New York: Holt, Rinehart and Winston. https://www.wtc .ie/images/pdf/Classroom_Management/cm6.PDF.

Schaeffer, Francis A. *Art & the Bible*. Downers Grove, IL: InterVarsity, 1979.

———. *He Is There, and He Is Not Silent*. Wheaton, IL: Tyndale House, 1972.

Schrag, Zachary M. *The Princeton Guide to Historical Research*. Princeton: Princeton University, 2021.

Schwartz, Daniel L., Jessica M. Tsang, and Kristen P. Blair. *The ABCs of How We Learn: 26 Scientifically Proven Approaches, How They Work, and When to Use Them*. New York: W. W. Norton, 2016.

Seidel, Leonard J. *God's New Song: A Biblical Perspective of Music*. Springfield, VA: Grace Unlimited, 1980.

Sergiovanni, Thomas. *Leadership for the Schoolhouse: How Is It Different, Why Is It Important?* San Francisco: Jossey-Bass, 1996.

Šimundić, Ana-Maria. "Lessons in Biostatistics." *Biochemia Medica* 18, no. 2 (2008): 154–61. https://www.biochemia-medica.com/assets/images/upload/xml_tif/Simundic _AM_-Confidence_interval.pdf.

———. *Start with Why: How Great Leaders Inspire Everyone to Take Action*. New York: Penguin, 2011.

Sire, James W. *The Universe Next Door*. 6th ed. Downers Grove, IL: InterVarsity, 2020.

Skinner, Burrhus Frederic, *Beyond Freedom and Dignity*. New York: Alfred A. Knopf, 1971.

———. *Walden Two*. Toronto: MacMillan, 1948.

Smart, Simon. *A Spectator's Guide to World Views: Ten Ways of Understanding Life*. Sydney, AU: Blue Bottle Books, 2007.

Smith, David I. *On Christian Teaching*. Grand Rapids: Eerdmans, 2018.

Smith, James K. A. *Desiring the Kingdom: Worship, Worldview, and Cultural Formation*. Ada, OK: Baker Academic, 2009.

Society of Health and Physical Educators. *Grade-Level Outcomes for K-12 Physical Education*. Reston, VA: Shape America, 2013. https://www.shapeamerica.org /uploads/pdfs/2017/Grade-Level-Outcomes-for-K-12-Physical-Education.pdf.

Souers, Kristin. *Fostering Resilient Learners: Strategies for Creating a Trauma-Sensitive Classroom*. Alexandria, VA: ASCD, 2016.

Sousa, David A. *How the Brain Learns*. Thousand Oaks, CA: Sage, 2017.

Sousa, David A., and Carol Ann Tomlinson. *Differentiation and the Brain: How Neuroscience Supports the Learner-Friendly Classroom*. Bloomington, IN: Solution Tree, 2018.

Spears, Paul D., and Steven R. Loomis. *Education for Human Flourishing: A Christian Perspective*. Downers Grove, IL: IVP Academic, 2009.

Spencer, Herbert. *Education: Intellectual, Moral and Physical*. New York: D. Appleton, 1864.

Sprenger, Marilee. *Social Emotional Learning and the Brain: Strategies to Help Your Students Thrive*. Alexandria, VA: ASCD, 2020.

Sproul, Richard C. *The Consequences of Ideas*. Wheaton, IL: Good News, 2000.

Tan, Amy. "Fish Cheeks." *The Brief Bedford Reader*, 2000. https://www.ncps-k12.org /cms/lib8/CT01903077/Centricity/Domain/638/LA/Short%20Story%20-%20 Fish%20Cheeks.pdf.

———. Biography: http://www.amytan.net/about.html.

Tokuhama-Espinosa, Tracey. *Mind, Brain, and Education Science: A Comprehensive Guide to the New Brain-Based Teaching*. New York: W. W. Norton, 2011.

Tomlinson, Carol Ann. *Leading & Managing a Differentiated Classroom*. Alexandria, VA: ASCD, 2010.

———. "Chapter 1: What Differentiated Instruction Is—and Isn't." *How to Differentiate Instruction in Academically Diverse Classrooms*. Alexandria, VA: ASCD, 2017.

Tomlinson, Carol Ann, and David A. Sousa. "The Sciences of Teaching." *Educational Leadership* 77, no. 8 (2020).

Tomlinson, Carol Ann, and Tonya R. Moon. *Assessment and Student Success in a Differentiated Classroom*. Alexandria, VA: ASCD, 2013.

Tregaskis, Sharon. "50 Years Later, Recalling the Founder of Head Start." *Cornell Chronicle*, May 15, 2015. https://news.cornell.edu/stories/2015/05/50-years-later -recalling-founder-head-start.

Tuchman, Gaye. "Historical Methods." *The SAGE Encyclopedia of Social Science Research Methods*, edited by Michael Lewis-Beck, Alan Bryman, and Tim Futing Liao. Thousand Oaks, CA: Sage, 2004. http://dx.doi.org/10.4135/9781412950589.

Tuckman, Bruce W., and David M. Monetti. *Educational Psychology*. Belmont, CA: Wadsworth Cengage Learning, 2011.

Tuttle, Harry Grover. *Formative Assessment: Responding to Your Students*. Larchmont, NY: Eye on Education, 2009.

Vatterott, Cathy. *Rethinking Grading: Meaningful Assessment for Standards-Based Learning*. Alexandria, VA: ASCD, 2015.

Von Glasersfeld, Ernst. *An Introduction to Radical Constructivism*. (Originally published in *Die Erfundene Wirklichkeit*, edited by P. Watzlawick. Munich: Piper, 1981). English translation in *The Invented Reality*. New York: Norton, 1984. https://app.nova.edu/toolbox/instructionalproducts/ITDE_8005/weeklys/1984 -vonGlaserfeld_RadicalConstructivism.pdf.

———. *Radical Constructivism: A Way of Knowing and Learning*. Washington, DC: Falmer Press, 1995.

Vygotsky, Lev. *Thought and Language*. Translated by Alex Kozulin. Cambridge, MA: MIT, 1986.

Watson, John. "Psychology as a Behaviorist Views It." *Psychology Review* 20 (1913). https://psychclassics.yorku.ca/Watson/views.htm.

Weinstein, Carol, and Wilford Weber. "Classroom Management." In *The Classroom Teaching Skills*, edited by James M. Cooper. Belmont, CA: Cengage, 2011.

White, John. *Exploring Well-Being in Schools: A Guide to Making Children's Lives More Fulfilling*. New York: Routledge, 2011.

Wiggins, Grant, and Jay McTighe. *Understanding by Design*. Alexandria, VA: ASCD, 2005.

Willard, Dallas. *The Divine Conspiracy: Discovering Our Hidden Life in God*. San Francisco: HarperCollins, 1998.

Williams, Robert Chadwell. *The Historian's Toolbox: A Student's Guide to the Theory and Craft of History*. 2nd ed. Armonk, NY: M. E. Sharpe, 2007.

Willis, Judy. *Research-Based Strategies to Ignite Student Learning: Insights from a Neurologist and Classroom Teacher*. Alexandria, VA: ASCD, 2006.

Wilson, Donna, and Marcus Conyers. *Five Big Ideas for Effective Teaching: Connecting Mind, Brain, and Education Research to Classroom Practice*. New York: Teachers College, 2013.

Wong, Harry, and Rosemary Wong. *The Classroom Management Book*. Mountain View, CA: Harry K. Wong, 2014.

Woolfolk, Anita. *Educational Psychology*. 11th ed. Columbus, OH: Merrill, 2010.

World Health Organization. Constitution of the World Health Organization—Basic Documents. Forty-fifth edition. Supplement, October 2006.

Wormeli, Rick, and Dedra Stafford. *Summarization in Any Subject: 60 Innovative, Tech-Infused Strategies for Deeper Student Learning*. Alexandria, VA: ASCD, 2019.

Zull, James E. *The Art of Changing the Brain: Enriching the Practice of Teaching by Exploring the Biology of Learning*. Sterling, VA: Stylus, 2002.

INDEX